TEXT AND TABLET

"Text and Tablet brings a logician's insights to bear on Biblical and Near Eastern traditions and on their modern interpreters. A bracing challenge to the negativity that governs much discussion, this book proposes original solutions to a wide range of problems. Significant progress has been made in recent years in archaeological general theory, logical analysis of narrative, literary study, and historical discovery. Exposure of hidden, or partial, assumptions in the Old Testament and Near East religion and archaeology leads to the need to re-interpret their own identities."

Robert Gordon, University of Cambridge, UK

Text and Tablet balances a blend of logic, post-analytical philosophy, French philosophy and literary criticism to carefully introduce some of these issues to the student and research reader. Just as writers such as Derrida and Kermode have been interested in relating religion and philosophy to literature, so this book extends the idea of multidisciplinary synthesis to connect ancient and modern issues. Linking philosophy to literature, Old Testament texts and studies, Near East archaeology, and Religious ideas and debates, in fresh ways, Gibson develops a critical debate with a variety of scholarly perspectives to present new and controversial insights. Specific and recurrently problematic ancient texts and sites are examined, as well as developing interpretations of some recent excavations.

Addressing issues raised by leading thinkers (Chomsky, Deleuze, Wittgenstein, Renfrew, Barr) on language, life and history, Gibson seeks to challenge many entrenched views based on familiar discoveries and proposes fresh engagement between the interpretation of Old Testament studies and archaeology, using a new, multidisciplinary analysis. This book will prove of particular value to those interested in theology and biblical studies, philosophy of language, archaeology, and modern comparative literature.

Arthur Gibson is currently at the University of Surrey, Roehampton, UK.

ASHGATE NEW CRITICAL THINKING IN THEOLOGY & BIBLICAL STUDIES

Ashgate New Critical Thinking in Theology & Biblical Studies presents an open-ended series of quality research drawn from an international field of scholarship. The series aims to bring monograph publishing back into focus for authors, the international library market, and student, academic and research readers. Headed by an international editorial advisory board of acclaimed scholars, this series presents cutting-edge research from established as well as exciting new authors in the field. With specialist focus, yet clear contextual presentation, books in the series aim to take theological and biblical research into new directions; opening the field to new critical debate within the traditions, into areas of related study, and into important topics for contemporary society.

Series Editorial Board:

Text and Tablet

Near Eastern archaeology, the Old Testament and new possibilities

ARTHUR GIBSON

Editor
Brook W.R. Pearson

Ashgate

Aldershot • Burlington USA • Singapore • Sydney

Published by
Ashgate Publishing Ltd
Gower House
Croft Road
Aldershot
Hants GU11 3HR
England

BS
1180
·G48
2000

Ashgate Publishing Company
131 Main Street
Burlington, VT 05401-5600 USA

Ashgate website: http://www.ashgate.com

British Library Cataloguing in Publication Data
Gibson, Arthur, 1943-
    Text and tablet : near Eastern archaeology, the Old
    Testament and new possibilities. - (Ashgate new critical
    thinking in theology & biblical studies)
    1.Bible. O.T. - Criticism, interpretation, etc. 2.Bible.
    O.T. - Historiography 3.Middle Eastern literature -
    Relation to the Old Testament 4.Middle East - Antiquities
    I.Title
    221.6

Library of Congress Control Number: 00-134433

ISBN 0 7546 1460 3
Printed and bound by Athenaeum Press, Ltd.,
Gateshead, Tyne & Wear.

Contents

PART II: OLD TESTAMENT AND NEAR EAST INTERPRETATION

List of Figures and Plates

Preface

The ancient Near East mirrors or exhibits many phenomena that various specialists, and philosophers, do not understand. Carefully composed analyses by biblical scholars can inadvertently obscure an unpredicted ancient world. Sometimes retrojection and regression simulate journeys to the past that unknown to us have no corresponding source. Fresh discoveries can have unexpected effects on current views and future possibilities, as can the new possibilities assigned to old sites.

Conversely, at some levels, the Old Testament and Near East tablets and narratives are known fixed bodies of data, though scholars variously assume that, for example Old Testamwnt books, have has lost weight, become obese, or are the product of cloning. The body is also replete with externally clustered or cloistered interpretations. There is always a danger in both subjects that external perception may be treated as a property internal to the body. Groups of interpretation congregate around, say theological, presuppositions or their negation or contraries. And we do not always know what a contrary is, nor what it is to be contrary. Such ignorance as we embody complicates attempts to discuss and assess ancient narratives, not least the Old Testament, in repulsive or attractive relation to its putative external historical references. A reason for this is that our perspectives can cut against the grain of fashion that construes itself as progress. This would be an odd reaction from those poststructuralists who prioritise difference, not progress, while their criticisms of protectionist conservative interpretation often are progress. Such is the universality of relativity. This book supposes that we may need a new blend of such elements whose sublime sum is an identity different from these sublimated parts.

Exposure of hidden, or partial, assumptions in archaeology sometimes leads to the need to re-interpret its own complexified life. The paucity and random unevenness of the discovery of sites, specific empirical data, or matching inscriptions render generalisation a perilous affair. In view of these problems, scrutiny of notions of inference, or the absence of them, in Old Testament studies and archaeology for assessment of the conjunction of these two unmatched mates, is a perennial task. A theoretical study burdened with methodology would not only be tedious; it would not relevantly assist with the interpretation of pragmatic issues. Nevertheless, significant progress has been made in recent years in archaeological general theory, logical analysis of narrative, literary study, and other areas such as historical analysis. It is important to assess the problems associated with introducing, suppressing, or unwittingly assuming measuring languages or criteria for empirical data, be the target empirical site or thory of language. At the side of such points stands the fact of the massive and exciting progress that has been made in excavations.

By way of reflection on the foregoing variety of considerations, we allow that we cannot always know how typical examples do affect, or could be countered by, *unknown* archaeology and *undiscovered* texts. Still, attempting to allow for this problem, a way to develop these issues in the present book is to encourage a sense of new typicality to emerge from those cases which attract, occasion agreement, and those that attract dissension, in relation to fashionable or traditional consensus. This provides a means to provoke fresh reflection on archaeology and the Old Testament, though in a framework of multiple perspectives. An attempt to choose examples employing the foregoing diet of concerns could be fraught with difficulties. It could also readily trigger undue moderation that would be prejudicial to a strong sense of adventure, and to traditional conceptions. Rather, this book boldly considers interpretations of a range of unstable exotic yet substantial issues, as well as (the perhaps recently neglected) strengths in familiar stabilised interpretations. These are integrated to contribute to the initial development of original synthesis for the engagement of four stately partners: archaeology, the Old Testament, Near East literature, and philosophy. Their involvement here varies, depending on many factors contingent on the uneven ancient world and our Third Millennium states of affairs. It proposes a *rapprochement* that develops multidisciplinary syntheses. The book amounts to a preliminary scenario for a new conception, one partly contextualized and expressed by an emerging string of other works (for example, see Gibson, 2000a).

Arthur Gibson
ag205@cam.ac.uk

Cambridge, August 2000

Acknowledgements

I am grateful to Professor Lord Renfrew: he first read the draft of the book, and his assessment was very helpful and encouraging. Later he facilitated my introduction to areas of archaeology and research, as well as meetings with a variety of archaeologists, quite outside the remit of his pressing responsibilities. His is a model of scholarly and humane care, of very special value. The first archaeology conference I attended, arranged by Professors Renfrew and Anthony Snodgrass, 'Future Directions in Greek Archaeology' (held at Clare College, University of Cambridge in 1986) stands out in my mind as an ideal example of distinguished sensibility and friendship with people from many countries.

Special thanks are due to Professor Robert Gordon for his examination of the first draft typescript and shrewd comments, for discussion and encouragement. Discourse with the following (some now deceased) has been a source of stimulus over extended periods or episodically: professors Lewis Binford, Sir Ernst Gombrich, Anthony Snodgrass, Edward Sollberger, and especially to Thorkild Jacobsen over a year. I am much indebted to Ilya Gershevitch, James Kinnier Wilson, Sir Harold Bailey, Walter Taunton, R. Y. Ebied, Jürgen Staark, Jack Plumley, Rosalie David, and briefly, but no less valuable, Sebastian Brock, who inducted me into the study of various ancient languages. The first three scholars later enabled me for over 20 years periodically to consult with them about the progress of various issues in my continuing research. I have many fond memories connected with this research, and space only for one such example. It was kind of Harold Bailey to allow my three month old daughter Lily to use his library for unscholarly activities, while we pressed on with research; perhaps the only time he risked dying prematurely was his absent-minded rediscovery of her, via a sudden cry. Earlier bouts of sustained periodic research or discussion with professors James Barr, John Chadwick, John Killen, Jack Plumley and Stefan Strelcyn are much appreciated. Some of my ideas started to form when Sir Frank Kermode guided me into research on English literature over an extended period; I began very much the novice, while he asked me to teach him Hebrew that strayed to include Ugaritic. George Steiner gave time to listen, criticise, and encourage. Over some years,

xi

the occasional enquiry to, or brief exchange with, David Daube, Maurice Haran, Sir John Lyons, Wilfred Lambert, Elaine Pagels, Nicholas Postgate, Chaim Rabin, John Ray, Lawrence Schiffman, and Gregory Vlastos, as with a number of others, always met or meet with valued responses.

Subsequent to writing this book, it had to be prepared as camera ready copy. I am grateful to Brook Pearson, who volunteered to do the first, more extensive and onerous part, of the crc processing, as well as standardising the Bibliography. (I impose the title of editor on him in appreciation of this role in the processing.) He drew my attention to contexts where I might consider adding further reflections; these I composed when I did the second part of the CRC process. Thanks also to Daniel Deme for checking some details for the Bibliography; to Roger Gibson for computer services and Ben Gibson for technical advice. Credit for the preparation of some of the plates goes to Hossein Majidi and his superb Digital Imaging Centre, Cambridge; for other graphics' computer processing and use of facilities, the Cambridge University Computing Service: Roy Barlow, Harvey Barker, and Stephen Burdett (now of the Cambridge University Law Faculty). Thanks to Sean O'Mahony, who retrieved the manuscript after someone had lost it. I appreciate the cooperative atmosphere accorded by various people at the University of Surrey Roehampton, Cambridge University, and especially Trinity College Cambridge, as well as a number of the latter's facilities. I am grateful to the following libraries, and to their librarians, for fine services and assistance: the University Library, Faculties of Oriental Studies, Classics, Cambridge University, and the Wren Library, Trinity College, Cambridge; also, the New York University Library. The University of Surrey Roehampton provided a research grant for a part of the cost of CRC typing. Many thanks also to Pauline Beavers of Ashgate Publishing for her fine editorial assistance.

I acknowledge use of the following illustrations: the Staatliche Museen, Berlin for the boundary stone; the British Museum for the Sumerian Seal by Adda the Scribe; the Brooklyn Museum for the Egyptian Hayes' Papyrus; the Leiden Museum (Rijksmuseum voor Oudheden) for the Egyptian Ipuwer text; Peter Moore for the Gebel et Tih in the Wilderness of Zin; the editors of the *Bulletin of the American Schools of Oriental Research* for the smaller Beth Shan stele; the Israeli Museum for the clay anthropoid sculpted Philistine coffins from the Beth Shan cemetery; the estate of Kathleen Kenyon for the Bronze Age house at Jericho; and Brill Academic Publishers and J. Hoftijzer for the Deir 'Alla Balaam Inscription; N. L. Falcon for the Saidmarreh Landslip in Luristan and the Naft Safid gas blow-out.

Arthur Gibson

List of Abbreviations

AA	Architectural Association Files
AS	*Anatolian Studies*
AV	Authorised Version
BA	*Biblical Archaeologist*
BASOR	*Bulletin of the American Schools of Oriental Research*
BCILL	Bibliothèque des cahiers de l'Institut de linguistique de Louvain
BDB	F. Brown, S.R. Driver and C.A. Briggs (eds.), *Hebrew and English Lexicon of the Old Testament*
BHS	K. Elliger and W. Rudolf *et al* (eds.), *Biblia Hebraica Stuttgartensia*
BJPS	*British Journal for the Philosophy of Science*
BJRL	*Bulletin of the John Rylands Library, University of Manchester*
CAH	*Cambridge Ancient History*, 3rd edition.
CC	*Communication and Cognition*
CTA	A. Herder, *Corpus des tablettes en cunéiformes alphabétiques découvertes a Ras Shamra-Ugarit de 1929 a 1939*
EA	W.L. Moran (ed.), *The Amarna Letters*
FO	*Folia Orientalia*, Kraków
JAOS	*Journal of the American Oriental Society*
JBL	*Journal of Biblical Literature*
JCS	*Journal of Cuneiform Studies*
JEA	*Journal of Egyptian Archaeology*
JNES	*Journal of Near Eastern Studies*
JSNTSup	*Journal for the Study of the New Testament Supplement Series*
JSOTSup	*Journal for the Study of the Old Testament Supplement Series*
JSPSup	*Journal for the Study of the Pseudepigrapha Supplement Series*
JSS	*Journal of Semitic Studies*
MEE	*Materiali epigrafici di Ebla*
NEB	*New English Bible*

OTL	Old Testament Library
RBI	*Rivista Biblical Italiano*
RILP	Roehampton Institute London Papers
SAS	*South Asian Studies*
SBLSS	*Society of Biblical Literature Semeia Studies*
SG	*Synographia*
SMS	*Syrio-Mesopotamian Studies*
STAS	*Studies in Theology and Sexuality*
TAJIA	*Tel Aviv, Journal of the Institute of Archaeology*
TD	*Theology Digest*
TM	*Les Temps Modernes*
TSAJ	*Texte und Studien zum antiken Judentum*
UF	*Ugarit-Forschungen*
UT	C.H. Gordon, *Ugaritic Textbook*
VT	*Vetus Testamentum*
VTSup	*Supplements to Vetus Testamentum*

For Kelsey Gibson

PART I
A CONCEPTUAL FRAMEWORK

1

Philosophical Archaeology and Ancient Texts

Introduction

The archaeologist Ian Hodder (1999: 20) states, 'It is remarkable that there is almost no literature available on how archaeologists come to their conclusions.' Within the present book's priority – that of the Near East and its relations to the Old Testament's narratives—this reported situation cannot be given the extensive attention that it deserves, though it serves to justify the book's concern with identifying and assessing relations between empirical data and conclusions which are said to follow from them. These data include site archaeology, ancient narratives, our contemporary mentality, and their relations; the present study is not primarily concerned with the investigation of methodology, however. The philosophical elements presented in this book are not intended as decoration secondary to archaeology and interpretation of ancient texts. They are there as practical functions in the study of the ancient Near East and the Old Testament.

The connections between data and conclusions are of central concern to philosophy. This interest is also partly a function of perceived relations between philosophy and the subject to which it is applied. A presupposition of this book is that a philosophy of a subject will include use of other subjects. This can sometimes highlight the need to introduce a feature from another subject as a component of philosophy itself. Some of the reasons for this are because we are ignorant of what the identity of philosophy is, and of what the identities of philosophies are. There is gross dispute over a range of fundamental questions about this sort of issue between many philosophers. On the one side, some philosophers claim that attention to the 'philosophy of philosophy' is futile. Against this there are many opposed theories within philosophy on such topics as logic, language, the history of philosophy, and philosophy of social theory. So an attempt to apply philosophy to other subjects will be fraught with problems.

An analogy is appropriate here: Nancy Cartwright (1999: 180) refines the idea of 'bridge principles', albeit, in her context, for physics and economics. She states that, 'theories in physics do not generally represent what happens in the world;...the fundamental principles of theories in physics do not represent what happens; rather, the theory gives purely abstract relations between abstract concepts... When we want to represent what happens in these situations we need to go beyond the theory and build a *representative* model.' Cartwright (1999: 181) notes that this notion reflects the sense of an '*interpretative* model' which operates by 'bridge principles' linking distinct fields of meaning. Obviously, there are a number of differences between philosophy of science and a philosophy of texts from the ancient Near East and Old Testament. Yet, we should be wary of dismissing all parallels between philosophies of sciences and humanities, not least since Cartwright's book proposes substantial parallels between physics and economics. Cartwright (1999: 201) refers to the notion of theory-nets, as opposed to theories. So one could say my argument would be that, within a spectrum of philosophical theory-nets, there is the potential for devising representational models that lead to the exposure of bridge principles for other subjects, which have interpretative significance for the ancient Near East. This perspective distances itself from commitment to a specific theory, and/or treats it as a phenomenon in need of bridging-principles. An explicitly developed (future) philosophy of the ancient Near East is more provisional than, and possibly at least as complex as, a philosophy of physics which recognises parallels with economics. The foregoing is not a proposal for a formal methodology. There are evident disanalogies, though the use of prediction/forecasting in physics and economics might be profitably compared to retrojection in archaeology and our interpretation projected into the ancient world.

Might this use of philosophy concentrate on method and technical terms, as well as a review of various theories? Rather, this book presents an applied engagement with a variety of actual problems within the studies on the ancient Near East and Old Testament material. This choice itself presupposes that other subjects have something to contribute to philosophy itself. Research on the ancient Near East and the Old Testament has benefited from the introduction of other subjects, such as literary analysis, aesthetics, history theory and scientific testing. So an attempt to produce some possible routes to a philosophy of these facets of the ancient world will have to reflect on such issues. Moreover, when the conjunction of philosophy and other subjects suggest a new interpretative state of affairs, there may be need to modify and propose fresh views in these subjects or with regard to how they impinge on the evidence. In a certain respect, then, we are faced with the need for a future Renaissance scenario.

Is it possible to handle some uses of literary theory by treating them as subsets of archaeological general theory, noting the archaeologist Colin Renfrew's (1982) concern to advocate research for an archaeology of the mind? Notoriously, Freud (1953) and the historian of ideas Foucault (1966, 1969) employed not only the metaphor of 'archaeology', but also some of its conceptual structure by which to construct concepts of mind and its relation to language.[1] May these writers have perceived or responded under the impress of some traces of mental elements in archaeological analysis and its historical retrojection? Some possibilities associated with this type of proposal are initiated in Gibson (1998b).

The Old Testament is a dense, and perceptually unstable, set of narratives. Traditions of institutionalism within and external to it have, to varying degrees, thwarted this apprehension by facilitating an imperious sense of predictable, normative meaning. The new hides within the old, however. Components of unacknowledged possibilities are ossified within the ancient text. One should not overstate the scale of such claims; yet may not modern alien perception identify unfamiliar ancient sense? Sometimes it is worth interrogating influential theories that have been adopted as the norm, and re-posing discarded or unlikely theories to test our assessment of our pasts as well as the ancient past. As distinguished scientists sometimes intimate (see Rees 1999: 145): good, even wrong, ideas are extremely scarce. They are needed to rival and test accepted hypotheses, as Popper (1982) explained, especially where the peculiar problems associated with retrojection are involved, as is the case in such widely separated subjects as mathematical cosmology, and investigation of the ancient world's narratives in archaeological contexts.

Adjacent to this perspective is the prospect that relating ancient genres to modern criticism could enrich both. Some French literary analysis (typified by *Les Temps Modernes*, for example, in the studies on George Bataille—*TM* 54 [1999] 602), suitably adjusted and qualified, might be re-deployed to ancient Near East narrative—and *vice versa*. Riffaterre (1991), among others, speaks of an intertext between narratives. Beyond this rudimentary idea, intertextuality ranges from (a) reference; to: (b) the weaker allusive relation or parody between the read narrative and texts which it presupposes. A quotation is an evident example of the former, while some other intertextual relations code complex nests of scarcely identifiable sources. Although one should map the limiting functions of intentionality, I suggest that the intertext can be conceived live metaphorically as a mirror of the contributing authorial (un)consciousness, semantically contracting schedules within and between narratives. One does not have to adopt an idea of a collective unconscious infecting texts to appreciate that ancient narratives often mirror the psychological archetypes ranging

---

[1] Although they employ this terminology in different ways, as Forrester 1997 shows.

through the societies in which narratives were composed. Certainly, problems of interpretation obtrude on attempts to retrieve a conception of which property of the unconscious is mediated by a symbolic transaction. Riffaterre (1991) proposes that, in French, highly disputed narratives can yield to decidable semantic assessment that will expose internal senses. Gibson (1997) has an original theory to realise this sort of situation in the Dead Sea Scrolls.

Signs to the External World

Such a conception is, I suggest, also applicable to a range of semantically informative physical objects that have been used as signs in the external world. To select a common illustration (to which we will regularly return in this book, in particular because of its common uses), how should we conceive of an ancient animal such as a lion when used in an ancient text, tablet or site? As Gombrich (1977) has shown, some mental states of sculptors and their worlds are, in complex senses, manifested in the 'lions' that they produce. In this situation, word and object share some common features, though discontinuities between them are informative mirrors of ancient imagination. Some features of myths and societies are condensed into similarities and contrasts embodied in the lion-type.

Livingstone (1986: 59-60) has, in respect of Mesopotamian influences, drawn attention to early provenance of the lion motif. For example, Gudea's presenting the 'mace [or axe], lion-headed weapon studied with *ḫalalu* stones', and Eninnu's fundamental use of it as early as the 3rd millennium BC. It appears that these types of usage were dominated by the seminal Sumerian term me, an expression for 'archetype'. It is significant that this term is employed, for example, to mark the perceived essence of what it is to be civilisation, among other functions. Accordingly, the lion was fundamental to the semantics of text, site and mentality in Sumerian and Akkadian. This is especially important in view of the Mesopotamian mythological me weapon text, discussed in Chapter 8 below.

Figure 1.1 depicts the Hittite Lion Gate at Hattusas, which, as Akurgal (1962) pointed out, embodies an archetype that, from early times, was influential long after the demise of the empire that constructed Hattusas. It is worth attending to this in the perspective of the pragmatics of producing such art and it site-realisation. Such lion figures, and the like, were often composed as substantial additions to buildings and gate-pillars, which therefore had to be structurally integrated precisely by the ancient architects. Eleanor Robson's (1999: 185-90) studies on Mesopotamian mathematics at the turn of the 3rd millennium BC demonstrate that such builders articulated geometric

Figure 1.1 The Hittite lion Gate at Ḫattusas

coefficients and, for example, equations for producing trapezoidal bricks. She proposes that such mathematical phenomena do not accord with our division of pure and applied mathematics, were quasi-algorithmic in nature, and related to mental calculation at junctures where we should have detailed written formulae to achieve such abstract calculation to implement building-plans. So, we should not accord to the characteristic Mesopotamian placing and existence of architectural symbols such as the lion some sort of casual and incidental significance. If we add to the building process, the role of the artist/craftsman as a functionary of this type of process, it assists us to recognise the complex and institutionalised position that sculptured architectural symbols occupied in ancient Mesopotamia. (Obviously someone might object that these symbols had a mere decorative purpose; yet the following and other investigations show that this judgement is not capable of explaining the close relation such symbols had to cultic and conceptual matters.) Clearly, the lion archetype was modified by many other cultural impulses, including earlier Sumerian, later Assyrian and Canaanite images. No doubt the use of 'lion' in, for example, Genesis 49, as an individualising ideal, and Daniel 7's use of 'lion' as a complex empire motif, are variously differentiated later ironising transformations of such early archetypal patterns. When different types of symbols (such as lion and iron axe) are combined, frequently there is an informative transfer and merging of types.

So it should not surprise us to discover a Hittite reference to a lion made of iron from the sky (cf. Kosak 1982). In turn, this complements the reference in the Sumerian Lugalbanda Epic: 'He took his axe made of meteoritic iron' (cf. Hallo 1983). This use of alleged 'meteoritic iron' (KU-BI AN-NA) may presuppose an early *imagined* knowledge of the putative 'celestial', as well as terrestrial, sources of iron, certainly by 1600 BC and probably before 2000 BC (cf. Muhly *et al.,* 1985). It seems evident that the celestial source of iron must have had its origins in astral cultic mythology, rather than any extensive empirical metallurgical sources. This cluster of relations, made in cultic astrology and war, is intensified when we consider later Canaanite iron axes. In Chapter 7 below, an Ugaritic iron axe, replete with lion-head, is discussed in connection with the background military and cultic polemics of the axe-raising miracle in Elisha's ministry in 2 Kings 6.

It will be helpful for handling the investigation of such examples, if the basis of an overall theoretical framework can be established, partially as an outcome of linking archaeology with such subjects as logic, linguistics, literary theory and aesthetics. I hope that proposals in this book will not only be helpful for its primary subjects (Old Testament as well as Near East/Mesopotamian interpretation and archaeology), but also for the development of aspects explored in other subjects here. There is no reason why one should not attempt to develop bases for a theory of meaning employing uses of language in subjects other than, for example, poetry.

Barthes (1977, 1985) derived insights for his theorizing from study of the Genesis Jacob narrative. Ingraffia's (1995) research, on the relation of postmodern theory to biblical theology, has not only shown how the latter can be revived by the former; he also obliquely demonstrates that theological analysis of narrative can contribute new theoretical insights for literary and philosophical theory.

Multi-disciplinary applications benefit not only the target-subject, but also the subject that is applied to it. For example, logic, when brought into archaeology, can derive new insight for archaeology respecting logic's (and logics') own developments. T.J. Smiley's (1982) exposition of the 'Schematic Fallacy' is pertinent here. Informally expressed, it is the use of—actually arbitrary—formal schemata as though they were *the* logical forms of sentences. Smiley points out that some distinguished logicians, who have constructed mathematical or philosophical logic systems, have fallen into this fallacy.

This fallacy can be reformulated as a corollary of Gidden's (1984: 180) critique of mistaken 'reification' in sociology. It is worth linking this parallel to the project of developing a facet for a sociology of archaeology, not only of ancient societies, but also a sociology of archaeology. Archaeologists impose their patterns of rationality on data and their discourses, just as literary expositors do. Further investigation of natural languages, *and* any other domains of semiotic expression—such as artefacts—is urgently needed to enable one to assess what basis there is for generalisation of logical inference over disparate subjects, as well as how individual subjects might contribute to the construction of criteria for reasoning. Conversely, extant versions of logics, when applied in this perspective, and even at the elementary levels, can excavate fundamental relations in archaeology which might have been silted-up by cultural ideology. The possible future definitive synthesis of almost any subject can be brought about by such multi-disciplinary—and not mere interdisciplinary—links, partly because one subject does not internally possess the criteria for its own complete definition. No slice of the world is logically an island, in the sense that even with random functions, they displace the empirical and/or conceptual space that comprises their contexts, and this produces functional relations, which prevents autonomy. I am not proposing analysis involving formal logic. Much of the scope of the term 'logical' here is sustained by making explicit consistent interpretation of the ancient data, and what is taken to follow from them.

Visual Predicates

The above listing of literary theory and aesthetics may seem novel, or perhaps only relevant for the history of art in archaeology. Rather, it will be maintained below that research ideas in such topics can be of explanatory value in archaeology. For example, what logical status do artefacts, such as religious centre statues or the above lions, have in descriptive power? Chapter 2, below, will argue that literary theory and aesthetics (and other subjects) can be formulated so as to occasion the exposure of a close logical relation between the logic of language and the logic of objects that depict identities.

The lion motif introduced above is a case in point: a stone lion is a live metaphor of an actual lion. There is a calculable mapping relation between the actual and the figurative; not only for the measurement of overlap respecting shared properties, but also respecting the contrasts which embody interfaces for measuring representation and discontinuity. I shall propose that this type of range of features can be logically characterised. A fundamental reason for this is that the identity of meaning is itself a type of live metaphor notion.

On the basis of this sort of approach, it eventually follows that the representational properties of artefacts are themselves tautologies, sometimes in counter-intuitive ways, with logical predicates, that is, logico-linguistic predicates. (See Gibson forthcoming e: Section I.2, for a detailed study of this terminology, and Gibson forthcoming c on counter-intuition.) Such an approach uses a relative identity theory, in which relations of identity have the form 'x = y' with respect to a predicate or property F (following Geach 1981). My treatment also implements a realist approach to language, integrated into a fresh theory of meaning, a view which is developed in the present book and Gibson 1997b, 2000a. A realist theory of meaning does not have to be a naive or self-evident correspondence of language with the external world. There are unexpected and counter-intuitive correspondences between language and its references. Consequently, we should develop this type of state of affairs as a counter-intuitive notion of realism. We should also allow for the obvious but sometimes-neglected features of logic applied to language. But some applications are quite basic; for example, logic represents false as well as true propositions (and other natural language expressions that can be paraphrased into logic). When 1 Kings 18 presents expressions used by Baal priests, it clearly allows them the claim that Baal acts in such and such a way; yet the narrative denounces such assertions as false. Consequently, a logic that accounts for these phenomena—correspondence and falsification—is not an artificial language. Rather, it is a formal language that matches, at points, ancient linguistic functions. We do well to notice, additionally, that ambiguous predicates can be logical, as Williamson (1996), and Rescher and Brandon (1980) variously show.

This sketch prepares the way for the thesis that visual, three-dimensional and behavioural properties which can be paraphrased into, or represented by, linguistic and logical description, can be used as a form of evidence that is quite as valuable as textual predicates. Might we say that this is not so because, for instance, with respect to a statue discovered at a religious site, it is often claimed that it is ambiguous as to whether such a statue was intended to simulate a god or a worshipper? The correct response to this would note that 'ambiguous' and 'intended' mark genuine problems, ones that are here tagged by two terms that indicate categories typical of literary problems. This is because the artefact embodies logical problems that are tantamount to such literary issues. Consequently, such ambiguity and intentionality are not grounds against treating artefacts under the rubric of logico-linguistic predicates, but are evidence for the equation, if analysis is carefully controlled. Such an equation will assist one to render explicit the function of controversial variables in the narrative and in analysis. Allegations of ambiguity in given cases could turn out to be a misleading way of obscuring an informative source of relations between the options of statue god and worshipper in statue. A case of ambiguity could be an intended or actual property of the statue's role.

The concept of what I have termed 'God-manifestation' (Gibson 1997a) is a theme in which predicable properties are shared between a god and a worshipper in whom that god is assumed to be manifested. Accordingly, some of these family resemblances are not evidence of ambiguity, or of a masked intention. They are the visual distribution of predicative levels of identity (or identification) between god and worshipper. In this way, the polarisation of choices between the god and worshipper categories masks the point that the correct choice would be the *conjunction* of properties shared. If this were true, its denial would arise via confusing visual surface grammar with the deep structure of visual sense. Of course, anthropomorphism itself is an extensive example of live metaphor. It is true that we do not often have the documented ritual *roles* that such statues played—where this category might be thought to correspond to the use of a term in language in this parallel between the visual and the linguistic. Yet language-codes can usually be deciphered even when inscriptions are fragmentary, so the absence of a full social anthropology of rite is not in itself decisive against the foregoing claim, while more extensive knowledge would be helpful.

Although the application of psychoanalysis to such topics is a precarious enterprise,[2] it is yet possible to infer some content for the mental states of which the statue is a product. Discussion of this topic will be resumed below, in Chapter 6, subsequent to suitable data having been examined. However, even with a coarse-grained approach, we can appreciate that the overlap of theistic and human visual predicates is a presupposition of god-manifestation. A collage made up of different people can be identified as just that: the sum of similarities and contrasts constitutes fresh identity.

---

[2] If we develop a flexible structure heeding the emphasis, if not the program, enunciated by Spitz 1985.

The logics and virtual reality of film are of some assistance here (cf. Gibson 2000a and forthcoming d), since its employment of visual metaphor parallels some ancient religious uses of images. Such ancient contexts also both linguistically and socially encode a sort of performance enactment that mirrors the function of performance in some modern visual media. Just as the filmic realm is a two-dimensional conceit to simulate a three or more dimensional world, so religious literature's uses of personification, metaphor and enactment serve as proxy for a slice of an imagined world.

A god-manifestation statue can accurately be interpreted as a three-dimensional collage employing a relative identity thesis: 'x = y respecting a set of properties F', where 'F' is the relevant narrative or behavioural means of representing the statue (cf. Gibson 1997a). I shall argue not only that this sort of analysis fits in well with available cultic texts and tablets, but that this case is typical of others. If one does not know the identity of the god, this does not prevent application of the foregoing. That is to say, the god's perceived identity is intentional: the descriptions attached to the god, and/or its cultic roles, and these comprise relevant aspects of its envisaged identity. On occasions we may not have retrieved relevant features from site residue, and therefore have a fuzzy concept of the purported identity that precludes our furnishing a criterion of a perceived deity's identity.

Archaeology and Theology

Sometimes, however, the conditions of adverse influence are intended properties of our own minds or culture. Kabbani (1986), among others, has shown that Europe's myths of Orient institutionalised many fictions about the Near East in Occidental culture over the last few hundred years. Solely admitting them does not shake off such presuppositions of influence. This is not the place to present a discussion about the application of Kabbani's view to an exposé of how Europe's myths of Orient would reveal some 19th–20th-century mainstream biblical studies as imperial cults equal to the rule of Empire.

This institutional pull has been mirrored in many studies of biblical cults and priesthood. These cults comprise a main epicentre of creativity in the Old Testament, by which other topics are often gauged in the familiar frameworks of biblical studies. Haran (1978) has, for example, advanced and practised the counsel that a course different from and earlier in date than, Welhausen's view can be produced for the origin of cults and priesthood in the Old Testament. Haran's view is a weak version of the type of revision in theories of a much more extensive reform that, I believe, could take place in the context of developments in archaeological science and linguistic theory, and literary conceptions outside of biblical studies. Nevertheless, R.E. Freedman's (1996) judgement—that we need to distinguish Haran's backdating scenario from Tigay's (1985) attack on the documentary hypothesis—is an important caution against any distorting generalisation of Haran's and other disputed positions. I will attempt to argue that a correct analysis of the biblical and archaeological data will revolutionise certain spheres. I do not adopt or adapt the sort of approach illustrated by Haran's work, but replace it and others with something much more radical, while construing Haran's work as a marginally typical case of moderated unease with some territory in a dominant paradigm. This paradigm is largely derived, with unexceptional modifications, from Europe's myths of Orient, even though episodically valuable site and specific research has been generated within this past, albeit still active, Occidental paradigm.

Gottwald (1979) explained that scholastic obstacles stand in the way of a comprehensive understanding of early Israel. He located the problems mainly in the arena of the difficulty concerning the nature of the ancient sources, and in the scholarly aversion to conceiving ancient Israel as social totality. Two points: first, in principle there are ways around the problems by correct use of inference. This suggestion does not stand in as a strategy to eclipse other non-logical approaches to analysis and perception. Although a wide variety of methods have been devised for examining the Old Testament, there has been little explicit attention given to analysis of logic in the Old Testament, or its theologies, or in methods applied to it. This also obtains for the relation of the Old Testament to archaeology, even allowing for Albright's study (see Gibson forthcoming e: 'Appendix'). Secondly, the possibility that ancient Israel became a 'social totality' is influenced by conditions prior to that totality. To gain access to knowledge of those conditions by inference, we need to keep clear of theological assumptions, while applying archaeological general theory to the excavations.

'General theory' is the framework of systematic analysis now being developed to imply conjectural knowledge about the societies that left the archaeological residue in the excavations. I suggest that Cartwright's (1999) idea, mentioned above, of the theory-nets, is helpful here, rather than the perspective of a single theory, or theory itself, being the arbiter for focus in grasping the role of general theory in archaeology. On such a view as I am proposing, the conjunction of theories and data comprise and are collected in theory-nets. That is to say, multi-disciplinary scenarios such as are being rehearsed in the present book require a more general framework than a given theory's approach to data, as perspective for self-assessment and fruitful use of interpretation. Archaeologists do not excavate conclusions. They excavate raw data from which, with very careful analysis, conclusions follow. But if one employs the wrong logic or uses no explicit framework of inference, one runs the risk, when adopting subjective inexplicit controls, of inventing a fictional ancient society for the site(s). Although there is something of value in Gottwald's hypothesis, his work seems to be a function of the obstacles to which he draws attention: detecting fatigue in traditional theological frameworks, he partially integrates their flaws into his thesis. For example, he supposes that Israel emerged from within Canaanite society, and not at all by invasion or immigration from outside Canaan. I argue below that this does not follow from the archaeological data and analysis (see Chapter 5). There are two further reasons for this situation: first, there is the, by now exhausted, history of conservative versus liberal polarisation in biblical studies which warps systematic analysis. We need to do away with this opposition; but not by absorbing both fixed positions as one. We should start again, differently. In some conservative theology, there is an obsession with assuming that an excavated site is itself a piece of theology. In liberal theology, there is a suppressed presupposition that a slice of the Bible is not exemplified by a feature of a site, or that this possible conjunction is irrelevant to the proper pursuit of Old Testament interpretation. Accordingly, there is a neglect of testing for, and reformulating of, the dimensions of the possible correspondence between narrative and its complex referents. Ideally, modern archaeology is concerned with the full use of a site's artefacts to infer whatever is its history, be it liberal or conservative. Tablets and inscriptions from sites need far more attention than they have been given, and also they require logical analysis of their various relations to biblical texts, which does not proceed with any theological assumptions—especially not as if they were law-like logic premises.

Archaeology of Cult

A valid criticism of Gottwald's enterprise is his assumption in it that biblical scholarship has devised a true account of cultic phenomena; yet there is much to do before we can achieve satisfactory understanding. Archaeology of cult and archaeological general theory proceed apace for various areas of the world. Multi-disciplinary analysis could benefit from a theory of how indeterminacy, as a feature of mentality, functions for religious centres. A theory of the presence of indeterminacy in some modernist literature and political order is a source for this (see Gibson, 2000b)

Greek site analysis and theory are well developed for the archaeology of cult, especially in the context of archaeological general theory. Here we are faced with opportunities and limitations. Renfrew (1982, 1985) argues that there is nothing inherently obscure or problematic about inferring religious institutions and spiritual life from archaeological discoveries. He states (1985): 'the problem is...that archaeologists, with a few honourable exceptions, have made little attempt to develop a coherent approach to the subject'. It is worthwhile discussing some of the issues Renfrew poses in his analysis in its contribution towards a framework for the archaeology of cult. The discovery and excavation of the cult sanctuary at the late Bronze Age town of Phylakopi on the Aegean island of Melos afforded Renfrew and others the opportunity to formulate an attempted framework. Some traditional extremes within archaeological interpretation are well known, and described by Renfrew; there is the apparent rigor of pedantic, scientific inferential argument, as opposed to the humane, imaginative response. Both extremes have generally been rejected by archaeologists at the policy level, though each seems to operate to depict personal tendencies among some archaeologists. Renfrew points out that few of the methodological problems have been tackled systematically, though at the time of writing he treated Ucko (1968) as an exception in general archaeological theory.

At the centre of this opposition is the problem of identifying continuity or change. The priority in this problem, as Renfrew (1985: 3) states it, is:

> continuity in religious practice does not imply lack of change in that practice, and it certainly cannot be taken as evidence of constancy of meaning. Unless the complexities are recognized, the interpretation will amount to no more than projection backwards in time of the customs and concepts which are documented for the historical period, and hence ascription to the earlier, non-literate society of religious beliefs and practices which may in reality have developed very much later. Instead, if valid inferences are to be drawn, the religious system of a given period has to be interpreted primarily in the light of the evidence available for that period, and not on the basis of subsequent belief-systems, however well documented.

The Middle East is less adroit than the Aegean. Biblical scholarship does not yet have corresponding researches with which to match Nilsson's (1971) *The Minoan-Mycenaean Religion*. This judgement is not intended to obscure the progress made in research into Middle East archaeology, however. In addition, theological speculation in biblical studies has played a greater role in influencing the production of interpretation than has Classical commentary diverted Aegean archaeology—sharp though the latter's disputes have been.

Renfrew's warning against backward projection of belief-systems is, I think, presented for application where later belief-systems are applied to earlier societies, and where no extant texts exist for the earlier societies. In biblical studies, there is a large class of quite different cases. This is where there are thousands of ancient tablets and relevant sites for the earlier period; but here theological literary commentators have consigned a biblical narrative to a later date than the possible earlier provenance of the narrative, on the basis of what may turn out to be incorrect theological assumptions. (Chapters 2 and 5 below respectively deal with examples in this class concerning the 3rd and 2nd millennia BC.) Consequently, while we should adopt Renfrew's warning without qualification, we can add to it a corollary for biblical archaeology (which also no doubt will apply elsewhere as well): theological evolutionary assumptions are consequent on and not prior to archaeological investigation. Therefore we should avoid dating-projection forward of a narrative's belief-system and text, if this is an inference based on a theological premise unattested by archaeological general theory, archaeological excavation and interpretation of a site.

Theology should be isolated in analysis from archaeological investigation much more than it is. In the context of the foregoing, there is sometimes a central opposition: the illicit projection backward in time of a later text, versus the illicit projection forwards in time of an earlier text. The often-elusive midpoint—the mean—is the tablet. Here I am concerned with ways in which it can be interpreted by archaeological general theory, and assessed by an appropriately developed means to expose some of its logic of contents. Resolution of the opposition also presupposes the smoothing out and identification of theological assumptions, so as to ensure that, at either end of the opposition, theology does not interfere with the conclusions that follow from causally accurate description of the information in sites and the Old Testament as well as other Near Eastern texts.

Logical Archaeology

The following offers a new interpretation for aspects of archaeological theory, though it does, I hope, usefully complement and contribute to some other theories. First, some aspects of hitherto opposed theories (such as Binford 1983 and Hodder 1985) can complement one another (see Kristiansen's 1998). Scientific archaeology has been much concerned with processual archaeology. This can be summarised as the analysis of the past using a general theoretical framework which interests itself in overall trends and patterns of distribution in the framework of measuring global patterns about similarities and contrasts. Binford has made special contributions to this arena, while emphasizing the role of analysis and generalised proof. Scholars in this area have been especially interested in applying induction to infer the (alleged) causes and effects of large-scale change. Mellor (1982) showed that some of this research confused statistical probability with causal probability. The latter constructs a probability from specific empirical information, with veridical links to the causes involved in producing effects. Conversely, much statistical probability is not nested in knowledge of causes; it is a subjective pattern of expectation. So, in this role, statistical probability is not a technique that can generate relevant knowledge of ancient causes. (Chapter 6 below partly operates as an attempt to identify grounds for a causal explanation of a state of affairs in Late Bronze Age Canaan.)

One peculiar characteristic of archaeological analysis is that it inverts the usual order of analysis of the external world. Archaeology starts with an effect (the unordered residual remains of a society), and this requires analysis so that we can construct its causal antecedents (i.e. propositional description about the things which caused the effect). A further problem here is that such effects are sometimes not the result of intentional action; or at least not the outcome of action intended by those causing the effects, for example, as illustrated by the case of the innocent victims in an invasion. This type of intentionality provokes a number of sharp difficulties for archaeological interpretation and its general theory. I argue that one can side step these difficulties in a number of areas by diverting attention to texts and tablets which manifest intentional states, and not infrequently ones about intentional action. It is my contention that knowledge derived from such narratives can break some deadlock tensions between problems in processual archaeology and the difficulties in attaining knowledge of ancient civilisation, without adopting a normative assumption about the nature of relevant culture. Of course I am not assuming that this will solve or oppose some general queries in processual archaeology. Indeed, research into the causal logic that would map such processes is still in its infancy.

There is also a problem of understanding what logic is. It is worth adverting briefly to what could be an interesting development for archaeology in logic research. 'Inference' is a relation, and one that can be defined from a number of vantagepoints, some of them unexpected. Shoesmith and Smiley (1980) have constructed a multiple-conclusion logic. It could be that this shows the way for developing part of the formal proof-basis for some topics in archaeology, since their work is a fine model for retrojection where plural possibilities obtain, as they do when a site is excavated. Normally in logic, a group of antecedents is used to infer a single conclusion. Multiple-conclusion inference can reverse this ordering: a single antecedent implies a block of multiple conclusions (some of which are not determined as to truth-value). It is worth noting that the standard logic and multiple conclusion logic can be relevantly interrelated, so that each system is complementary. Smiley's logic can be adapted as a type for the historical time-sequence forward from the earlier single original state to that state's later multiple conclusions, if it can pattern the appropriate causal relations. (The single antecedent might characterize an individual event or a law-like state.) Standard logic, with its multiple antecedents and single conclusion, would be applied first to the site-data, to construct an inference to the earlier multiple historical causes. So multiple-conclusion logic could be implemented and interrelated with the standard logic. Although the present work is not concerned to implement a logic program, issues connected to logical judgement will be considered even if off-stage from analysis, and introduced if relevant to applied analysis.

It is helpful to have both an explicit grasp of logical issues as well as a strong grasp of the various main options and possibilities which complicate this situation. The ordering of antecedent and consequence of reasoning may seem a formalist preoccupation: this is not so, in particular where we are uncertain which way around to start or select evidence and reason. Outside of our subject, there are basic problems of ordering analysis, with, for example, relations to some social anthropology in which the epidemiologist Wyatt (1977: 81) stated: 'here are some answers. What are the questions?' Or, as Finley (1985: 104), a historian of ancient Greece stated: 'The historian's evidence...propounds no questions.' We sometimes presuppose almost unconsciously, or are dimly aware of, or imperfectly formulate, our own assumptions. This disposition is often also implicitly parsimonious. This often-covert reductionism accordingly renders invisible a whole series of incomplete or omitted tasks. There is no such thing as the single antecedent proposition, as it were—a generalised proposition about a relevant single historical truth which was a cause of facets of the multiple sites. Yet we often make this sort of move or there are movements of such propositions herded to a single conclusion. It is at least equally valuable to recognise that such a proposition would be a subset of a general archaeological theory we should seek through specificity and criteria of application.

By the same token, narrative inscriptions from such sites could yield a singular generalised knowledge about some ancient minds. Research into the basic properties of religious language, for example in Kirjavainen (1982), could serve as a starting-point to describe the intentional logics of many cultic descriptions. This would be at the same time processual archaeological knowledge, and archaeology of the mind. So, a contribution I wish to suggest is that the ancient world furnishes data that can yield causal knowledge of individual situations and mentality through scrutiny of propositions and linguistic fragments in tablets and inscriptions. I believe that this cuts through some restrictions imposed by processual archaeology, but that it can also place one in a better position to harness and generalise some features of processual and postprocessual archaeology.

Dan Sperber (1985), the French philosopher, has argued that some domains of cultural beliefs are semi-propositional. It might occur to someone to use this viewpoint to oppose the above claim that one can logically describe texts that state or involve such beliefs. Sperber elegantly draws attention to the intentional element in belief, and his criticisms of relativism are important. Just because a belief is itself vague, however, it does not follow that one cannot logically describe it in propositions. Geach (1972) has proved that even quasi-names of primitive contrary deities are susceptible of logical scrutiny, and vague predicates can be represented in some standard logical calculuses. An example, to be dealt with in Chapter 2 below, falls into this category: the god Ninurta in the Sumerian creation fragmentary inscriptions from 3rd millennium BC Syrian Ebla. These are composed of quasi-propositions for which, despite severe analytical problems, there are determinate propositional senses.

As with many, Hodder (1985) heralded the emergence of work designated 'postprocessual archaeology'—which he thinks is needed in the light of the state of affairs in processual archaeology. Hodder has argued that processual archaeology locates attention on the (alleged) merely passive nature of humanity, as the mere subject of worldwide processes. In contrast, Hodder wishes to stress the importance of individuality and the dynamical identity of societies. Although I approach the conflicts and analyses very differently from Hodder, I broadly agree with his interest in individuality.

Binford seems in some ways to oppose claims about insights into ancient cultured mentality, and appears to presuppose that a scholar who moves from the archaeological material to describe some ancient minds has falsely adopted an un-provable normative foundation. This criticism may be true where archaeologists make strong assertions about specific aspects of the postulated primeval human groups. But this book attends to literate humanity, and claims that this interpretation of Binford's view is generally inapplicable to literary or conceptual residue of humanity.

Of course, if someone wants a strong mystical version of 'ancient mentality' that encodes a private language-game that we cannot scrutinise, then this would fail to locate my evidence. Such an objection does not have an answer, however, to Wittgenstein (1958; and see D.G. Stern 1995) in his demolition of the private language argument. Accordingly, the enterprise being developed in these pages relies on the results of the contrary thesis of the communicability of sense, while taking account of the severe problems in the arbitrary signifiers in ancient sign systems.

Riffaterre (1991) has shown to some extent that expressions with apparently undecidable meanings can be measured with some certainty in context where intertextual relations occur. The complex intertext for *Text and Tablet* is formed between excavated tablets/inscriptions and the Old Testament, as well as other narrative records in the ancient Near East. I argue below that the problems with dead languages can be overcome in some spheres, with revised use of current techniques applied to live languages. What Allon White (1981) showed in the perspective of English literature, particularly regarding Conrad and Henry James, can be applied to many ancient narratives. That is to say, 'ambiguity' is not sufficiently analysed, and it can itself not infrequently be disambiguated, as Empson (1953) in some ways showed. Ambiguity is distinct from and easily confused with 'obscurity'. White (1981: 21) stated that William James, 'associates, at some deep level, the idea of obscurity of information with purity: if meanings are so elliptical that they remain "intact and inviolate".' (Of course, this purity is the 'purity' from the standpoint of the role of the narrative voice, and, though it may violate the sensibilities of the reader, the internal dynamics is what may yield to measurement.)

We can add other aspects to this thesis. First, to *recognise* that an expression is obscure is already for one to have shown or presupposed that the expression employs a category of sense whose violation of apparently transparent sense-boundaries delineates contrasts that throw light on the form of the obscurity. Secondly, if that 'meaning' just is in principle obscure, in the sense of having no measurable semantic identity, then, on an intentionalist view of meaning, that obscurity just is, or partly is, the conceptual state of sense imparted by the writer, or that of the limit of his ability to condense his intention to become text. Consequently, further resolution of the obscurity into an over-determined semantic sense would not lead one to the author's state of mind, but to a fiction of his mind.

So, on the one hand, those who are intentionalists have to argue that a mind is obscure, and thus there are limits to such clarification; to describe fog precisely is not to disperse it into a clear day. On the other hand, intentionalists—and anti-intentionalists—should allow a related point: writers play around with ambiguity, obscurity and the arbitrary possibilities of randomness in signifiers. An upshot of this is that one cannot move simply, from anti-intentionalist recognition of the arbitrary signifier, to a conclusion that we do not have a capacity to infer knowledge of the mental states of ancient or modern authors. One reason for this is that, if an author or editor is playing with his own indeterminacy of sense and his exploring the scope of obscurity, this will be an intentionalist internal to the narrative. Thus the narrative will have a mapping relation to the author's mental state. Therefore, on this analysis of merely one feature of deconstructionist or structuralist meanings, anti-intentionalist meanings may have an intentional relation to the mental antecedents that gave rise to them. This seeming paradox clearly also spins back on the authorial role of deconstructionist critics: we appear to know what they are explaining, so there is a discrete limit to the generalising power of deconstructionist theory.

Nevertheless, this is not to set up a carping relation between the present author and deconstruction, especially in view of the value of Derrida's *The Truth in Painting* (1978). A force of the above discussion has been to maintain that allegedly competing theories may well have to merge their programs. When they are interfaced with the ancient worlds, they have to confront more extreme forms into which their respective theses are pushed. The result of this, we have seen and will see, is that a realignment of critical relations and new syntheses, will be more than the sum of its critical parts. Intertwined within these considerations is the view that such reflections can lead to improvements for critical theories for our contemporary literary criticism.

This is distantly analogous with the relation between the Big Bang and the modern world: in the heart of the start of the universe is the unified state of local physics today. Although not drawing a law-like parallel between the ancient and modern narrative worlds, nor supposing that we can have a grand unified view of literary and linguistic theories, the position of this book is that the neglect of contrasts and comparisons between ancient and modern literature can hold up progress in refining understanding of both modern and ancient literature. The helpful application of modern literary theories to ancient narratives also provides insights for modern literary theory.

For example, given the poststructuralist interest in semiotics and the extension of the concept of linguistic symbol, ancient symbols themselves can now more readily be seen within a combined framework in which icon and linguistic sign are co-extensive forms of creativity. The literary theory of ancient texts, I suggest, is of merit as a subset of archaeological general theory of the Near East. Correspondingly, literary theory for ancient inscriptions and iconic or semiotic functions is itself a projectable development from such possibilities and conjunctions, a proposal which the present work attempts to initiate in the perspective of archaeological theory and Mesopotamian literary analysis.

Hodder (1982) has advocated an idealist framework for archaeological theory. A standard description of idealism would show it to be pluralistic, with generalisation limited to epochs, subjects or domains, with contrary generalisations admissible for other sets of epochs, subjects or domains. (On this view a thesis is not essentially true or false.) Binford (1982) has strongly criticized Hodder's approach, on the grounds that empathetic insight into past mentality is not generally possible, and subjectivism is incorrect. I think that there are strengths in both writers' views, though it seems that both fail, if construed as generalised explanations of archaeology, while they present insights of considerable significance for our progress. Kristiansen (1998: 36-37), while also being influenced by their conceptions, has demurred from the need to speak within terms of some of the new archaeology's confrontational contextualisations. He situates such debates as functions of cyclic shifts between generalising, teleological frameworks and particularising, non-deterministic ones, with middle positions occupying versions of functionalism and structuralism.

It is important to distinguish between (a) our adopting or believing a framework defined in terms of and sharing in idealistic and subjectivist presuppositions characterising idealistic phenomena in the ancient society; as opposed to (b) our measuring idealistic assumptions of the ancient society by use of non-idealistic objective measuring criteria. I believe that the chapters below obliquely show (a) to be false and (b) to be true. For example, Chapter 6's section: 'Biblical and Ugaritic Gods' demonstrates how idealistic and subjective assumptions about existence in Canaanite mythology are explicitly present in Levant narratives and ritual sites, in the course of which it is proved that relevant details of them can be represented by deployment of bivalent logics. The resulting study shows that some scholars have allowed these subjectivist assumptions to thwart accurate control of these functions in analysis, partly by conflating aspects of (a) and (b) above. The result has been that the idealism in a textual presupposition has regulated scholastic parameters outside of the immediate scope of the target text. Logical assessment of the text, its archaeology, and the scholastic assumptions needs to be objective and non-idealistic if it is to expose and correct such distortions, identify idealism in the ancient world and control it in archaeological assumptions.

Processual archaeology is holistic, as for example Kristiansen (1998: 40-41) presents it. In the context of philosophy of social theory, S.D.T. James (1984) has proved that holism and individualism are not contrary, at the structural level. She advances a thesis that preserves both principles. It is clear that her work could be used to develop further integration between processual and postprocessual archaeology, if reformulated along the present lines, employing the approach here proposed. I have reasoned elsewhere (Gibson *forthcoming e*) that meaning itself is not constructed holistically, though it articulates syntactic and semantic universals (an example would be the category of proper name). A severe restriction on a strongly holistic form of processual archaeology should be recognized. If such holism be true, a single feature of one site can be understood only if all such features on all sites are known, or a given site should be typical of all others. This is a strong form of holism, however; a problem is that the stipulation of what is 'holistic' can be so weak that one senses some scholarly uses of it are tinged with metaphor. Of course, the presence of metaphor is not in itself bad, though its unnoticed presence as a shifting goalpost in technical usage is contrary.

In logic theory of meaning, in contrast, for one to know a language holistically, is to be in a position to define a single sentence, by virtue of which one would have defined all sentences. As Dummett (1975) and Gibson (*forthcoming e*) argue, we can understand single sentences (i.e. molecular semantics) and not all others. Consequently, universal semantic holism for all natural languages is false, and the linguistics of all expressions in ancient languages should not therefore be stipulated in advance of empirical research, not least since we may not have typical samples.

There is also a neglected value of the synchronic orientation in relation to logic, which Bucellati (1996: 10) well characterises, in a way that is applicable beyond the scope of his remit in grammar of Babylonian:

> A synchronic description…views the language as a working system, in terms
> of the logical connections of its component parts, and regardless of how they

> come into being through time. Synchrony is not a small slice of temporal
> development, it is rather a logical system viewed outside of any temporal
> development.

Certainly, we may sometimes be unable to determine the synchronic phase, and what it
is to be a 'logical system'. This is problematic, but we can identify domains for some
temporal boundaries, and, as Gibson (2000: 'Prologue') demonstrates, the more
advanced research on such a system gives way to formal properties that are helpful to
natural language narratives, not adverse to them. Consequently, logical theory can be
of importance for understanding ancient semantics and narratives.

To the extent that texts and tablets inform archaeology, a non-holistic
foundation will be true to archaeology. Also, given that processual archaeology has,
without exhaustive veridical knowledge of some of its domains, generated valuable
understanding, this state of affairs resists the assertion that 'true' archaeology is
universally processual, by *reductio ad absurdum*. If, therefore, we reduce the strong
form of holism in some processual archaeology, to accommodate postprocessual
developments (while qualifying their subjectivism and global claims), we will discover
that this complies with the positions I have assigned to the archaeology of text and
tablet, within the scope of their contribution to archaeological general theory, to
construct an archaeology of individual minds. The huge amount of texts discovered in
the ancient Middle East requires a somewhat larger role for the archaeology of text and
tablet in relation to the archaeology of the mind than for some other countries or
epochs. The project to construct archaeology of mind, and a philosophy of it, is
important (with qualitative variation) for any sites where linguistic data are unearthed.

A sensitive balance is needed to steer through trends in archaeology, to
preserve the insights achieved in scholarly debates, while not allowing polarizing
tendencies deposited by fashion to distract from the value of unexpected or familiar
types of exploration. In maintaining this balance, Colin Renfrew (1982, 1987) has
pioneered a perspective and distinctions by which to frame research for attempts to
retrieve comprehension of some ancient mentality. Renfrew (1987: 10) introduces the
term 'mappa' to designate the conception marking an internalized cognitive map of the
world. Renfrew (1994) develops the focus of this approach, and shows the need for
further attention to make explicit the role of reasoning and how to expose the identities
of ancient mappas. Such concerns are functions of the conjunction between our
techniques of analysis and ancient traces of mappas in archaeological data. My own
philosophical position (detailed in Gibson 1998b; 2000a) is that the world is
realist—often counter-intuitively so—while the uniqueness of what it is to be
consciousness in its expressive identities, stands qualitatively in enormous contrast to
inorganic processes. Consequently, if the expressions of mappas have, even to some

quite approximate degree, been expressed by ancient people, the empirical and logical significance of the resulting properties have two qualities in contrast with inorganic data. First, since they are manifestations of intentionality or intention, they will have a conceptual fingerprint that relays some function of a mappa. Secondly, since expressions of the logic (even) of intentionality crucially differ from non-conscious causal effects in the ways in which they betray 'fingerprinting' by their causes, there will be traces of rationality that can be tracked for evidence of rationality in ancient consciousness. Certainly, the ingredients will vary in quantification and quality, depending on whether the data are uses of language or material, and what their proportionality is to their varying capacities to act as signifiers. Occasionally, the arbitrariness or inefficiency in the signifying medium may seem to resemble the inorganic domain's non-semantic status; but usually, the context of the archaeological data or the mappa's internal identity house criteria of *différance* that yield identification of sense or no sense.

It is important, if the above approach is right, to separate out the differences on the interface between processual archaeology and the integration of information from ancient inscriptions. A reason for this is because the subject-contents of ancient narratives and idealistic features of ancient societies should be described, though they should not be allowed, where we can prevent it, to infect the metalanguage and criteria of measurement which represent them.

Clearly, these issues directly lock into the problem of truth. Much of this book is concerned with explaining the structures for identifying truth in various ways. Chapter 3 addresses criticisms of and evidence about the causal explanatory grounds relating the Bible to Egyptian archaeology. In this context, I reflect on aspects of J.-C. Gardin's (1980) significant study, as well as other approaches. But I should here take issue with Gardin's (1980: 15) concession that: 'Our analysis cannot...pretend to be a logical one, in the technical sense of the word, nor a formal one, except in a metaphorical sense.' If the logic were only dead metaphor, that would be a worry. Rather, logic can apply to metaphor, and use live metaphor, which is a distinct issue (see Gibson 1997a).

Gardin (1980: 15 n. 1) offers a footnote explanation of this technical sense in the course of which he cites the work of the German logician Frege, as a typical example of the specialist use of 'logic' that does not, in his view, apply to theoretical archaeology. I submit that, while this may be true of Gardin's book, it does not have to be true of archaeology or Near East historical research generally. In a sense, Gardin is right, however. Frege's interpretation of some logic does not go in the right direction, or far enough (see Dummett 1981,1993). Some of my recent work (Gibson 1997a; 1998b, 2000a) amounts to a preliminary attempt to apply logic and logical linguistics to typical ancient and modern narratives. What Gardin approach hopefully allows for is the new project that new philosophy of exotic pure mathematics (say of super string theory) has unexpected relations to the logic of creativity in some literature (see Gibson forthcoming c-e).

Three other points indicate the way to obviate or focus Gardin's apprehension. First, there are many specialist senses for the term 'logic', usually deriving in various ways in analytical philosophy from Russell's and Whitehead's *Principia Mathematica*; and Frege's work on which Russell founded his view of analytical philosophy. Secondly, for example, Binford's use of the logic of hypothetico-deductive inference derives more generally from Popper (1972), whose logic is also concerned with binary (true/false) logics, despite his empirical concerns with science. Thirdly, there are fresh developments in analytical philosophy's logic research (for example Lewis 1980, 1986), which typify progress as well as logics of surprising sorts. This also applies in quite separate ways to some French research, for example by Bouveresse (1995). The present work will select from these and also develop its own philosophical approach.

Such trends move against traditional mechanistic formal assumptions about what logic is. A characteristic of such research is to place a question mark in opposition to the implicit and often-unconscious assumptions scholars of the bible and of the Near East deploy. The production of new insights in logic is partly a metaphoric process. This itself relates to a large arena for research in logic to which I here only allude. L.J. Cohen's (1993) study of metaphor can be adopted for this purpose, though he does not deal with this type of issue or explicitly analyse live metaphor. Gibson (1997a) develops a logic and linguistic theory for this distinction, in the contexts of the Dead Sea Scrolls.

Binford (1982: 161) suggests that, 'the accuracy with which we can infer the past is directly related to the degree that our uniformitarian assumptions are justifiable'. This is an important point, but it is compatible with the thesis that a uniformitarian assumption is one in which idealism and relativism are historical functions of the ancient world and its archaeology. For example, consider the uniformitarian principle that all female consort deities are idealistic and entail a partner-deity. Chapter 5's examination of 'Aserah' and' 'Yahweh' at Kuntillet Ajrud furnishes evidence for this claim. So, one's having an idealistic presupposition with which to infer knowledge of idealism in an ancient culture is consistent with having uniformitarian assumptions. A number of studies in the following chapters are to some degree concerned with showing that we can infer knowledge of ancient mentality by the correct juxtaposition of idealistic cultural referents using objective inference. Binford has developed middle-range theory—the conception of theory building in which there are revisable competing theories tested by causal inference. Binford (1977) states that the development of middle-range theory should grow in firm combination with general theory in archaeology. In conjunction with this position, we should maintain the following, when we are studying literate humanity: middle-range theory, archaeological general theory, postprocessual theory, and archaeology of the mind cannot definitively be generalized without relevant analysis of text and tablet, and it needs integration of its results into these subjects, and vice versa. A consequence of this situation will be the outcome that we can have true perceptions of the ancient world.

Catastrophe Archaeology and Mental States

Crudely put, a uniformitarian presupposition is a proposition with the quantifier 'all' prefixed to it, or propositional tautologies of that form. For example, 'All the universe is subject to catastrophe at some time' can be logically parsed in many ways, though this range of quantification need not preoccupy us in the present contexts. Geophysical catastrophe is a subset of processual archaeology. Perception of such catastrophe is a subset of the archaeology of mind, and of postprocessual archaeology. The conjunction of the three spheres is a subset of archaeological general theory.

Yet how does this conjunction pertain to uniformity in assumptions about literary typology? In the *Poetics*, Aristotle subordinates the actor to the tragic action, while representing the universal in the particular, whereas Henry James (1986) inverts the relation and makes the action subject to the individual. The prima facie reality in catastrophe is that, for example, geophysical catastrophe facts are, at best, Aristotelian, while the psychoanalytic universe is that of Henry James, in a manner of speaking. But Mesopotamian gods are 'psychological individuals', and they may, as with the devil god Pazazu, subordinate their inventors in worship. (Regarding the relation of Mesopotamian mentality and gods to modern philosophy's categories, see Gibson 1998b.)

Thom's catastrophe theory has been refined by Zeeman (1979) to apply in ideological theory as it relates to the residue of societies researched in archaeology. He argued that there is no historical law to specify some particular evolutionary sequence of ideologies, though he identifies sociological invariants of perception in populations that change. Conversely, as McAllister (1986) has proposed, progress in science and its past historiography reflects a realist and objective basis for theory appraisal of the physical world, though we should qualify this with the point that one can have a nonrealist presentation of realist data. So, the measurements of comparison and contrast in the social and scientific domains are productive for generalisation.

It is a significant topic for research to discuss how this type of catastrophe theory relates to psychoanalysis, with its attention to collective trauma and primordial chaos (cf. Lyotard 1984). It was more than a playful slip that induced Freud to compare psychoanalysis with archaeology. Freud's (1959) study of myth in relation to poetry and primal crisis can lead to illumination in Sumerian archaeology. Hutcheon's (1984) examination of Mauron's relation to Freudian thought, and to Mallarmé, serves as a useful refinement for background work on the roles of poetic texts in this perspective. Valuable also is Bouveresse's (1995) study of Wittgenstein's criticisms of Freud for raising questions about mythology of the unconscious (cf. also Bouveresse, 1997). Central to future questioning concerning the issue of ancient catastrophe and collective trauma is the problem of what counts as an unconscious causal experience. This itself impacts on the problem of what it is to have an unconscious pain and its relation to consciousness. We cannot at present answer such questions, though there have been refinements in formulating the problems, particularly by Wittgenstein (1995).[3] For analysis of relevant formal logics, see Gibson (2000b: 'Prologue' and forthcoming e).

Some myth comprises itself to be the stage marking the individual's (or an individuality's) emergence from the group's psychology, in which his imagination breaks from the 'Father-God' which provokes his (or persons') heroic deification. The relation of myth to the unconscious and the latter's ontological status are problematic. But even if we consider only a typical imagination, its relationship with, and reaction to, the world, as ways of determining in some limited senses the functioning scope of the relation to its conscious manifestations, then we need not enter the disputed arena of a mystical unconscious. That is to say, our assessment of the existence of the unconscious can be struck in relational and functional terms: the external manifestations of conscious experience are to be interpreted as signs of internal activity such as dreams, forgotten yet implied data, etc. As Forrester (1980) has argued, we do not have to follow Jung to discover that psychoanalytic theory of myth and culture are inextricably tied into the theory of symbol. The links between dream and myth, Forrester shows, were derived from close attention to philology by the early analysts.

We might here extend Freud's figure and comparison of detective work in archaeology with psychoanalysis. We should allow for the transition of analysis of the individual mental to its partially metaphoric application collectively to general aspects of cultures (and ones remote from Freud's Europe, on which see Bowie 1993: ch. 4). Psychoanalytic processual causal laws could be formulated as a set of preconditions in the mind, and, by inference, in the unconscious mind. Semantic axioms could then relevantly associate them with the conjunction of archaeological general theory and an archaeology of the mind (such as Renrew, 1982 sketched), appropriately interpreted by

---

[3] All references to Wittgenstein are based on the Wittgenstein 1998–99 CD-ROM transcriptions or to the actual MSS; but since the Basil Blackwell (Oxford) translations are sufficiently precise for the present purposes and the CD-ROM version is very complex for referencing, the dates and sections refer to the Blackwell editions.

an archaeology of text and tablet. My own additional preference, while accepting many Freudian insights, is to qualify their claims by concurring with Wittgenstein's (1958: 15, and *passim*) criticisms, that, on occasion, Freud's use of reason and attendant distinctions are inconsistent, for example his confusion of a reason with a cause in inference statements. The study of Bouveresse (1995) is one instance of how one might come to some accommodation on this conflict. Wittgenstein's respect for Freud's and Breuer's (1893) research directs one to a source for further alignment, and Drury's (1981) discussions with Wittgenstein, as well as Drury's (1973) own study, are helpful in this regard. This overall strategy isolates linguistic use and pre-Greek symbolic value more than Freud did.

There is a close connection in Sumerian and other mythologies between psychological (including psychotic) fantasy and perceptions expressed about geophysical realms. It is an interesting project for psychoanalytic research in relation to ancient Mesopotamian imagination for catastrophe theory to be applied to mental topology.[4] Most of these areas are new to research, so it is worth sketching a route for future work. Typical Mesopotamian mythology has a strong relation to certain modernist forms of surrealism, especially in the arena to be considered below—that of perceived historical catastrophe and demonology. As Descombes (1995) explains, modernist writers such as Sartre and Merleau-Ponty were averse to the Freudian analysis of society, but the surrealists were perceptive to a Romantic strand in Freud's approaches, and they incorporated elements of his work into their programs. As Bowie (1991, 1993) has pointed out, it was left to Lacan (obscurantist and overstated though his treatment sometimes is) to insist that Freud has more central significance for the relation of the past to the *future* than Freud himself appreciated. In a sense (regarding the functions of obsession, trauma and religious symbol in demonology), Sumerian demonology parsed uses of the unconscious that held later Akkadian and Canaanite cultures in its sway (cf. Gibson 1998b).

A plausible way of attempting to link ancient with modernist surrealist symbolism influenced by Freud is to consider psychoanalytical research on the art of Max Ernst. Although there are, without doubt, vast differences between ancient and modern worlds, there are similarities in their use of categories and motifs mirroring unconscious types. Apart from the obvious partial similarities between their use of male and female identities in traumatised and schizoid states, what Elizabeth Legge (1988), in her important analysis of Ernst's work, terms 'deadpan' style and

---

[4] One strategy here, developed by various writers such as Mallarmé, in *Un Coup de Dés*, and Gibson 1987, is to introduce geophysical phenomena as motifs for mental states, as did ancient writers; but in the latter case this is as live metaphors to depict a model for representation of the mental.

'exaggerated lack of inflection' in his Freudian paintings has some parallels with the inertness of Sumerian pictorial and pictographic depiction of catastrophic phenomena. To be sure, part of this equation is eclipsed by 'accidents' and limitations imposed by the media of representation; but equally, artists and traditions respond to thwart such limits. Catastrophe theory in textual archaeology is a subset of cosmogony. In cosmogony, the origins of the universe are, as it were, functions of gods who mirror the human psychoanalytical patterns of their composers and historical contexts. Gwendolyn Leick's (1994) study of sex and eroticism in ancient Mesopotamia, for example, reviews the Eridu model of cosmological articulation of sexuality, and supports the view that, peculiar to it is ENGUR both as a personification of the goddess Nammu, and as a motif preceded by the signs for the 'sweet water ocean', etc. Nammu is a goddess who gave birth to the heaven and earth, the gods, and, as such, is the self-procreating womb. Some of these associations are stitched together over the use of E.engura as the term for the main temple in Eridu. Leick's employment of Lacan's psychoanalytical theories, according to which the unconscious is textual, assists us to recognise a way in which such disparate semantic and symbolic values were presented as coincident in Sumerian fields of meaning. No doubt there is much further work to be done here, not least in judging to what extent Derrida's (1978) deconstruction theory has a lodgepoint in such matters.

Human reaction to geophysical catastrophe is a fruitful sphere for research, especially in the perspective of catastrophe theory being used in physical science to measure earthquakes. These interrelations may be novel, manifesting a cluster of exotic and problematic phenomena, but they are substantive. These involve data which are at once causal, intentional, processual, postprocessual and entrap ancient collective as well as individualist mentalities. In this sphere of unexpected connections, it is well to make explicit a stylistic device internal to the subject and to be used here: the digression. One person's digression may be another's sense of relevance. The boundaries of relevance are often counter-intuitive to our expectations. Although one would not wish to allow irrelevance to have dominion over judgement, there is a genuine sense in which we do not know in advance of our cultural futures, if a digression will turn out to be a direct route into a substantive arena of research.

It is worth exploring Marian Hobson's (1995) research on the 18th-century French writer, Diderot—concerning his use of digression to surprise readers with a new perception of a central topic that constantly outraged institutional sensibility. Hobson explains that such digression is internal to understanding of the subject. Perception of the visual world is not always reliant on visual experience. Analogy between two disparate topics can discover new knowledge where there is only apparently irrelevant difference between them. In considering the relations between the Old Testament and the ancient Near East, it is worth assessing the possible matches between data in the two zones, and the not unknown irrelevance of such putative matching to the significance of a specific text. But it is also of exploratory value for understanding of the Old Testament to position a set of texts at a great distance from it, that nevertheless have indirect impact on the two zones' conflicting worldviews.

It is also profitable to select a case that most extremely embodies, in content and scholarly interpretation, an example of digression and stretched analogy. In short, a situation that would have pleased Diderot, and which will disturb consensus; a purpose here is to question our confidence that we have determined the limits of grounds for surprise and ignorance. The consequent disturbance is itself a fertile ground for reflection on, and reflecting, senses. In the perspective of stylistics, we might profitably view such digression, relevantly used, as a function of creativity. So, for example, the Prague 'school' of stylistics argued for 'style as deviation'. This overstatement should be ecumenically counter-posed against the Roman Jacobsen view of style as 'recurrence or convergence of textual pattern' (see Tova Meltzer's, 1995 helpful survey for further detail). Presumably, part of the answer to what the identities of originality in an ancient tradition are, is the counter-intuitive conjunction of something akin to the Prague as well as the Jacobsen approaches to the issue. Digression is internal to a narrative's creative form (even as a subplot or tonal function). If it is relevantly recognized by a later reader's sensibility, then this state of affairs has significance for the narrative external relation to other textual traditions and their innovatory or institutional identities. Thus we can suitably consider an exotic scenario concerning ancient Mesopotamia whose identity and relevance to other subjects are problematic and obscure.

It would be less profitable to choose a secure uncontroversial topic as an example of present concerns, and thereby, with ease, avoid being held as a hostage to fortune, to trim the book more readily to engage approval; conversely the present writer has no desire to foment controversy for its own sake. In fact, just as Christopher Ricks attracted a furore when he wrote of Keats and Embarrassment, because he employed his own embarrassment as a device to evaluate Keats's perception of emotional psychology as a function of his poetry, we should wish to avoid controversy as functions of a desire to criticise or reduce a writer alienated from one's sympathy, while yet boldly addressing issues of disagreement.

These observations serve to introduce the tantalising topic of the mentality involved in both ancient writing concerned with trauma and catastrophe, as well as modern scholarly assumptions about them. James Kinnier Wilson (1979) presented a revolutionary interpretation of the early Sumerian Ki-bala ('Rebel Lands') tablets. His views were critically received, and both his preoccupation, as well as the sharp responses, may well embody the psychological presuppositions of authors that are not all together internal to the objective empirical assessment of the subject. Such a state of affairs is itself a sensitive matter; but in Foucault's (1976) *The Will to Knowledge*, exploration of such matters brings priority and perspective which at most is implicit or confused in debates like these. The Rebel Lands literature considered below has only indirect relevance to the Old Testament. However, its influence in Mesopotamia, as well as its mediation to other genres, and its employment here as a token typical of some others, constitutes it as a primal source of collective influence in the relevant ancient cultures and traditions. Our autobiographical concerns, obsessions, or proclivities will tend always to infiltrate and predispose the subject of investigation. Whether or not Kinnier Wilson's original work reflects a personal concern with origins and a motivation based on psychiatric and medical priorities derived from his father, Samuel Kinnier Wilson (the neurophysiologist who discovered Wilson's Syndrome), it should not obscure the significance of the issues and perspectives he raised. Whatever the status of his conceptions on such matters, the hostile reception of his book in 1979–80 mirrored the absence of, and probably ignorance about, psychoanalytical/ psychiatric research applicable to the subject, in contrast with the explicit and developed approaches of such research which were well under way and applied to, for example, French literature (cf. Bowie 1972; 1978; Foucault 1961; 1963; 1969; 1971). At the side of the book's characteristics, we should position the roles of conformity and individualism. Shapiro (1997: 34) deconstructs both these polarities, and shows that the conformity can be built on rubble, while individualism should not be an expression against conformity; that said, he emphasises that genuineness can too readily be under threat where originality is concerned. An upshot of this is that we should consider to what extent the unusualness of his *Rebel Lands* is a function, not so much of its author, as it is to do with the psychodynamical turbulence and obsession with origins which are internal to the 'Rebel Lands' tablets. In short, mirroring and inversion are psychological features of narratives as well as of authors. And of course, critics.

In certain respects, the 'Rebel Lands' is chosen here because of a wider problem. In attempting to understand the ancient world, we all have more extreme forms of problems than those with which we grapple do in our contemporary and ordinary typical human areas. For example, following Wittgenstein (1995: sec. 83), we can have non-verifiable sensations in which we 'perfectly well identify' a matter, though there are either no objective external criteria, or there are difficulties in formulating them. This type of problem has special significance for the reportage of unusual phenomena or records which themselves are deviant, non-standard, unstable in ideological position in relation to others in their environment, as well as bizarre or abnormal semantic fields. What comprises being these, of course, is itself often a matter of presupposing that from which some groups would demur. Within such a priority, however, there are some well-developed interpretations of distinctions, even though there is argument about how to resolve some of their difficulties. One set has been explored by, for example, Dan Bar-On (1999). This has to do with how to classify and interpret the impacts of trauma. Internal to this area is the role of silenced information, facts, data and assertions. Trauma paralyses responses, often by redirecting them through 'institutionalised' routes. The role of 'institutionalised' here not only concerns the effects of abstract functions concretised into a social institution, such as an incorrect politically conceived record of past traumatic history. It has to do with the ways people cope with trauma by artificially framing memory, experience or interpretation so as, for example, to by-pass or neutralise deleterious impacts. Near East study is at a very early stage in addressing these issues, and one can hope only to introduce and suggest ways forward in these areas. Certainly, it would be inappropriate and misleading to treat all ancient literature as traumatised tropes. Conversely, beneath many sites and between intertexts there have been or are traumatic states. The ancient world seems to have been much more regularly traumatized individually and collectively than, for example, the contemporary USA is, untypical though the latter may be of other areas of the world. The central problem in such traumatization is how to expose implicit or over-stated functions. Bar-On (1999) recommends addressing these issues by bold presentation of alternatives, and relevant insights from personal and social psychology. He notes that there are problems linking these areas, and in any case they are beyond the scope of the present book. Nevertheless, his work is important for the present analysis, and we should look to ways of avoiding underestimating how these issues of interpretation obtrude on the study of the ancient world, since we are, even outside of abnormal contexts, concerned with the functions of 'silencing' and institutionalization of the past. So both areas have lessons relevant for each other.

The tablets of the 'Rebel Lands' themselves embody a semantics that is unstable, and frankly, the themes seem so soaked in psychotic fantasy that empirical measurement of them is a problem. They reflect a deviation from much Sumerian and Akkadian literary sensibility. The tablets are exotic, unstable and controversial in their status, and, as such, they reflect some of the types of considerations delineated above. The Rebel Lands tablets, in seeming accordance with their title, were taken, until Kinnier Wilson (1979), to be concerned with people who rebelled in the target lands.

The Ki-bala tablets describe a primeval conflict between the gods and the earth, in conceptions that were later to spread through Sumerian to Akkadian forms and their editions. I here offer a brief presentation of Kinnier Wilson's views, as well as my own interpretation of the tablets. Once upon a time, in the Inanna and Ebih story, a mountainous location near Mount Ebih was involved in catastrophe. The mountain range split in two, and one side of the mountain range moved and destroyed Aratta, also attested in the Ebla archives. In the gods' underworld, fires broke out. Ninurta (in the legend *Nin-me-šár-ra*), in the manifestation of a liquid Serpent-god, spewed mucus all over the mountain range. The wind gods and demons came up from the underworld; the wind gods poisoned people.

Although this narrative contains myths, Kinnier Wilson presents evidence to argue that the tablets relate to an actual geophysical location where there was a geophysical catastrophe, coded into the collective memory of the Sumerians. He attaches this to the emergence and evolution of Sumerian and Akkadian mythology. Since there are not only Sumerian but also Akkadian versions of these narratives, it seems clear that certain scribes and readers in 2nd millennium Mesopotamia attended to these stories derived from earlier memories and re-used them. In view of this, it is worth noting Foster's (1996: 12-14) cautious response to some of the other Mesopotamian catastrophe traditions, which he considers when assessing the prospects for ancient Mesopotamian treatments of volcanic phenomena that might also parallel in some ways to the Thera eruption (ascribed to the possible low date of circa 1515 BC). Foster concludes that there are no explicit references to a volcanic catastrophe in Mesopotamia, though he hopes that such data may be retrieved. Foster does not refer to Kinnier Wilson's study or the Rebel Lands tablets. Although these appear in particular to refer to earthquake and landslips, they include the types of phenomena Foster includes—fire-glow, atmospheric dust, etc. So the following can be taken to adopt aspects of Foster's unrequited interest.

In their scientific survey of Persian and related earthquakes, Amraseys and Melville (1982: viii-ix, 37) consider that, though scattered indications of earthquakes survive from the 3rd millennium BC, there was no adequate documentation of earthquakes until the advent of the Islamic period in the 7th century. They cite an Arabic source that, looking back from AD 872, states: 'On Sha'ban 258 an earthquake devastated the region of Saimereh...about 20,000 people were killed...the shock was possibly felt in Iraq at Wasit and at Basra, and was also responsible for large-scale landslides in the Saimareh valley' (1982: 6; variant spelling 'Saimareh' = 'Saidmarreh'; latter employed hereafter). Amraseys and Melville also note that the sole surviving earlier record of a major earthquake in the relevant area—the Zagros—was precisely the location Kinnier Wilson (1979) cites, that of Saidmarreh. They (1982: 31) report that it existed from prehistoric times as an enormous landslip of 20,000 million cubic metres.

The Ki-bala tablets cannot readily be dated, but they appear to typify contexts that had extensive influences on later perceptions and contexts in Mesopotamia. The proposed geographical location—Saidmarreh—is outside the inner circle of Mesopotamian culture. Yet this should be balanced by Guillermo Algaze's (1993:2) perspective, in his study of the dynamics of expansion in early Mesopotamian civilisation, using the Uruk world as an index. He states that,

The only proper framework for the study of the phenomena connected with the rise of Mesopotamian civilization, then, is one that takes into account the likelihood that sources of disequilibrium external to the alluvial system of southern Iraq were as influential in explaining the particular political economy of civilization there as the internal sources illuminated by recent research.

I propose that we should aim at constructing a cultural and psychological framework of influence and disequilibrium at the side of this approach. The Ki-bala tablets comprise a possible, exotic, start for such a framework. Their uncertain identities and disturbing possibilities are as much a function of their subject matter and archetypical functions, as they are problems for researchers. As such, they have potential for the generation of a framework to engender fresh insights into mentality, as much as they have propensities for ambiguity and perplexity.

As mentioned above, in choosing Kinnier Wilson's study, I have explicitly considered and am mindful of the perplexing role, especially in this example, of autobiographical presuppositions in scholarly writing. A scholar can tend to overstate the scope and significance of a neglected or hitherto unattended feature or interpretation of his subject. Preoccupation with catastrophe, particularly relating to seismic activity, is an arena attractive to eccentric and obsessive attention. Conversely, highly refined institutionalised scholarly traditions of reading narratives can err by deeming unexpected deviance from our critical canon to be evidence of impropriety in the capacity to make value judgements, and possibly a sign of personal imbalance. So boldly to proffer a scenario such as Kinnier Wilson did is a risky venture.

For those who are instinctually averse to novelty, it is worth their reflecting on the notion of digression. The symmetry between Diderot's use of digression and originality may violate an unduly restrictive criterion of acceptability for theory by a scholarly tradition, since the latter is partly a function of the coincidence that such a tradition is the manifestation of true collective judgements. Aberration is a function of not only innovation, but also tradition. At the side of this, we need to allow for the often unpredicted and unrecognised ways in which ancient trauma imposes a blackout of irrelevance by virtue of what trauma is. As the psychoanalytical theorist Kennedy (1998) explains, there is an elusive relation between people who are traumatised (here, in the vehicle of their literary creativity) and how external observers are cognisant or ignorant of the products of trauma. Central to this in terms of the ancient Sumerian world and us, are two states of affairs. First, we do not know the identity of degree of absorption by ancient people of displaced fragments of trauma that was the result of transmission of earlier trauma. This mediation from the traumatised victim to people who are not themselves the recipients of trauma, is regarded as an important way in which trauma itself, and not just its memory, is transmitted. That is to say, ancient scribes preserving the creative results of trauma are themselves likely to have been influenced and affected by the scholarly depiction of trauma. Just as the use of ill-placed humour by a victim can be a troubled mask by which to distance the apparent effect of trauma so it is with the ossification of trauma into stylised chaos or catastrophe genres. They themselves yield witness to the disturbance of an artificially, and therefore psychologically unresolved, distance between the traumatic origin and its continuing mediated influence. In some other more distant sense, which it is not appropriate to discuss in the present context, we may also note the ways in which modern scholars may be attracted to consider such cases because of obliquely connectable autobiographical considerations.

Such element in the study of trauma, as it relates to the present concern with ancient Mesopotamian demonology, poses somewhat of a difficulty for assessing the criteria of relevance. This is precisely because, in a genuine sense, the too-ready adoption of a canon of apparently tight relevance is itself a manifestation of the need for criteria about excluding matters whose connection are only cognisable over a larger and deep structure contextualization. One such evident, though general, function is simply the point that somehow the whole of Early Bronze Age Mesopotamia probably produced a demonological environment which pulsed far and wide in its unpredicted and extensive influence, causally modifying the most unexpected, as well as familiar, areas of human psychological experience. The upshot of this for the creative emergence of the Old Testament is an amazingly complex and incompletely sketched domain. On the one hand, traditional scholarship has tended to speculate with uncontrolled synthesis that attracted, for example, James Barr's (1961) ire. On the other hand, not least in the perspective of some deconstructive criticism (see Gibson forthcoming e), we should be wary of a too ready tendency to deem it that such a type of speculation has closed down, in principle, by analysis, what in fact only has a contingent and not necessary detection-procedure for identifying forms, and not a full range of possible reconstructed synthetic theories. Advanced uses of critical theory and fallacy have to be aware, and wary, of the fatality for theorisation of articulating fallacy and negative induction, in the absence of an objective sympathy for theory construction and objective conjectural knowledge.

With these sensibilities, and others, then, the present author plays hostage to fortune by reviving and speculating an unstable exotic trauma scenario from Sumer which undoubtedly had an extensive influence on later traditions, and indirectly probably mirrors other counterpart competing traditions. Moreover, it is presented because such a demonological trauma seems to be presupposed in incompletely perceived ways by some of the Old Testament's own demonological and cultic polemics. In this perspective, then, at some levels, appropriate features of Old Testament contexts hide dislocations, disruptions and a mythomorphic mediation.

Figure 1.2   **The Saidmarreh Landslip in Luristan**

Figure 1.3   **An example of the Rebel Lands' catastrophe debris**

Various proper names and designations can be assigned to geographical locations. For example, Mount Ebih = Jebel Hamrin, and the Diyala Gap into the Zagros mountains). The principal centre of this area that Kinnier Wilson proposed is about 160 miles due east of Baghdad, in the Iranian province of Luristan. This area is an extended part of the oilfields, where the oil-bearing Asmari limestone (a rock reservoir associated with the Middle East oilfields) comes to the surface. In the center of this location is the Saidmarreh Landslip, well marked on standard maps.

Within this region, there is a section of a mountain range, about two and a half miles wide, nine miles long, which has effectively disappeared, except for the debris partly composed of gigantic boulders as large as houses on the basin floor. Apparently, an earthquake redistributed this large segment of mountains of solid rock that is some 300 to 500 metres thick. There is evidence of gas blowouts whose occurrence long antedates the Sumerian period's oil/bitumen seepage, and bleeding from subsurface pockets of oil which, on the surface, turned into detrital bitumen. In ancient times, Gudea and others are known to have collected this type of bitumen. Figures 1.2-3 documents the present state of the Saidmarreh Landslip (note the horseman in each picture, for scale), and Figure 1.7, below, shows an oil fissure blow-out, with a flame of about 1000 feet.

Kinnier Wilson adduces a range of texts to demonstrate that the above geophysical picture is repeatedly and explicitly designated in the Sumerian and later Akkadian tablets in the context of a primeval cataclysm, as well as later being a much-feared area of danger. It seems evident that the surrounding peoples were plagued with gas and oil blowouts, drifting clouds of poisonous gas and periodic earthquakes. Various terms in the Sumerian and Akkadian for seismic cataclysm, and 'wind/gas', 'fire-lights', 'clouds', 'firebolts' are obviously being stretched by the ancient scribes beyond the terms' usual limits in the Sumerian and Akkadian semantic fields.

Here are some samples (using Kinnier Wilson's translations as a basis for my own rendering):

(1) Nin-me-sar-ra (Kinnier Wilson 1979: 9):
usumgal-gim kur-ra ušₓ (KA X SU) ba-e-sì

In the form of the great Serpent you (Inanna) deposited (oil)-poison across the mountainland.

(2) For text, see Kinnier Wilson 1979: 18:
When the heavens shook back and forth and the earth trembled and quaked.

(3) Based on Kinnier Wilson 1979: 29
kur-*ra a mi-ni-íb-láḫ... giš-šegbar mi-ni-íb-ùr
[*ina šadê mê*]

ki-a su bí-ib-dar GIG-ma
(var.: g [ig-g]ig ba-ni-íb-gar [*ina erṣeti*])

He dried up the mountainland, obliterating the undergrowth,
Made a rent in the earth and set poison therein.

i-ne-eš ud-da a-ša-ga úḫ-ge₆
[*i-na-an-na hi-*]*sib eq-li* x [ ]

The produce of the field was now (a slick of) black poison.

(4) SLTNi 61, ll. 17ff.:
ur-sag kurgul-gul
uru-laḫ₆-laḫ₆
ki-bala-se bi-du₇-du₇

O Lion-head that destroyed the mountainland,
That destroyed the city,
Raging madly against the Rebel Lands.

(5) CT 16,15, iv 60ff.:
ur-sag-[imin]-na a-du min-na-mes,
qar-ra-[du si-bit] a-di si-na su-nu.

e-ne-ne-ne lil-la-mes bu-bu-<da>-mes
su-nu za-qi-qu mut-tas-ra-bí-tu- ti su-nu

The Lion-heads, seven times two were they.
All of them are become gas-demons;
Gushing (columns) are they.

(6) See text based on Kinnier Wilson 1979: 128-29:
{a} the lofty Hursang [= East part of Zagros Mountain Range]...
He moved to earth as a great sheet(?) [of rock]
across the heart [of the mountainland].

{b} The mighty stones of the Hursang
that moved of their own accord,
Which...turned altogether into dust.

Text and Tablet

Figure 1.4   **A boundary stone featuring the ur-sag**

(7) Text based on Kinnier Wilson 1979: 24-25:
{a} I, Mugab, was the blazing fire which rained down upon the Rebel
Lands.

{b} As the fire of the Flame-flare began to burn them,
The fires of the Conflagration were ignited, one by one.
The fury of its radiance enveloped the land.

The expression ur-sag (= *qarrādu, qurādu*), here rendered 'lionhead(s)', and
traditionally 'hero', Kinnier Wilson (1979) takes to be the representation of a burning
gas fire column. 'Ur' is a normal term for 'lion' in Sumerian, yet it is sometimes
employed in contexts about 'fiery lions'. On BM seal WA89089, the term is also used
to depict the ascent of the goddess Inanna in flames. The god Ninurta is characterised
as a 'shining Lion-head' (ur-sag-pa-e-a). It is probably Ninurta who is delineated on the
seal impression reproduced in Figure 1.5, produced by the (BM WA89115) seal of the
scribe Adda, which is depicted in Figure 1.6.

Porada (1980) suggested that the layout of the Adda seal reflects the style and
proportions of a major composition such as a temple wall painting, though no Agade
period sanctuary with evidence has been excavated to test the view. Gibson (1998b)
provides a new interpretation of the Adda seal to typify the psychological function of
such visualisation. If Porada's view is correct, it emphasizes the earlier catastrophe in the
Rebel Lands coded into the cultic memory of later periods. Although this is
hypothetical, and modal fallacies are not easily avoided when studying such
indeterminate functions, it is worth attempting to develop a functional typology for
such possible cultic architecture on the analogy of similar sites in Sumer to furnish a
framework for the above suggestion by Porada.

I suggest that we can explore the prospects for a link between nihilism and
paradoxical representation in poststructuralist monumental architecture. This project
could be modified for application to Sumerian temples, and it can be integrated with
Porada's view of the Adda seal. This association would probably have the force and
significance of the arbitrary and instrumental manipulation of iconographic motifs, etc.,
as a mirror of priestly and political will. This itself encodes the operations of semantic
indeterminacy parading as the single authoritative sense which, in widely different
contexts, Kermode (1979; 1996) has exposed. This approach to comparable modern
three-dimensional cases would lead to an interpretation of such data—presented as the
single sense-significance of an entity—as a covert movement to nihilism, though the
superficial roles were imperialistic. It would seem that the obsession with death in birth
on the seal and its related mythology amounts to a Romantic nihilism in a crucial stage
of transference.

Figure 1.5   The impression from the Sumerian seal by the scribe Adda

Figure 1.6   The original Sumerian seal by the scribe Adda (BM WA89115)

In such Sumerian catastrophe scenarios, the nihilistic theme is carried by ur-sag, when it is employed as a class designation for some of the gods who emerge from the earth under the mountains. Some of these gods (for example Ama-usumgalanna) come to destroy the Rebel lands. But they succumb to their own nihilism and become 'dead Lion-heads' (ur-sag-ug[6]-ga) and 'dead gods' (dimmer uggu). This Nietzschean end complies with the view that the gas column leaks eventually burn out. On the seal, the birth of the gods is overseen by a deity who simultaneously presides over birth and hopes to devour the divine progeny, and thus parodies the death of the gods.

Ingraffia's (1995) research on postmodern theory and biblical theology is a far cry from the Mesopotamian contexts here. Even so, his isolation of a modernist nihilism within Christian misappropriation of biblical narrative, that lays stress on the alleged death of God as a function of observing nature, has some resemblance to the crisis of the gods in the Rebel lands, though we should allow for differences in notions of modernisms.

Gibson and O'Mahony (1995) have suggested that elements of a nihilistic modernism attend the 'Sumerian Lamentation over the Fall of Ur', in which a crisis of nature and deity is discernible, each of which is coincident with the other. Barr's (1993) demonstration of the territorial overlap between, and interdependence of, natural theology and biblical faith, is distant from the present concerns. Nevertheless, it is evident that his concern to highlight natural theology categories within the semantic presuppositions of revelation in Old Testament narrative, indirectly mirrors parallel intersections in a variety of competing Mesopotamian perceptions. The Rebel lands tablets are perhaps the most eccentric of these, though in a familiar way they directly merge notions of nature and transcendence.

These phenomena and explanations, in conjunction with the texts cited above (p. 38), harnessed to the geophysical data described in the foregoing (originally highlighted by Kinnier Wilson), provide a theory which has causal explanatory power. Its borders may be of uneven value, and its internal structure will require refinement; yet, dismissal of it in principle may have mores to do with the institutional presuppositions from which it deviates, because of its drawing attention to a new sphere of psychopathography of psychotic catastrophe theory ossified in ancient institutional art, than to some inherent lack of viability in the potential of the thesis.

The above case is an instructive example to relate to the concept of what a parallel is in archaeology. The term and notion of 'parallel' are multifarious in Old Testament studies. 'Parallel' partially has a conservative provenance, which should not be conflated with the present book's usage. Conversely, just because some earlier employment of the term was associated with polemical forcing of alleged matches between biblical text and alien tablet, it should not catapult scholars away from the tenability and complex rationale of what it is to be a parallel. The heart of the matter of parallel is often taken to be either self-evident or resolved; the issues are less obvious and more complex than such responses allow, however. The concepts that can be associated with 'parallel' are often counter-intuitive and deconstructive, while also possibly realistically empirical. So I ask readers to rethink with the present analysis whether or not we too readily engage in covert negative ideological reading according to which we tend not to recognise the complex internal evidential force of some parallels because of the understandable aversion to their *misuse* in some conservative theology. It is not a sufficient condition for rational judgement that one simply walks away from the causal interlocking of textual and archaeological evidence because of one's taste as a function of, say, literary emphases. If someone responds that they are not very impressed with the whole project of discovering parallels between the Old Testament and the historical world external to it, then this presupposing that they have a (negative) decision procedure on the basis of extant scholarship for what it is to be a parallel. But there is no such achievement in past research, and theology is far too unstable a basis for inference to warrant the exclusion of reference to empirical properties on internal narrative grounds. Rather, and consequently, we should allow the growth of a subject to be freshly developed: what it is to be parallel between Old Testament narrative and external historical environments. Obviously, in many areas we will not find any; this should not be a product of a reductionist ideology, however.

In terms of logic, we have a basis for explaining a parallel as follows: if there are two things that embody a criterion of identity, then they constitute a parallel. A parallel implements (instantiates) a criterion of identity. Clearly, the same criterion of identity can be realised in two things that do not share identity in other respects or domains, such as fraternal twins who are male and female. (The notion of criterion presupposed here is further formulated in Gibson forthcoming e: secs. 3.1, 1-2, and forthcoming a; and Chapter 6 below applies the distinction to topography.)

A parallel's criterion of identity is formed by a (logical) predicate. This criterion descriptively isolates that to which it is applied, or of which it is true, so that references can be made to the states or objects comprising the parallel, as a defining function of the parallel. What quantity or type of data will be required to identify such a parallel will vary in accordance with the defining properties of the parallel. In an (extended live metaphor logical) sense, all of Part One of this book is about what a parallel is. At least two sorts of parallel can be envisaged. One type is a parallel resulting from two sets of phenomena which are unmediated and not causally connected, which can be termed an acausal parallel. Hence, if the wheel was invented in more than one society without cross-influence, this would be an acausal parallel.

But the issue of influence relating to being a parallel is more complicated than these brief comments allow. For example, there is a revival of some Sumerian and Old

Babylonian in the Neo-Babylonian period, which biblical writers might not only be influenced by, but also self-consciously emulate for purposes of irony. Middle Assyrian is an example of a language only indirectly acquainted with Sumerian, yet one which draws on semantic relations ebbing and flowing from Sumerian in contrary tides ripe for pun and polemical allusion. Within such indeterminate semantic fields, Canaanite Hebrew mediates for its own multiple identities and cultic priorities. The emergent biblical Hebrew styles are partly crafted from disputed contexts preserving some Mesopotamian theistic trends, while attempting to cancel such influences. Consequently, behind an acausal parallel there may be a common ancestor for two causally independent parallels. The 'burning mountain' in Jeremiah 52, apparently speaking of Babylon, seems to trigger a network of allusions to the, albeit temporally remote, narrative Rebel Lands type of catastrophe, possibly derived from revived Sumerian motifs—a fashionable craving in the Neo-Babylonian period.

The second type of parallel is where there are grounds for linking the two sets of shared properties causally. Both types of parallels break down into further subsets. The causal parallel has relevance for the above Sumerian and geophysical sets of data, if the above type of interpretation is sustained. Here the subset would be a parallel between geophysical phenomena and literary as well as glyptic data. Even so, both sets contain asymmetries because of the uneven content of the two subjects and their states of preservation or otherwise. The sorts of causality linking the two are, of course, asymmetric: literary aesthetic in one set and geophysical in another. This is rather like the difference between a distorted holographic and its physical counterpart.

The above evidence is in need of development and qualification in a variety of ways. Whereas Sumerian does not offer precise geophysical scientific terminology, this does not entail the explanatory failure of a literate society attempting to use iconographic symbols and literary motifs. This would seem so even with a disadvantaging mythology programmed in them deployed to encapsulate the nervy physical reality of geophysical dislocations breaking through the countryside order of their environment, and probably dreams. Such a viewpoint is not to commit one to suppose that scholarly imagination could replace historical discovery, however. This is enforced by the 'catchword' nature of Sumerian writing that has no thoroughgoing phonetics in relevant fields. Despite this dilemma, there is a core of seismic geophysical category expressions in the literary samples cited above which, conjoined with the topographical data, and literary analysis of them, appear to have a causal explanatory power.

Might it be argued, however, could not the Rebel Lands texts be composed of dead metaphors or idioms that do not convey semantic contracts mirroring any memory of or contact with actual geophysical information?

Figure 1.7 A gas blow-out at Naft Safid similar to the ur-sag manifestation

Even were such a judgement to be true, this response, though reflecting a mythological sensibility, is a judgement that does not easily eliminate other classes of use, such as reference to physical events. A presupposition of some quite distinct diachronic linguistics is that historical—'literal'—usage came before, or is first in respect of historical development. If this is generally correct, it adds to the point that metaphor in the above Sumerian does not in principle exclude a probability of literal usage. 'Literal' itself of course decomposes into a problem for definition. A neglected category within metaphor is that of live-metaphor. This function is employed widely in representation of gods. Many of the examples discussed in Chapter 8 below fall into this class, and I offer a theory of live metaphor in Gibson 1997a, which covers the relevant needs of the present work in this regard

In grading priorities in usage about metaphor and literal classes, it is important to give special attention to the above early Sumerian, and its absence as well as presence from the later Akkadian, modified or mediated, recollections or reflections applied to the Sumerian tablets. This situation might be viewed as a function of both alienation and attraction. The presence and absence of the Other language from Sumerian and Akkadian standpoints is at times indeterminate to us, because of our ignorance; and probably, in some cases, the ambiguities are internal to the intended narrative play. In other words, the phenomenon of multilingualism has peculiarly complex relations to the users' perceptions of their own monolingualism. To varying degrees, both standpoints overlap with one another, whether it is a matter of diachronic and/or synchronic loans, or the psychodynamics of conceptual cross-cultural influence.

Metaphorized later Akkadian mythological extensions of the Sumerian are consistent with the foregoing point about literal sense. Through certain sorts of metaphor we may apprehend probable 'literal' (i.e. actual) origins. So we need not eliminate metaphoric, nor idiomatic, senses in the Sumerian material in our evidence. It merely emphasises the priority of the Sumerian level, which even if it is retailing a sense of a past ending (reorienting Kermode's, 1964 use of the expression to include the impact of past/future crisis on a present existential crisis). Although the Akkadian is in some ways linguistically clearer than the Sumerian, the traces of the psychopathological turbulence and the seminal force of the Sumerian often make the latter medium more suitable as a set of complex mirrors to mediate the dynamics of the past crisis.

Here Derrida's (1998) concerns with the prosthesis of origins in the debates on the roles of multiple linguistic influence are important. There is difficulty in conceiving the identity of functions of Sumerian as a multicultural influence on the identity of the Akkadian languages. This difficulty is a focus for attempting to infer the conceptual shapes of further problems concerning how language contributes to the emergence of cultural senses of identity in the 2nd millennium. As Derrida argues, concerning some Franco-Maghrebian influences related to Arabic in the middle and second half of the 20th century in Algeria and France, so it is with particular strands of Sumerian–Akkadian relations at the beginning of the 2nd millennium BC: it is possible to be monolingual and to speak and/or write a language which is not (entirely) one's own. This perspective can be (to use Deleuze's 1994 expression) a plane of immanence by which to construe the written transmission of a Sumerian language in crisis, and to construe its tablets which mediate geophysical cataclysm as complex figure for the partial displacement of a collective personal identity. Emerging around 2,300BC, the Akkadian fed off the Sumerian partially as a function of the former's concern to assess both its archetypal dependence on, as well as differentiation from, the latter's placement as the past sense of an overlapping ending of the Akkadian's beginning. Akkadian came to be a paradigm for control of origins as a means to govern the present, challenged by a century of temporary renaissance of Sumerian about 2,100BC.

With the discoveries at Ebla (dealt with in Chapter 3 below), it would be sensible to be cautious about Sumerian/Akkadian and other Northwest Semitic relations, tentative, as most of the Ebla interpretations have to be. Even without Ebla, these relations are very complex. As M.-L. Thomsen (1984) supposes, there appears to have been a few hundred years overlap when Sumerian and Akkadian were both spoken. Sumerian seems to have been used as a live literary language within that overlap. Biggs (1974) and others indicate the Semitic loanwords in Sumerian at Abu Salabikh, which assist structuring a lexical interrelation between these two phases. Ebla usage presents us with a Semitic Canaanite or Old Assyrian language in use at the same time as early cuneiform Sumerian. There are many fields of meaning required to structure a generalised claim of cross-fertilisation between Mesopotamian and the literary sources for aspects of the Old Testament.

For example, in one arena, that of 'wisdom', Lambert (1995) has plotted some empirical links between the two. Although the exact routes taken to reach, and forms of influence on Hebrew of Sumerian and its mediation through Akkadian are unclear to us, yet there are sufficient continuities and empirical lexical and thematic identities to support the conclusion that the Old Testament mirrors the impact of such influences, not least through demonology and religious references. Within Sumerian and Akkadian at an early date, there is already evidence of transfer of sense, and consequent influence, regarding demonological mythologies. Such mobility is partly a result of response to the needs of varying socio-cultic contexts, which perhaps is a function of and/or need for a theme's extended survival and influence. That is to say, the internal semantic dynamics of a primal narrative internalise properties that facilitate its transmission to other cultures and minds. Research on Spinoza by Gatens and Lloyd (1999) is applicable here. They develop the way Spinoza's use of the imagination impinges on the material world and body. In Mesopotamian propositional attitudes, we find a merging of the imagination as a property of material phenomena. Although any mirroring by theory of ancient text must allow for *différance*, we do well to ponder these relations. This type of historical situation, together with the foregoing data and Rebel Lands citations, is a complex set of premises to imply the empirical probability of the mediation of some features at least of the Rebel Lands to new cultural arenas.

One detail of this type of field in meaning is, for example, the term ur (Sumerian 'lion') in ur-sag ('Lion-head'), used in texts (4) and (5) cited above (pp. 38-39), which was anciently perceived as a live metaphor for certain forms of light manifested in the contexts of the above cited Rebel Lands texts, and extends my earlier comments on 'lion' as a type. In this way, these semantics include the possibility that Sumerian ur ('lion') is being punned upon with the added Akkadian homonym ur ('light'). If one wanted an illustration in another, later, context to exemplify the character of such a semantic pun relation, the ironic lion/leopard masks in Euripides' *The Bacchae* are apt choices (cf. Foley 1988); but, of course, the overall case does not depend on the viability of this association.

Another possibility, which could be confirmed, if the basic foregoing thesis about the location of the Rebel Lands is correct, concerns the hitherto unidentified city and land of Aratta. In the Inanna and Ebih story, it is stated that a catastrophe destroyed the (hitherto undiscovered) city of Aratta: 'And the mountain itself will I remove afar unto Aratta…Like a city cursed by An, none shall raise it up again.'

So this city may lie under the Saidmarreh Landslip, or further away adjacent to the eastern side of the Landslip, if the Sumerian texts are interpreted together on the basis of the above thesis. The figurative and idiomatic pasts and Semitic futures of the Sumerian theme, transporting the Rebel Lands' legend and myth, are central. If Kinnier Wilson is correct, even in some extensively revised form, the Rebel Land catastrophe yields an origin for some demonology. The cited Rebel Lands texts evidently manifest a genesis and crisis for some demons and gods, which mirror human psychopathography in trauma. This directly relates to, and complements, the study below in Chapter 3 on the Canaanite *Repha'im* and the underworld. The development of a psychodynamics of demonology maps into catastrophe-theory and imaginative creativity. Yet, it also yields a credible internal explanation of the mistaken ancient ascription of transcendental causality to the natural world by means of mythology, and has some significance for an archaeology of the mind. In addition, it provides occasion for showing how the conjunction of processual and postprocessual archaeology can be achieved.

This approach complements Rorty's (1984) argument that explains the philosophy of history within terms of and by vocabulary employed in that history. Complementary to this is Kermode's (1985) view that 'the text is a world system'. If the above hypothesis is correct, then the world behind the Sumerian texts was deforming in accordance with conditions accessible to interpretation by means of archaeology of the mind. Such a strategy can utilise geophysical catastrophe coded into mythology. The text entraps the dynamics of human collective religious psychosis and personal trauma attendant on it.

Lambert (1995) assessed the possible grounds for a Sumero-Babylonian tradition for specific features of Ecclesiastes, considerations that would do something to change the usual stress on the Greek influence for the book. Other themes in the book generally concur with the above perspective, epitomised by Kermode's view, though mediation of them is at present undetermined. Ecclesiastes affirms that: 'the world [*'olam*] is in their heart' (Eccl. 3:11). (The translation 'world' here attempts to render the Hebrew *'olam*; this rendering leaves out the semantic value of 'age', together with some sense of 'duration'.) This later aphorism encapsulates traumatised foundations of creativity which have considerable significance for the psychoanalysis of ancient narrative in many perspectives, not least of which is the contribution such study can make to the social anthropology and genesis of ancient mentality.

20th-century AD theology has increasingly been absorbing secularised mythological categories, partly derived from the literary influence of such figures as Nerval, Verlaine and more importantly Baudelaire (for which see Hiddleston 1999)—allowing for the demythologising effect which such authors have on theological traditions which have been encompassed by poststructuralism. This may have some, obviously incomplete and involuted inverted mirror parallel with some Mesopotamian Akkadian scribal sensibilities. We may well find that such Sumerian apprehensions have a structural and mythological modernity about them which has an aura of the familiar in ways that are not entirely our imposition of Europe's myths of Orient (while yet very much agreeing with the accuracy of Kabbani, 1986 outlined above), as we view our own conditions for destruction and renewal in our third millennium.

Perhaps remote in the past, conjectural though the Rebel Lands' origin is, there was a transference and fixation for their prescient sense of the ending—a terminus which was mirrored in the future Semitic responses to alienation by the Other when gross disruption of narrative order by divine intervention was perceived to be required to challenge monotheism and its hold on natural theology. This is not the occasion, however, for a general review of evidence for the links between the early Sumero-Babylonian polytheism rooted in the Rebel Lands and the Canaanite pantheism which the Old Testament targets.

There are many, admittedly quite unstable, data by which to adduce some Sumero-Semitic connections. For example, in respect of puzzling yet clearly cross-fertilised mythological terminology, 'Baal' occurs at Ur; a Canaanite Dagan at Ebla and Ur to distinguish it from Mesopotamian ones; and *Repha'im* appear outside of the

Levant, as we shall see below. The cultic and omen prohibitions of Leviticus, together with instances throughout the Old Testament of disputes with polytheism, and familiar spirits introspecting the underworld, typify a complex website point of relay between Hebrew and Sumero-Babylonian theologies, no doubt with complicated and oblique mediation. The range of seismic vocabulary in contexts such as Ezekiel 38–39, and Daniel 12, coming as it does from historical influence in Neo-Babylonian at a time of the revival of Sumerian motifs and terminology, are not directly coded into the same sort of Rebel Lands mythology. Nevertheless, there are firm parallels, with regard to divine judgement and intervention via catastrophe deploying mountain and seismic imagery, to sustain relations of allusion and irony. With the role of a theology of divine censure in the destruction of Sodom in Genesis, we have a more explicit usage of the seismic phenomena as a medium for divine wrath.

The overall point of such relations is one of a parallel for internal Old Testament exegetical purposes of contrast. A general emphasis seems to be a proportionality function: to the degree that the monotheist worshipper has demeaned herself by influence from external tradition, to that degree the external narrative functions which are her purported source will be engaged to characterize her deconstruction. Of course, even if true, this bare recipe is susceptible of all manners of local deformation and modification. Clearly, imaginative whim in contexts of religious centres will never exhibit universalised conformity to a formal rule; yet the social needs of cult control and psychological influence display evidence of some shared patterns between Sumero-Babylonian and Hebrew Canaanite religions.

The distant relations between the Rebel Lands tablets and the Old Testament seem in certain restricted ways parallel with the concepts of images and text representing the unconscious in relation to the conscious. If this is the case, in the Rebel Lands there are ingredients for a typology of trauma in polytheism that holds a position of primal fantasy metaphorized as social and psychological upheaval. These tablets are like the bedrock of typology rather than token values of it, somewhat like the distinction between a metalanguage and an object language. This would account for some of the asymmetry between Rebel Lands as source and as influence, as well as the disappearance of a schizophrenic god such as Usmu in later Mesopotamian usage. These remarks are merely a preliminary for further research. An immediate task in the perspective of the foregoing is to consider the relevance of the role of the future tense in the psychoanalysis of literary culture, for example as developed by Malcolm Bowie (1993).

Tablet and Text

Archaeological excavations expose only extant, static phenomena. But these phenomena are, in multiple senses, intentional products: they have internal properties of identity that are themselves often-unconscious interpretations or mirroring conceptions. They are constructs of a complex equation between their originators' consciousness and unconsciousness. People lived there; their lives are the dynamics which archaeology tries to retrieve from their static leftovers. There are remains that such people did not intend as an account of themselves (the contents of a rubbish tip, a building fallen in siege and never rebuilt). In contrast, there are excavated writings, inscriptions and material religious symbols, and distinct yet intentional artefacts such as walls, which societies leave behind. These latter products are not invariably communications that were intended as an explanation of the people who produced or composed them.

Killen's (1985) analysis of the Greek Linear B tablets is an exercise in detective inference to show, among other things, that the Mycenaean economy was an 'Asiatic classical bureaucracy'. The accountant writers of the tablets did not intend to communicate this insight—they were themselves ignorant of the fact, and they were unaware that their records would continue to exist beyond the end of the financial year; but the tablets were preserved because of military destruction of their societies. So here is a case concerning which we know more about an ancient society than, in these relevant respects, they did, as a result of our inferences operated on their data. Consequently—though we should assess the probable measure of our ignorance—surprisingly clear and forceful, albeit provisional, conceptual insights can be gained into the ancient world. For example, this can be accomplished by examining often quite apparently unpromising and crude inscriptions, in a framework derived from semantic theory, literary analysis harnessed to psychoanalytical theory, general archaeological theory, and culture theory.

If we place together two sets of evidence from two sites in separate civilisations to construct a parallel, we can use the resulting conclusion to generalise the foregoing argument. This benefits both the student in search of particular knowledge of a society and a person interested in archaeological general theory. Chapter 6 below demonstrates that one narrow aspect of the Linear B archives (tablets An 261 and As 1516) matches at relevant points the narrative accounting style in Joshua 12. This shows that Killen's derivation of parallels between Minoan and Near Eastern economic systems is enhanced to complement some analysis of aspects of Near Eastern Semitic societies, and some Aegean notions of origin can be traced to the Levant.

There is also the pertinent question, addressed below in Chapter 6, concerning the possible date of the original composition or source(s) found in a site or text. For example, in the latter class, the book of Joshua is usually consigned to a period much later than circa 1250 BC. Yet destruction of the Mycenaean Greek society that employed customs that are depicted in the Linear B tablets, have accounting parallels with the book of Joshua, which presents its allegedly firsthand contact with customs in Canaan, at a time significantly prior to the standard form-critical dates (which are after 1000 BC). Clearly, this could have been diachronically mediated, though the Bronze Age II existence of the linguistic data obviously supports in principle contemporary practice for Joshua; also, the absence of parallels in other Levant literature does not augur well for arguments that this approximately synchronic relation between Joshua and Minoan Linear B societies exists because of mediation through Canaanite customs. This illustrates how literary, as well as historical, inferences can be devised for two distinct cultures by placing archaeological discoveries in a refined analytical framework to achieve a decision-procedure for likely interpretation. Cultic symbols often intertwine with religious inscriptions and narratives. Although the meaning of semantic sign may arbitrarily be given that meaning in ancient society, yet it can be employed to convey a definable meaning, as Renfrew (1985:13-14) proposes. This point follows on a number of grounds. One of them is that, though the meaning of an inscription may be arbitrary, its internal linguistic and external empirical relations are not. For example, a proper name is a determinate thing, while its referent may not exist or may be incoherent. And, as Chomsky (1995) points out, a concrete referent, such as a city, is often constituted by not only physical constructs, but also inheres as complex abstract series of properties and relations. This sort of mixture of functions enables one in principle to tackle and resolve what a text means, within approximate limits, and yet the arbitrary content of a text prevents construction of a mechanical decision-procedure while description and logic can yield one.

So summarily stated, the idea of a successful analytical decision-procedure is straightforward in principle, even if problematic in certain contexts (or the absence of them) by which to practise: it is the application of two linked techniques—that which is paraphrasable as logical functions or accurate description, and the perceptual judgement with originality which mirror some features of the referent. The conjunction and application of these techniques is rather more complicated than the idea of them. Of course, perfection in understanding and applying these techniques is not within scholarly grasp. Yet the gap between some misuse of and weaknesses in reason/prescription of texts and what is possible, reflects a situation in which large gains can be made by attending to the needs of logical analysis and description, though one would not want to handle these elements as a fetish obsessed by 'method'. At the other extreme, confused dogmatism, obscured by unspecified assumptions, sometimes achieves the level of an implicit method. The last section—'Editorial Disagreement'—of Chapter 3 below gives an example of the effect such a 'method' has on assumptions about a decision-procedure. One type of confusion which frequently distorts a decision-procedure is the use of what is actually a random association whose randomness is disguised by it being masked with some cultural ideology. Finley (1985) criticises generalised examples in this class; John Chadwick (1985) has warned against allowing this tendency to become respected as 'the associational method'. Some of the associations of this type of method are actually superimposed functions of ideology which are conflated with (what seems to be) the empirical data. Analytical deployment of any associations should be sharply regulated by empirical knowledge and inference. But this does not in practice deny that we can achieve knowledge of that which is not always explicitly present in a symbol or artefact. For example, Chadwick mentioned the Minoan 'priestess of the winds' (a-ne-mo- i-je-re-ja), and infers that: 'a priestess implies a divinity, so we must add Anemoi = "the Winds" to our list of deities'. Here we can infer that there is a deity from the presence of a priestess; and we could do this even if there is no mention of the deity's 'name' ('the Winds'), since a priestess presupposes a notion of a deity by the nature of her function.

Even if we adopt the idea that there is some shift of meaning or new nuance in some uses of a symbol, we have in the above examples of economic tablets and the priestess role, sets of functions that identify various, and varying, dynamic properties of the society which left the phenomena behind. These examples also briefly exemplify how different types of data can be tackled using related or identical methods, while logical association of them in analysis produces understanding for archaeological general theory in which individual questions can thereby be answered.

Part of the difficulty of examining ancient texts is that we need to be wary of presupposing that there is to be had, or that we have, an account of the 'nature' of what meaning is. I return to this issue below in connection with linguistics and logic; but for the present context it is worth noting Skorupski's (1976) research on the structure of meaning in relation to social anthropology as well as philosophy. The extended use of 'meaning' in anthropology involves not only the senses of words, what they refer to and what they are true of; anthropological 'meaning' incorporates the associated actions (rites, etc.) which comprise the symbolic structures of social actions. There might be a problem about the prospects of identification here. It might be helpful to express it in the following way, using points from Skorupski, but developed to reflect current interests. The meaning of a symbol is under-determined in its use and associated actions. That is to say the significance an ancient religious centre that its initiates presented to themselves—its perceived priorities—was an incomplete account. This lack of completeness is not merely a matter of the need to add other sentences to fill out the description of a religious centre within a society. Rather, it is that such a function with a particular symbolic meaning does not contain a code telling us how to define and apply the symbolic meaning. (Just as if you are given a sentence describing what a priest is, then this may not enable one to go out in the street and identify a passing priest, unless you are in a privileged circumstance to observe the relevant dress or actions or testimony.)

If we have suitable contexts by which to grasp the functions of analysis and inference in application to the external world, as well as attempt to reach conclusions about the meaning of actions in cult societies, it is important that we do not thereby presuppose we have all relevant theoretical assumptions for understanding the target elements of the ancient world. We need further thought-bridges to handle the gaps between symbol and significance. That is not to disagree in principle with Binford (1983), who has used the environments in modern societies, which are parallel with ancient societies, to test and infer understanding of empirically documented practices of ancient societies. We require, however, proof external to their poststructuralist postulated theoretical counterparts to measure the relations, positions and force of such mapping claims. Analysis, that neglects the sphere covered by social anthropology, does not utilise resources for overcoming many problems in defining symbolic action. Davidson's (1980) philosophy of action, if not his theory of truth, also highlights the thesis that the correspondence between language and action is a key to discovery about the structure of action.

For example, it has been customary to ignore as unhistorical the report in the book of Daniel that Belshazzar was king of Babylon prior to its fall. Chapter 9 below attempts to expose the historical linguistics for the claim that Belshazzar was king, if we care precisely to understand aspects of the narrative's own background social anthropology. The cuneiform coronation records contain regal and religious evidence about the social dimensions of the coronation. If these are accurately linked to the language in the book of Daniel, which clearly mirrors them, we discover that the rightful king Nabonidus passed his son the 'kingship' (sarru-tam, etc.) to Belshazzar his son because Nabonidus wished to remain away from Babylon. In such case we see that the ancient language corresponds to the world it represents. Occidental scholastic reductionism invents a clash between the narrative and its target. This error arose for three reasons: first, uncomprehending linguistic analysis in which 'modern' imperialistic cultural assumptions masked the narrative's sense. Secondly, the anthropology of the symbolic action recorded in ancient style was a neglected inferential dimension. Thirdly, the linguistic axis was not related and integrated with the anthropological one.

Such conclusions can be produced for more elusive, mythological, symbolic action contexts. An apparently very obscure symbol can, upon examination in a general framework analyzing its contextual connections, be a key to a whole web in a complex set of relations. For example, Renfrew (1985: 23) proposes that the smiting figure position—with arm raised, which depicts a power-role, should be associated with a god, and not with a votary representation of a worshipper, in the bronze smiting figurines discovered in the Philakopi sanctuary. Such a thesis blends in well with the Canaanite and Egyptian god smiting figures. Canaanite Baal smiting god figurines (to be dealt with in Chapter 8 below, and presented in Figure 8.2) were systematically classified by Negbi (1976). He provides a refined framework for the thesis that successfully sustains a probable indirect mediation between Canaan and the type of site exemplified by Philakopi.

The smiting god figure symbol directly interconnects with another symbolic sphere. In Chapter 8 below I explain how the Baal smiting god stance is connected with the 2 Kings 6 text. This passage is perhaps one of the oddest narratives in the Bible. It recounts that an axe is borrowed; it sinks in the Jordan, and it is raised to float, by Elisha. Some of the archaeological data for determining the cultic anthropology behind this type of narrative typology were published as far back as 1949 concerning Ugarit, where a ceremonial war axe was excavated on which 'lion' and a 'boar' motifs appear. Inscribed tablets were found with the axe; they provided cultic information concerning the axe's functional symbolic military and mythological significance. In this way we are suddenly transported into a world in which obscure, bizarre detail is inverted by its ancient symbolic function in which the axe was, in that Canaanite society, a constant, central to 'normal life', marking also that society in its ecumenical relation to, or conflict with, surrounding kingdoms and gods.

The long history of the axe symbol and its varying detail with recurrent elements, such as the 'lion-head' mouthing the axe blade (see Figure 8.1), mirror the transmission of concepts, of symbols from Sumer, as an emblem of the goddess of fertility and war. One strand that was aired above is the Lion Gate at Hattusas. Clearly this architectural iconography is temporally remote from much of the Old Testament. Nevertheless, integrated into the old Syrian and Assyrian connections with the Hittites, who built the Lion Gate from where the motif was later mediated (see Ozguc 1980), these traditions are direct antecedents of the later Canaanite stereotyped 'lion' archetype. This archetype is also manifest in the use of a lion, with its flame-throwing mouth to personify divine mountains (Amiet 1980). Such a cluster of motifs complements the remarks on the 'Rebel Lands' mountains' ur-sag (Lion Heads). These associations are typical of other later ones (see Frankfort 1939). We do not, of course, have to suppose that these items are explicitly being alluded to in 2 Kings 6 to recognise that they support an allusive tradition that is being parodied in this narrative. This is primarily because the conjunction of the contemporary employment of the archetype in 2 Kings 6 and other relevant Old Testament passages yields the same criteria of identity and thematic use of cultic material.

According to Riffaterre (1991), the forces of a literary culture's own contemporary intertext—that is to say, the group of relations between text, tablet and cultic images—draws on the collective memory. Such catastrophes as the Rebel Lands' Lion-Heads typify this thesis. If we adapt aspects of the writings of Freud, in particular as interpreted by Lacan (see Bowie 1991) in their emphasis on the external world as a mirror of the ego, we can readily position, even in a coarse-grain way, a successful interpretation to contribute to the explanation of some of these conceptual forces. The primordial Sumerian selves are projected, by transmission, onto external geophysical events, and these are mirrored back to confirm and modify the pulses of the cultic identity. Later narratives absorb and twist these features through an involuted mirror that is focused to military and fertility wavelengths.

2 Kings 6, Chapter 8 claims below, is the result of a narrative pulse that has deeply mirrored the symbolic psychology of a military and mythological cultural complex that was in unstable transition. In 2 Kings 6, grim irony decodes and decomposes some of the ancestral mythology nested in contemporary life, opposed to the worship of Yahweh. So, if readers minimise and parody the 2 Kings 6 text for being bizarre, trivial, eccentric, irrelevant or marginal, then this misses the mark of the punning focus. It is precisely the bizarre state of affairs, which is being focused for a critical attack, through pun, in 2 Kings 6. Nor would it be subtle to respond that, since it is pun, it is secondary, for many narrative themes have their identity over the disputed sense of a pun. The irritating presence of the seemingly miscast, hardly relevant, axe in 2 Kings 6 is an original narrative device which mirrors and encapsulates aspects of Canaanite mentality, prone as it is to polemical exposure. This sort of prose is peculiar, and set in a world often presupposed to be remote from modernist Europe, with its use of apparent irrelevance, that strikes many a reader as bizarre.

It is not entirely dissimilar, however, to some of, for example, Mallarmé's symbolist uses of allusion and parody in his *Un Coup de Dés*, in the way in which detail is first viewed by readers as unconnected with its context but subsequently internal to a theme. Here a presupposed type of reader is, as it were, taunted by assuming a naive or linear reading, only to discover that the parameters or relevance concerning interpretation shift. Accordingly, such a semantic texture is susceptible of fresh characterisation about the role of consciousness in relation to the putative backcloth of the narrative. The prospects of synthesis for such nuances are attractive, especially if one combines the foregoing analysis with Chapter 8 below: this attests to the explicability of the archaeological materials in the light of their anthropology and the tablets' literary properties.

On the edges of the immediate scope of this book, is the further issue in such contexts as to whether or not, and if so how, something akin to features of a modernist alienation, and the collision of monotheistic versus other ontologies, partly reminiscent of 19th-century AD Eurocentric modernisms, have parallels with some Iron Age religious confrontations as well as their more extended societal backcloth.

In this perspective, a raft of interpretations of archaeology and text can, with suitable modification, be redeployed as theory-nets to contribute to the archaeology of the mind. This complements and extends the senses that Renfrew (1982) proposed in archaeology for this type of enterprise, in the recovery of aspects of the products of ancient consciousness. In philosophy, as Anscombe (1957), Hacking (1994) and Blackburn (1998) have and variously argued, the philosophy of mind contains as yet intractable, or only partially solved, issues central to what mental is. They also consider that other problems in philosophy depend for their successful treatment on how we resolve controversies in the philosophy of mind. In this respect, then, the archaeology of mind can have a significant role to play in certain areas of research into human mentality, in particular as it pertains to the history of ideas and philosophy of history. Contiguous to these, this book displays some areas for investigation in which traceable expressions of ancient minds have informative, and frequently puzzling, resemblances to what have sometimes been assumed to be the quite other more civilised evolved cultural states of modern humanity. Although this use of 'resemblances' and other forms of measuring language themselves require further examination, yet it seems that in a variety of ways humans were always modern.

2

The Old Testament and Literary Theory

Tablets, Texts and Literary Theories

Although valuable work has been done in relevant Near East and Levant studies, little research has been achieved to develop a literary theory of inscriptions and tablets as literature within the perspective of a modern literary critical framework. Particularly is this the case in relation to the narratives and literary remains of archaeological sites, which predate the Greek Classics, though we are challenged with various intriguing problems if we are to relate literary criticism/theories to tablets and inscriptions. Access to insight into mental elements motivating and moulding ancient culture can be achieved to varying degrees by analyzing the ancient literary remains.

This is not to presuppose a naive formulation of the view that we know what the uneven relations of the intention of the writer(s) to the text was. Instead, it should presuppose an informative link between what a writer intended to state, and what we can retrieve from what he stated in the mediated forms that the relevant ancient narratives embody. We here have the dualism of differing authorial intentions: ancient writer and modern scholar. In full-time professional scholarly criticism this dualism usually exponentially transmogrifies into a skyscraper of intentionalist layers, smoothly retailed in simplified packages of carefully regulated

Such a scenario is readily unpredictably affected by invisible turbulence, even when there is a style of calm measured judgment. For example, Loughlin (2000: 87) states that:

> Except for the biblical story there is no literary evidence that there ever was an Egyptian Sojourn and Exodus as described in the Bible. This is true regardless of the date one assumes for the event.

Loughlin certainly fairly interprets some of the typical canon of scholarly oppositions. That is not what I wish to encourage us to rethink. Rather, it is the presuppositions of rational choices disguised by fairness to critical canons. What status has his term "true"? For example, how has Loughlin managed completely to obliterate any even marginal hypothetical function whatsoever for the Ipuwer text? If we take his language "there is no literary evidence" to be precise (he did not state "no literary facts"), then it is accurate to replace his "true" with "false", since on some scholarly *interpretations* there is such evidence. (See 4 below.) Obviously, Loughlin's qualifying phrase "as described in the Bible" appears to rescue his judgment. Contrariwise, this itself depends on a naïve-universalized presupposition of *interpretation* of all or a sufficiently extensive (unstated) chunk of interpretation and not "the Bible" itself. So, we are left with unquantified and unqualified assertions. Perhaps, we are supposed to scan them by some sort of consensus to the effect that, crudely, anyone in her right mind would not take the sort of arguments thus discarded beyond what Loughlin's boundary of possibility marked by "is true regardless of the date" takes them to be. This turbulence is mirrored in the odd stylistic dislocation, in his writing of the double subject "Egyptian Sojourn and Exodus as described in the Bible" and his immediately reducing them to a single "event": "This is true regardless of the date one assumes for the event". Unless this is a stylistic slip, only if one is not neutrally assessing the identities of disparate data would one reduce narrative that purport to cover hundreds of years, and with two complex series of asymmetric processes (sojourn and exodus) could one so reduce two subjects. That Ockham articulated some six contrary versions of his Razor (see Gibson, 1998) may itself betray the point that attempts at such reductionism have confused complex antecedents, as I suggest Loughlin has here. Furthermore if one ever met the scholarly archaeological players, and heard their lectures, in the scholastic history partly presupposed by Loughlin's seeming irenic use of "true", it is a struggle to discover the presupposed objectivity. For example, the visages of Dame Kathleen Kenyon and James Callaway recall the nostalgia of pioneering functionaries of competing world empires, rather than the smooth prose of Loughlin's otherwise helpful interpretation (cp. Kenyon, 1960; Callaway and Weinstein, 1972, 1977, 1985; and chapters 4, 5, 6 below). Clearly one does not have to assume the negation of Loughlin's assessment disinterestedly to investigate the options he from of his judgment. Compare two possibly partially parallel situations in other subjects. First, in epidemiology, Wyatt (1977) reported that J. R. Paul had, early in the 20th century discovered a polio vaccine; due to various factors this was lost, and much later rediscovered in various forms. Imagine its 'status' in a sort of Loughlian rationality: 'Except for J. R. Paul's story there is no evidence that he ever did describe a polio vaccine. This is true regardless of the date one assumes for the discovery.' Secondly, consider a possible reaction in 1927 to the earlier the publication of Hitler's *Mein Kampf*: 'Except for Hitler's psychotic autobiography there is no evidence that there will be a Third Reich and extermination of the Jews as described by him. This is true regardless of the date one assumes for the aspiration of the Jews to return to Palestine.' (For relevant analysis of indeterminacy in the interpretation of Hitler, see Gibson, 2000; Young, 2000.) The identities of historical probabilities are more unpredictable than Loughlin assumes. Reductionism smoothes away evidence of indeterminate perturbations. Our interpretation of the past has an unstable counter-intuitive future.

Three central questions act as boundary markers for the construction of this arena. First, how does literary theory apply to tablets, inscriptions and symbolic expressions that have been described in archaeological analysis? Secondly, how does literary theory apply to the Old Testament? Thirdly, in what ways do the archaeology of the mind and these two literary projects interlock and contribute to each other?

The Status of Literary Theories

Adjacent to the above enterprise about archaeology of the mind, are complementary questions for research. Can modern literary criticism and literary theories be used to derive understanding of ancient inscriptions? And how might this project interact with the application of modern literary theories to the Old Testament?

Can we get a lever on this latter question by adverting to some recent research in the Greek Classics and the application of literary theories to them? Goldhill (1984) has claimed that Derrida's deconstruction can illuminate ancient tragedy when deployed to investigate, for example, Aeschylus's *Oresteia*. Goldhill (1986) develops this type of deconstructing approach for other narratives. Deconstruction is a mood about reading that clusters around the reader, rather than author, and on what is absent from the text as signalled by the text. We should be aware of the need to allow for a restricted sense of generalisation in which the multiplicity of semantic variations composed in a narrative resist uniform reductionism. The complex functions of semantic features manifesting deconstruction can cut a text off from its past, and yet require the reader's imaginative ability to produce patterns for the text, while forming intertextual contracts with culture external to the text. Hobson (1998) has termed such complex causal, specific yet indeterminate semantic patterns 'micrologies', because of their networking signals through complex detail. Deconstruction is whimsical and random, not unlike competing interpretations of causal indeterminacy in quantum physics. Deceptive perceptions are seemingly recognized as myths to guide one to the text. An objective knowledge of meaning is thus denied since there are many senses ascribed to or recovered from the text.

Perhaps it is not entirely impish imperialism to suggest that some deconstruction is similar to the Babel theme's world-view of Genesis 11. Its deconstruction of the single-sense language, its non-standard ironic folk-etymology for 'Babel' and 'confusion' take us into the heart of deconstruction in a way that structures more than literary play. Part of the comic irony is a slip of classification. One can adjust Whedbee's (1998: 56-59) view of this to note that the Babel people want a name for themselves within the one language, yet end up with Yahweh's name and another language. As suggested above, with regard to Derrida's 1996 study of monolingualism, in connection with the Rebel Lands' tablets and their primal discontinuities, Genesis 11's engagement with language mirrors much later concerns with the role of monolingualism in competition with multilingualism. For both, and not merely for the form linguistic singularity, monolingualism hovers under the textual presuppositions of an author's assumptions of fluency within a perceived cultural ethos.

A narrative is a residue of a live language just as archaeology is the reduced remains of a live society. In this perspective, deconstruction, especially as structured by Ward's (1995) study, isolates ironic deferral of final meaning attending a narrative. That is to say, expressions in a text are a presence, which obliquely advertise the absence of codes that originally implemented their native usage. This advertises the beginning of an indeterminate regress: ambiguity was contiguous with the native use of such language. Subsequently, the regress retires to the psychogenesis of inscriptions and ancient literature. In such an explanation, as noticed above, there is a parallel with narrative sense and archaeology. Each is a residue that regresses to the mental. A further absence is the intertextual relation between narrative or inscription and the societies whose residue is interrogated by archaeology. Accordingly, in an extended and uneven sense, which of course needs monitoring and measuring, irony in language closely resembles the identities of language itself and its relations to its referents.

Historically, this type of theme occupies the position of the subversion of the referential historical subject external to the presence (i.e. language) which displaces it. A familiar trend in poststructuralism presents this subversion and indeterminacy in language as a new revolution original to postmodernism. As Andrew Bowie (1997) in German Romanticism, and John Milbank (1998) in European theology show, such doctrines predate the 20th century. F.H. Jacobi (1787) employs effectively the same conceptual strategy and microstructural approach to combat Kant and Hume. Certainly, one does not have to pander to the desire for employment of a heavy and formally novel terminology to sustain the foregoing sort of thesis. And if one wishes to argue that an ancient narrative inheres by the deployment of such literary devices, it is as well not to require such terminology, though rendering distinctions and functions explicit by such crafted terminology is an aid to clarity and exposition. A similar conclusion may be derived from some medieval narrative analyses, for example in Chinca's (1997) study of Strassburg's *Tristan*. In short, my subplot here is to invert a facet of contemporary literary theory debate by suggesting that some post-structuralist theorizing, in concentrating on the indeterminacies in modernist discontinuity and deconstruction, inexorably leads to identifying functions of continuity in ancient texts.

We need, obviously, to qualify, adumbrate, and supplement these remarks. Irony has a role in such narrative to which we can apply a revised deconstruction, as illustrated at the end of Chapter 2 below. On the present analysis, deconstruction applies to elements in ancient narrative intertextual relations only if one qualifies and transforms Derrida's overall view in this sphere. Deconstruction matches some elements in some levels of Genesis 11, and not because one can universalise the scope of the theory. Of course, a deconstructionist may retort that incomplete ungeneralised application of this Derrida (1978; 1982; 1996) philosophy is precisely what deconstruction is; but in rejecting this emphasis, one can argue that competing theories can be used to characterise the other levels, complementarily operating alongside deconstructionist functions in the narrative.

The position being advocated here is that a given literary theory reflecting one 'school' or movement is not successful if elevated to the status of a global narrative law specifying the meaning of a narrative. The pretext of literary theory is not only narrative context bound; its scope is a facet or levels of sense within a narrative. To use terms and theses such as 'deconstruction', or 'structuralist', is not to deny that its properties may well have been noticed and explained in previous eras. Of course, the scope and form of definition will have varied, and, no doubt, originality plays a role, as 20th-century literary history deforms conventions quantitatively further than has been achieved before. It is worth bearing in mind, however, that the producers of new literary theories, including the one outlined in these pages, are usually too strongly prepossessed with the seeming uniqueness and explanatory power of their own innovatory assumptions. In Cartwright's (1999) terms, we need to think in terms of theory-nets and criteria to be devised to assess degrees of effectiveness in application of theories.

'Unique' modernists usually have sometimes neglected precursors. An aspect of Roland Barthes' (1970, 1985) structuralism typifies this point, albeit as an off-centre case. We can find parallels between him and, for example, the late 19th-century AD biblical commentator, E.W. Bullinger's (1898) (arbitrary) ascription of exotic structures to the biblical narratives. As Harland (1987) proposes, we might profitably employ the term 'superstructuralism' to depict Barthes' and other poststructuralist positions, in view of their assimilation of semiotic, anthropological and philosophical elements into analysis of the text, in ways similar to allegorising biblical commentators such as Bullinger. Bullinger alleged that he discovered acrostic, symmetrical and asymmetrical patterns in Bible narrative; but actually he was often composing (as we should now say), almost deconstructing trajectories from his theory-laden imagination. To be sure, Barthes and Bullinger differ, in that the former discards the claim that we can get back to the author's intended meaning, and Bullinger would have denied this thesis; yet both in their varying styles are seeking to systematise the significance of suppressed symbols. A purpose here is to draw attention to the specified similarity in some structural patterns between Barthes' playful *exposé* of mythologies and Bullinger's expository typologies, both of which are directed to heighten consciousness of the perceptually 'hidden' elements in examined discourse.

My contrapuntal and ironised use of Bullinger as a scholar presupposes knowledge of Bullinger's now anachronistic erudition. We could consider many biblical expositors to exemplify the foregoing point. In a study linking literary analysis of the Old Testament with other spheres, in particular archaeology, it is of some value to make explicit certain issues of influence and assumptions about cultural progress. Such elements not infrequently remain unconnected with applied exposition, whilst they sometimes invisibly coerce the (actually vastly complex) presupposition of relevance and structure in what constitutes the activity of biblical interpretation. The notions of historical progress which smooth out partially dissimilar critical literary analyses in different generations using presuppositions of progress and anachronism, do not easily account for overlaps and similarities. Indeed, these are sometimes obscured by superficial differences whose significance should not be under-estimated. Culture's initial absorption of and engagement with a new influential novelty, such as Barthes' structuralism, has often preceded a down-grading re-assessment of the value of a new movement, as Thody's (1977) belittling conservative assessment of Barthes illustrates. Barthes' writings are not the institutionalised structuralism that sometimes directs trends in academia, however; one is wise to return to his original writings, as we attempt to do with all assessment of sources. Barthes' (1977) treatment of the Genesis narrative of Jacob fighting with an angel is an instructive piece of what may be designated as tantamount to an ancient subversion of an institutionalised use of structuralism. It is clear that structuralism, as practised by Barthes in his later writings, was tending to invite its own implosion. Theologians and expositors of the Old Testament absorbed with structuralism do well not to neglect this feature, and accordingly integrate indeterminacy into their hypotheses. It is worth noting the parallel between Barthes and Sartre in this regard: as Cumming (1992) has shown, Sartre absorbs and subverts Husserl's application of intention to genre in ways that are parallel with the approach Derrida (1967) took. An element of Sartre's later existentialism codes in a feature of indeterminacy that is a component in the drive to deconstruction. Khalfa's (2000) analysis of Sartre and his relation to Deleuze affords a basis to use Deleuze's theory of image to depict ancient personificatory functions, for example, Jacob fighting with an angel (see Gibson 2000a).

Mental Causes and Indeterminate Texts

Such considerations as those above may mask the partial derivative aspect of these theories, and conventional prejudice may distract the author from recognising his own illicit over-generalisation. Steiner (1990) is suspicious about the foundations of cultural 'academies' which attract and influence high profiles for literary theorizing. One has to guard against a contrary assumption: that sense is transparent and intentional, while a mean between the two points, which cancels out originality and unexpected synthesis, is not the consequence of implementing the previous points.

Anscombe's (1970) study showed, among other things, that it is possible for a thing to manifest indeterminacy and also exhibit causality. A narrative displays these phenomena: characteristically, it is a product of mental causes, and, if we follow Frank Kermode (1990), the product of such mental acts and states includes indeterminacy. He combines this notion with the pluralising use of literary theories, adjusted to meet various narrative qualities. I wish to propose, however, that such functions of indeterminacy do not, as it is usually supposed, lead to the conclusion that we have no relevant objective knowledge of the intended sense of the narrative. The roles particularly of originality and its associated deployment of deviance from, or modification of, antecedent traditions or uses, break out of the uniformity in a semantic field that draws solely or centrally on the indeterminacies of traditions. The conjunction of these two aspects facilitates the inference that there is a causal relation between author or editor and his composition. This bond is strengthened in contexts where intertextual relations occur, since they are made to generate bonding between an authorial reading of a prior narrative and the author/editor's own later narrative, which is coded to introduce a semantic contract between the two texts. But this sort of refined balancing of factors requires allowance for the narrative's employment of originality or deviance from traditional patterns. Such a type of consideration is as much to do with the impact on an established usage of an expression or context of an original or deviant detail, as it has to do with the function of these latter two features.

Many Old Testament passages which have some vexed relation to history manifest the need for implementing fresh approaches sensitive to the above texture of considerations, yet they also display problems of deviance from presuppositions of relevance and propriety. The examples are noteworthy in Psalms 34: 133, and 1 Sam. 21:13, where David seems to enact a deranged character, having spittle to run down his beard. The tonal punchline is that this phrasing is unexpectedly akin to Psalm 133, with its poetic ritualising of Aaron's anointing, with the priestly oil running down his beard. In 1 Samuel 21, David invades the priest's role, by commandeering the tabernacle showbread for his military men, before Ahimelech the priest. Ps. 34:1 (the heading of the Psalm in translation) recounts this event from 1 Samuel 21, yet ironically 'changes' (*ta'am*) and uses this term for David's behaviour) the name of the king of Gath from Achish before whom David stands (in 1 Samuel) to 'Abimelech'. The similarity to the name of the priest 'Ahimelech' should not be lost to the satirical movement in narrative pun. In Ps. 34:8 there is the famous passage, '*Taste* and see that Yahweh is good' (alluded to in 1 Pet. 2:3); it employs the same Hebrew term (*ta'am*) which is rendered 'change' in Ps. 34:1.

To return to the relation of Old Testament and Near East narrative to the scholarly use of theories to expound such narrative, we should forefront the problem of the conflict between the multiplicity of literary theories. A factor in the production, and/or survival, of literary theories may be that each one isolates a facet of a narrative. Each theory over-generalises beyond its functional fit with the data. For example, Barthes' structuralism identifies properties of narrative indeterminacy and patterns of perceptual mythology, as well as their relations to non-literary eternal semiotic functions; but structuralism itself is not a, or the, theory of what it is to be narrative. This point obtains generally for theories. So, consider the following impious thought: a literary theory is truly positioned when it ceases to be believed as a, or the, generalised theory for its target set of narratives. With some literary theories, a stronger version may be apt: the only good literary theory is a dead one. This is not to consign literary theory to the grave. Only when a literary theory has ceased to be normative in activity is 'the theory' given its proper level of generality and its true perspective. The focus here is the view that a literary theory should be a subordinate element in other literary analyses. Thus literary theory, on this view, maps a strand or point in a narrative, and often has the prior role of rendering explicit the reader's disposition towards narrative. In this situation, features other than the one(s) successfully delineated by the literary theory are mapped by a plurality of other literary theories or reader presuppositions.

Of course, since there is no final decision-procedure or criterion of application for implementing any literary theory, scholars will differ as to what constitutes the identity and applicability of a theory in some states of affairs. This variance concerns the status of theory itself in this sphere. The idea of a theory thus warrants some brief attention here. A theory, roughly, is a universally quantified set of descriptions whose domain is literature, in a strong sense of 'theory'. My use here deforms this presupposition about theory into a recipe that episodically fits fragments of a domain in a narrative. Impressionistically summarised, this amounts to the following. The mind has an imaginative faculty that produces both creative fiction and literary theories. I propose a mental causal link between the two enterprises. This causal link can be termed that of a causally anomalous nomist. (I here modify Donald Davidson's (1980) use of this designation), and I suggest supplementing this notion by use of David Lewis's (1980, 1986) counterpart theory to construct a theory of psychological domains or 'worlds', though I do not adopt the latter's thesis on existence. Creative fiction is the mental landscape. Literary theory is the geography. There are enormous territories of different varieties to be mapped; there are proportionately immense literary theories to account for these worlds. Clearly, same maps will be bad, wrong, good, prejudiced, true, or false; but what tends to happen is that a literary theory (or its school) waxes imperialistic and over-generalises the scope of the theory. No doubt some literary theory only succeeds in mirroring its author's approach to literature, rather than imaging literary narrative. A given theory properly only fits one slice of literature; or perhaps only one level within one type of narrative or sentence: a street map for part of a city, as it were, has been attenuated to mimic the globe. It may be that a theory properly maps only one feature within one level of a type of sentence. In this way, a restrictive, eclectic use of available literary theories is correct. Obviously, this distorts, questions, and reformulates the aims often advertised for many theories of literature.

Kermode (1979, 1983) subtly revised and advanced the indeterminacy of narrative thesis. He is sensitive to the need to allow theories that conflict, since on his view the senses of narrative are open-textured and contain no self-determining procedure for reading the intended meaning. Other scholars such as Iser (1974) have contributed to the emergence of this type of notion. Kermode is, of course, aware that the idea of indeterminacy obtains in varying degrees. Thus Kermode is perhaps the most ecumenical of theorists sharply conscious of and focused to the importance of allowing uptake of potential for new competing theories. Since such indeterminacy and its degrees are contingent, it is not a necessary (i.e. internal) property of a narrative that it has to be indeterminate. This leaves it open that there can be narrative that is not indeterminate, and/or that narratives may mix determinate sense with indeterminacy. We should also be careful not to neglect a difference between indeterminacy and density in meaning. A text may be so richly dense in sense that, if incorrectly represented, it might be misperceived as indeterminate. Here some multiple senses, which may function consistently, might be inaccurately submerged by a critical requirement and mistaken for indeterminacy, though many narratives and parts of narrative are indeterminate.

There appear to be distinct brands of indeterminacy. Literary theories have sometimes crafted their notions of indeterminacy from physics and cosmology; so it is worth a quick glance in those directions. First, quantum indeterminacy: this can be parsed as a pure chance concept, or read as a disposition of the indeterminate (i.e. semantic) object, or interpreted as a causally determined (not deterministic) consequence of ambivalent senses (after the manner of Everett 1973 and Hawking and Penrose 1996). Secondly, this ambivalence can be classified as an expression which has two or more determinate values, but which are not calculable from, or expressed in the immediate context, or where the values alter when cited in two contexts. A case of the latter appears to be in Job 5:13 ('He takes the wise in their own craftiness') cited in 1 Cor. 3:19, where the reported speaker in the former is Eliphaz, but Paul in the latter—with a switch in presuppositions about 'wise'. It is important to isolate ambivalence from ambiguity because of their different status in theory of meaning. Sometimes an expression might by ambivalent but not ambiguous, while yet a commentator might incorrectly treat it as 'ambiguous'. Mitchell (1985) points out that the level of ambiguity in relations between language epochs (Old and Middle English) are often underestimated, because no single criterion can be or has been formed to isolate one from the other. We could adopt this point both for diachronic linguistics, as well as the semantic fields on which they impinge in Old Testament and Near East literary counterparts. Thirdly, there is the indeterminate narrative that is indeterminate because it is incoherent or contrary. There are other varieties in a different sphere that can be grouped as inconsistent (and Rescher and Brandom 1980 could be employed to construct such cases, for example).

The Principle of Excess

Kermode (1997) has also formulated a 'principle of excess' for sense in narrative. This proposal advances the idea that expressions contain more sense than their immediate employment in the narrative advertises. In this way, later users can quote from a narrative and 'find' new meanings 'in' it, which were not intended by the author. Such a view engages with the thesis of under-determination of meaning. Expressions in a narrative, according to Kermode, are open-textured. Consistent with this condition, Kermode has the related view that in some narrative there is vacant suggestive space for fresh sense or original interpretation. Kermode's (2000:311-12) exposition of Shakespeare's language concludes with an assessment of ways in which the playwright seems to engage with tantalising calculations concerning his audience's endurance: rather like a reader's attempts to master what at times is the incomplete work of life and transformation in the crafting of language. This interpretation looms large as an area for special care when approaching texts that were already ancient by Shakespeare's time. If at times we do wish to endure the effort of interpreting ancient language, we might thereby incorrectly assign obscurity to the narrative. Sometimes it is obscure; but our attention is too readily subject to our perceptual entropy induced by a sense of superiority. Our assumption that the narrative is obscure may be, of course, our failure to recognise that the need for a disposition of endurance when reading it is a mirror of a reality that had to be endured in its origins.

Culler (1980: 46) states that: 'we will have to recognise that the "openness" and "ambiguity" of literary works results not from vagueness nor from each reader's desire to project himself into the work, but from the potential reversibility of every figure'. Here Culler is expounding an aspect of his view of deconstruction, though it seems that his view contravenes one interpretation of deconstruction in this use of 'reversibility', while his judgement has an important insight. 'Reversibility' appears to be a compatible change of sense: reversible opposition, inversion, contrariety, and other such phenomena, are all mirrors of what they alter.

'Mirroring' is a subtle notion, yet it appears fairly clear that these phenomena code into their sense a decision-procedure of some sort, by virtue of retracing the semantics of what they alter. This is like a dual carriageway (and not a one-way street) in our desires to disambiguate the senses of such terms. The quantifier 'every' in the quotation from Culler, though qualified by 'potentially'—and yet whose extension is thus unclear—commits him to a strong thesis about reversibility of figures. Although Kermode's principle of excess is not of course tied to Culler's sort of view, that view can contribute to pointing a way forward in its explanation. Kermode's principle may apply to one broad type of use, mapped by a theoretically vacant semantic space in the topology of meaning, which can be represented by Culler's reversibility thesis.

Chapter 7 below can be construed as just such a use of this semantic space, in many respects, which employs presuppositions about King David's biography in 1 and 2 Samuel in conjunction with some scholarly exegesis of it. When 'oppositions' are controversially interrogated and resolution is presented, as it is in biography of David, some standardised readers, not sharing the resolution's presupposition, might deem it 'ambivalent', while it might be secure, or vice versa. This is part of a general problem with characterization. For example, in Eliot's *Silas Marner*, Silas is subject to trances. Shuttleworth (1984) notices how some critics take this to be evidence of Silas's unaccountability, in tension with the stable function of the character. But use of this trance feature as indictment of Silas's character presupposes a concept of normality and position for trances which Eliot puts aside, probably because of her own presupposition about development and catastrophe. Yet she does not finally harmonise the ambivalence in Silas's character. This may defer the scrutiny and/or cause of the ambivalence to 'chance'—interpreted as 'opportunity'—in the novel. The narrative presuppositions in the Samuel narrative of the witch of Endor, though from a vastly different universe of discourse from 19th-century modernist social realism, nevertheless code certain similar functions. The witch's trance function (along the lines of Eliot's usage, yet in opposition to some of her critics) is taken as an indictment of the witch—and Saul—because she is still accountable though abnormal with respect to the standard didactic norm presupposed by the Samuel narrative.

Likewise, study of the deep structure of David's biography, particularly in relation to Saul, shows that what may seem ambivalent excess space functions as a set of determinate presuppositions, if one follows Chapter 7 below. Accordingly, not only terms but also thematic groups of expressions, pressed into reverse by a narrative biography, can take up unexpected excess space while sensitively questioning assumptions about normality. Saul's own reversal will have an impact on the inversion of adjacent terms, and these will trigger perhaps surprising new semantic borders in hitherto unused semantic space impacting on characterization, in proportion to an author, editor's or literary critic's resourceful originality. In short, reversibility in the excess principle contexts have forms which are assessed by thematic modes that can in turn be measured, but whose central difficulty in many narratives is recognition of and allowance for presupposition which run contrary to the reader's mores, rather than to intractable barriers to interpretation. Within this sphere of difficulty resides the basic tendency we have to re-interpret biographical features or flaws, so that they seem to be more accessible to critical reduction than they are when viewed in their world view, in privileging our worldviews as functionally prior to and supervening over the narrative world we try to enter.

Ignorance and knowledge are mixed in narrative, however. One of the classes in which this occurs is irony. A by-product of Chapter 5's analysis below is to show how grim irony takes up unexpected semantic reversals in the book of Exodus by creating new space in extending semantic fields. Thus a principle of excess sense should allow for an ancient author's or editor's original creative ability ironically to re-write the topology manifested in semantic fields, as with the biography of David. In contrast, it is not quite pointing to a strawman to warn ourselves of a modern literary analyst, deadened by presuppositions supposedly identifying the serf-like stolidity of a scribe's purported allegiance to mainstream traditions. The possibilities of ambiguity in irony include the function of understatement by an author, a function that perhaps intentionally leaves open space for the over-competent reader to miss what has already been similarly neglected by the ancient author's, or critic's, target audience.

In contrast, ambiguity can occupy the function of a deep structure within a narrative, in which gap-filling and reversal are typical devices to sustain closure and focalisation of the development within the narrative's theme, as G.I. Davies (1992) shows in his study of Exodus 1–2. To his contribution, we can add a somewhat different, though complementary, perspective in which the narrative's deep structure creates a narrative conflict by allusion to narrative fields perceived to be external to the authorial voice.

The Plagues narrative in Exodus embodies a polemical war. The narrative battles with pharaonic interpretations of mythology and cultic politics. Its intertext's presentation of the purported Egyptian observer's readings of the Plagues—like some Unconscious hovering dislocated between text and perceived event—wildly differs from the authorial voice of the Exodus text, while yet seeming to occupy the same semantic module. Pharaoh tells Moses that he will not see Moses' face again, with the prospect of Moses' certain death if this imperative is not heeded. Moses' inverting irony retorts with invisible non-compliance: 'You have spoken well' (Ex. 10:29). The surface reading of the module is Pharaoh's threat, with Moses' agreement. Underneath, the intended penalty is turned on Pharaoh in his own words, because it is he who is to die, when there is a semantic reversal from master to victim. This ironic reading is partly made possible by pitching the scope of the module by reference to its larger sequential context in the Plagues' drama. In this type of usage, it is the authorial selection of priorities and skill in a state of affairs that should not be conflated with indeterminacy and/or application of a principle of excess. Consequently, such ironic reading really is an internal function of the narrative's semantics.

For each class of applications of the principle of excess, there is a corresponding class which may appear to satisfy the principle, but which does not. Two sorts of circumstances, at least, would produce such a group. First, the situation in which a critic's presuppositions did not expose the determinate nature of the narrative. Secondly, when irony or truths in the narrative were ignored by critical dissent. To be sure, someone might wish to respond that, if critical scrutiny judges that a narrative is indeterminate and susceptible of the principle of excess, one might suppose this to be an incorrect judgement. In this situation, one's objection has the suppressed premise that the narrative actually is indeterminate, because rational critics have an observational basis in the text for their views. This does not have be the case, however; for it would have to lead to the implication that each time there is a dispute about a text among competent polarised critics; both sets of critics would be correct, because any competent judgement is a candidate for this tactical move, not merely an objection to indeterminacy. A misplaced insight may be presupposed behind such a move.

My proposal is that narratives are theoretically pluralist. That is to say, the substructures of a large range of ancient Near East texts contiguous to and polemically intertextually subsumed in the Old Testament manifest in their semantics no single logical grammar, nor presuppose a common thematic mentality with respect to their underlying evidence of psycholinguistic phenomena. Although this may be thought to be a fairly obvious point, stated like this, the way the opinion is expressed is calculated to defend the notion that compositional activity has plural causal relations to author and written narrative, not merely to a reader's indeterministic projection on to a text. This itself is to support the idea that the varieties of logics conceived by humans in complex ways are mirrors of a variety of our psychological characteristics. No doubt cultural evolution, diachronic differences, and the disparate roles of editing, scribal paraphrases, and institutional censorship, together with many other influences, often vastly complicate such activities and linguistic states. But this is the obverse of the trend criticized in Barr (1961) and Gibson (1981, and forthcoming e) in which hypostatization and confused generalisation are shown to be presupposed as functions akin to rather badly depicted semantic quasi-Platonic Forms. Conjecture, explicated by logic and evidence, is not being opposed by this criticism, however.

A reason why some critics are at loggerheads is because they have variously conceived elements within the narrative, yet over-generalised an element as if it were a global view of the whole narrative. On this view, it would be an improvement to distinguish partial functions, and boundaries of nuances that support particular types of theories. Sure, it would be mythology to universalise this thesis: not all-critical imagination has a counterpart in all or some text somewhere. Nevertheless there is some evening-out in literary theorists' diets of interest. They can yield a wide array of strands that may be retrievable for reconstruction into global pictures of meaning. In this way, the opposed choice between semantic universals or relativistic semantics may be misconceived, as with the often institutionalised clashes between formalist and *avant-garde* options.

It is helpful in studies of ancient literatures to compare and contrast them with some activities in modern literary creativity and research. The case of Mallarmé's poetry is instructive here; in particular if one also compares it with some of the prose in Ecclesiastes, and the Rebel Lands' tablets. Concerning Mallarmé, Davies (1953) in combination with Lloyd Austin (1987), holds traditional formalist positions, in contrast with Malcolm Bowie (1978; 1982), who stresses the disrupting revolutionary potential in Mallarmé's poetry. Is Mallarmé's poetry a deconstruction of categories so that indeterminacy is an ineradicable property, in agreement with Bowie; or is his poetry much more classical in construction and formal precision with regard to standard French grammar, as Davies and Austin suppose? This opposition might at some levels conceivably be unnecessary, at least for some types of Mallarmé poetry (for example *Un Coup de Dés*), though it could leave the standard grammar as primary. Reading Sumerian is sometimes an experience not unlike arbitrating on this sort of debate. Mallarmé's own comments on his adherence to standard grammar would seem to support the view that internal to tradition's rules is a randomness.

Such a literary perspective pertains quite closely to another realm of critical perception, that of philosophy applied to language. The foregoing concurs with Wittgenstein's (1958: secs. 1-110) paradoxical discovery that 'following a rule' is not itself a rule (cf. Boghossian 1989). Could not the reason why two leading groupings of scholars disagree about the basis for assessing Mallarmé be because both scholars are correct at complementary levels, if either or both viewpoints are re-qualified? An upshot of such disagreement appears to be that, just because the form of a narrative is heavily ossified and uniform in style, this has little bearing on its capacity for multiple levels of sense and even irony. So simplicity of style is compatible with elusive complexity in semantics. A corollary of this can be argued to the effect that the psycholinguistic origins of such phenomena are complex and variable in ways easily omitted from later supervening modern treatments that presuppose a stress on primitivity and linguistic rule-based grammars. This would unpack into a specific thesis, but first we need some talk about models of meaning.

It is sometimes assumed that sense is linear. Such a notion is sometimes implicit and unformulated, yet it accords with the ways in which narratives are treated. This tendency might be characterised along the lines that, just as language is written two-dimensionally, so is its nature. Even without questioning such a disposition, it is problematic as to how one might, within such a formative idea, express what abstract sense in a narrative is; and this is not only the concept of modern abstract features, but ancient informal uses of abstract elements. Rather, graphics is deceptive: the way linguistic expression is written is obviously not symmetrical to its contents. Gibson (forthcoming e: Prologue, and 99; 1998b) argues that some logic, though remote from the self-consciousness of ancient writers, could be a route to suitable abstract conjectures by which to attempt some mapping of the semantic topologies of Near East creativity.

Holographic Meaning

Distinctions between form and content in meaning are not easily sustained, however. There is, of course, enormous distance between natural and formal languages, though Gibson (1997a) develops a view of live metaphor which allows for this gap, while supporting the utility of relating the two sorts of languages, often for purposes of measured contrast. In such a framework, form is the typology of sense. A holograph is an apt entity with which to highlight this relation of form to content, in which 'form' is a live metaphor for a typology in a certain realm of sense, as illustrated below. It catches structures of meaning, with its three dimensional ghosting of its subjects (cp. p.46 above).

Following Rorty's (1984) view that definitional vocabulary should be drawn from the narrative being examined, it is an interesting exercise to utilise a narrative's own linguistic figures, as a resource for trying to mirror ancient internal narrative presuppositions about such language. Isa. 57:15, 'dwelling in eternity', employing *skn* is a rare collocation—so much so that Barr (1964) leaves it out of his stylised treatment of words for time; yet it stands in splendid isolation as a temporal abstraction utilising language normally for a fabric dwelling. It marginally indicates the possibility of vast shifts in sense's sensibility in Old Testament semantic transmission. This type of shift may mirror or anticipate and complement an aspect of John 1:14's drawing on Old Testament tabernacle motifs and lexical stock (*škn*) in affirming: 'And the Word became flesh and dwelt (*skenoo*) among us.' Here metaphor is programmed with a pun that transforms a tabernacle ontology. Architectural and residential models form strands of such meaning that is therefore in the use itself. Consider that semantics is itself an abstract set of dimensions, though of course what it represents often is not. One might, without lack of sensibility, combine the building figure of meaning with the holographic live metaphor to explore the thesis of meaning as an abstract medium with metaphoric structures within it: foundations, levels, and branching structural connections. Of course, there are many qualifications to add to such illustrative models, and it is a sensitive matter to use it without overstatement, but the exploration of an internal dynamic unnoticed by an ancient writer in his narrative space is both a puzzling and a fertile sphere of possible insight. The occupation of an untypical linguistic borderland by an expression can be utilised as a profitable listening post for fresh signals in narrative terrain that not infrequently have been so drenched with critical noise that ancient senses have to be retrieved by indirect observation.

In contrast Kermode (2000: 68-82) has beautifully delineated in Shakespeare ways that, using an element from Rabelais, words spoken in cold weather that freeze, later thaw. He thinks of it as an allegory of the way in which certain words thaw out in the course of an early play such as *Love's Labor's Lost*; and he notes that such a device become central for Shakespeare This can be employed to refine my idea of holographic sense, in which nuances and inner senses thaw when deployed to intimate a rich array of senses, as with *skn* (rather akin to puns in and out of idioms, developed in Gibson forthcoming e). Kermode (2000: 69-74) adds to this theme reflections of Shakespeare's "The Phoenix and the Turtle", to adduce an awareness of how the playwright has a deep concern for introspection on the semantics of identity, with play on substance, shadow, where a single motif transcends to be two. This type of insight profoundly directs us to areas of the significance of double and multiple meanings. The motif of 'holograph' may be a helpful ragbag term to encapsulate central pulses of such senses.

Yet we are rightly sensitive to equivocation. Conversely, we should discriminate between two zones of literary significance. There is the traditional issue of equivocation, and one should not balk at denouncing actual slips in this group. Beyond this, however, there is another sphere, which I take to be that of Frank Kermode's concern: in great creative narrative there frequently is a piling up of levels of sense, a merging of distinct semantic values for thematic purposes and nuance. These may be regarded as using or related to sorts of polysemy, metonymy, synecdoche, and the like. Certainly some literary uses drift free of logic. And in such cases one would hope to measure the distance between such linguistic phenomena and logic. There is, however, an uneasy and yet fecund borderland between the two. We do not yet understand some of the areas of formalism (say, fuzzy logic, relevance logic) always to denounce these as illogical, though, clearly, there are established foundations for many areas of logic.

Another feature of logic could be borne in mind, perhaps to distract from a mechanistic tendency and to unsettle confidence in logic as the objective science of measurement. 'Counter-intuition' in pure mathematics is when a mathematician conjectures a solution to a deep problem whose answer defies extant solutions, and finds that his answer is the contrary of the correct answer. Gödel's research to the effect that the foundations of arithmetic are unprovable is such a counter-intuitive state of affairs. Gibson (cf. forthcoming e, 1998a, 1998b) suggests that much of great creative narrative may well structurally occupy a comparable position in the theory of literary understanding. Consequently, if such considerations apply to ancient tablets, their texts, and Near East creative literature, then we will have a highly complicated situation that probably violates Ockham's Razor. As Michael Tanner (1979) shows, it is a quality of great art that it attracts opposed judgements about its significance and centrality. If we add to this the notion of the Lacanian motif of the human unconscious as a disruptive narrative force bursting on the conscious use of language, we may have to release hold on many ideas about simplicity and lawlikeness in language studies.

The intractability of an ancient tablet or narrative will in part be a product of the gap between our knowledge of linguistics and it: a result of political editing or scribal stylisation whose aura obscures perception of the society behind the narrative. Beyond that, it may just be that there is no nature to language as a holistic phenomenon. In such a priority, academic norms may be artificial psychological restraints fighting against the admission of the creative power of ancient semantic disruption. Successful scholarly reaction to this may have to rely on unexpected pluralism, some merger of creative work with critical method, and a chess-like skill avoiding limiting restrictions, with a mathematician's artistry in using an indirect route to achieve an apparently impossible end. To be sure, scholarship has practised many skills like these. The focus at issue is, rather, the original integration and transformation of these variables in isolating new identities. The above enterprise aims to pull together logic, truth, and literature, but in some respects not in usual ways. Logic and mathematics get more and more counter-intuitive the deeper discoveries go. This is because creativity in the structure of the subjects themselves looms nearer in the formalisms as we reach deeper into the functional dynamics of ancient narratives.

A note on the relation of logic to informal narrative is relevant to the connection here between form and function. As logic and its functions are analysed in greater depth, the concern for correct form generates paradoxes that break down the validity of formal generalisation for subjects other than formal systems. At such junctures, the importance of semantic originality may involve paradoxes reinstated as a presupposition tantamount to logic's paradoxes. Logical inventiveness is thereby, in principle if not in theory, circumscribed by logic when one attempts to resolve such paradoxes or at least assess them. Such are the outer borders of 'correct form' by reference to which formal linguistic theory has a limiting case that collapses. Attempts to reconstruct a route around deconstructing paradoxes in logic generate the need for arbitrary inventiveness, even in the case where one wants a universal logic. It is as if Augustine and Aquinas, or Plato and Aristotle had come to an impasse, and had to agree on a joint attempt to provide a unified field theory to account for the integration of logic with literature.

Adopting Gibson (forthcoming e) as a premise to combine with the present analysis, my point amounts to the claim that ancient literary uses are a formally unnerving manifestation of human creativity, which resist programmatic resolution by either formal grammars or literary theory. They seem to require a fresh type of engagement between a new conjunction of both fields that then require bold revision. A reason for this is that a narrative that survives to achieve cross-cultural generalisation and collective influence in alien cultures outside of its origins is deep and completely simple in paradoxical ways. In addition, its semantics are accordingly both great art and original logic, even where institutional conformity is a property of its histories. So we need new theories of the conjunction of logics and literatures. In this perspective, as one digs paradoxically deeper—more simply and with increasing complexity—logic becomes more artistic. A counterpart of this state of affairs, I suggest, is that, correspondingly, literary creativity is in some respects thereby nearer in structure to the counter-intuitive areas of logic than many might dare to expect. This is not a proposal that amounts to mechanising ancient narrative by something that is insensitive from a creative and advanced logic perspectives, for example syllogistic. Rather, it involves (in Gibson 2000a, and forthcoming e) the notion that logic has to be overhauled to be more sensitive to some of the logical features already in creative language and also in very advanced mathematics. (In the latter, the ideas of a proof and formal consistency are very problematic.)

Concerning some of these matters, it appears that Aristotle's *Poetics* and his *Rhetoric* have neglected contributions to make. Burnyeat (1994) has argued that we should recognise that in Aristotle's conception of the enthymeme we have features of deductive situated in natural language. Following on from this research, Gibson (forthcoming e, f) argues that logical deduction, rhetoric, and creative literature can to some extent be integrated and be found in a range of uses in ancient texts. Adjacent to such an enterprise Lear (1980) showed concern to demonstrate that Aristotle was occupied with metalogical issues in his research into syllogism. In view of this, and given the plausibility of identifying the enthymeme as a category of deductive (not incomplete syllogistic) reasoning, I suggest that we can readily appreciate that one aim of Aristotle is a first step in the direction of a philosophical logic of creative literature in the *Poetics*. I keep this focus in mind when investigating other ancient creative literature.

Now let us return to the earlier discussion of Mallarmé's poetry, presupposing such considerations, as a mirror to reflect some perennial concerns in our approaches to ancient literary issues. It may follow from the above that both some deconstructionist and some of the more classical grammatical views are correct, but only when they are realigned with new theories. For example, imagine a single line of ancient Semitic narrative or one of its terms, and consider the prospect that it is an instance of multidimensional polysemy that requires characterization as a three-plus dimensional function—rather like a building. We could regard levels within Mallarmé's typical poetry as having such distinct contributions stacked in hierarchies.

Consider, to begin with, the elementary, albeit dense representation the Old Testament uses of *rwḥ*—the Hebrew word-form for 'spirit', 'breath' and 'wind'. In some contexts (for example Gen. 1:2, 'And the Spirit of God moved upon the face of the waters'), it appears that sometimes these senses are allusive levels all functioning in a single use. In the manner of Gibson (1997a, forthcoming e) we could identify the various senses as multiple levels of sense coincident in one use in a narrative, if suitable contextual evidence supports them. Without wishing to commit us to equivocation, this thesis could be used to imply that the theories of homonymy and polysemy need at least supplementation by hypotheses to account for the causal contiguity of different semantic values as a function of thematic nuance of a word in a single context. Analyses or translations compete with one another when actually they are indiscreetly pulling apart a continuum of stratified senses—levels within the word. Just because a confused diachronic etymology has discredited previous assumptions about multiple senses, it does not follow that multiple senses in one word in a specific context do not exist. Yet such a view is not committed to generalising this multiple-sense thesis over all uses of a term merely because there are multiple senses in a particular usage; generalisation will be bound by the occurrence of the phenomenon.

Within a world of meaning where multiple senses occur, there will also be complementary syntaxes with multiple functions. Such syntactic operators are polysyntactic variables; as with word-senses, such syntax will have multiple levels of syntactic meaning nested into its scope. The Hebrew *'elohim* (God/gods) is a case in point (see Gibson 1997a). The case ending is identical for singular or plural. A number of Old Testament passages employ this polysyntactic variability to harness themes about God's manifestation in agents (Gen. 1:26-27; Ps. 82:6, etc.), in which emphasis on divine manifestation in agents also complements reference to God. Of course, due regard has to be made for ossified homonymic case-endings, though the existence of these does not rule out the possibility that their common form can be used as a bridge to create a pun or irony.

There are grounds for some generalised theory about multiple levels of meaning over syntax. Here, the formal patterns of mathematical logic could be used to flesh out the levels and transformations. Gibson (forthcoming e) explores some grounds for this type of thesis, as well as proving that some formal logic distinctions apply to actual Old Testament usage. The following chapters episodically utilise such insights in an informal presentation (for example the final two sections of Chapter 6); and the last section of Chapter 3 below explains how one can locate multiple senses in a biblical narrative, by noticing that some hitherto opposed interpretations of the narrative are really two complementary levels of multiple function within the one narrative. This is not to universalise relativity, nor to assume that all interpretations are right.

The foregoing lays a framework for aspects of, for example, Alter's (1981) work on biblical narrative, in which creativity and multiple internal mirroring of biblical dialogue are stressed. As Hammond (1983) noticed, Alter's view complements Kugel's (1982) study on the nature of the Psalms. Kugel argues that the various standard parallelistic formulae for Psalm linguistics are incorrect. He maintains that, in the Psalms, we should see an extension and intensification of high prose: a parallelism is a dynamic addition and development in the relation between first and second lines, not a static 'synonymous' identification. If we combine these aspects of Alter's and Kugel's views with the present sketch of literary sense, we will see that the above diversion from narrative to poetry interrelates properly at the suggested levels. Yet we may need to adjust Kugel's criticism of some traditional views of parallelism; it seems that it is the articulation of the idea of a synonymous parallelism in the Psalms, rather than the notion itself that—closely regulated in application—is at fault. Some aspects of the traditional views (though they would benefit from improved formulation) could combine well with some features in Kugel's approach, if we posit the concept of multiple levels of structure and sense within the parallelism.

This reverts to the type of question provoked by the disagreement between linguists over Mallarmé's poetry. It can consistently be proposed that, in such cases (but not all cases), equally distinguished scholarly dissent about classical grammar and styles in poetry do not have to be mutually exclusive ways of assessing that poetry, though they may have to overlap counter-intuitively. The same point could also apply to other genres. Classical grammar subsuming Mallarmé's poetry and some deconstructionist patterns overlaying it may be apprehended as distinct domains or levels within the poetry, although such phenomena will no doubt obtain unevenly and suprisingly even with regard to their own mannered ways.

Semiotic Serpents

A consequence of the foregoing is that it generates another literary thesis: literary theories sometimes map the same creative territory from different standpoints and levels, and thus a group of apparently competing theories can be complementarily applied to a narrative if suitably qualified. A scholar, who holds to a single-sense of a narrative or to one, perhaps presupposed, single theory will misconceive the impact and status of a pluralist approach to literary theories.

For example, in Chapter 4 below, it is argued that the Exodus 7 serpent-rod polemic in the Court of pharaoh is a complex symbolic narrative that has many levels of parody, irony and allusion. The serpent may partly correspond to the cobra sign on the pharaoh's headdress, given the scope of the original terms. We could introduce Eco's (1984) semiotics here; Eco is concerned to present language as a series of symbolic interactions between the sign, the world it depicts and with which it merges, and the reader. Based on C.S. Pierce's (1931–58) research, Eco highlights the communicative properties of phenomena, and how language participates with these pieces of the world to produce signs. On this scenario, Exodus 7 represents how the magical, numinous interconnections of sign and society code one another.

Lacan's (cf. Bowie 1991) use of mirroring is pertinent to the serpent. The external world is the ego's mirror, and artefacts in it code the identity of the observer. Linda Hutcheon (1984) uses the *mise en abyme* as a displacement device. Here the ureaus on pharaoh's forehead is the incarnate condensation of father-god Ptah. And the serpents in Exodus are used playfully in the narrative to deconstruct what is taken to be the mythology linked to the political power in the personal confrontation between Moses and pharaoh. The stable universe of courtly myth is disrupted like a dream from the unconscious by the rod undergoing transmission to become the serpent.

This type of emphasis facilitates our applying some of Derrida's breakdown of 'meaning' for creative narratives. Nevertheless, the above critique of thematic elements opposes one's universalising a thesis about deconstruction: (a) Derrida discounts the possibility of objective sense; (b) Derrida is incorrect not to allow mimesis and other literary theories to complement his own views, though his objections are forceful. Derrida showed that, for example, in Descartes' writings, he selected only one of many possible sets of interrelations within his own writings, and omitted or minimised the role of other nuances or themes which have dispositions to run counter to his thematic priority. Likewise with the Exodus' narrative, according to Derrida (1978), institutional commentary tends to seek the mirror of its own preoccupations in narrative prescriptions.

'True' Interpretation

Hovering around the above concerns is the question of just what is the 'meaning' of a narrative? Does narrative have a single sense or multiple senses? And does this binary way of posing the issue presuppose or render circular the measurement of meaning? We can see some parallels both with the standard Exodus commentary-like institutional reading both in Descartes and in recent work such as that of the Germanist P.D. Juhl (1980). Juhl argued that there is only one single interpretation of a narrative. Kermode (1983) proposed that there are sharp difficulties in Juhl's thesis. Their disagreement typifies a common problem, and there is the additional difficulty of presentation, which also relates to presentation in ancient narrative such as the above Exodus case.

A concept about meaning may be developed with a form of presentation which is subtle, persuasive, deep and strong. Conversely, a competing thesis, which may be in principle true, might be disadvantaged by a weaker formulation being associated with it. Rhetoric may not symmetrically mirror the strength of the argument it retails. Again, an intrinsically weak thesis might be strengthened so as to display illusory explanatory powers. As the philosophical logician Lewy (1976) maintained, there are strong concepts of a concept, as well as weak ones. Critical realisation, or its opposition, in a phase of debate may not be sufficient, or may be too incisive, to present the full-blooded formulation of its potential. For example, did James Barr (1961) demolish in principle the possibility of a reconstruction of those mangled concepts of meaning against which his book inveighed? This is not to oppose the truth of its criticisms, nor to suppose that a negative answer would automatically warrant a reversion to the modes of institutional conservatism that it attacked. Barr's book did not dismantle in principle its targets, but only their contingent versions.

In commenting on these literary policies, the aim has also been to relay the resulting balance of options to guide interpretative pathways in approaching the Exodus and other narratives. Certainly, the iconographic features contingent on the sense of 'serpent' may be neglected or overstated. The present book suggests that integrated disparate techniques, priorities and theses will form the most effective composite theory as a means to identify ancient senses in narratives. In short, the single sense of the narrative, if true, would be a multi-dimensional stack of levels of meaning co-ordinated into a literary unity. The single sense thesis, in this viewpoint, would be proscribed as an overstated device which distortedly focused on thematic unity as the criterion of meaning, thus not being tuned to apprehend the cement bonding of the shifts of sense which are the levels of sense.

Contrariwise, multiple level, or deconstructionist, hypotheses might be so stimulated by the plurality of nuances, and possibly misread them as indeterminate textually external options, that the critic is not user-friendly about the ancient narrative.

One might deploy this vantage-point as a device for defocusing and tuning away the unified bonding in a great narrative, by too great emphasis on strands and levels of sense, yet offer a concept which is so impoverished a view of thematic semantics and terminological pinning in the narrative, that it does not expose the dynamics of the roles. Such internal properties of meaning as there are will further complicate matters by the use of irony, parody and allusion to combat contentions anciently deem to be illusions. A reason for this is because irony, for example, shifts the semantic position of a term and thus displaces a point in a theme. This deformation may either go unnoticed or be overstated as something that fragments the unity of the narrative. Consequently, the role of 'force' and rhetorical functions in a narrative are like quicksand in relation to a too uniformly conducted discussion of alternatives between single and multiple-sense discussion of ancient texts, particularly when nontextual semiotic iconographic targets are sought by the ancient narrative and the critical reader. In the Lacanian role, as critical readers, we may inadvertently find our egos employing the narrative at which we connive as a mirror whose distortions are reflections of the disruptions which our unconscious bestows on the narrative senses. Particularly is this the prospect when we are dealing with an ancient narrative whose primordial disturbances question the archetypes that our rational orders presuppose.

How does the above point about single-sense narrative apply to the Old Testament? It is an evident point that, at some levels, Old Testament narrative presupposes perception of a unique viewpoint for its legal authority, counsel, or origin, for example Elijah's presupposed supervenient function in 1 Kings 17–18 over the Baal priests. Such an authorial voice, to some extent, matches a claim to be 'the' single correct interpretation. We should be wary of defining this point by approximating it only to the nearest available current theory; however, it is of interest to have a literary formalism which can be of use to make such assumptions explicit. A distinction between a given Old Testament narrative's authorial standpoint, as compared with its propositional attitude reporting or quoting actors and world views opposed to the authorial voice, is enormously important here.

The Old Testament is clearly pluralistic in its containing complex reproduction of dissenting world-views. To this extent, plural models of free indirect discourse will be needed (cf. Banfield 1982). Many semantic narrative fields of the Old Testament contrast the plural worlds own universes of presuppositions, putatively with a single correct premise. Although many scholars will be disposed to interpret such situations in opposed ways, and want to argue that, within the Old Testament, yet there are distinct modes of presenting this single correct interpretation. Monotheism versus polytheism is one of the obvious cases of this type of opposition but part of the Old Testament's internal voice which uses a type of single correct interpretation requires precise reproduction, especially where it is considered to be inaccurate as a voice of the historical past.

The state of affairs in groups of Old Testament semantic fields seems, roughly speaking, an internal bundle of pluralist models wrapped around externally by a single-correct interpretation model. Evidently, this single interpretation presupposition is not to be equated with a self-evident 'establishment' conservative recipe. Yet ancient presuppositions of 'revelation', rebuke of inspired agents, and a host of other thematic pulses place the Old Testament in the class of what could be called, clusters of counter-intuition, though one should be careful not to suppose that ancient textual phenomena are exhaustively or entirely neutrally depicted by such tags. The foregoing claimed that literary theories might be used in a pluralist way to map creative narratives, and also finds a carefully guarded place for the notion of a single correct interpretation. 'Correct' here is of course a function of a narrative's own assumed worldview.

Interrelated with these two facets is the problem of true or false measurement of texts, when scholastic assumptions sometimes operate incorrectly. For example, Chapter 7 below considers the life of David, as scholars with distinct theories have variously interpreted it. The Old Testament privileges David, as opposed to Saul. Some scholars have attempted to rebalance this opposition, and salvage Saul from dishonour. The problem is to judge which theory or commentary accurately represents itself. Chapter 7 below attempts to show how one can logically expose some features involved in assessing the multiple meaning of the text to resolve this tension. Basically, literary theories are posterior to narrative investigation. When the narrative is analysed, some literary theories will fit over the results. Unfortunately, theological theories are sometimes adopted as true assumptions prior to analysis of the text. We can use relevant logic as one means to sorting out probable interpretations.

Polyphony, Fantasy and Mimesis

The Russian formalist Mikhail Bakhtin can be introduced to explain how narratives might be misread (esp. Bakhtin 1984). Bakhtin sought to identify the unity in variety, while opposing the notion of a single truth, yet tied to a theme of binary opposition. A central aspect of this program is 'polyphony'. Bakhtin identified this in the novels of Dostoevsky, in which, though each character seems to be bestowed with equivalent moral or 'logical' weight, each differs from the others. The notion of good versions of bad, and feeble realisations of good, are themselves variations within his theme, and as such are parallel with the above description of weak and strong versions of a concept, as exemplified in the philosophy of Lewy (1976). Bakhtin finds it impossible to isolate Dostoevsky's preference because he had none (or so it seemed).

Unlike the author of the life of David on one standard view, Dostoevsky smoothed his authorial view out of sight behind the inequalities of the characters. Bakhtin added to this world of polyphony a concept of binary oppositions, good/bad, pure/impure, and light/dark. This was enriched by the notion of counterfeits of the opposed values. Statues of humans have no orifices, one of Joyce's child characters announced in ruder terms in the British Museum.

In the universe of binary relations, Bakhtin viewed social history as a series of inversions and tensions about alternate choices, placed against a background model of the ancient carnival of the night. In this model of the carnivalesque, the grotesque battled with the 'pure form', often with inversions of role, to code the constant flux of historical forces. As Jerome Gâme (1998) explains, Bakhtin's concern is with form to propose that a style of oblique concern, by sideways-on vision through multiple voices. Here irony inverts expectations. Great as Goliath appeared as champion of Dagan, the characterization of David with grim carnivalesque irony presses Goliath into the role of a dysfunctional counterfeit warrior by David rejecting his companions' attempt to push him into counterfeiting—invalidly miming—the warrior ritual trappings.

Bakhtin's patterning of narrative reality is usable to sketch and tune distinctions between competing motifs and their contrary polemic copies. In particular, it is helpful as a means to map the scholarly rationale that prefers to privilege one hermeneutic side of the binary relations. Often hidden within such polemical theological wars, there reside presuppositions about what it is for a narrative to manifest such coded oppositions, and, sometimes-suppressed manifestos about the nature of the text. Chapter 7 below scans the study of contradiction and contrariety in theological discussion of the books of Samuel and Chronicles about the characterization of David. The narratives ironically mirror ancient assumptions concerning kingly identity, neglect of which can derail correct representation of binary oppositions and allusive use of polyphony.

In a Rabelaisian world, Bakhtin saw a transformable means for rendering the world intelligent. The world is a collection of metaphors that map the unconscious and their competing opposites, with the grotesque as a route to purity, with counterfeits as roads to reality. Assyrian state archives catalogue a relevant binary that pervaded Mesopotamia: "1 one-column tablet, antiwitchcraft" (Fales and Postgate, 1992:64). 1 Samuel's witch of Endor, with king Saul seeking binary displacement in the dead of night, by enlightenment from the chthonic grotesque, presents Samuel possibly rising from the dead, with an ambivalence that codes Saul's indeterminacy of conviction about the binary conflict in the narrative. Not infrequently, one might slip into posing the alternate status of Samuel as risen and as ghost as exclusive alternative ways to read the narrative. On this Bakhtinian scan, this would have displaced the irony employing allusion to mirror Saul's binary illusion in the night. The theme of Saul's journey, to ask if a battle can be won, is dislocated and overridden by what the narrative voice poses as the true point of the battle: Saul's counterfeiting of and opposition to his role model. His literary archetype thus psychotically condenses into fantasy. Bakhtin's theory can be positioned as a backcloth of which the logic introduced in the present book is a corollary.

In Chapter 6 below, the examination of biblical God versus Ugaritic gods can be positioned as a complex example of the arena in which Bakhtinian binary functions operate and can be paraphrased as logical polemics. It is maintained in Chapter 6 that a number of scholars have misunderstood such binary oppositions, specifically in contexts where the biblical narratives are ironically punning in deadly seriousness upon a mythology offered, so to speak, as a carnival of the night. Bakhtin was not writing of carnival as a dead metaphor. Rather, he held that festivals encoded a psychology of powerful fantasy that could be used to liberate or imprison the reader.

Kathryn Hume (1984), in a non-Bakhtin perspective, has provided the work for further treatment of fantasy by linking it to the topic of mimesis. She claims that fantasy can be a device for representing reality when associated with mimesis. She does not address biblical examples, but this work would serve as a starting-point to investigate, for example, Old Testament representation of Canaanite rites and festivals. A central case for study is also the narratives about the Egyptian Plagues, dealt with in Chapter 4 below. Here the carnival of the night metaphor can be compared with a structural function, centred on night, death and the god of Egypt. In this perspective, we can discover that the theory of fantasy and a concept of mimesis can be interconnected with elements of historical analysis to retrieve some understanding of the ancient Near East.

Psychological Conclusion

One of the aims of the foregoing has been to sketch projected links between archaeology, literature and ancient mentality. A stress on the archaeology of the mind stirs deep and controversial waters. Freudian psychoanalysis is relevant to the extension of this subject, and it is appropriate in such a perspective to develop, among others, points introduced above concerning catastrophe archaeology. It has been widely recognised that Freud raised important questions respecting the abnormal mentality simulated in some Classical Greek literature; yet what of the analysis of mentality for periods long before that, as evidenced in much earlier literatures and pictorial art?

The foregoing considerations point to and reflect archetypal foundations if we divert them to new areas for research in Mesopotamia—the ultimate source of many later Greek themes. True, the Greeks made mythology articulating their specific identities, and we should be careful when generalising over diverse cultures. As with the first reading of a narrative, however, to come upon original historical and psychological causes of mythology and its attendant creativity in the Near East will not only mirror a cradle of civilisation, it will advertise the arrival and perhaps growth of the foetus there. I have claimed elsewhere (1998b) that the two-faced Roman Janus god of entrances will have been fathered by its Sumerian twin god, Usmu, in the psychodynamics of the unconscious. In the Adda cylinder seal (BM WA89115, Figures 1.5-6 above), the double-faced god Usmu stands to the far right in epiphany attending the birth of Ninurta, or possibly his emergence from the Rebel Lands. Amiet (1980) suggests that the Adda seal may be conceived as a celebration of a union in divine marriage, which, if true, would enable a link to be, forged through the Adda seal between marriage and its birth of a god's motif.

Freud (1960) only reached as far back as Janus: his 'Janus' is a double typology for jokes, and this does not exclude tragic satire. For Freud, 'jokes' here is a simile for reflections in the mirror of social progress or regress. Freud argued that the third person indexing of Janus is a cipher for the first person user. If this holds for the Sumerian god Usmu, we will have an access-point (if suitably characterised) which mirrors a facet of the mentality of its composer(s). This will enable us, if we can generalise such a link over other phenomena, to discover some of the content of Mesopotamian archetypes with which to fill the unconscious mind into which Jung poured pale shades of its derivative social escalation and progress. Ian Hacking's (1994) treatise on the emergence of multiple personality in the modernist world, as an unintentional function of a mass media semantic contagion, could be reformulated as a conceptual formalism by which to model some psychodynamics of Near East trauma.

The above discussion of Kinnier Wilson's (1979) study of the Rebel Lands tablets, with their alleged attention to actual cataclysm, is important as a basis for theorizing about dreamscapes, in the perspectives of their mirroring some ancient anxieties and trauma. The relations of such phenomena to trance have yet to be addressed in research, though Gibson (1998b) has offered a theory of some features. Trance and trauma are intimately connected, as are the ways in which dreams are parasitic on such phenomena. Although the Old Testament is some distance psychologically and culturally from such dreamscapes, yet they clearly played roles in the emergence of its folk-psychology, legal prohibitions, and religious mentality.

The role of shared or collective amnesia is also a relevant consideration in analysis of trance, both specifically and generally. The role of both male and female typologies are relevant to such issues, but to women especially in the present context, where the misuse of women is particularly in evidence in the ancient world. In Mesopotamia and the Old Testament, there is implicit and explicit concern with themes of sexuality and childbirth in, for example, the Adda and other seals, as well as their conjecturally contiguous literary contextualization. This state of affairs should give us cause for pausing to reflect on the presuppositions about women and their distorted identities by such metaphorised fields of significance.

Although in principle male and female are equals, women are at risk in ways men are not. One unexpected instance of this asymmetry concerns the result of research by Daniel Schacter (1997: 72-73) which demonstrates that in situations of trauma and abuse, women suffer acute loss of explicit and declarative memory abilities. This occurs because of the volume reductions in the hippocampal regions of the brain-volume needed for such memory functions. The resulting loss of orientation and increased disadvantage for women in such traumatic situations serves as an explanation for part of the reasons as to why women readily function(ed) as victims in, and of, religious activities as well as possession states involving witches (see Abusch, 1995).

Obviously yet fundamentally, concern with the woman as an individual human identity in Sumerian and Akkadian histeriographic spheres was an archetypal, alien absence. Pioneering investigations are needed to examine the absence of such relevant identities, and what that amounts to, for women, by being women, in ancient Mesopotamia. Theses are largely uncharted areas; we should be wary of the influence of our own as well as ancient intentionality. It is certainly a complex, involuted and provisional series of routes that would take us back to knowledge of such ancient women. Frevel's (1995) explorations of the roles that sexuality has in Mesopotamian fertility traditions and attendant prostitution, together with their probable traces in the Old Testament, provide elements of the background to launch areas of such investigations. Haley's (2000) research on Hebrew contexts enables us to harness a measured assessment of how some Canaanite background involving the worship of Asherah and her some of the sexual proclivities of her worshippers are mirrored in the Old Testament.

We need to interrelate these insights into the extent to which the diverse and only partially understood Sumerian, and Akkadian, metaphoric realms of discourse presuppose physical sexual counterparts in some texts and societies. This situation is also affected by the differing ways in which the employment of gendered metaphors personifies perceived forces and significance of the external world. Allowing for the qualifying effects of such factors, the study of ancient human mentalities by their expression in functions of metaphor are important corollaries to aid interpretation of how women were perceived, how they and their social contexts absorbed their negative self-images, and how they were treated.

For example in the perspective of assessing the part played by lion and bull metaphoric functions in Sumerian and Akkadian societies, Watanabe (1998: 148) highlights situation of collective coercion, suppression and exclusion of dissenting people. The above study (pp.32-48) of the goddess Inanna presented her role as sexual motif and Sumerian archetype (me), as well as lion. Watanabe (1998: 104-7) extends this focus of the bestial symbol as a map for human sexuality by documenting Inanna's song for her vulva: she invites the lion to plough her vulva, while in some contexts 'plough' is replaced by the ox as a metaphor for intercourse. We are to some extent unclear about the degree of overlap between the images of women in ancient Mesopotamian cultures and the experiences of actual women, though the asymmetry of power, and its impact on sexuality, between men and women seem similar to the relations to which women have been generally subject throughout history.

Fundamental to research into the denial of women as individual, and use of them as sexual commodities, is the sort of framework furnished by Martha Nussbaum's (2000: 246-51, etc.) analysis of the principle of each person's capability. This pertains to a woman's identity and family, society and state, not least in relation to women's specific vulnerability over and against men; for example, in issues of sexuality and violence, as well as economic inequality (see Nussbaum, 1999:276-98). The male domination of women who are deformed to become commodities of prostitution and rape assumes new dimensions of trauma in a Mesopotamian context of ritual sex as well as sacrifice.

The above aspects pertain to my suggestion that many males, children and women in environments associated with or subject to a domain of control and regulation, in certain ancient Near East social groups were in continual or recurrent states of extensive individual and collective traumatisation. Such states would not be dissimilar to, and at least have some continuities with, the types of traumatisation involved in our own worlds of experience. Perhaps we have tendencies merely to assume that what was normal for 'them' should classed as an index for what was acceptable to them, since they experienced it as standardised reality. There is need to go beyond this. We should analyse what it is to be human and deviation from even an approximate grasp of being a human, so that we might to some degree measure and range of the psychological distances and differences between the 3rd millennium B.C. and the 3rd millennium A.D. A human in the ancient world might well be unaware of the abnormal, yet politically 'normalised', forces that operated on her to minimise or destroy her perception and awareness of the prospect of her individuality. But conscious ignorance does not entail unconscious impact on her. It will be helpful therefore to encourage a perspective in research that employs what, hopefully one might claim, is the rising contemporary awareness of gender justice. As Nussbaum (2000: 298-99) contends, however: "The outrages suffered every day by millions of women – hunger, domestic violence, child sexual abuse and child marriage, inequality before the law, poverty, lack of dignity and self-regard – these are not uniformly regarded as scandalous, and the international community has been slow to judge that these are human rights abuses." We seem, after all, still to share something with very ancient societies; this should be factored into our presuppositions of difference and absence when presuming to look down history.

Perhaps surprisingly, some traditional euorecentric interpretation of modern mythology and culture might nevertheless also partially be reinterpreted and deployed to assist and evoke an apt sense of alarm for our focus, in our attempts to grasp the abnormality under which women laboured in a range of these ancient traumatic conditions. Donnington's (1979) deployment of Jungian psychology to Wagnerian mythology, Freud is clearly more central and seminally primeval. The foregoing comments about the Adda seal indicate this enriched Freudian focus in the ways that such parallels begin to emerge, not least with the implicit birth and sexuality motifs. Other characteristics of the seal extend the parallels. The god standing next to Usmu is most probably Ea (cf. Frankfort 1939), the god adjacent to the water stream which often personifies him. In company with the goddess Nintur, Ea devises a birth control plan (in the story of Atrahasis; cf. Jacobsen 1976). An upshot of this plan is the creation of the Rebel Lands demon Pashittu, who destroys children as they are born, as a function of Ea's counsel. So the child as victim of a male has ancient provenance; this sphere is potentially turbulent with deep trouble, however. Hacking's (1994) drawing attention to child-abuse as a property of the abnormal psychology which attends the extreme schizophreniform of multiple personality opens up a vast area for research on this paternal theistic dynamic. Since sadism is an internal property of the perverse euphemism 'paedophilia', which has causal relations to certain sorts of erotic data here obliquely considered, there is the possibility that the ancient phenomena associated with Usma or the like included such features. This would be a project for a quite different enquiry from the present one. On the Adda seal, the split-personality god Usmu attends Ea; therefore Ea and Usmu depict a sinister twisty risk in the epiphany of the gods on the seal, with Ninurta's emergence from the hole in the mountain summit being attended by an ambivalent divine trainer of midwives, so to speak. The implicit theme involving symbolic misuse of gynaecological trauma is not without its counterparts in our world of war and media (cf. Bono, 1999).

    In addition to the evident relevance of these sorts of feature to general theses in Freud psychology, there are other tantalising relations in what some might only notice as borderline detail. For example, Freud's (1953) equations between birth fantasies about life in the womb and being buried alive; the Adda seal certainly echoes many such themes when it is related to Sumerian literature, exampled in the underworld universe which seems to mimic the unconscious dream world. In this sense, we will find some truth in the proposal that primarily it is art and practice that inform psychoanalysis and not the latter the former.

In contexts like these, what is sometimes deemed borderline detail may actually be an unnoticed function that is central. Kermode (1985) notices this in connection with Freud and Hamlet: 'If we were now to construct our own *middot* [hermeneutical guidelines], one of them might well be: what has been thought marginal may belong more properly in the centre.' (Cf. also Kermode, 2000: 106-10) Conversely, we do *not* want to be dominated by a merely Freudian novelty that is paraded as *the* method for interpreting ancient texts. Use of Freud may be apt for only some possible clusters of sense in a theory about the archaeology of mind in the study of meaning. Certainly, we should not underestimate the difficulties in achieving a true synthesis. Yet ancient symbolism furnishes us with the possibilities for archaeology of some Near Eastern mentalities. It consequently contains data for some psychodynamics of the societies which gave birth to it, though we should take due note of Kirk's (1974) reasons which explain (at the time at which he wrote) why the harvest for Greek mythology from psychoanalysis has been somewhat slim. Perhaps the foregoing contributes to showing that part of the reason for this paucity is wrong or insufficiently refined analytical framework and theory. Although we should not conflate psychoanalysis with mythology, we can ascertain that there are some close links between them because of the central role of language-typology, albeit sometimes in different ways. The multitude of interpretations which might be constructed to envelop these proposed links, and the mass of speculative conflicting psychoanalytical schools' claims, are legion; but my approach turns the possibility of such links on their head.

Many French psychoanalysts, particularly within the orbit of Lacan (cf. 1991), have given enormous emphasis to the equation of language and the Unconscious. Such an equation holds the status of a live metaphor, if correctly stated, and if my above outline for what it is to be meaning is right (also cf. Gibson 1997a, forthcoming f, 1999b). Lacan's sexualization of logic and language can readily attract the charge that he was philosophically psychotic, if one adopts as a mean many standard Anglo-American analytic viewpoints in logic; and it is an unusual characteristic of Lacan's (1976) views in psychoanalysis that he applied the term 'psychotic' to himself. This type of deployment of clinical terms like 'psychotic' to claim a parallel measurement in the composition of a contrary world-counterpart in a non-psychoanalytical subject involves exotic calculations. (A systematic venture explicating this sphere could use Fine's (1985) research on arbitrary objects as a point of departure.) This exotic use of 'psychotic' is no less problematic, however, than Lacan's (1991) sexual incursion into mathematical logic and associated departure from standard logics, in which he sexualises inference. But his revision of the Oedipal schema, as revised by Forrester (1997: 114-61), seems to fit well with the Adda seal's bonding of marriage and gynaecological functions. Given the abnormal psychological data present in Mesopotamian mythology, which model patterns of irrationality in their composers, any pertinent modern figurative extensions of 'psychotic' and similar terminology, may hold illuminating parallels for representing aspects of ancient mentality. Clearly related to this program would be the need to assess to what extent ancient mentality shared abnormal patterns in relation to the differing cultural presuppositions of the ancient and modern worlds, not least of Lacan's psychosis. For example, if classifying a symbol as 'psychotic' were a result of neglecting to account for ancient ignorance about scientific causal relations, then the classification would be incorrect. Yet, for some explanatory categories, such extenuating explanation would be overridden, for instance, in the case of a type of perversion that would be so judged if displayed by any human agent irrespective of epoch or context.

It is interesting to relate this collection of issues to my foregoing discussion about the Rebel Lands tablets, in which some of the probable origins of demonology can be explained in terms of geophysical cataclysm. Details were, of course, located by the author(s) or scribes of Rebel Lands' tablets, but the phenomena there depicted were incorrectly isolated and falsely merged with mythological elements. Another way of construing this situation is to claim that ancient scribes and priests invented a 'psychotic' scenario of causal relations and personal identities. Here psychosis—as the construction of a fictional world, which is misperceived to be coextensive with the physical world—is an especially apt category for characterising features of the artificial worlds of Near Eastern primitively perceived personal experience in mythology. This sort of interpretation might only apply to some (possibly earlier) phases of the history of 'psychotic' motifs; it is quite probable that metaphoric revaluation of earlier 'literal' uses places a ban on some psychoanalytic interpretations of the ancient world. No doubt, there are also vexing problems about marginal cases, together with the problem of religious art merely simulating abnormal ecstatic religious experience. Even so, in the latter instance, metaphoric reproduction of previous literalistic symbolism displaying abnormality is still valuable as a way of gaining evidence of the mental activity from which it derives. There is also the perplexing topic concerning the status of a rational mentality that has a diet of metaphoric discourse—classifiable as 'psychotic' if taken literally. In this perspective, one might consider some Mesopotamian literary contexts that elevate perversions to morality (for example, the human sacrifice rites and attached symbolism present in a number of sites mentioned in Chapters 3, 6 and 8 below). Of course, there is the danger of not rightly slicing the division between an imagined ancient cosmos and the actual historical world; yet that error is not the sole prerogative of archaeologists, as modern politicians illustrate.

It is worth considering more closely the possibility that, if there is an alignment between elements in psychoanalysis and ancient mythology, consequently the actors or roles associated with psychoanalysis and ancient mythology in the archaeology of religious centres also thereby display some alignment. If Lacan's positioning of language, in close relation to the unconscious, be entertained as a myth—leaving aside the question of the coherence of his thesis about it—it is conceptually apt, though provocative, to try and locate a parallel between Lacan (and a number of other psychoanalysts) and ancient priests, as well as between Lacanian treatises and priestly or scribal mythological narratives in ancient Mesopotamia. Noting that the role of ancient priest was sometimes intended to be psychiatric or medical, such comparisons are not solely impish or metaphoric.

A parallel of a priest with aspects of a psychoanalyst is significant for exposing levels of sense. Lacan defined transference as a 'substitution of a being for another being' (cf. Lemoine-Luccioni 1985–86). The alignment proposed above can be construed as a function of this substitution-transference. This substitution can hold both ways: the transference-relation between psychoanalyst and patient, in which substitution is central, might be viewed partly as a device for representing the psychoanalyst as patient. Clearly, if the mental ideology which the psychoanalyst presupposes is itself an inaccurate typology, then the psychoanalyst's 'normalisation' of the patient to the psychoanalyst's ideological stereotype will merely be a measure of the psychoanalyst's own abnormality. So, whether or not a psychoanalytical theory and its practice are true or false, it consequently mirrors both patient and clinician. In this way, psychoanalysis is rather like mythology. The psychoanalyst plays god and manifests himself in the patient under the pretext of the patient existentially realising herself. This has some connection with a priest standing both for a god and for his worshippers, in which the priest goes proxy for the god. Sometimes this relation is presented as incarnation, as with the god Ptah in pharaoh (studied in Chapter 4 below), where priesthood is not involved in the equation; but frequently there is a priest-king who doubles as a twin substitute for a god and people. In a typical mode, the priest is a double substitute. Purported mediation and healing are of course the stuff of both ancient mythology and modern psychoanalysis; yet the questions of who are victim and who are healer are sometimes satisfied in the one individual.

The above parallels are not without some ironic similarity to one's regarding an ancient author or editor and psychoanalyst as a patient or victim, and not master, of his imaginative creativity. Such a judgement complements an interpretation of Muriel Spark's novel *In the Driving Seat*, according to which the author is playing a goddess who aesthetically rapes and kills the reader. The reader has a mirrored inversion in the book's characters, in which the seducing men entrance the plot's driver into killing her. The dead victim is the controller of the plot, though subservient to it. These phenomena find parallels with Sumerian and Akkadian gods who manifest and fantasise their composers and 'readers'. Some structural similarities between the dense, highly involuted and opaque literary styles of Lacanian and much Mesopotamian scribal commentary on myths are also not without point. If we identify a collective state of cultic abnormality, psychoanalysis of this type will be a subset of that society's readerly or functional social anthropology. One example, where human sacrifice is a perceived respected normal and normative rite is 1 Kings 16's foundation sacrifices for Jericho. This state will thus have mirrored an element in and of ancient consciousness, which may be not unlike Hitler's use of Wagner at Bayreuth and his policy at Auschwitz, exposed by Kershaw's (1998) structuralist depiction of the latter two instances, and Gibson (2000d).

In many ways, the Sumerian Adda seal appears to offer a condensation of the foregoing points. The epiphany of gods on the seal and its attendant narrative corollaries display the symbolism of transference in which substitution performs an explanatory role. Here, the theme of polytheistic god-manifestation comes into play, in which substitution (at the linguistic level) by live metaphor is a convention to mark substitution of one identity for another, made explicit with the double-faced Usmu on the Adda seal. Although in subject-matter this type of seal is dissimilar to Euripedean tragi-comedy (cf. Foley 1985) and Socratic irony in *The Banquet*, yet the application of Lacanian psychoanalysis to these two latter genres by Lemoine-Luccioni (1985–86) reflects the possibility of intricate transference-relations between Classical Greek and earlier Near Eastern cultures, though this need not involve direct mediation.

Nevertheless, there are evident fundamental differences between ancient and modern mentalities, although a precious sense of the uniqueness of modernity is a fiction that has no part in assessing such contrasts. One conjectured contrast may be worth weighing: just before 2000 BC, the Ur III empire ended in catastrophe. From being the dominating cultural language, Sumerian very quickly died as a living language. I should like to tie this historical circumstance hypothetically with another problem, that of the evolution of the unconscious. Although evolution has yet to account for the origin and emergence of human consciousness, the evolution of the Unconscious is a somewhat neglected topic. When the latter is discussed, it is frequently assumed that the unconscious was formed very early on in evolution. It may be that discussion of a single origin for the origin of the Unconscious is akin to ideas about the wheel: as mother of necessity, perhaps it spontaneously appeared in many places. Possibly, as Apollinaire ironically noted, when he offered to explain what a metaphor is: when people were thinking of how to imitate walking, they produced a wheel (i.e. a circle of feet walking).

As such, a seminal context like the Rebel Lands in Sumer may betray part of the route to an origin of the unconscious. Part of my thesis is that the origins of the Unconscious could be caused by cosmic trauma, and possibly, consequently, associated with concomitant permanent collective amnesia—in the sense that the unconscious largely just is this amnesia. Such a state of affairs could be a relatively recent affair in human history (see Gibson 1998b). The currently perceived uniqueness of the Sumerian language and much of its visual symbolism tied to language complement this suggestion. The trauma may have been long antecedent to the high point in its culture (if so, celebrating cataclysm long gone by 2,300 BC); or one to be associated with the traumatic conditions of its sudden demise. Clearly, one may have an amalgam of such traumas, with parallels from elsewhere. The main point with the presupposition of such a conjecture is that the origin of the unconscious is a function of conscious experience *and* its deliberative reaction to crisis. If so, the contents and/or the profile of the Unconscious are a retrojective function of conscious society. This would make an enormous difference to the identity and susceptibility of cultural language to analysis as an exemplification of typical trauma and amnesia, as a means to reach a general understanding of religion in relation to culture.

For example, human consciousness may have become transmogrified into becoming its own unconscious, with attendant semiotic programming and deconstruction of religious memories. A domain of mythological consciousness abruptly slipped under the surface of ancient mentality, becoming the Unconscious. Cataclysm, at many levels, imploded into apparent oblivion only to re-emerge as the imagined world of demons. This would give a collective autobiographical twist to Sartre's view that hell is other people (cf. his play, *No Exit*). If these sorts of hypotheses turn out to be near the mark, Freud's book *Moses and Monotheism* would be even more obviously relevant here than usually. It is a subversive attempt by Freud to escape his own autobiography by competing to become a replacement for Moses.

In such a perspective, likewise, the author(s) and ancient editor(s) of the Rebel Lands texts seem to have been implementing their psychotic traumas as control mechanisms for urban dwellers who feared losing their social fabric and its structural archetype—the complex notion marked by the Sumerian term me. It is important to note that this archetypal me is also said to be possessed by goddesses such as Inanna and Suen, conditionally given to the male god An. The ancient Mesopotamian world was constituted by collections of me. They comprised a complex mythological, psychological as well as political typology—a code for what it was to be such a world. This contrasts with the Old Testament, which manifests at least an indirect rejection of the ethos of the Sumerian sets of me and its Akkadian counterparts. The Mesopotamian city Ur was one of the main instantiations of the archetype me. In Genesis 12, Ur is the point of demarcation and rejection for Abram's biography and world.

As Delaney (1998) shows, the influence of modern culture on our grasp of Abraham is a function of our distorted concerns that dispose of evidence concerning, say, the roles of gender in Genesis. We may employ this situation as a generalised figure for our initial sense of an ending here: what is most familiar may be the least comprehended. In concluding, we are challenged to begin anew.

PART II
OLD TESTAMENT AND NEAR EAST
INTERPRETATION

3

Does Genesis Contain
3rd-Millennium BC Text?

The Ebla Texts

Dalley *et al.* (1998), a leading non-biblical Mesopotamian scholar, demurs from some typical mainstream Old Testament scholarly tendencies to late-date aspects of the Old Testament narratives. In this respect, the present writer brings a Mesopotamian, as well as an archaeological general theory, perspective for assessment of the Old Testament. A. Mazar (1993: 225) found the Levant Middle Bronze II similarities to the cultures illustrated in Genesis too close to be ignored. Bimson (1978) developed a case to show that the patriarchal narratives in Genesis display a setting in the 21st to 19th centuries BC. He employed a survey of the Palestinian archaeological evidence to support this case. Abraham's migration from Ur via Haran, on this analysis, would not be more recent than 2092 BC, thus placing Abraham, if we move from narrative information to historical ontology, in the Middle Bronze I period. Bimson's treatment proceeds by, in part, identifying archaeologically supported expressions in Genesis, so it is empirically relevant to raise the question of the possibility that such linguistic items in the texts hold this position because they have a provenance contemporary with what they narrate: Middle Bronze I and II language. Bimson's treatment does not embrace a direct consideration of any Ebla material (see Conti 1992, for a comprehensive list of cited sources); but the Ebla archives overlap the relevant periods. So it is appropriate to discuss in a preliminary manner the possible connection between Genesis and Ebla. The available Ebla data warrant exploratory hypotheses regarding their possible relations to Genesis 1–14, though this is not the task to occupy us here.

Since Bimson depicted some parameters of the above discussion, later excavations and analysis have facilitated the constructions of related theories. The frequently problematic new discoveries at Ebla are not the only source of evidence for

Figure 3.1   The Ebla administrative tablet TM.75G 1769 1207

a Semitic language in the 3rd millennium that would give a contemporary linguistic framework for some features in Genesis 1-14. One important study is that of Catagnoti (1998), supported by Eidem (1997) and D.M. Matthews (1997), based on 3rd-millennium onomastic material from the Habur region. This proposes that the earliest, pre-Sargonic, data attest to the existence of an independent Semitic dialect in the Habur region. Accordingly, as Eidem (1997: 307) notes, this case for a 3rd-millennium Semitic dialect is founded upon linguistic evidence distinct from the Ebla, Mari, and Kish sources. Although one should proceed cautiously here, bold hypotheses are not improper, if we are to make progress in retrojection from archaeology to ancient society. Matthews (1997: 2-5) warns us of the complex differences and overlaps between, concepts of 'context' in chronology, glyptic, inscription matters, together with the problematic issues of assigning the term 'culture' to archaeology, site, society or ethnic grouping. There is, however, evidence of a complex administrative structure and recording procedures at Ebla (see Figure 3.1) that document extensive relations with the Levant, some other parts of the Near East and Mesopotamia.

There is the added discontinuity of the putative biblical characters in Genesis, for example Abraham. I can here only advert to the need for fresh explorations to, for example, the role of travel as a device for composing a dissenting world-view that places alienation at the centre of originality—for example, Abram's journey through Genesis, from chs. 12 to 22. We should re-commence our research programmes on Abrahamic travel narrative by study of Ian Hacking's (1998) fresh investigation of the 'dissociative figure': why 'unaccountably' a person exits from a society. What are the traceable mental of behavioural states associated with such rupture, and how do they come to be depicted in ancient narrative? The linguistic and/or pictorial residue of an ancient site is probably a trace of high culture and its attendant people. The presupposed ontology in the narrative of Abraham rarely, if ever, occupies this functional slot, though its literary aesthetics do. Consequently, one would hardly be correct to expect the random ancient archaeological residue that we possess to be compliant with, or contain relevant traces of, the 'low' ontological culture of Abraham. Even so, the foregoing pattern of data in archaeology enables us to make some progress.

Chapter 2 of the present book considered the role of Freud in relation to scholars' motivation for examining ancient texts. Since the discovery of the Ebla archives, they have held an especially exotic position in institutional polemics. Attempts to avoid excess in theorizing can accordingly easily err on the side of making no progress in the attempt to avoid association with those who manifest apparent instability of interpretation. The psychodynamics of innovatory thinking, however, while attempting to avoid literary psychosis, should bravely explore the possibilities of what may be thought to be fantastical historical realism, or no history at all in narratives, even if only to measure the marginal boundaries between history and imagination. Pettinato may well have unwittingly invented a putative ontology for or of irony, whilst thinking that it was narrative history. But we would do well, in avoiding such evangelical confidence, to refrain from replacing it with its unimaginative totalitarian antithesis.

For example, one possible way of reconstructing relations between Genesis and Ebla narratives, if there were an empirical text link, could be to regard Genesis as a Hebrew polemical satire, due to the presuppositions of Syrio-Canaanite myth-building when those societies wrote history; for example, as if it were the purview of Baal Dagan's cosmology (cf. Gibson forthcoming e). And it is important in this perspective that we should note that, in the Middle Bronze Age, Baal is attested as god's name at Ur, as well as in the Levant. In such a scenario, parody would submerge illusion as allusion, and opposition would seem to mimic likeness. To exercise Platonic disquiet on this form of art would be preferable to dumbly reading Plato as if he were canonical, whether the reader is Pettinato or Matthiae. (This relates to the further explorations of 'illusion' in the sections *'True' Interpretation* and *Contradiction*.) A central fragment of recurrent concern, however, is summarised by stating that what was true of 18th-century France, and its illusory conditioning on us, may speak to our contemporary forms needing a new renaissance. Marion Hobson (1982: 307) argued that 'illusion' for the 18th century was an answer to the problem of representation, by displacement. Knowledge of this inverted relation has tended to designate and to shape our conception of that problem. To be aware of its history is to be more be in a position to apprehend what it attempts to exclude, and perhaps to be more prepared to understand those artists and critics who have made it their business to break through its restrictions. One fundamental feature that can be excluded by over-statement of the undoubtedly central function of illusion, is the function of exposing what is true. Having advanced beyond both fundamentalisms and nihilistic postmodernism, it would be helpful boldly to position both truth and illusion without the influence of institutionalised traditions.

Amalek, Sodom and Gomorrah

It has been suggested that Gen. 14:7-8 have later glosses; these are the verses which use the proper names 'Amalek', 'Sodom' and 'Gomorrah'. Pettinato[1] has proposed that they appear in the Ebla texts. The proposed occurrences are: si-du-mu ki and e-ma-ra,

---

[1] Pettinato 1980b: 148, 103, for A-ma-lik, and si-da-mu ki in TM.76.G.524 (see MEE, 1, no. 1806), v. I (cf. Pettinato 1979: 260). Compare Archi 1981; Pettinato 1977: 235-36.

for which see tablet TM.75.G 1860, though there are problems of such a reading.[2] Pettinato (1977: 235-56) announced the appearance of the two proper names with other names of the cities of the Plains, though he later revised some assessment of his claims. Unfortunately, Pettinato's presentation and interpretation are polemical and analytically insensitive; but it is hoped that possible parallels will not be discounted because of the way they are coloured by such presentations. If the terms do in fact have this 3rd-millennium provenance, on the sort of analysis offered in inductive theory by, for example, Cohen (1977: 211-13), it gives a strong inductive weight to an inference that this portion of the chapter is from that period. The possibility of the equation appears to stand irrespective of whether or not one construes the Eblaic as an Old Akkadian, Amorite, Hebrew or Ugaritic-like language.[3]

There are some problems of orthography and interpretation, however. We need to have data from other Eblaic texts to support an identity between a in Eblaic and 'ayin in Hebrew for A-ma-lik; si or sa with Hebrew samek, for sa-du-ma; and the sign e to match 'ayin or gayin, Eblaic e-ma-ra to represent Hebrew *'amorah*. These difficulties are not viciously circular, nor insurmountable, but could be clarified by future research publications. Even so, with live language and graphic limitations in representing proper names, which are after all usually ossified semantic items which do not always or easily graphic or reflect or are characterised by their host graphic or semantic field, some variation between two widely distinct graphic systems of indicating language is to be allowed for. Archi (1979: 556-66) prefers to vocalise sa-du-ma as such, whereas Pettinato has si-da-mu ki.[4]

In the press of discussion about such questions, and noting that the alleged five cities of the Plain are on two tablets not one, with uncertainty about some of the remainder, there is need not to allow these considerations to eclipse the foregoing threefold occurrence of extremely rare names in one context—Genesis 14—and, with appropriate qualifications, in the Genesis text's assumed Sitz im Leben reflected in 3rd-millennium texts at Ebla.

In addition to this, there is the possibility of an empirical hypothesis to fill out this linguistic theory with historical body. In a general vein, W.C. van Hattem (1981: 87-92) has drawn attention to the Rast-Schaub survey (1973: 5-54, 175-85), as it could affect attempts to identify some of the cities of the Plain. The Rast-Schaub report is susceptible of supporting Bab edh-Dhra', Numeira, es-Safi, Feifeh and Khanazir as likely remains of the cities of the Plain, although Sodom as Feifeh could dismantle into a location south of es-Sag. Such a series of links is highly unstable. Clearly such

---

[2] The notion of inductive weight adopted here is developed in Cohen 1977: 6, 211-13.
[3] Cf. the preliminary review of Gelb 1977: 1, and Pettinato 1981: 59-66.
[4] Pettinato (1980a: 213) comments on Archi's vocalization in relation to his own approach.

evidence may only support an inference yielding a group of conclusions rather than one single solution, in the present state of knowledge. A multiple-conclusion logic (cf. Shoesmith and Smiley 1980) with uncertain relations to singular inferences is apt for such a state of comprehension, and thus is appropriately restrictive for such data. This situation also has something to do with the restrictions in archaeological science and the modesty of the survey, rather than the nature of the attempted identifications. That there are possible locations provides an increase in the probability of the Eblaic possibilities.

Nevertheless, an information-theory principle is relevant here: the information-content in a term's use is inversely proportionate to its probability of occurrence.[5] General terms such as 'walk' are less informative than are rare words like 'Sodom'. It is the very rarity of the proper names which could lead to their being contextually loaded with information, in particular if the Ebla uses of the proper names can be logically and empirically linked to the Genesis narrative fields. Related to this is the logical principle that proper names in any case provide exact parallels in a way that phrases or their components often do not. Writers such as J. Van Seters (e.g. 1975) attempt to late-date Genesis, largely by appeal to parallels between predicate fragments in Genesis and later uses elsewhere. However, these types of parallels are logically inept as a proof since they are incomplete expression variable and indeterminate to the sum of their contexts, whereas parallels between a proper name's uses are comparatively immensely informative, not least since a proper name is a sort of universal, itself carrying, in usual circumstances, a criterion of identity. The reason for this is, of course, because a proper name's primary meaning is its identification of the bearer of the proper name. Clearly, sometimes two different subjects might have the same name in the sense that their names have the same spelling (on proper names and criteria for identity, cf. Gibson forthcoming e: Chapter 3). Edward Sollberger[6] contended that there are a number of occurrences of terms that (only) have the same form as proper names of the cities of the Plain in the Ebla archives. In addition to those Pettinato originally picked out, Sollberger's inclination was to regard these proper names as referring to sites in Syria, and not to the Cities of the Plain, though he offered no analysis of this proposal. But there is no known site called 'Sodom' in Syria. Sollberger's claim has no contextual backing: the tablets on which the proper names occur do not indicate or require a Syrian location, and other names there have sites outside of Syria. The point that the Genesis' narrative uses names which are written in the same way, given the extreme rarity of their occurrence, together with the export/import context of Tell-Mardikh and many of the relevant tablets, raises the

---

[5] The principle deployed here is that as formulated by Lyons 1977: 42-44.
[6] Based on discusion with Sollberger prior to his untimely death.

probability of the thesis that the Ebla uses refer to the same location as does the Genesis' narrative to well above half.

It may be urged that the form-critical consigning of the biblical Sodom to the realm of myth or legend furnishes a basis to infer the massive improbability of an empirical reference to Sodom, even though Sollberger said that there were some 16 references to a place called 'Sodom'. But even if consensus probability was the criterion of the estimated non-existence of a biblical Sodom, which would be a very degraded logic, we should consider the significance of the elements in the nature of probability. We may be dealing with the psychology of expectation implementing fragments of institutional ideology. Popper (1972) demonstrated the logic for 'very improbable things turn out to be true', and this may relate to the structure of some standard biblical literary criticism which has no logical procedures for testing empirical improbabilities. The basis on which such a reduction to a later date has usually proceeded is to assume that the possibility of a 3rd-millennium background to be outside of the boundary of probability.

The above situation has an obscure and peculiar relation to our natural instincts and the empirical data on to which it latches when we have no empirically veridical framework with which to surround theorisation. For example, Barr (1961, 1968) had rightly exposed the severe problems in the use of nonempirical conjecture to produce a purported explanation of synchronic comparative philological relations while ignoring the diachronic separation of evidence. But now imagine a situation in which, concerning two temporally remote and little known allegedly synchronic parallel yet entirely distinct languages, comparative philological identities are asserted, which cuts across the grain both of our state of ignorance and what theories have been formulated to account for the data. If the form of presentation is good, we cannot accuse the protagonist of fallacy or etymological impropriety, other than to argue that the equation is highly improbable. As Popper argued, however, the most improbable things turn out to be true. If, as Wittgenstein claimed (cf. McGinn 1984), the empirical approach to meaning is an interpretational conception, it could be: either, the case that Popper is right and we should be much more wary than we are of our empirical instincts—because they are simply the relaying of psychological patterns as if they are the (actually only seeming) map of the external world. Or, that some people in some habits of mind which cut across the grain of empirically framed custom, actually do, in some states of thinking, locate a highly unexpected equation which violates the drift and state of established theories. Such alternating options, of course, may dwell in all of us, and be quantified in their recurrence and distribution as a function of our taste, education and unconscious influences.

This discussion has an unusual and perhaps untypical application to one of the great Sumerian scholars, which is chosen precisely because of his impressive achievements. In Sumeriology, Noah Kramer is not usually neglected. Within biblical studies, however, Kramer's (1963: 298-99) proposal, that the proper name šēm in Gen. 10:1 semantically overlaps as a loan-word with the Sumerian term sumer, has not been integrated into Hebrew studies; perhaps not surprisingly. No doubt it is a somewhat bizarre unstable equation. But given Kramer's distinguished reputation, it is worth considering his proposal, if only to unsettle our sense of conceptual exclusion. He noted that the final -er would not have been pronounced in Sumerian (i.e. before expressions commencing with a vowel, and in which the equation 'sem = sumer' displays the unexceptional expected change from 'u' to 'e' between the two languages). One does not have to assign a high probability to the proposal being correct to give it the weight it deserves as a firm judgement by such a distinguished scholar. Beyond the scope of a straight comparative linguistic transference, the equation could impinge on intriguing and unexpected relations, including a Sumerian strand mirrored in Genesis, or a Hebrew stratum ironically alluding to a Sumerian tradition. This, Kramer claimed, corresponds to a Semitic ethnic element in Ur, which maps onto the ethnology in the Genesis narrative. It could equally reflect a much later nuanced deconstructing Hebrew attitude to Sumer, a conceit to deprive the dead Sumerian empire of its place as original source of a patriarchal identity.

It is the improbability of Kramer's equation, rather than its straight empirical possibility, which is attractive as a disrupting function in assessing our claims to understanding relations (or the lack of them) between Sumerian and Hebrew. But we should allow (if only) for the empirical possibility that the equation embodies Popper's stricture for structure: namely, that the most improbable things could turn out to be true, given that sometimes induction is a function of the psychology of expectation rather than an empirical property. Popper's (1994) work gathers together his various theories to sustain the conclusion that there is no framework for foundations, which is not conjectural.

Kramer's deadpan confidence in the Sumer/Sem relation is underwritten by its counter-intuitive instability—scanned by us as the high improbability that guarantees its absence from scholarly consensus. Although we may not accept Kramer's view, it is worth engaging with it to query our confidence in our empirical framework of historical relations at this level of specificity. It is precisely at the interface of such ignorance that we have no firm grounds to ban Kramer's thesis; it also presupposes a scale of assessment that may measure our uncertain attempts at criteria by which to assess new discovery.

The more general theoretical and empirical framework for such exploration should of course include the direction and diachronic identity of linguistic evolution and development. So, for example, S.R. Rao (1994) rehearses the scenario that 3rd-millennium Mesopotamian Semitic and Sumerian influences impacted on or contributed to the development or emergence of the Indus Valley and Harappian Scripts, as well as, separately, Dravidian. As Parpola (1994: 130-32) notes, we find such names as cuneiform *Meluḫḫ...e*, which at least partly seems to indicate areas of the Indus civilisation. Although in its current formulations this is an unstable and unworked hypothesis at the requisite levels, as with other proposals, it would enable some hitherto undeveloped Semitic–Sumerian or Sumerian–Semitic relation to be introduced into Kramer's suggestion, as a minor function in a Levant to Southeast axis for linguistic influence as well as diversification. Lest, however, we underestimate the stability of the prospect that there certainly were some semantic tides of influence and exchange of terminologies between India and Near East Sumerian, it is worth drawing attention to the research by Blazer (1999). He identifies traces of interaction between Sumerian and Dravidian, via Elam and Elamite. This contextualization itself contains empirical grounds for broadening and stabilising concepts of cross-fertilisation of extra-regional semantic functions, rather than our attempting to narrow this sort of exchange as a product of exception. For example, Blazer offers evidence that the occurrence of afro-Asiatic terminology in Elamite tablets into Sumerian indicates an unexpected cross-link for these relations of influence between India and Sumerian in Elam. Consequently, we may provisionally place the possibility of an Ur Semitic Hebrew-type of influence on Sumerian (or vice versa) in a broader framework of synchronic and diachronic multilingual influence.

Kramer maintained that the Genesis *Šinʿar* ('Shiner') corresponds to the Sumerian-Akkad territory of the 3rd-millennium civilisations. It is interesting in view of this that Gen. 10: 10 mentions one of Sumer's most important urban centres—Erech (Uruk). The narrative places this city together with other influential cities such as Babylon and Akkad, as seminal foundations of Sumer. It may be viewed as mischievous to refer to *Šinʿar* to introduce historical discussion about its relation to complex historical issues, but counter-intuitive probing is what is appropriate to perturb some states of our confidence.

Uruk level IV and later periods, albeit with their little understood linguistic data, portray evidence of their having powerful functions in Mesopotamia in founding centres comparable to the function given it in Genesis 10 (cf. Falkenstein 1936). Here the concept associated with a 'centre', however, is problematic. Postgate (1992) has presented fresh evidence and re-analysis of older results to expose a complicated picture of evolution and expansion which problematizes a simple idea of central functions. Algaze (1993) also enhances this picture with a complexified concept of the Uruk world system, according to which we are not dealing with an informal empire, but a world-view perception of complex expansions into Anatolia, the highlands above Mesopotamia, and entrenched developments in Iran. The forms of expansion, he argues, in places such as the Tabqa region, show explicitly similar organisation to the

Uruk city-state. This is not a kin-based Old Assyrian trade model, but fresh use of notions of export, the establishment of regional centres and cities mirroring Warka and related sites. The restrictions in knowledge of the relevant writing make any proposals provisional; yet we should note the importance of material culture, and redress a certain tendency to neglect the informative functions of such cultures when contrasted with language. As Tilley (1999) argues, material culture had a metaphoric function for ancient cultures, and functions of difference and similarities can to some extent be assessed in such phenomena. Hypotheses about these above issues warrant fresh assessment and exploration of how Uruk pertains to our perspective about Mesopotamian relations to Europe, early though it is in research to air such issues. Such reflection is of significance for philosophical scrutiny of scholarship's perceptions because it adverts to the roles of our own metaphors and our consciousness of them in the production of scenarios contrary to our intuitions of history and axis of progress/regress.

The European sites in Tataria, Romania, and near the Danube, excavated by Falkenstein and others, yielded apparently Uruk level IV types of tablets in ideographic Sumerian from the 3rd millennium. Renfrew (1973) judged these not to be evidence of Sumerian residence. There is, with the inscriptions, pottery evidence of some sort of occupationthat is undoubtedly Sumerian. Obviously there is uncertainty about the precise properties of the Uruk and Tartaria ideographic Sumerian, because there is no general agreement on its decipherment. It is possible that the tablets and artefacts could be evidence of a Sumerian group, perhaps migrating or fleeing from Mesopotamia. These issues clearly open up a cluster of deep problems for the migratory data in Genesis 10, as well as the suggestion of Babylonian parallels with them. If there is a source-relation between the Tartaria and Uruk tablets, this does not of course have to be linguistic influence, directly or causally, direct in transmission. There may have been many intermediaries, not known by us, which produced a causal loop of transmission, mediation or education; and these do not of themselves exclude migration from and/or return to Mesopotamia.

Walton (1981: 207-208; cf. Jacobsen 1939: 70ff.) argued that the decimal chronology in the Genesis 5 genealogy has its counterpart in the Sumerian sexigesimal King List; he suggests that the relevant differences are due to misunderstanding of the arithmetical conventions in one of the systems. Although Walton does not relate this to the 3rd-millennium question about Genesis, it is clear that, if a Semitic group is established for this 3rd-millennium epoch, then the Genesis 5 system could theoretically pre-exist the Sumerian List. Particularly is this the central point, since, given Walton's hypothesis, the arithmetical relations in the two Genesis and Sumerian lists appear to require confusion on the part of the Sumerian scribes. This is not to isolate the Semites as a collectively dominating influence; but it rather gives one a basis from which to question the Sumerians as the role model and sole archetype of Semitic and Hebrew narrative in the foregoing context.

We may need, according to Matthiae (1990), further to revise views about literate culture in third millennium Syria, and position the significance of the fact that the then economy of northern Syria was strongly integrated within the Mesopotamian economy. Such a scenario, of course, points up a framework in which Northwest Semitic reminiscent of Hebrew could have had direct contact with and interaction with Sumerian. It is interesting in view of the above perspective that a new version of the Gilgamesh Epic was found at Ebla. This form of the Epic treats of relations between Uruk and Aratta (the latter probably located in Afghanistan, cf. Pettinato 1981: 238). This text exemplifies, for the first time in the relevant sense, a geographically apt provenance for a Sumerian text which is said to have parallels with the biblical text—a text which presents itself as having a provenance in that area, namely the Levant. This renders mediation and contact that was previously interpreted as indirect, and thus stemming from later Sumerian, Hebrew or Semite literary relations, as possibly adjacent and contemporary. Such a reorientation raises issues about whether or not there could have been a Semitic influence contemporary with Sumerian or prior to it.

The Ebla linguistic material clearly gives weight to such questioning. If, hypothetically assuming a historical feature, the translation of *miqqedem* is 'eastward' in Gen. 11:2, and one supplies the subject of 'they' in that verse (by adopting the Semitic group preceding it in Gen. 10:21-31), then it would follow that ch. 11 presents a terminus for Semites in migration from Palestine to Sumer. This would comply with the idea of an emergence of an Abrahamic element from Ur at a later date. The use of 'Zoar' is with the present tense: 'comes to Zoar', thus supporting the possibility that this part of the narrative was composed when Zoar still existed, unless editorial anachronizing style is the cause. Ebla furnishes us with a use of za-ar ki (MEE 3: 18, 14, 2), which appears to parallel the biblical Zoar. Alternatively, if one posits Sumerians as the topic of 'they', then this may force the sense 'from the East' for miqqedem. Although with the discovery of epigraphic Uruk IV Sumerian in two parts of Europe, albeit in puzzling locations for Sumerian data to be found, it is possible that a group of Sumerians migrated to Europe and subsequently returned eastward. And perhaps one should not rule out the possibility that they could have had their provenance in a Tataria-like relation, and emigrated south/eastward. Of course the latter possibility (ungraded as to probability), is part of an awareness that we know little as yet about relations between Europe and Mesopotamia in the third millennium, and should allow for scenarios that are not a consequence of what is know about the Near East. The sense 'from the east' would also concur with a west Iranian (or perhaps Caspian Sea) location for Aratta.

Gurney's publication of the second part of the epic tale 'Enmerkar and the Lord of Aratta' (Gurney and Kramer 1976: 48, no. 2, ll. 136-62) illustrates, albeit through the opaque lens of mythology, the 3rd-millennium challenges from Uruk to Aratta, which might just embody some allusion to an earlier home or staging-post of the, or a, Sumerian group, without supposing that these options are exhaustive. Gurney's text also locks into elements of the theme of Genesis 11.

The king of Uruk is presented as aiming to capture stone masons and others from Aratta to aid his building of the atsu temple. He points out that it is his god who changed the language of humanity from one into a babel of languages. Of course this feature maps directly on to the context of Genesis 11 as a consequence of the Sumerian settlement's building activity. The complementary levels of historical and conceptual patterns clearly match on significant items between Genesis and Sumerian texts. With the Ebla Gilgamesh Epic's (cf. Gurney and Kramer 1976: 1-2) presentation of relations between Uruk and Aratta, one can estimate that knowledge of this type of interrelation was widespread in the second half of the 3rd millennium, reflecting as it does some basic facets of Sumerian society and cosmology. If these strategies for inference are right, then the bedrock of Babel is not editorial conflict over thematic nuances; it consists in reflecting a set of pervasive political, military and cultural conflicts. Within the orbit of this type of genre, and the set of priorities which it presupposes, the occurrence of references to Sodom in chapter 10 has a cumulative value for assessment of aspects in the Genesis text, especially since, if the homonymy does not block connections, Sodom is mentioned at least six times in Ebla material. In Gen. 10:19, the border of the Canaanites is given by reference to 'as you go, unto Sodom' (bo'akah s^{e}domah). This is written in the present tense—hence, in at least the presupposition of the narrative, with Sodom still existing. If we assume a date slightly before circa 2300 BC for the Ebla use of sa-du-ma, and adopt Pettinato's equation of it with the biblical proper name, we have a premise for inferring that the relevant portion of Genesis 10 was written while Sodom still existed as a city.

Although there are obviously unstable empirical variables here, this is a function of most other hypotheses attending the material. Certainly, as Matthiae (1997: 78-79) observes, at this time Ebla was in some substantial control of the transfer of raw materials, for north and south—a function that sustained its political influence and extended relations with some of Mesopotamia and remote parts of the Levant. The import of raw materials from Sodom is consistent with pattern. Sargon of Akkad's military intrusion on Ebla's affairs in circa 2300 BC probably had something to do with a decision to reverse this economic super-state's progress in favour of his vassal states. Matthiae (1997: 83) suggests that this was a result of the increased prosperity late in Irkab-Damu's rule and in the reign of Ish'ar-Damu. Such types of interpretation of Syrian and Sumerian material supply empirical presuppositions enabling one to infer a starting pointing for the thesis that early parts of Genesis were composed, or utilise literary elements composed in the 3rd millennium.

The sorts of parallels exposed above between other information and Sumerian as well as other sources provide a matrix and context for generalising the viability of this thesis to other parts of the Genesis narrative. Anachronism has been alleged against it. One such instance is the term 'Canaanite' in the verse that mentions 'Sodom'. But it is by now obvious that the Ebla texts use this term in the 3rd millennium. For example, in the Ebla text TM.75.G.1376, rev. III 3, we have:

> n i—b a d be ka-na-na-im
> [a] gift for the lord of Canaan.

So the occurrence of the expression parallel with 'the Canaanites' (*hkn'ny*) in the immediate context of 'Sodom' is the opposite of proof of anachronism. Many commentators have not permitted this term to exist anywhere near the 3rd millennium, supposedly grounded on other competing assumptions. This in itself advertises the unstable inconsistency of these assumptions. Even so, such analysts as J.A. Emerton, in his treatment of Genesis 14, did not rule out in principle the possibility of supplying a 3rd-millennium background for that chapter, though he did not raise or construct the possibility.

Matthiae (1997) has offered a provisional chronological framework within which one can attempt to construct such a background, although Pettinato (1981: 253) prefers a slightly earlier starting point.[7] This is of course sharply different from, for example, Albright's type of thesis reflecting the Mari provenance, though the situation does not in principle oppose some conclusions that were proposed earlier, from Albright's sort of view, such as E.A. Speiser's opinion that cuneiform sources might underlie Genesis 14. Not only do we have Syrian Sumerian at Ebla, but also now we certainly have a new Semitic language at Ebla (cf. Picchioni 1997). These considerations, including the foregoing analysis, and other archaeological data, facilitate preparation for some revolutionary constructions in an attempt to gauge the historical and literary backgrounds against which to match the earlier chapters of Genesis. Even if the claim that Eblaic is a language with only Northwest Semitic similarities to Hebrew is correct, then this still affords us premises for discounting the limitation of any Genesis Hebrew *Sitz im Leben* to the late 2nd millennium. This state of affairs furnishes a strand of a 3rd-millennium confirmation for some of its information and also cultural ethos, together with its stable interpretation, at the linguistic level in Genesis. It also opposes the Albright view that no Akkadian

---

[7] See Pettinato 1981: 72-74.

cuneiform script was employed regularly for writing Canaanite. Theoretically, Eblaic could be associated with the possibility that Hebrew was first written in cuneiform.

Pettinato claimed that, read as Old Akkadian or Sumerian, some of the Ebla expressions possesses no sense, but they do when West Semitic stems are recognised in them. For example, the Sumerian values gal and balag together have no meaning, yet these signs regularly represent the syllabic values ik and tub. These produce the West Semitic verb ik-tub which Pettinato (1981: 55-56; but cp. Gelb, 1977) maintains is not in East Akkadian.[8] The stem in ik-tub clearly parallels k-t-b ('he wrote') in Hebrew and some other West Semitic languages. He notes that on some tablets there is an ending in Sumerian, d u b-g a r ('tablet written'); and argues that, on some other tablets, the text is ended with the foregoing ik-tub which apparently performs the same role as the Sumerian terminating expression. No doubt we need to continue questioning such equations, and reformulate interpretations of the data. There are problems with attempts to generalise over even the available phenomena. Some standard categories can be interrogated by careful use of interpretation of Ebla data, so limits to generalisation in Ebla, and other studies, are not self-evidently incorrect, nor a failure in principle of the West Semitic mode of explaining Eblaic. If it is sought to oppose this connection by identifying Eblaic as a close relation of Old Akkadian, the similarities between Eblaic and Ugaritic are not thereby discredited. The view that Ugaritic was not a Canaanite dialect is not credible, though there are some areas of uncertainty about Eblaic's relations to Ugaritic as well as Amorite that limits synthesis on either interpretation.

The *Repha'im*

Despite these restrictions, the foregoing is a logical paraphrase of a causal explanatory basis to characterise some mythological and administrative elements that occur in a Canaanite environment of the 3rd millennium. The appearance of the 'Canaanite Dagan', ᵈBE Ga-na-na-um, is an unexpected case, as is one thesis supplied by Matthiae, not incautious about Canaanite–Ebla relations, namely the archaeological evidence of a religious centre devoted to the dead at Ebla, which Matthiae explicitly associates with the considerably later Ugaritic *rp'um*. Matthiae may prefer to develop this interrelation in the absence of any biblical relations, but other scholars have accepted that the Ugaritic *rp'um* have direct family semantic relations to the biblical *repha'im*. For example, L'Heureux (1979) shows that the biblical God (*'lhym*)/angel agency functions hold for the Ugaritic *rp'um*. (On the relations of this function in early

---

[8] See Pettinato 1981: 59-66.

and later Hebrew, see Gibson 1997a). So if one attests a 3rd-millennium Ebla relation with Ugaritic cultic phenomena, and if there are references to *repha'im* in biblical texts which can be considered for 3rd-millennium provenance, it is an empirical logical relation to regard the equation of Ebla with the Bible at the foregoing scale to be correct.

Matthiae employs Healey's publication (1978: 89-92) of the *rp'um* text, of which the following is a selection of lines:

1. Ritual of the sacrificial meal of invocations.
2. You invoke the Rephaim of the land (earth).
4. He invokes Blkn, the Rapha.
8. He invokes the ancient Rephaim.
20. After the owner of your throne, after
21. Your throne's owner descends to the land (earth)—to the underworld.

Matthiae thinks that this text matches a cultic centre at Ebla which is displayed in the temple B1, sanctuary B2 and the Great Temple D of Tell Mardikh dedicated to Ishtar. B1 contained evidence that it was used for ritual banquets of the sort presupposed in the quoted text. Seven sacrifices are listed in portions of the Ugaritic text, which fit in with this scenario. The regal banquets were held in Temple D, with the *Repha'im* religious centre of practice impinging on the dedication of the dead king.

Matthiae's (1997) valuable virtual reality construction of the temple and cult area at Ebla can serve as a presupposition for extending one's interpretative framework: from virtual site archaeology into virtual reality retrieval of narrative themes. This is an entirely fresh arena for theorisation; so suggestions have to be provisional attempts to match architectural premises with logical premises. At the side of the now fairly well established activity of computer-generated, and interpreted reconstruction in virtual archaeology, is a complex challenge of attempting to reproduce features of the conceptual world which were concurrent with ancient sites. Renfrew's *Towards Archaeology of Mind* (1982) is a presupposition for such a programme. The expression 'archaeology of mind' is that of Freud, employed as a metaphor for psychoanalysis, mirroring his private fad for collecting archaeology. We would do well, however, to heed Forrester's (1997: 109-11, 122-23) cautionary tale of Freud's inability to do anything other than analyse the art in archaeology. And Freud's claim to be able to totalise a subject is almost Platonic in its failure to allow for future changes, different empirical contexts for cultural functions, or deviations from his awareness of empirical functions.

In proportion to a narrative use of visualising poetics, or expressions in narratives susceptible of reifying retrojection to their purported ancient uses, we may retrieve empirically based virtual realisations of properties contingent on the type of site and milieu Matthiae architecturally exposes. There are various formal ways of developing such possibilities, many of which are paraphrasable into one another. Ross (1997) advances a semantics of media that partially absorbs David Lewis's (1986) theses. Basically, these formalisms are said to realise the possible or retrojected actual world (or subsets of both, mixed) of a linguistic medium. In the present context, a medium is a complex presence of biblical and Near Eastern narratives, some features of which are construed to map on to pragmatic and/or aesthetic artefacts (statues, etc., as well as inscriptions) excavated from the generalised empirical environments of target excavations. Gibson (1997a, 1997b, 1998b) proposes some interpretation of logic suitable for reproduction of identities applicable to such phenomena. The semantics of media in a number of spheres (as cited above in Ross and Lewis) complement the virtual reality processes used in virtual archaeology. Although in the foregoing I have exhorted us to avoid totalising assertions for theorizing over empirical data in the manner of Freud's archaeology of the mind, yet some progress can be made under constraints, and tricks of inference and creativity may yield counter-intuitive routes to understanding. Possibly, virtual archaeology can be operated as such a tool.

Hesse (1995) has carefully highlighted the need for modesty in the presumed exposure of past realities, while noting that 'poststructuralist' recognition of relativity appeared prior to 19th-century modernism, as Andrew Bowie (1997) has shown with the occurrence of concepts anticipating postmodernism's relativity in Jacobi's conflict with Hegel. On the one hand, therefore, Hesse is aware that poststructuralism is not a uniquely new pressure to force admission that we cannot have knowledge. On the other hand, her personal preference is for a nonrealist approach to retrojective inference. My own argument embodies the position that there is another option. This is a counter-intuitive realism that incorporates live metaphor as an account of language and visualisation. My point is that this is especially strengthened and complemented by virtual reality and virtual archaeology in particular. In a sense, virtual reality is a type of unexpected visualising poetics. The designed route of my theorisation, then, is to acknowledge the problems exposed, and developed by poststructuralism's utilisation of extensive metaphor, while attending to the structure of live metaphor and virtual reality as combined devices. The aim is to side-step and by-pass obstacles such as the uncontrolled employment of metaphor in theory-construction, as well as some of the limitations of irrealism, while benefiting from the criticisms of these two other competing approaches to crafting constructions of past realities.

Although Matthiae's site is unusual in some ways and esoteric, its rich discoveries and subtle analyses have centralised its use as case study for some future generalisation. In the foregoing use of the Rapha' tablet from Ugarit, Matthiae has himself provided a premise for generalisation and causal connection with data outside Ebla in the present context. Related connections between the Ugaritic *Repha'im* and the Old Testament have been proposed and developed over a number of years (e.g. Gray 1965: 127ff.). If a *rp'um* Ugarit–Ebla equation advanced by Matthiae is accepted, then it can be used to infer an equation between Eblaite uses and certain early biblical occurrences, if a Ugaritic–Bible link has been demonstrated. Clearly, such an equation will not be simple, nor be a covering law for all *Repha'im* contexts. Since Matthiae places the scope of *rp'um* in a social and political situation, it is of some interest that Gen. 14:5's military and social allusions employ the term '*Repha'im*'. If this is not a homonym of the Ebla usage, whether or not it has an identical mythological force, the Ebla context as interpreted by Matthiae furnishes us with a contemporary 3rd-millennium background for this term, as well as some of its other Old Testament cultic allusions; as is likely, some metaphoric shift attends these relations.

The King of Giants

Given the religious role and military associations with *rp'um* at Ebla, as with other comparative uses, there probably is a complex interplay of various types of metaphoricity, since they seem to participate in thematic cross-fertilisation of topics and functions, including royal allusions. The hypothesis of a strong family relation between Matthiae's Eblaic *rp'um* and biblical *repha'îm* can be highlighted and developed by the following sketch, which synthesises aspects of the later of transformation and puns upon these traditions in the Bible (Deut. 2:20; cf. WozÅniak 1979: 171-74). These traditions draw on a broader field than we see at Ebla, but the Matthiae hypothesis for Ebla can be shown to stand in the mainstream of such allusions Attached to the Ugaritic phenomena, these developments in interpretation give cumulative weight to the probability that the Gen. 14:5 and 15:20 uses derive from, or informatively relate to, 3rd-millennium mythology and culture impacted by military and cultic associations.

Such antecedents are remote from Iron Age II; their mythological influences seem to have been incarcerated in religious narrative throughout the intervening epochs. For example, why is one of the Hebrew and other Northwest Semitic morphemes for 'dead' parallel with this term *Repha'im*? The purported military context of Goliath's scenario presents a whole Israelite army afraid of him (1 Sam. 17:24). This perhaps strays beyond even Jewish humour, unless there is another reason. Possibly the cultic and otherworldly associations with the dead, highlighted by Matthiae, strike even much later into military legend or propaganda. Certainly the transcendent eternal giant and a kingly role were components in the collective (un)conscious of Canaanite culture by the time of Ugarit (cf. J.C.L. Gibson 1978: 102-22), and in some ways for later periods:

> Rapha king
> To thy Lady, to thy betrothed
> With the strength of Rapha', eternal king
> With his protection...
> To the Rephaim of the land
> Thy strength, thy protection, thy patronage
> May thy terrible splendor be in Ugarit...
> All the good years of god.

Side-stepping the metaphysical problem of the bad years of god, this Ugaritic paean to oversized military protectionism perhaps ironically inverts the biblical 'land of *Repha'im*'. Scattered in bizarre contexts though they sometimes are, biblical references to giants pin the militant feature of this propaganda: 'and there arose a war at Gezer...at which time Sinnechai...slew Sippai of the descendants of the Rapha' (1 Chron. 20:4). It may be that 'Og's funeral couch, with its dimensions reproducing those proportions of a god's funeral couch, resting in Rabbath of Molech, is polemical mythology overlying the obtrusion of rare, overstated, genetic mutation. There are thus prospects of discovering that *rp'ym* is an almost Bakhtin carnivalesque binary semantic value: a polysemic function mapping giantism and death to and/or from a single complex function. Where the giantism is functional, the demise is tonal; and *vice versa.*

In such scenarios it is important to position, so far as we can ascertain, the probable roles such functions had in the ancient consciousness. Matthiae (1990: 47; cp. footnote 100) draws attention to the probability that at Ebla two royal figures are repeated mirror-like on each side of a sacred tree on the back of the Ebla throne (based on a reconstruction of fragments). He notes how this type of style incorporates the Egyptian personification of Osiris as well as the Old Syrian cylinder seal found at Damanhur in the Delta (see TM.88.P.564). Matthiae (1990:48) suggests, "It is likely that the two king figures, which quite probably were representations of royal ancestors, the Ugaritic *rapi'uma* adored in the Old Babylonian period from Mesopotamia to Syria, were followed by two divine figures, wearing the two plumes tiara, facing each other." Here three-dimensional articulation of polysemy seems to code in the type of complex nuance I termed 'holographic meaning' (above pp.75-76). The Ebla kings themselves appear to have been actors in personifying such identities, and consequently we should formulate a live metaphor process for the representation of mythological categories in the functions of the royal human, as depicted in the range of texts depicting such mergers. This somewhat scrambles the modernist distinction between demythologisation and beliefs, if taken as a model for the manifestations of consciousness in such humans, though it may be that ritual forms associated with this type of symbolic order were entertained as metaphors or partial-belief states. The totalising engagement with death in some of these contexts, however, seems to limit the scope for a demythologising scenario.

A Giant Obituary

Eight passages employing repha'im in the Old Testament are usually translated by the term 'dead':

> Dead things are formed from under the water. (Job 26:5)
> Shall the dead arise and praise you? (Ps. 88:10)
> For her house inclines unto death, and her paths unto the dead. (Prov. 2:18)
> But he knows not that the dead are there. (Prov. 9:18)
> The man...shall remain in the congregation of the dead. (Prov. 21:16)
> Hell from beneath is moved for you to meet you at your coming: it stirs up
>   the dead for you. (Isa. 14:9)
> They are deceased, they shall not rise. (Isa. 26:14)
> And the earth shall cast out her dead. (Isa. 26:19)

In short, all these passage translate 'dead' for a word that elsewhere in the MT and Near Eastern texts is a term for 'giant'. We have seen that non-biblical uses of *repha'im* have associations with death in contexts that embrace religious centres and their mythologies. It seems that this sort of English translation emerges from a tradition of translation that was sensitive to the thematic context of death and 'poured' this into being the meaning of repha'im, since the necrotic cult background of the repha'im was not appreciated or correctly positioned. The main LXX translation of the above uses of repha'im has the 'dead' sense (five times), once with the value 'ungodly', twice with 'physician'. Some non-standard versions resort to some such sense as 'shades', which reflects a sensibility to the binary use of the Hebrew. Isa. 26:19, noted above, has 'and the earth shall cast out her dead', with the terms for 'earth' and 'dead' contiguous in the Hebrew narrative. The same two expressions are to be found in the same order in Deut. 2:20: 'land of giants'. The LXX main text follows this sense. Pearson (1999) argues that the LXX translator reflects a Greek cosmological model, with the Titan mythology in view. He further suggests[9] that the LXX translator is explicitly aware of this Semitic background, thus making his choice of Titan mythology the closest equivalent available to the Hebrew.

Within a variety of Canaanite worldviews, typified in Eblaic and Ugaritic, the sense is transparent: the giants, descended from the gods, and so imbued with divine

---

[9] In discussion with the author.

power, symbolised the supreme state of man's physical stature, graced with eternity and virility. What more appropriate figure for the Psalmist to draw upon to tell of human transience and weakness than to evoke the dead: 'shall the *repha'im* arise and praise you?' Proverbs speaks of the way of lust and false wisdom: 'For her house inclines to death, and her paths to the *repha'im*'. The burden of these passages with their cultic network of puns appears to be that those, once deemed giants, the epitome of power, are dead.

Fertile Giants

But there is a further source of thematic interplay. *Rapha'* in the singular has the well attested value of 'heal'. The LXX translations support this on occasions. Elisha is said to have healed the spring at Jericho which caused the women to miscarry (2 Kgs. 2:22). God healed Abimelech's wife and his maidservants, subsequent to their infertility (Gen. 20:17-18). This type of use is not universal to the term, yet it pervades many. Whether or not the root *rapha'* is homonymy or polysemy for the two senses 'heal' and 'fertile', is not known; yet from the foregoing data they seem to interact. Such a contract of interplay would work whatever the origins. The Old Testament perception of repha'im clearly reflects a culture of original fertility and giantism immortalised in cultic adoration, with a later phase of the unthinkable death of these beings. In a sense, Goliath is the incarnation of the aspirations of early Canaanite myths of the giant, but one who falls, in accordance with the biblical terminal history of anyone descended from Rapha'. Thus, the translation of the repha'im as 'dispensers of fertility' (cf. Gray 1965: 131), trades on a theme of divine origins and gigantic power that even so terminates in its antithesis: death.

    The cultic centre at Ebla, in Matthiae's treatment, consequently has an ironic relation to its future shadows in Old Testament use of Canaanite *repha'im*. We do not know to what extent the *Repha'im* in Genesis 14 were apprehended as an allusion to manifestations of this cultic theme. But the Genesis 14 placing of an invasion of repha'im a hundred or so miles away from a then infamous religious centre of repha'im, to secure a hero motif around 'Abraham',[10] in a chapter replete with its own competing religious symbolism and polemic, is a piece of grim humour. This is a genre whose latest form attests to the extinction of the repha'im, for that is what Isaiah 14 later appears to circumscribe concerning another invader from the East: 'Hell from beneath is moved to meet you at thy coming'. The subplot in each narrative is also pertinent to the *repha'im* theme's other biblical contexts.

---

[10] For the characterization of 'hero motif', see Emerton 1971: 431-34.

Within the narrative world of the Old Testament contexts, they are taken to be some sort of spiritually mutant alien group from outside of the faithful's territory that invade this domain of God's people, bringing a world destructive of God's teaching. We should be able to pinpoint how the Repha'im sustained their claim to divine descent. Notoriously, the Canaanites regarded the cycle of nature as supported by the gods—the gods provided the fertility for the revival of the earth after winter, Ba'al himself accommodatingly 'died' at the end of each year and was 're-born' at the beginning of the new year when he was enthroned as king of the gods. The *Repha'im* played a major part in this drama, claiming to be the personification of Ba'al's fertility because of their perceived stature, which was also evidence of their descent from Rapha' the eternal king. Hence, the giants, imposed as figura on rulers and deities alike, as sons from divine parents, were focal points for expressions of fear and adoration by the Canaanites; for they saw them as holders or custodians of two primal powers of the world: godhead and fertility. And the warrior and priestly garbs with which the giants clothed themselves adequately advertise the functions they claimed to perform. Thus, the Canaanites in every sense would associate the giants with the gods, eternal life, and fertility. It may more readily be appreciated how apt a reference to the *Repha'im* functions in the passages that were examined earlier: the giants were seemingly deathless, infused with the gods' own nature; but the giants still died and decayed. The later uses of rephai'm mapped a grim pun on the moralising mythology from incarnation to grave.

Matthiae's (1989) exposition of the religious centre at Ebla is directly relevant to the above complex of mythological nuances; for, although the later Old Testament allusions are refined and stylised by centuries of usage separating it from Ebla, Matthiae's own thesis has a striking relation to the Old Testament motifs. For centuries after the attack by Sargon in 2300 BC, Ebla and parts of its temple and palace complexes continued to be used until well into the 2nd millennium. Presumably, this was concurrent with the survival of elements of the Rep'um rituals and/or cultic memories. So the diachronic gap, even if one were to dismiss a 3rd-millennium linguistic source for the biblical repha'im, does not dismantle the prospect for a later date for influence. This amounts to a strong inductive base for associating Ebla and the Old Testament when one articulates the previously advanced interrelations adduced by a number of scholars between Ugaritic and Old Testament repha'im. These linguistic and iconic elements thus pass through the linguistic history of the term repha'im between Ebla Early Bronze Age usage and later Old Testament literature, with Gen. 14:5 standing in the middle or earlier phase of the linguistic history. If one wishes to stress the close linguistic affiliations of the Semitic Eblaic to Ugaritic, such equations of an Ebla religious centre for *rp'um* gain a causal linguistic connection from the Ugaritic narratives on *rp'um*.

In terms of virtual archaeology and the semantics of media, this cross-fertilisation is fundamental to reconstruction. When two functions housed in asymmetric media are shown to have even partial functional identity, the inferential benefits are significant. An aspect of this suturing together of disparate functions which has been developed is that of characterisation of individuals in relation to historical biography and the extension of this into an ontology of the actual world. This is not the occasion to develop an analysis along these lines, but a few comments are apt relating to the role of Abraham as character.

The enfolding of a narrative's other-worldly presuppositions (such as transcendence and revelation) with assumptions of historicity are of course perplexing, though we should allow for, for example, a qualified parallel with other worldviews such as a modernist ideology in which fiction and fact are welded into polemic. Aristotle had already addressed some of the pertinent issues long before modern concern with the division of labour between ontology and imagination. Weidemann (1994) attempts to show that Aristotle's notion of possibility is committed to possible world semantics, though of course he did not develop one. A fundamental reason for this is that Aristotle's possibility is concerned with both the actual possible circumstances which obtain on a logical semantics, as well as those (theoretical) possibilities which may obtain (cf. his *Metaphysics* IX 3, and *Prior Analytics* I 13). This picture should be supplemented by introducing Aristotle's conception of the enthymeme as a deductive rhetorical notion that can be applied to some ancient narrative contexts, as argued in Gibson (forthcoming f). Attempts to reconstruct by virtual archaeology a given property of the ancient Near East from site and text have to attempt to differentiate the two forms of possibility. The conjunction of narrative biography (such as Abraham), or collective religious centre biography (such as the rites of the *repha'im*), and historical semantic values in ancient texts with site representation in archaeology, is an important complex in producing a possible actual world for application to the past reality. The way film is composed, we see from the research of Deleuze (1985), is a form of virtual reality. The idea of a film visualisation, if we are careful in qualifying the relations of representation, has similarities to the Levant world's use of visualisation in both religion and politics. A subset of this concerns how one may reinterpret ancient archaeological and linguistic phenomena using visualisation to mirror such styles. Gibson (1997a, cf. 2000a, Part 1) proposes models to develop this approach, particularly regarding representation of God and people. Such an approach to conceptualisation of ancient narrative creativity can be interpreted, in terms of policy, as a corollary of Matthiae's deployment of virtual reality formalism to represent facets of the external ancient world of Ebla.

One way to test such conceptual conjectures as virtual reality and its association with history is to build a retrojective prediction into the scenario, to be assessed by future discovery or by the emergence of some proof beyond the point at which the scenario has been applied. Hesse (1995) faults Popper because his logic of scientific discovery was not a test incorporating predictive power. In virtual archaeology, the requirement of retrojection is itself a form of predictive experiment, not unlike astronomical interpretation which observes the past. In archaeology and astronomy, the residue of the past is reconstructed to yield an identity of which it itself is a small subset. Virtual archaeology is a device to generate this exponential increase in informability, derivable, with theory, from an empirical identity other than the concept that, hopefully, is its consequence. Matthiae's attempt to select a 'fit' between site architecture and textualized ritual, employing a complex mythological *rep'um* concept, is such a case of extrapolation, whether or not one finds the proof-procedure weak or strong. Counter-factual, subjunctive conditional, representation is accordingly required by investigation. The difference from established history is that we do not, on occasions, have cognisance of the criteria that identify the difference between the actual and the possible. Ideology subsumed as dogma and/or (falsely) as neutral description of site, artefacts or texts, can do much damage as a distorting function on theory-construction in virtual archaeology, quite as much as loose speculation or postmodernist freeplay.

Sumerian Creation at Ebla?

One such sensitive arena is creation. As Rogerson (1991) elegantly shows, the earlier chapters of Genesis are by now heavily governed by distinguished exegetical policies that police the limiting or limited boundaries of possibility. Unfortunately, this situation is not infrequently attended by an absence of explicit logic or neutrality to assess the relations of possibility to actuality in these spheres. Protectionism against radical interpretation goes well beyond what is sustainable by advanced techniques in formal analysis and scientific discovery. This does not assign Pettinato, the original epigraphist at Ebla, dismissed by Matthiae, to the realm of bold precise theoretician championing the truth, however; even so, one should not be embarrassed boldly to address what is by now a politically charged debate, nor feel obliged to join a particular camp. Since there are as many theories of literary Sumerian as there are Sumeriologists, it is not unexpected that dispute and uncertainty have attended the Sumerian literary tablets in a dialect related to but different from the Fara Sumerian. In this vein Pettinato's publication of what he takes to be a creation hymn has some importance, although Archi[11] has criticized Pettinato's interpretation, with replies by Pettinato (1981: 208-13). Even though Pettinato's exegesis is not inviolable, I will assume that he largely met Archi's criticisms, while yet Archi and Pettinato have not exhausted the possibilities surrounding the interpretation of the tablets. Pettinato suggests that the unusual collocations in the Sumerian indicate that they should be read as copies for expressing Eblaic. There are two and one part copies of the text, TM.75.G.1682, M.75.G.2196, and TM.75.G.2500 respectively. 2196 is reproduced below since it is the most convenient for present purposes, reflecting some of Pettinato's translation, though my rendering below attempts to integrate lines 1-4 with 5-12 in a way Pettinato does not:

Ebla Creation Tablet:

1.	l u g a l—a n—k	I Lord of heaven and earth,
2.	n u—g u b k i g i n_7	You had not made the earth exist x you created (it),
3.	n u—s i g u_4—i a g i n_7	You had not established the solar light you created
4.	zu-ur_5-ra n u—t u k u_x	You had not (yet) made exist the morning light.
5.	l u g a l i n i m—k a l	Lord: efficacious word,
6.	l u g a l h e—g a l	Lord: prosperity,
7.	l u g a l n a m—n i r	Lord: heroism,
8.	l u g a l n a m—x	Lord:
	[n u—g a l n a m—r i , s u -m a, in TM.75.G.1682]	
9.	l u g a l m u—d a—k u s	Lord 'independent',
10.	lu g a l m e—a m	Lord: divinity,
11.	l u g a l p a	Lord who saves,
12.	l u g a l HI—z I	Lord: happy life.

A first reaction to this text and translation might be regarded as a competing theory against Pettinato's basic interpretation. Is not this Sumerian text more akin to a list of titles for a god than a creation hymn? It is true that there is no god's name to open the possible list. However, this objection would not be insurmountable, for there are precedents. We know that the subject of CT 42, 37, 1 is Ninurta, but the name is absent from the head of the list. An objection to this line of argument might be that the above Ebla text has a literary descriptive and no titular opening. Contrariwise, this is exactly what CT 42, 37, 1 has:

---

[11] See Archi 1979: 561-62. Archi neglects Eblaic uses such as ti-'a-ma-tum/tihamatum (cf. tehom, 'deep', in Gen. 1:2).

ur-sag eaX (E)-ni-ta a-ma-ru ki-bal-a-ta x [x]

The lion-head when he arose [was] the Floodstorm which [swept] over the Rebel lands.[12]

It is sometimes said that such title lists were also furnished in order that the people might learn the value of the titles.[13] The appearance of the multiple copies at Ebla would comply with that function; and one might wonder if the variant closely related copies might not have something to do with scribal practice and a didactic circumstance, on this approach to the text. Pettinato assumes that the mythological introduction of lines 2-4 is incompletely presented; but of course we have no other text which presents a more (allegedly) complete form of the introduction. So his suggestion has no empirical foundation.[14] Another facet of this interpretative argument is that lines 5 to 12, even on Pettinato's analysis, comply much more with a title-listing sequence rather than a literary text, though the alleged hymnic genre could mitigate this criticism if one construes the lines as a coda to praise the deity by use of his titles.

These factors do not neutralise the considerable body of exposition that Pettinato has brought to bear on the text, but rather qualify the level of probability. If one adopts his overall view, this does not entail having to accept all his interpretation of individual items. The lack of inflection of the Sumerian renders the second person characterization uncertainly based, even allowing for line 4, and it could be read as third person. A genitival rendering could be introduced for lines 5 to 12 (by, for example, reading line 6 as g a 1 a), taking them as accusative. Consequently, the following rendering attempts to integrate lines 1-4 with 5-12 in a way which scanned as Eblaic, the text might be translated as follows:

> The lord of heaven and earth
> It existed not,
> Then he created the earth.
> Light had not been formed, then he created it.
> He had not made learning's light.
> Then the Lord manifested the Word:
> The Lord's fullness,

---

[12] Pettinato 1980b: 244 offers a revised translation of part of this tablet. Cf. Kinnier Wilson 1979: 19-20, 52.

[13] A case is cited in Lambert 1960: 40 1. 30. He has the translation 'provoke', but surely it should read 'taught'.

[14] Pettinato, at the time of writing 1980b: 244, assumed that line 5 opens up the 'homogeneous section of the epithets' with an epithet; but this line can be positioned as the pivot on which the epithets are seen as corollaries of lines 2-4.

       The Lord's omnipotence,
       The Lord's headship,
       The Lord's own counsel,
       The Lord's divinity,
       The Lord's salvation,
       The Lord's fortune.

There are here a number of semantic properties which have partial parallels in Genesis 1 and other parts of the Old Testament, though it is important to qualify these relations as well as to note the non-Syrian Southeast Sumerian parallels which also, albeit incompletely, obtain for this Ebla tablet. This latter point itself, though, should be modified by, for example, Kramer's (1968: 291-92, 294, 297-99) recognition that within the Sumerian tradition there are already parallels which link up with aspects of the Genesis narrative, in which, of course, he took the Genesis relations to be from post-Sumerian periods. Kramer said that these relations were mediated indirectly, except for whatever direct influence one might be able to isolate for the Abrahamic–Ur history. Now with the Sumerian at Ebla, whether or not one posits an underlying Southeast Sumerian literary influence in the Ebla text, the probability of a 3rd-millennium basis for Genesis 1-2 is increased by the existence of such a tablet in the geographical orbit of the Abrahamic historical setting. Also, the Ebla text is more explicit on creation than any hitherto extant Southeast Sumerian narrative. This should be allowed to quantify the strength of the tablet's relevance for giving the Genesis 1 composition a 3rd-millennium origin.

     The contrast of a created earth (l. 2b) with a prior state of its not existing (l. 2a) explicitly mirrors Gen. 1:1-2. Likewise, the contrast over light's creation (l. 3a, b) semantically reflects Gen. 1:2. If Pettinato's suggestion (1980a: 212) of (l. 3a) 'solar light' enables one to discover an underlying nuance about, or derived from, ^{d}Aya, the companion of the Sun god, then on a number of interpretations this would yield a value that partly matches the making of the sun and day in Gen. 1:14 and 3–5. The sense of 'teaching-light' arises from the Semitic expression (l. 4) zu-ur$_5$-ra (with zu-u$_9$-ra in TM.75.G.1682), subject to the condition that one can compare this to the Hebrew morpheme z-h-r, also in other Semitic languages (cf. Ugaritic zhr, 'brilliant'). Pettinato (1980a: 212-13) proposes the Hebrew zohar, giving it the sense 'splendor' (as well as offering sahar and sohar as possibilities). But z-h-r appears in two homonyms or polysemes in Hebrew (a) 'light, shining', and (b) 'enlighten, instruct'. I conjecture that some suitable merger of the two senses could account for the Eblaic uses, if in fact this stem is in line 4, in virtue of the associative semantic interplay which probably occurs there. This could act as a fulcrum to connect the thematic senses and transformation from creative cosmology (ll. 1-3) to its instrumental theology and adoration (lines 6-

12), with zu-ur₅-ra dual sense, or tonal value,[15] acting as a live metaphor to catch the transfer from physical cosmology in creation to its personification. This complex of relations is asymmetric on some counts to Genesis 1's usage of a speech-act agency, yet there is an extensive conceptual parallel with regard to the two narratives: the 'Word' is the causal agent in a context of creation identified with the Lord's person and action. If it is correct to construe lines 6 to 12 as the exemplification of or corollaries to the 'word' in line 5 of the Ebla text, then this aligns Genesis with the Ebla narrative indirectly, yet substantively, on the verbal medium as manifestation of the Lord's personality.

The creation of man, with its imaging of man in God's likeness, is absent from the text. It is interesting to notice, however, that a deity at Ebla is di-mu-tu that appears to relate to the Hebrew *dᵉmut* ('likeness') in Gen. 1:26; we do not have to conflate, for example, Dahood's (1979: 308) dogmatic formulations with such options. May be hypostatization in the use of *dumut* reflects a ludic influential phase in some relations between Semitic and Sumerian vocabulary. Pettinato leaves line 8's r i—s u—m a untranslated, for there seems to be no legible parallel transcription in the texts which would aid analysis. However, one may conjecture the possibility that if this expression is not logographic, the ri-su formation partly conforms to the requirement for a proposed Eblaic Semitic stem *r*'s (Assyrian *resu*). In the Zenjirli dialect, we may have a precedent for the elision of ' in the Panammu inscription (cf. J.C.L. Gibson 1975: 80 l. 12, 84 n. 12), or we can suppose for analogy a value indicated by the Ugaritic *i* behind *ri-*. If we take the value n a m in the parallel text (of lines 7-8), the sense 'headship' or 'beginning' can be derived as a valid inference from this cluster of relations. This possibility would attach itself to the foregoing level-specific parallels between the Ebla tablets and Genesis, subject to refinement and fresh discoveries: as Lord of creation the deity is also thereby its head and beginning.

'Ur of the Chaldees'

Van Seters (1975), T.L. Thompson (1978; cp. 1999) and others have claimed or assume that 'Ur of the Chaldees' is a misnomer. Certainly there are problems. They view it as an anachronism, believing that it was not associated with the Chaldeans until the 7th-century or 1st-millennium BC 'Chaldea' renders the Akkadian *kaldu*, reflected also in the later Greek transliteration; it certainly appears in 1st-millennium texts, as witnessed by Ashurnasirpal II's annals (cf. Saggs 1962):

---

[15] For the theory of tonal meaning, see Gibson 2000b: 48, 59, 103, 130, 157-64.

I established power and might over the land of Suhu...
and the chilling terror of my arms overwhelmed
the land of Chaldea.

This inscription is from the period 883–59 BC. The earlier periods are not absent of relevant material; but the issue is controversial and disputed. The above writers fail to outline this situation, which forces qualification of their assertions and blocks their own theses about the expression. Dalley (1998) observes that an Aramaic association for 'Chaldees' would indicate a 1st-millennium date. But the Hebrew *kasdim* in Genesis is obviously not the Hebrew form of the Akkadian *kaldu*. It is too easy to submerge the former term as if it were the latter word. It is appropriate to offer a review and interpretation about the state of analysis concerning 'Ur of the Chaldees' in an attempt to clarify some relations and contrasts. Of course, as one would expect, at Ebla the proper name 'Ur' (urki) occurs (see Pettinato 1980b: 90 and TM.75.G.1647), and it appears in Southeast Sumerian and other texts of the Ur III period (often as Urim, cf. Buccellati 1966: 84-86). In a somewhat problematic Ebla tablet (TM.76.G.521 v.IV and v.VI), graphic parallels for a postulated 3rd-millennium equivalent appear for 'Chaldea', although with different senses (Pettinato 1980b: 259).

'Chaldea' transliterates the Septuagint's transliteration of the Akkadian kaldu. This latter term itself predates the 7th century BC, appearing in the 10th century, which at that time supersedes the designation 'the Sealands'. There is no evidence that this terminological change marked an alteration in the identities of the tribes inhabiting the relevant areas; and it is reasonable to suppose that this ethnic stock goes back to the 3rd millennium, albeit with some additions. 'Ur of the Chaldees' is not a proper name, nor solely one name, but it is composed of a proper name and geographical or ethnic designator. Uses of this compound expression may not possess the identical ossified association that some commentators ascribe to it; nor might it be a designation that was in use, or common employment, in Sumerian. It could, nevertheless, exhibit a West Semitic stylism for separating out the northern from the southern Ur by a territorial or ethnic modifier 'Chaldee' (*kasdim*). So the absence or unavailability in extant texts, of the form 'Ur of the Chaldees' is not necessarily evidence of anachronism. Furthermore, the occurrence of such terms as Haran (har-ra-nuki) at Ebla (e.g. in TM.75.G.309), in a genre in which 'Ur' appears with other names that are used in the Genesis narrative that includes 'Ur of the Chaldees', shows at least a framework of selected proper names consistent with 3rd-millennium usage, thereby depicting acquaintance with it, if taken in conjunction with the foregoing 3rd-millennium data.

Long before 2000 BC, not only in places south of Ur, but at Ur itself, there was proper name evidence of a Semitic element in the population (e.g. king Sharrum-kin). Hence, one over-reaches the inferential scope of the evidence if one uses

'Chaldeans' as a narrowed, ethnic term. In this respect, then, it is inaccurate to assert the conjunction that: Ur was one of the city-states of Sumer *and* to suppose that it did not become associated with the Chaldeans until the 1st millennium, because the texts do not require that; and tendencies in the data can be constructed so as to oppose the judgements (see Saggs 1962: 55). It is certainly incorrect to believe that Ur had no association with the country of south Babylonia to which the term 'Chaldea' is applied, because, from the first Dynasty of Babylon onwards, records inform us that this geographical location was administrated principally by Ur (see Saggs 1962: 79). This at least gives a circa 2,000 BC administrative-political basis for accepting that some connection with Ur and (the area at some time termed) 'Chaldea' (kaldu) existed. So, 'Ur of the Chaldees'—even if a use of 'Chaldea' with the -l- formation, and not -s-, is hypothetically postulated for the time of Abraham—is historically credible as an equation, and not self-evidently inconsistent with other known historical situations for the Abrahamic period.

But there is some indication of a need for suspension of other judgements in this area, partly because of an assumed change in the Akkadian and its relation to the Hebrew. In translations, 'Chaldea' stands for the Old Testament Hebrew *kasdim*, whereas the later Akkadian (it is assumed to reproduce or match in function) is kaldu. The difference in 'l' and 's' is usually assumed to be explained by a shift in Old Babylonian and later Akkadian from *kasdu* to *kaldu*, because in some dialects of Akkadian an 's' before, for example, a 'd' can be exchanged for 'l', as in *kasdu/kaldu*. But this explanation is a theoretical calculation inferred from some empirical evidence for this term kaldu, applying to other words that display the change. That is to say, the linguistic situation for the proposed change in specific texts from *kasdu* to *kaldu* is not extant. If such a change happened, it might be merely a sound change; on the other hand, it could carry an alteration in the scope or role of the term(s). Certainly, the form *kaldu* appears to parallel the Hebrew *kasdim* in later uses, for some contexts.

We should notice Saggs' (1962: 555) comments, however, to the effect that the two terms kasdim/kaldu are not synonymous in all contexts. Even with the same form of a term such as 'Israel', there may be an alteration in functional scope (as with its use for the whole of the Hebrew tribes, and later sometimes for the northern tribes). When we are ignorant of the possible scope of a posited original form *kasdu*, even hypothetically as a name for the rough area *kaldu*, but prior to *kaldu*, it is not a balanced judgement to insist on a conclusion that the Hebrew for 'Chaldees' (*kasdim*) in Genesis is anachronistic.

It is possible, as a hypothesis for investigation, to propose that, since *kaldu* is late and the Old Testament Hebrew *kasdim* corresponds to a postulated Old Babylonian form (circa 2000 BC) *kasdu* from which *kasdim* is said to derive, *kasdim* is not anachronistic, but originally contemporary with a circa 2,000 BC use of 'Abraham'.

Strictly, it is *kaldu* that would, according to extant texts, be anachronistic, if applied to Abrahamic times. But Genesis does not employ that term for its internal presupposed early dating for the Abrahamic narratives. It utilises *kaśdim*, which is not only a different term, and a distinct language, from Akkadian *kaldu*; it corresponds to the posited Old Babylonian form *kasdu*, which belongs to a period (circa 2,000BC) of development contemporary with Genesis, originating from 3rd millennium history. This is a function of evidence easily neglected about 'Chaldea'. Nevertheless, in Sumerian for this period there is a pertinent form of consonants exemplified by kildu. This proves that the relevant formal pattern of consonants is not anachronistic, and is attested for the appropriate time at the end of the 3rd millennium. (If kildu is taken to match kiśadu, it has the values 'throat', 'besides', 'arrive', etc., so I am not of course assuming that there is a full semantic alignment here—cf. Deimel 1947: III, 2, 199.)

In this state of affairs, it is 'the' or a (pre-Christian, pre-Dead Sea Scrolls version of the) Septuagint Old Testament Greek translation which may have produced the anachronism by rendering the Hebrew *kaśdim*, parallel with an Old Babylonian form, by the incorrect transliterating Greek *chaldaioi*, though the latter was then current in Greek. I do not assume that this rendering is in fact wrong. Even so, there are undeniable differences at a linguistic level that have been obliterated by the type of polemics, for example, of the sort that Van Seters and Thompson offered. When such states of affairs are exposed and smoothed out descriptively, instead of prescriptive censorship, one can find that the map of meaning and its geography in ancient history do not have to yield anachronism from the Hebrew Bible in this case. They ignore the obvious point that the situation could be a product of anachronistic translation, together with such treatments neglecting to register the force of the *l/r* change in Akkadian and its relation to the Hebrew.[16] Decisive solutions to this problem should await further discoveries and results; we should not prejudge scholarly history of the future over this issue. In view of the importance this question has for the Abrahamic era, it is odd that there has been a trend to omit and failure logically to assess these data.

C.H. Gordon (1958: 28-31) proposed that 'Ur of the Chaldees' is not the Ur in Southern Babylonia, but one in northern Mesopotamia: Ura in Ugaritic texts, under the control of Hittites. Gordon (1958: 30 n. 7) suggested that the terminal 'a' in 'Ura' can be accounted for, and its appearance is evidence of the Aramean background of Chaldeans. He claims that the northern route Abraham took would have been odd if he lived at southern Ur, by going to Haran; this route is reasonable however, Gordon suggests, if the northern Ura site is accepted as 'Ur', because this is probably 200 miles north of Haran. Saggs (1960: 200-209) produced a detailed demolition of Gordon's

---

[16] The Akkadian s is different in value from the Hebrew; this might betray that there is some further evidence of differentiation and separation of the terms.

thesis, to which Gordon (1963) has responded. 'Ur' occurs at Ebla, and this gives an early Sumerian basis in a Semitic context for the term in the south, that seems to destroy Gordon's theory. Although Saggs is correct in his criticism, he neutrally cites the old etymology of 'Arpachsad', which is still accepted in the work of Simons (1959: 9-10). This etymology traces the second component in 'Arpachsad', that is, *kaśdim* (excepting the plural termination -*im*). The component '*kśd*' has the same consonants as the posited Old Babylonian *ksd*, with 's' rather than 'l', as explained above. In Gen. 10:22 where the name 'Arpachsad' appears, according to Simons and others, it takes the role of designating Babylonia in the table of the nations. Such an interpretation would strongly support the previously mentioned change in scope of '*kasdu/kaldu*' compared with Neo-Assyrian 8th-century usage.

Editorial Disagreement

The foregoing discussion in part drew attention to the scholarly treatment of the patriarchal narratives that ascribe to them a mainly nonhistorical status. This was illustrated by reference, for example, to Thompson and Van Seters[17] though they disagree with one another over significant issues. The status of such scholarly disagreement can, obviously, be a sign of merit in open discussion. As when, for instance, Thompson (1978: 76) claims that: 'The...attempt by Van Seters to set the Abrahamic stories of Genesis in the mid-1st millennium BC and to establish an exilic or post-exilic date for the "Yahwist" is unsuccessful.' This situation is so familiar as to render a resume of the wide variety of different approaches to Genesis unnecessary, since I now address a current concern untypically instanced in an unusual facet of feminist studies.

There are many types of re-assessment of biblical themes, including the deployment of feminism by, for example, Meyers (1988). Subsequent to such developments, the new sort of enterprise was launched by Harold Bloom's and Rosenberg's (1990) untypical thesis which placed the early part of Genesis in the hands of a feminist author of the same period. It proceeds with the discovery that God's female gender (Bloom and Rosenberg 1990: 36) has lain hidden beneath the edited subtext of the Old Testament, and this author is a woman in the Court of David. My own view is that Bloom's imperious, unconventional, brilliance may have unwittingly isolated some presuppositions of the feminist psychology that Genesis was *countering*, and so ironically mirroring. On this view, then, Bloom's view is not correct as he expresses it: his insight has located a presuppositional detail of the communal purpose

---

[17] This is not to oppose their criticism of misuse of Nusi data.

of the text with which he confutes a Mesopotamian female function. Bloom has examined and reconfigured with originality some mainstream expositional schools expounding an ancient Mesopotamian female god, such as Inanna. The latter deity is splendidly framed and characterised by Leick's (1994) study. In short, at most Bloom has detected an ironising polemic against a Mesopotamian female deity competing with Yahweh behind Genesis 2, but he has not exposed a semantic function advocated in it. Consequently, Bloom has confused oblique critical dismissal of a competing alternative to the text's worldview, with the (incorrectly aligned) possibility of the text's absorption of the competing presupposition.

Nevertheless, I suggest that Bloom's exposure, if modally restructured, is subtle and has a kinship with Forrester's (1997) analysis of Freud's presuppositions: Freud unconsciously 'leaked-out' in his strictures examining, and to some degree, repressing, women whom he purported to cure. Bloom's study of J might be such an act of transmission. J could be a type-name for the influence of a large set of feminising predicates. In this scenario, I could still to some degree be under a wide variety of male-dominated Semitic scribal traditions in the Levant which were, as we know they were, heavily influenced by Mesopotamian mythological mores, even when seeming to compete with them. My interpretation could employ the type of 'mirror' notion developed by Lacan (cf. Bowie 1990, 1993). On this view, Bloom's acuity has detected (yet transformed in a manner not allowed for or recognised in his interpretation) some culturally external feminist figural presuppositions to which the Genesis 'J' is responding. In Bloom's intended sense, then, his thesis is incorrect; but with a retuning, it has application to the foregoing state of affairs. I choose this example to highlight how the function of detail, or a detail, adjusted to the authorial or readerly presupposition of a biblical narrative, can almost totally change the direction, status and value of a scholarly interpretation, and in a fashion rarely allowed for by scholarly activities.

It would take a separate book to generalise this sort of claim, but it may meet the present purpose to offer a brief additional, controversial, prospect for analysis. Imagine that the above re-interpretation scenario is generalised to some standard scholars and their treatment of the purported editorial subtext of the Old Testament. J. Rogerson (1991), cautiously reviewing a whole variety of approaches to Genesis 1–11, shows the prowess of source-based literary studies, while balancing Near Eastern historical background. Rogerson refrains from proposing a synthesis yet helpfully notice the general conclusions from past and contemporary scholarship. What if 'J' itself in these scholars is deconstructed into, and/or originally was, merely the set of stylistics internal to one author's semantic field in Genesis? That is to say, what if J never was a set of editorial functions external to the text? What if we retune scholarly source criticism into literary criticism of networked themes counter-poised by the original author(s) in composition with other (perhaps neglected) narrative functions and nuance? This would be rather like restoring Shakespeare as the author of King Lear after it had been deconstructed by poststructuralist theatre directors, and Beckett subsuming aspects of it in *Endgame*, if the latter had been wrongly conflated with Shakespeare.

Within the sphere of inference and probability, there is a sharp problem of how, or if, such conclusions follow from evidence. On the one hand, the wide conflicting varieties of hypotheses appear to exemplify a situation in which either conclusions are not secure or the standards of reason are not sufficiently high to imply conclusions. Logical grounds for this analysis appear in, for example, Gibson (forthcoming e). My claim is that there has been no relevantly explicit exposure of assumptions and their relations to support and accompany such types of editorial procedure. One response to this may be to assume that this is a matter of mere re-presentation with the added bits of logical trimming to strengthen claims with enhanced rational presentation. This objection inaccurately overstates the role of method in logic, whereas inference, properly understood, espouses the status of relations independently inherent to empirical and conceptual content. In sum, the objection fails to recognise the point that, in advance of not having exposed the status in reason of grounds for a conclusion, it is questionable to assume in this sort of case that what it is or can be is demonstrable by nonlogical means. This is complicated by the obvious truth that there are layers of later composition using earlier material in the Old Testament. Yet this is not itself the correctly qualified argument which would support the generalised concept allegedly accounting for almost all Old Testament narrative. It is quite possible that the amount of generalisation about editing and its identity are tantamount to modernist mythologies provoked by Enlightenment assumptions. The steady accretion over the last 150 years of yet more generalised forms of editing hypotheses may merely be a function of the modernist cultures which have spawned such assumptions, rather than a discovery procedure adept at exposing the quite different ancient world cultures.

Astruc's (1753) *Conjectures sur les mémoires originaux dont il* first proposed the distinct Yahwist and Elohist sources. Astruc requires a separate study to appear elsewhere, though it is relevant to sketch a view here. Ernest Nicholson's (1998: 6) review of Pentateuch research, following others, passes off, unanalysed, Astruc's idea as a 'discovery', which, linked to Eichhorn's work, 'did not find recognition' until 1853; and he notes that Astruc was a medical doctor in Paris. I have no wish merely to quibble over terms used by a subtle scholar such as Nicholson. Rather, we have a substantive problem here. These measuring terms and Astruc's techniques are Enlightenment myths of premodernist Empire. The expression 'invention' might be a suitable replacement for 'discovery', and for 'recognition', 'acceptance'. Astruc was a doctor serving Louis XIV's Court, and was a famed authority of venereal diseases.

Certainly, we should not fall into a genetic fallacy of confusing the nature of scholastic source with the quality of its result. But a study of Astruc's identity is long overdue. He was an internecine force mirroring the establishment in the Court that attracted to itself the French Revolution. If many of the techniques internal to Enlightenment projects, modernist Marxism and European imperialisms are now exposed as anachronistic adventures of over-universalising presumption, there is no reason to assume in principle that Astruc's 1753 initiation of a yet future contagion of editorial synthesis is immune to the vestigial narcissism of his medical context. This is fighting talk; deconstruction of myth is not merely a cure appropriate to cure fundamentalism, however. Specialist French scholars of the period recognise the need to do much more research on Astruc; so why theologians have transcended this requirement is odd.

That there was editing of the Old Testament does not entail that the degree and nature of modern perception of it has discovered its identity or scope. The evidence for many editorial theories is not attested by separate unedited early texts. This is a vicious circle: no unedited narratives of the Old Testament is tantamount to no external proof for editing at the scale of carving up Genesis into distinct origins. Editing of detail occurred; but this is not the relevant domain. We are here talking of origins of books from separate sources. This absence poses severe if not chronic problems for the state of the art. Kermode (1979, 1990) has discussed lack of rigor in some analysis of Christian editing; I argue that this criticism applies even more to earlier texts. If the criteria for testing the possible falsehood of a thesis cannot be produced, then the proof for the thesis cannot be adduced (cf. Popper, 1953). Postulating hypothetical sources has to be taken to be a predictive foundational claim. This fits with Popper's (1972) procedures, as Hesse (1995) refines them. With regard to P, for example, no such distinct source manuscript has been discovered from Old Testament eras. This blocks a proof claim attached to such retrojective failure. Sure, the survival of appropriate narrative is highly unlikely. Tough. We need to join the real world. Absence is the presence of no testable hypothesis. Some scholars merely weaken the grounds of proof *whilst* writing as if their reasoning and terminology were parallel with theories where subject testable for falsifiability. In this situation the undoubted technical skill is like reading livers. It is a metaphoric ornamentation, intransitive with respect to the actual world of proof and history. Unless there is proof from within early texts for the existence of two historically distinct narratives, the absence of unedited narrative is absence of requisite proof for editing. In this perspective, the possible underestimation of the function of creative originality in the composition of relevant ancient texts may be a result of undue stress on overstatement of, and eclipse by editing theories that some scholars have perhaps too readily redeployed from their own cultures.

In Genesis 11's Babel narrative, we have what is often considered to be evidence of editing. In this view, typically, the narrative is said to be composed of two stories which originally emerged from Sumerian, more fully present in Akkadian: (a) 'Babel' means 'gate of god', and uses an etiological strand rationalising the function of ziggurat cities. (b) 'Babel' means *balal*, and is employed to explain the confusion of languages and dispersion of peoples around the world. With regard to (a), it is clear that no Hebrew word for gate (*ša'ar, deleth, pethah, saph*) is reminiscent of the connection. The Akkadian *bab-ili* can mean 'gate of god'. But form is not a criterion of semantic transmission and preservation of sense between two languages; two related languages often have the same morpheme with opposed meanings and unrelated semantic fields positions.

Concerning (b), the Hebrew writer in Gen. 11:9 presents his use of 'Babel' with the folk-etymology *balal*, 'confusion', and locks it into subtheme (b) above, rather than differentiate it from another adopted story line in Genesis 11. The point is not that there is no relation, but that inexplicit assumptions illicitly infer a thematic relation through etymology. If parody were operating between the Akkadian and Hebrew elements, then the relation would not secure the transfer in the way required. As Goldhill (1990: 210) says: 'parody, like irony, establishes an unsettling possibility of reading otherwise that becomes finally difficult to control'. New discoveries, such as those at Ebla, are opening up quite new pathways to construct intertextual relations involving parody, as well as affording pitfalls for speculation. More precise methods are needed, together with original inventiveness. The discovery, for example, of a deified [d]EDEN (= wa-pi₅-um; cf. Pettinato 1979: IV 290, no. 807) is a tantalising item for relating to the 'Garden of Eden', but it awaits the development of literary as well as textual insights which would warrant controlled explanation.

In characterising and assessing the sort of links that (a) and (b) posit, such synthesis has to take on board a large set of problems, many problematic elements of which are in the Akkadian and Sumerian and not only Genesis. Kramer (1988: 108-11 and 1983: 114-21) points out the complex puzzles and blocks on certainty in these relations. The relevant passage in the Sumerian 'Enmerkar and the lord of Aratta' presents the confusion of tongues as the result of jealousy by Enki for Enlil, a theme entirely absent from Genesis. Klein (1997: 77-92) has successfully refuted objections to Kramer's earlier view that the story has reference to the past, rather than future. Klein refines the force associated with a difference between Genesis and the Enmerkar narrative: the spell of Nudimmud enabled Enmerkar to speak with the lord of Aratta in another language, and the poet ascribes the invention of cuneiform to Enmerkar. Elements in this tradition have surfaced at Ebla, as discussed above in 'Psychological Conclusion'. There are in the relevant southern Sumerian and Ebla texts series of related specific semantic and conceptual themes that have parallels in the semantic field of Genesis 10–11, even allowing for the varieties of divergent value-judgements and subplots in these genres. Such relations all include proportionately similar and qualitatively different uses of the subject and themes in each of the traditions, including their distinct uses of the material. Each tradition presupposes disputing ideologies and theologies that exhibit evidence of contemporary interlocking disputes. It seems problematic to distance the relevant comparative features of Genesis to a temporally remote point so that all interactions are due to indirect mediation through the much later Iron Age and neo-Babylonian sources in the exile. There is no proof of the alleged probability that the foregoing types of intertextual engagement and causal influence could arise in such temporally separated modes. Such arguments as there are seem to be circular, by presupposing the conclusion required in what needs proof. Some of the data in the relevant part of Genesis appear to require construction as evidence of some synchronic influence, interaction, reception or synthesis with Sumerian and Ebla type of sources or polemical targets in circulation centuries before the Iron Age. The heavily modified later scribal revision and alteration of much later Mesopotamian sources do not contain the functioning type of intertextuality contained in Genesis and its 3rd- or early 2nd-millennium Mesopotamian counterparts. In this perspective, the notion of dependence is much more complex and counter-intuitive than is traditionally allowed in discussion of the earliest provenance for parts of Genesis 10–11.

Rogerson (1991: 75-77) suggests that the relations between the proposed J source and Pg source exhibit, as he terms it, 'unevenness', and he introduces the familiar two-story origin of Genesis 11, from which Genesis 11 is said to derive its material. He observes that, 'Whether or not this is convincing, it draws attention to elements in the text.' However, given the subtle counterpoint and allusive use of elements, as well as subplot lateral weaving of nuances between themes, such unevenness has nothing in semantic functioning which displays evidence of disparate origins; and indeed Rogerson carefully side-steps and qualifies the status of such views. These views amount to a segmentation fallacy of slicing separable functions in a narrative and recombining them through equivocation. A literary consideration could operate here: unevenness is precisely what makes up thematic progress and tragic reversal in creative originality. The unexpected, the sudden change of indexical attitudes within a narrative, are components in unitary originality resulting from a single author, not necessarily the work of an editor. Consequently, this aspect of the two-story hypothesis is heavily infected with presuppositions external to the narrative.

An upshot of this is surely that it is incorrect to affirm, 'Whether or not this is convincing, it draws attention to elements in the text'. 'Drawing attention' is a presuppositional activity, and elements in a text are accordingly masked or exposed by the assumption chosen to interpret them. A theory which inculcates questionable or misleading assumptions into reading of elements in a text is not thereby drawing attention to them, but falling into generating a familiarity with textual data while distracting from their identity, and in the perspective of false-footing the reader with a distraction which may prevent her from regaining a suitable degree of disinterest (cf. discussions above, pp.55-56, 68-69).

Instead of absorbing and merging two stories, the authorial voice in Genesis 11 could be deconstructing (see Derrida 1983) Sumerian ideology and asserting its own singular tradition. On this view, new use of a Hebrew tradition's unstable vectors discovers a trajectory provoking contrary disjunctions with Mesopotamian traditions (see Hobson 1990: 111-39). Here, attempts to trace two source stories would be to have displaced and misunderstood the univocal creative mode of complex pun. The foregoing observation about a narrative 'false-footing' a reader may have some significance here, particularly in relation to the absence of punctuated narrative and its connection with irony in possible apostrophe in Genesis 11. In some poetry, for example in Apollinaire's poetry (*Alcools*) which influenced a whole way of composing poetry (e.g. Jean Tardieu 1991: 103-31), line-structures, the absence of punctuation and a visualising theme are employed to destabilise, question, or redirect a reader's expectations. In such compositional narrative universes, apparently unconnected or displaced lines are left to run together, which, when related, generate recognition, or attract ironic contrast, enforcing the dislocation between two opposed or closely connectable yet apparently contrary subthemes. In the admittedly very different climates of Sumerian and ancient Hebrew, it is problematic to reconstruct and retrieve a probable ancient reading. We have to reconstruct suspensive syntax and an account of its force, in relation to *enjambement* and its association with equivocal syntax, intended or otherwise, employed in a narrative that sustains contrast, tension and climax. This is especially true for Genesis 11, regarding the question of the status of such functions in the narrative. The proposed sources J and Pg manifest the above deconstructed phenomena, and so they could be interpreted as two internal narrative strands whose contrasting elements in rhetorical dance are unified, not displaying an 'unevenness' providing proof of editorial sutures.

Kramer's revised study of 'The Sumerian Deluge Myth' (1983: 114-21) points out that its long lacuna's content (lines 51-84) is in fact difficult to surmise, though scholars sometimes assume that it narrated the happy return of mankind to Sumer, in which it is supposed to hold the position of Genesis 10's migrations. Kramer stated that it is dubious to follow Jacobsen's (1981: 513-29) suggestion that another earlier 36 destroyed lines contained the calamitous dispersion over the face of the earth (cf. Genesis 10). The point of mentioning these two topics is that, with their possible non-existence or the theoretical conditionality of them, there are few points of straight similarity in the Sumerian narratives on which to presuppose relevant causal relations between them and Genesis 10, and consequently the differences correspondingly hold substantive positions of significance in marking contrasts.

Reverting briefly to the above discussion concerning Bloom in relation to the previous paragraph, the Sumerian Enki's creation of mankind with the assistance of the goddess Nintu begins to look much like Harold Bloom's thesis on J, and one might suggest that Bloom has inadvertently written a book about a feature of the literary psychopathography of the Sumerian tradition, and not one which fits the biblical data. He may even have been misled by scholarly editorial assumptions that ignored the contrasts internal to Genesis. Perhaps unconsciously, he responded in a sympathetic way to Sumerian possibilities. Although Bloom is uncharacteristic and extreme in relation to the centre of Old Testament scholarship, his book about J consequently highlights (more transparently and eccentrically than more moderate hypotheses) tendencies to conflate distinctions in the desire to invent new histories for Genesis. Later Akkadian tablets use elements, possibly missing in the Sumerian tradition, that align with points in the Genesis 11 Babel theme, which scholars have sometimes hypothetically imposed on the earlier Sumerian forms. Such guesswork sometimes works; yet it is hardly a basis, when theoretical, to be employed, as it sometimes is, with the status of a discovery-procedure. In contrast, see George's (1999) fine study.

But then, given the prospects of Hebrew elements in the 3rd millennium BC or early 2nd millennium which could predate these Akkadian forms, the temporal ordering of them is crucial to the questions of originality, dependence, and parody. Of course, early Sumerian forms of myths are discovered at times. Yet editing within the Sumerian and Akkadian traditions themselves subtly loops around or papers over twists in the revisions of archetypal stories, for example in the conjectured over 20 or so ancient revisions of the Epic of Gilgamesh. The whole area is very unstable, and since relations between texts in different languages are polemical, with narrative detail being used to generate competing cosmogonies, the occurrence of parallel morphemes does not support the thematic weight placed on them.

4

Egyptian Texts and the Old Testament

The Presence of the Israelites

The scenario of a late 12th century dating of the emergence of the Hebrews in Canaan dominates the field. It is healthy for objectivity to test how secure this view is by assessing criticism of, and some evidence for, an earlier date. Sometimes rational categories in scholarly assessment of biblical relations, to express it politely, operate as metaphoric uses, though this is not infrequently an unconscious or at least an unacknowledged tendency. It extends to the ways in which literary categories are merged and I argue incorrectly distinguished, and historical domains are conflated with literary histories.

One move to refresh this debate is to scramble the battle lines, and accords the marginal a central place for argument. This is not solely a concession to improbable scenarios by which to secure equal opportunity for free speech acts. It is not impossible that the following is an accurate characterisation of some established positions. First, many senior scholars mirror the presuppositions of those who appointed them, though there is sufficient dissent to obscure to what this degree this obtains. Secondly, these presuppositions are thereby assigned roles of high probability that refined empirical analysis could not justify. Thirdly, possibilities outside the scope of, and therefore in competition with, these presuppositions are accordingly demoted to low probability. Fourthly, this third device is inaccurately interpreted so as to confer such a status as 'contrary' on the relation between established presupposition and marginal option. Fifthly, points one to four happen, in complex ways, to coincide with, or mirror, dominating cultural paradigms upwardly mobile trends.

Clearly these points have different realisations in different cultural contexts. These manifestations tend to have discrete sets of oppositions that replay the points, though opposed schools of thought tend not to even out by sharing marginal and central presuppositions. Certainly this stylised account has exceptions: randomness indeterminacy are also functions of cultural order (Gibson, 2000b develops this concept). Rather, the foregoing five points are intended as a model of tendencies, among other factors. Furthermore, it is evident that in the situations where the five points operate at some levels, this is not itself evidencing the merit of a theory external to their scope. So, for example, the dominance of the Iron Age date against the Bronze Age date, favoured in this book, need not be a product of these points. Rather, the type of realisation the points may enjoy empirically, even in a weak form, complement a deconstruction of arguments and data in ways unfamiliar to us. Just because some hypothesis has been associated with marginal or governing presupposition or person should not count as part of its conceptual identity.

A conception of analysis that should be added to this (advanced elsewhere in Gibson, 1981, 1998b, forthcoming a, c, e) are, the idea of counter-intuition (see above pp.10, 77-78, 84), and the notion of a misleading working approximation or counterfeit (see p.161). Obviously, the latter term is not presented so as to suggest that that term incorporate an intention to deceive. We all operate with approximations that sometimes turn out to be different from our assumptions about them. Rather, the issue is, is the assumed degree of accuracy for a function different from the actual function to the degree that we are incorrect to suppose that our explanation is confirmed by the data. This may be a matter of unexpected micro tuning. Perhaps we present a banknote to a bank, under the impression that it was issued by the legal fiscal source marked on it (while possibly registering a query about that source's own confident use for it of 'In God we Trust"), only to discover that it is a counterfeit. It will have been true that we rationally trusted to our capacity to observe it as evidence of the genuine thing. And it will also be correct to conclude that we had inadvertently trusted in a counterfeit (even if we had queried the source's assurance of its divine reliance). In other words, if we do function as rational beings even at the relevant given spacetime, we and the data have dispositions or propensities to assume that things are as they are not.

My point, however, is not baldly merely the upshot of the five points. It also covers the idea that, because of this state of affairs, we are far more prone than we think to assigning confirmation and conceptual self-evidence to our own concepts than evidence and reason permit, especially in contexts of dispute. (That counter-intuitive states seem to be entrenched features of new science in some areas (see Gibson 2000a), supports the prospect that the present remarks may reflect states of affairs generally, and in certain spheres of science.) Consequently, we have even more of a disposition to assign disconfirming properties to those choices we are not disposed to adopt. In the light of this, it would be safer, of course, for the present author now to say nothing. Presupposing that this would be less boring than giving the reader further opportunity to disagree, the author continues to be at risk.

D.B. Redford's (1992) *Egypt, Canaan, and Israel* has attracted controversy (see Rainey 1995, and Redford 1996). Its study of 'the Joseph story' has the merit of treating the narrative as a candidate for singular authorship. It proceeds immediately to use this as a ground for classifying the Joseph story as non-history. To be sure, if none of the narrative is historical, one would wish to recognise this, but confusion of the significance and implications of literary analysis are not *the* helpful relations and devices to achieve this. Of course, Redford does not present matters in this way; he proceeds by autocratically presupposing questionable distinctions as if they are self-evident truths in literary criticism and in its relation to theological motifs, though varieties of literary research know nothing of such dogmatism. For example, the preference for a generic 'god' terminology, and other features, are supposed to contribute to the 'placelessness' of a dehistoricized novella, though no proof is offered. There is no logical connection between such a proposed element and the use of 'god'. And, in any case, the whole narrative is explicitly set in Egypt. So Redford's attempt to foist placelessness on the story is contrary to its identity. No explanation is given as to why the Genesis theme might presuppose other obvious reasons for embodying the avoidance of generic theistic terms; of which there are many. For example, it may simply be a function of the desire to generalise the theme for applicability to any who would accept a deity, rather than the covenant YHWH; or it may be that the theme stresses the absence of a generic focus because of the Hebrew people's or the brother's situation, or their trial, etc. Redford (1992: 423) remarks that, 'admittedly, as the story is now placed, it takes place in Egypt; but the basic shape of the plot does not demand a Nilotic setting'. His style is one of innuendo, when instead explicit analysis and reasoning are rationally required. He side steps the problem, while conceding a mere fraction of its size.

Redford has offered the judgement that 'the Joseph story' is a product of a single author, 'and few extra-biblical works can rival it for excellence of style and composition. The story is constructed around a beautifully turned and symmetrical plot that displays a unity and integrity that bespeak single authorship' (1992: 422). So why use the assumption above, namely: 'as the story is now placed'? No explanation or justification is given for the suggestion that this placement is 'now'. 'Now' as opposed to what? We are not supplied with the answer, except for the inexquisitely oblique, 'it takes place in Egypt; but the shape of the plot does not demand a Nilotic setting' (1992: 423). Redford's '[it] takes place in Egypt' clearly falsifies his claim of 'placelessness', yet he writes as if this is mere whim by overriding it with 'the basic shape of the plot' and its not having a 'demand' for placement. No proof is offered for this, only policy assurance which are internally contrary. There are no criteria in literary analysis reproducing or implementing Redford's judgmental terminology. So we are supposed to accept this series of opinions as authority for their truth. Whatever function this ruling term 'demand' is supposed to have, it cannot extract its purported role from Genesis since Redford has admitted that the story actually is set in Egypt. The use of 'Nilotic' is strange, falsely specific and over-determined: the 'Joseph story', is set in Egypt. Accordingly, the subject has the geographical Nile as one of its components, and therefore it cannot logically, empirically, or aesthetically have its placement-identity indexed as Redford asserts. Further, since the Egyptian Court, the dungeon, the royal administration areas, and Joseph's travel-patterns, in exercise of his diplomatic duties, are the domains of placement in Genesis, it is at least bizarrely peripheral to the story to invent an excluding 'Nilotic setting' at all, let alone as a criterion for seeming to falsify the story's own placement function. In short, Redford's eccentrically critical discourse subsumes a disruptive and irrelevant irrationality as an apparently orderly customising of the story for purposes of subverting its acknowledged identity. This is sad, especially since a deep deconstructed and reconstructed literary assessment of such a beautiful theme is urgently needed to expose relevant areas of its creative identity in relation to historical interpretation.

Lichtheim (1976: 203) notes the uncanny resemblance between the narrative of Joseph and Potiphar's wife, and the story of Bata and his brother's wife in Egyptian literature, which notoriously raises questions about the possible contact between the two literary worlds from which the texts emerged. Possibly the occurrence of Hebrew-like proper names reflects a Hebrew presence in Egypt which helps to account for the resemblance. Gardiner (1961: 157) observes that scarabs of the period, which may pertain to the foregoing, mention such Semitic names as 'Jacob-her', and finds he cannot reject the view that the patriarch Jacob is commemorated in this name. If this type of equation is correct, it may be extended and generalised.

Comprising a list of 95 slaves, the Hayes papyrus (Figure 4.1) is a record of people living in Egyptian, 37 of whom have Semitic names. Albright (1954: 222-53) identified a large proportion of the Semitic names to be Hebrew. Of course, one cannot prove that the bearers of these apparently Hebrew names were Hebrew; but the onus is on a disputant opposed to this view to present evidence to the contrary, since, for this period, non-Egyptian names appear to depict ethnic minorities in Egyptian. Although of course there were vogues for foreign names, yet where the context specifies bearers such a pattern does not seem to be present in the Hayes' papyrus. In any case, it would be a peculiar practice for Egyptians to name themselves after their slaves.

The name of one of the slaves on the List is 'Jacob'. The name 'Joseph' is also employed to indicate a Semite in Egypt during the period that Genesis presupposes for it setting (cf. Save-Soderbergh 1951: 53-74; Kitchen 1997: 68-69). R.J. Williams (1983) has shown that Semites, probably with named Hebrews among them, served within the Royal Court of Egypt in positions of influence in the time prior to the Exodus. Further, as K.A. Kitchen (1997: 68) points out, the name 'Abraham' probably occurs in local Egyptian dialect form (where *m* and *n* are frequently interchanged), in the Egyptian Execration texts as 'Aburahan'. The word *'prw* is used in Egyptian during and before the Late Bronze Age in the time of the Patriarchs, to designate a group living in Egypt in subjection to the Egyptians. There have been some problems over the exact sense of the equivalent of this Egyptian term. However, Cazelles' (1973: 25) distinguished research, drew on then hitherto unpublished texts. He concluded, albeit tentatively, that, 'The Hebrews of the Bible, *'ibr(iyy)im*, can be identified with the Hapiru of cuneiform texts, the *'prw* of Egypt and the *'prm* of Ugarit'. This judgement reversed the trend to dissociate the biblical Hebrews from the Egyptian *'prw*.

These uses and their plausible interpretations require one to question the confidence Mazar (1985: 58) expressed for a theory of the late composition of elements in Genesis in which he took *'bri* in 'Genesis, Exodus, and 1 Samuel to be pronounced identically'. This assumes that: (a) current scholarly phonology satisfies criteria for MT phonetics; and (b) that the criteria comprise implicit decision-procedures for all relevant ancient oral differences and similarities in pronunciation of the term. Rather, this batch of presuppositions is false. A problem with such a distinguished authority as Mazar obviously is, is that a quite imperialist style of presentation has an almost complete absence of explicit proof. Instead, there tends to be an in-house display of conceptual policy-networking loosely tied to overall opinions that are taken to be the 'information' to which one appeals. The general impression is of self-evident coercive certainty, supplemented by peer agreement. Closer scrutiny seems to reveal no unquestionable or proved basis of assessment.

The Status of 'Silence'

Sometimes the silence of a narrative—that is, the absence of expected items—may result in one losing track of the regress of premises that maintain a thesis, in relation to their contrary effect on a remote conclusion. For example, Redford (1992: 257) states, 'Of the latest and most disastrous migration of the 2nd millennium, that of the Sea Peoples, the Hexateuch knows nothing: Genesis and Exodus find the Philistines already settled in the land in the time of Abraham (cf. Genesis 26 passim; Ex. 13:17, 23:31). The great Egyptian kings of the empire, the Amenophids, the Thutmosids…are absent'. On the last point, only if Redford's ascription of the biblical Exodus to a late date is correct, does the 'pharaoh' of the book of Exodus cease to be a reference to a member of one of these royal lines; so his argument is viciously circular. Moreover, the absence of a proper name is not the absence of a reference to the ruler, and there are many references to the ruler of Egypt in Exodus. Consequently, at least within the chronological worldview of the Old Testament,there are numerous biographical and

Figure 4.1 The Egyptian Hayes' Demotic Papyrus

political references to that royal 'king' of the Egyptian empire. Therefore, deconstructed of its circular premises, Redford's account, chronology apart, is simply incorrect propaganda.

In addition, since there is evidence of Philistines in the land at the time of Abraham, how is this supposed to be a demonstration of the absence of historicity in the relevant theme of Genesis? Further, Redford does not make explicit a contradictory feature of his comments in conflict with his criticism of 'silence'. Although Philistines are mentioned by Genesis to be living in the Levant during the period of Abraham, there is no reference to them in Genesis for the immediately subsequent period, at the time in the eighteenth century when Sisostros III's military campaign led up into the Hittite territory. This and other data give some grounds for exploring further the notion that the Philistines migrated at the beginning of this period. So the absence of reference to the Sea Peoples after Abraham and before the earlier Bronze Age rather than Iron Age date complements this absence. Either way, the absence of reference to Philistines in Genesis for this period is worth more extensive examination, and to investigate evidence of narrative consistency—a neglected possibility. Redford also fails to allow for the consideration that a narrative's thematic priority does not have to extend to an ecumenical inclusion of worldview slices of its putative contemporary (and, for our extant) world's synchronic information as proof of the narrative's grasp of its own history.

The foregoing criticism implements a concern of what it is to be relevance-conditions, quite absent from Redford's study. Two factors in this perspective are the roles of focus and presupposition (see the researches of Rooth 1996, and Horn 1996). Semantic theory in these topics is variously concerned with narrative in an object-language, such as Genesis, and the distinct sphere of the metacritical status of a scholar's own language. Redford has no explicit logical descriptive methods or analytical procedures in either arena, and consequently he has no account of how the two domains interact. One is not expecting formal semantic theory of course, since this is not his priority. But there is no requisite attention to the pertinent distinctions. It would appear obvious that in Genesis we have focus-sensitive constructions (to theme, time, intended world-view collisions in perspective and truth-claims) whose presuppositions rule out as irrelevant the sort of material discussed above, the absence of which in the biblical narrative Redford alleges to be evidence of a nonhistorical genre. Redford has here incorrectly exchanged a presupposition of external irrelevant Egyptian historical material as if has to be a criterion, for the testability of internal Genesis-Egyptian presuppositions of focus. Certainly, the paucity of explicit Egyptian evidence for the Genesis Egyptian presence is a difficulty. But it is not the problem Redford construes it to be—that of the issue of absence, to be resolved by the straightforward presence of that absent documentation. Thematic focuses and presuppositions in competing histories (Egyptian material and Hebrew narrative) are asymmetrically and complexly related in ways almost totally ignored by Redford. Rooth's (1996: 283-88) helpful formulation of 'scope islands' of focus is applicable here. There are structural and quantificational restrictions implementing narrative concerns of focus. In certain contexts, an internal Egyptian perspective expands attention to a theme or concern, whereas the asymmetrically functioning Hebrew narrative (partially matched with the Egyptian perspective) may operate focus and presupposition which reduce attention in narrative composition or editing to zero. Neglect of this Hebrew reductionism will simply result in a commentator confusing a focus eliminating internal irrelevance with his focus which is a fiction unrelated to the text's semantics.

Related to the semantics of 'focus-islands' is the way in which the absence of information in Egyptian and other texts or artefacts corresponds to a presupposition in, say, Exodus. It is helpful in this respect to discriminate between two senses of 'silence' teased out by the following statements:

(a) Absolute historical silence where there is no original historical event or artefact in Egypt that is parallel with the Old Testament's proposal.

(b) Ignorance of the initial original historical situations produces a gap in Egyptian history at the point where the Old Testament depicts some state of affairs.

(a) and (b) clearly often resemble one another, since it is frequently impossible to obtain exhaustive explanation of the actual Egyptian history. The archaeological theorist Jean-Claude Gardin (1980: 5-120) warns against hasty attribution of falsehood to a text in such a circumstance. It is profitable to employ some of his terminology to display the issue. Parallels are highly theory laden interpretations which require unpacking into physical data, events or functions, the explanation and historical inferences which are assumed or merged with these series of analytical factors. Such a complex type of analysis assumes a conceptual grid (which can be presented graphically) into which biblical claims are placed. The Egyptian data that are expedient to match Old Testament narrative claims occupy confirming or justifying slots parallel with the biblical propositions. It is inconsistent to infer from an empty position in Egyptian data that the allegedly corresponding slot occupied by another (say, biblical) proposition is thereby false (on inconsistency, cf. Gibson forthcoming e: 35-38). The absent material leaves a vacant slot that is to be represented as a conditional question, not an inferred falsehood.

For example, when Dothan and Dothan (1992: 205), in their valuable review of Philistine excavations, assert that, 'There is an anachronistic reference to "the land of the Philistines" in Exodus (13:17-18)', this ascription of chronological deviance rests on a complex group of presuppositions whose antithesis needs more explorations than has hitherto been offered. What if, in the turmoil following Thutmosis III's death, some Philistines regained control of a portion of territory, perhaps returning from Crete or Turkey, or, in attendance as vassals of Egypt, took advantage of other external pressure on Egypt from the North and East? Or, on another scenario, what if the term 'Philistine' was not an attempt to index the then contemporary ethnic grouping, but an ossified use derived from an earlier, then redundant, ethnic label? (I return below to the question of the Philistines in Canaan.) At every point, such possibilities are pertinent to a final judgement of nonhistoricity and/or anachronism, even before we attend to the ironic use of language in socio-political and religious contexts that also employ in such irony collision of historical categories and functions. These matters are far more unresolved and complex than many surveys and speculative deconstruction, as well as conservative reactionaries' histories, allow.

Sometimes there exists extant indirectly relevant information that can affect the assessment of this type of perspective, which might be neglected. This category is akin in some ways to that of a mathematician's indirect route to a solution. For example, in many areas of proof in logic, it is not possible to mount a challenge to achieve a direct interpretation to resolve a problematic topic. This does not entail that a solution cannot be obtained by an indirect assessment; nor does it have to imply that an indirect proof lacks consistency or provability. On occasions, there is a deep elegance and counter-intuitive significance in such indirect methods. The solution to Fermat's Conjecture was an example of an extremely tricky indirect set of complex methods that yielded, finally, a solution in the face of apparent contradiction to the very presupposition that there is a proof. This reference to Fermat's Conjecture (cf. Singh 1997) is not to suppose that analysis of the ancient world is either of the same order as proof in this topic, nor is it to assume that a slice of the ancient world is susceptible to the same sort of strong proof as mathematics. Rather, it presupposes that one should allow that a messy proof procedure is not necessarily evidence of proof in a mess. Since mathematics is a sort of paradigm instance of proof, it is worth our here noting that it is too easy for a scholar of the ancient world to conclude that the idea of proof or rational demonstration for remote epochs involves 'proof in a mess'. Not so: a messy proof can contain fine rationality. Moreover, just as a standard value for a 'metre' will rarely be conformed to in practical areas where it is presupposed, *that* standard should be made explicit. One should agree, however, that this parallel, of a standard value for scrutiny of an ancient text, is less helpful than Fermat's Conjecture, since the latter requires extremely complex, sometimes experimental routing of hitherto unknown procedures. As a live metaphor for the complicated and messy interaction of multiple disciplines comprising Near East studies, this parallel is helpful as a pattern of rationality. No doubt, in the course of developing such proofs, sometimes by intuitive moves, and incorrect and valueless sequences, we should aim to isolate and avoid confusing arbitrary opinion and conceptual ideology with reason, as well as misconstrued or neglected data. Quantification and regulated generalisation of such matters is a function of incomplete knowledge that can mislead us.

The ancient alteration and destruction of annals and domestic records are variable types of such a state of affairs. Redford (1967: 52 ff.) has given some attention to this sphere, usually as a strategy in his dehistoricization of the Old Testament. Yet he does not offer a reconstructing analysis quantifying the positive arguments in favour of historical biblical reconstruction of the relevant material. Quantified qualitative analysis of the destruction and defacement involves a form of counter-intuitive retrojection that is subject to problematic and unpredicted variables. The topic of quantified analysis in relation to qualitative description and inference is a complex arena with disputed issues. As Stephen Shennan (1997) argues, there are ways of harmonising interests and emphases here. Quantitative analysis should be given due weight, while some of the problems discussed in the present context concern the ways that Redford neglects to provide all the relevant quantitative data, with the effect that aesthetic and evidential aesthetic interpretations are skewed by absences.

It is incautious as well as evidence of a fallaciously formulated project seemingly to entail negative conclusions from the absence of data, especially if there is proof that the data have been infected by ancient subjects or players who manifest the contradictory of the hypothetical data. Relying on official Egyptian annals for Hebrew information is like inspecting Swiss banks for Second World War gold teeth. The aesthetic of this is a simile just questionable enough properly to disrupt our composure, subsequent to our assuming we are sufficiently critical to recognise the invisible.

The case of Thutmosis III's erasure of his mother-in-law's and uncle's names, and other alterations of inscriptions (as in Figure 4.2) are striking instances of an imperious violation of the representation of the past. Thutmosis rendered his past history fictional in the interests of doctoring his image, relations and relationships. As Redford (1967) himself shows, this type of alteration is systematic. If the presupposition of the book of Exodus is in some form accurate—that Moses held a function and relationship in the Egyptian Court, and especially if Thutmosis III pharaoh was ruler—then this ruler, or even another pharaoh, would have had special reasons for wishing excise any reference. In particular 'Moses' indexed a biographically proximate namesake who had competed in some way (not necessarily documented by Exodus), with public success, to demolish Thutmosis's own 'image' and reputation.

Figure 4.2 Queen Hatshepsut's cartouches, replaced by those of Thutmosis III's

Literary research of Exodus has regularly eclipsed exploration of possibilities of an empirical basis for narrative polemics and ideological conflicts in relation to Egyptian royal political and military biography. We have only a little developed investigation of what the criteria for identifying and mapping such possible literary historical structure might be, especially where the function of imperial censorship has (possibly) written out one side of the history.

Other pharaohs of this epoch, for example Amenophis IV (Cf. *CAH*, Ch. 19), practised the same 'art' of historical 'editing'. So a possible source of important records concerning these pharaohs is sometimes destroyed by their peers or near-contemporaries. Redford (1973) has documented this activity respecting the temple of Osiris at Karnak; Porter and Moss (1982: 148) studied the extensive damage to Thutmosis III's funerary temple at Thebes (see Figure 4.3). There were some names found in his tomb at Biban el-Motuk (Winlock 1948), and these are probably Hebrew. Accordingly, I argue that there is a probability, of higher than half, to take consider in this controversial period and royal context. It affects the functional identity in inference and significance for the function and degree of silence concerning the thesis of Hebrews in Egypt (for this use of 'probability' see Gibson forthcoming e). And there is need to construct a new theory of a concept of Egyptian internal and foreign policy propaganda before we can adequately continue to quantify the distorting function of the erasure of Hebrew traces. If we position the purported escape of the Hebrews from Egypt, selecting even a part of their portrayal in the Old Testament, taking it in some way to be an empirical possibility, then the political and theological import of such a revolutionary breakout would be exactly the type of situation which Egyptian officials were not pleased to preserve or at least record objectively.

Molyneaux's (1997) study of perceptual and visual presuppositions in late 18th-dynasty Egypt cautions us about the invisible effects of ideology. He cites Baines (1989: 132), who states: 'official ideology presents human action as royal; humanity is almost excluded and its position in the scheme of things poorly understood'. Molyneaux (1997: 110) adds:

> Such political misrepresentations of cultural life do not allow for the possibility of alternative points of view. This omission is important, as Baines (1989: 11) observes, because it should not be assumed 'that state-imposed burdens were universally accepted.' And yet, finding evidence of resistance to the state in official art seems impossible.

These functions of ancient Egyptian censorship should be introduced as central defects in the case for the internal Egyptian absence of evidence as disproof of Hebrew dissent and emigration, prior to one's attempting to quantify the significance of the absence of evidence for elements in the Exodus narrative. Since, according to Molyneaux's view

Figure 4.3 A sculpture of Thutmosis III, defaced by a later pharaoh

degrees of distortion and omission by the Egyptian hierarchy are often undecidable; yet obviously massive, it is incoherent to assume the probity of a demolition of all evidence for a Hebrew presence in Bronze Age Egypt in the context of an almost totalitarian control by Egypt of depiction of its social and political history, and other factors (discussed in Chapter 5 below). Since Egypt's own dissenting citizens, scribes and artists were not allowed to be portrayed, nor question regal authority's disagreeable past, then it is very unlikely that foreign slaves, who confronted and violated Egyptian religio-political traditions, would be recorded. (Cf. Gibson, forthcoming e, for an account of generalization relevant to the foregoing).

General and Specific Evidence

A specific piece of information may have only illustrative general value as support for interpreting a narrative. This is the case with the well-known wall painting at Beni Hasan: it depicts 37 Semites with laden donkeys entering Egypt, and it is usually dated to around 1890 BC; it is frequently employed to represent a family 'like Abraham's'. It has been proposed that they are carrying lead sulphite, yet this has been objected to by claiming that they came not from Canaan, but from the Red Sea, because lead sulphite was mined there. This ignores the point that lead sulphite was mined elsewhere, and in Canaan (Forbes 1965 and Oppenheim *et al.* 1970). So the ascription of lead sulphite leaves a possible causal relation between the painterly subject and Canaan. This is an unconditional association with Semites going into Egypt at the relevant time-point for the link with patriarchal narratives, though it does not precisely fit the date presupposed for Abraham in Genesis. The data exhibit necessary yet not sufficient conditions for the historicity of the relevant narrative information.

Even so, the specificity of this sort of evidence increases the causal probability supporting the historical relations in the narratives. The weighing of such data is cumulative. For example, Kitchen (1990: 635-43) publishes for the first time the contents of a Middle Kingdom stela about 1760 BC held in the Brazil Museu Nacional. This stela, part of a collection with similar intriguing data, has at least three, but probably four, West-Semitic personal names, which are probably Hebrew, of workers who appear to be stonemasons. The transcription of one name as Twti is almost certainly 'David'; another *'pr* (= 'Eper', as with Gen. 25:4). In the stela, the latter's mother is said to be *'ibi* which is well attested in Egyptian among Semitic slaves. The stela thus has specific evidence of a Semitic presence in the period of the patriarchal narratives, which combines well with the Beni-Hasan painting. This is characteristic of many other pieces of evidence which undermine the use of an anti-historicist 'folk-lore' literary motif after the manner of Van Seters, incorrectly used by him to dislodge the probability of a historical ontology for some patriarchal elements. As Clements (1977: 90-92) observed of Van Seters' book *Abraham in History and Tradition* (1975): 'in its evaluations and methodology it is noticeably oddly balanced...its polemical tone and tendency to assert rather than to set out a careful balancing of arguments become noticeably self-defeating'.

Purely Literary Grounds?

In view of these sorts of interrelations between narrative and history, a purely literary approach to the assessment of the patriarchal narratives should be questioned if employed to deconstruct historical claims. Van Seters is typical of one approach in this perspective, in which the neglect of historical and archaeological information is combined with a particular set of assumptions about repeating patterns. This type of claim proceeds by noticing that some of the patriarchal narratives depict, for example, the separate but similar themes attached to the Genesis characterisation of Abraham, Isaac and Jacob going into Egypt and returning to Canaan. The argument builds on the parallels between stylistic motifs in each account that are attached to these figures. Such an argument then concludes that, in view of the repetition, the motifs are literary and not historical.

Since history, and not only literary fiction, contains many such repeating patterns, where famine, displacement, migration, and not least the agricultural economics of local topography, impose repeating strictures on populations which provoke similar reactions in different times, it is incorrect to infer nonhistorical status from the recurrence of phenomena. The conjunction of narrative patterns with specific and general historical data that satisfy criteria of identification respecting the narrative's presuppositions is tautologous with a causal link between theory and its testing data. Consequently, this conjunction has the force of a causal explanation with a supporting inference about the historicity of elements in a narrative.

Such evidence can be derived from a number of narrative directions and historical relations. For example, the above cited examples of Semitic names in Egypt are matched by names being found in Canaan written in Egyptian hieroglyphic, some of which are Hebrew, in the time-period proposed for the patriarchs (see Giveon 1976: 127-34). At Tell Kabri in western Galilee, in a tomb occupying the latest phase of the Middle Bronze II, two scarabs with this type of inscription have been found, and documented by Kempinski (1990: 632-34). The name on the two scarabs is 'Yakubum', and this name with variant forms is known to occur on some 17 other seals. It may be too much to link this with the Hebrew 'Jacob' (with mimated ending), though there are a number of Semitic verbs from which one can derive the name. In whatever way one wishes to construe these data, the scarabs typify a large group of data that complements Semitic elements in Egypt, by indicating the influence of Egyptian–Semitic associations in Canaan in the pertinent period which are neglected by the prioritising of literary motifs in the absence of historical analysis.

Of course, there are many other issues to examine that will contrast with the facets of analysis being discussed here. But a modest upshot of the foregoing is to notice that the relations between relevant features of the patriarchal narratives and Middle East history undermine a literary perspective which neglects this conjunction by presupposing the explanatory priority and historically reductiveness of literary patterns.

An Egyptian Parallel with the Plagues?

The occurrence of a parallel between two texts does not entail a causal relation of dependence between them. Nevertheless, when a complex group of literary interrelations and terms occurs in two texts, the probability of their having a direct causal relation increases in proportion to the shared incidence of terms and collocations of expressions. Accordingly, a non-chance link of complex senses between the Ipuwer text and the Exodus plagues' narratives supports causal probabilities with explanatory power. (Concerning the formal analysis for this type of reasoning, see Mellor 1982, 1995).

Even if there is a correspondence of dependence between the two texts, this may be a complex one, and not simply a relation of quotation. For example, one might agree with Parkinson (1997: 166) that the poem below is not historical—but in the version we have it is in the style of its first or some early institutionalised typical contextualizations. This is no bar to posing for the Ipuwer text a radical rcontextualization that historicizes it for hebraized application at a later (Late Bronze Age) date. Consider the possibility, then, that the Exodus Egyptian plagues' narrative re-uses and transforms an earlier Egyptian prophecy of doom composed, let us assume, at a time of cataclysm in the 6th dynasty. The functional load that the Exodus' narrative could carry in such a derivative relation would be highly allusive and prone to misconstruction. It might be misinterpreted as a set of two contemporary texts each representing one state of affairs, or the priority of dependence might be inverted.

Below there appears a set of quotations from the text that might be a candidate for this type of complex counter-intuitive parallel. The linguistic context of the Egyptian text need not be parallel with the context of the alleged parallel in the book of

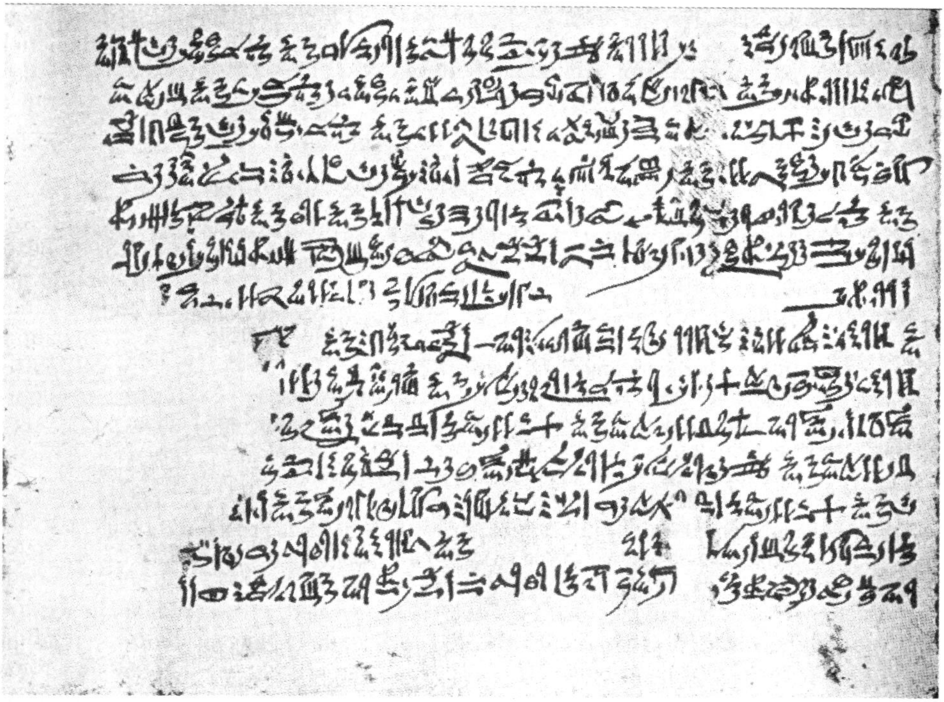

Figure 4.4 The Egyptian Ipuwer text

Exodus, for there to be a parallel, since the presuppositions of the Egyptian and Hebrew genres are dissimilar to one another in many ways. The quotations cited below are from the Egyptian text, and they correspond to expressions in Exodus with the Exodus' reference being cited in brackets. The text is the 'Admonitions of Ipuwer'; the only copy is that dated by Gardiner to around 1350 BC.[1] If we assume a late Bronze Age chronology for the contextualization (either original, or later re-use), this text could date to the early Judges period. Ipuwer is speaking in a dramatic present tense customarily used to describe past events, as, perhaps, he looks back at the Plagues to warn the pharaoh of further judgements. Or, at the time of the occurrence of such doom, as a fulfilment. As, for example Parkinson (1997: 171) translates part of it (1.12-13): 'what the ancestors have foretold, which has reached [fruition...]'. He is presented as if speaking in the Court of Pharaoh (commencing at Ipuwer 2.10):

> Woe, the River is blood; people [still drink/]shrink from drinking it. (cf. Ex. 7:20-1)
> All animals hearts weep, cattle moan. (cf. Ex. 9:3)
> Cattle are left to stray; there is no one to take care of them. (cf. Ex. 9:21)
> The land is without light. (cf. Ex. 10:22)
> Woe [the great stronghold...], doors, columns, floors are consumed with fire. (cf. Ex. 9:21)
> No fruit nor herbs are found. (cf. Ex. 9:25-31)
> Woe, trees are destroyed woe, grain is ruined on every side. (cf. Ex. 10:15)
> The children of nobles are dashed against the wall...children are laid out on high ground. (cf. Ex. 12:27)
> He who places his brother in the ground is everywhere. (cf. Ex. 12:30)
> Wailing pervades the land, mixed with lamentations. (cf. Ex. 12:30)
> Behold, something which has been done which never happened for a long time: the pharaoh has been taken away by poor men. (cf. Ex. 14:28-15:4).

The last part of the above quotation could be construed as a euphemistic way of describing the death of pharaoh in the Red Sea at the hands of *'apiru* slaves (as Egyptian scribes may have couched it)—opaquely represented by 'poor men' (for which see Exodus 14:23-8). It should be mentioned that the few scholars who have given the Ipuwer text some examination prefer to interpret it as a late copy of what was written in an earlier period. However, this is not in the perspective of their finding a defect in an Exodus period application of the Ipuwer text. Some scholars are disposed

---

[1] Papyrus 344, Leydon Collection; published by A.H. Gardiner as 'The Admonitions of a Sage' (Gardiner 1900). An English translation of parts of the text translated in the present book is a modified form of that in Pritchard (ed.) 1969 and the translation by R.B. Parkinson (1997: 170-99).

to a 17th-century BC date (Kitchen 1997: 58), whereas others, for example Van Seters (1964: 13-23), prefer to lower the date; yet Gardiner chose a Sixth-Dynasty origin for it. There has been a trend to drop the text's date towards the Bronze Age. With the sole copy being dated by all to 1350 BC, theories about earlier as well as later dates are prima facie unstable. If such a date, as a context for authorship, were correct, then one would have a premise for developing Ipuwer as a direct link to Hebrew contact in Egypt. What if one were to agree with, for example, Gardiner's assessment and place some of the Ipuwer language in the Sixth Dynasty? It would be consistent to use such a view to interpret the extant Ipuwer text as a refined or reconstructed and expanded product of the more ancient source, allowing that it also contains evidence of its final composition. For the precedent of such a genre from the later Middle Kingdom, however, it is conceivable that archaic language was imitated in its composition *circa* 1350 BC. Furthermore, on this hypothesis, we would consequently have a text of causal metaphoric power evoking some of the events behind the final phase of the postulated Hebrews in Egypt. There is a puzzling reference (in Ipuwer 15.2-3) to, 'What is now happening to the land is letting the Syrians know how to govern it'. Parkinson (1997: 199) plausibly interprets this as a warning to Egyptians that foreigners are becoming aware of their troubles. The odd reference to a Canaanite location and the choice of the Egyptian for 'Syrians' here may mirror the theme Egypt's own Semitic slaves as a source of revolution. Such expressions as 'the land is without light' and the significance of its biblical context may reflect a common type of source as that of the *Tempest* stele (lines 8 and 12). Using the new Ritner translation (Polinger Foster and Ritner 1996), we have:

> The gods [caused] the sky to come in a tempest of r[ain], with darkness
> in the western region...a torch could not be lit in the Two Lands.

Polinger Foster and Ritner (1996) assign it to the time of Ahmose (1515 BC is plausible). Could the Ipuwer text embody traces of psychodrama, as an impact of revolution? If the degree of trauma memorialised by the Ipuwer text, or by the Exodus narrative, has *any* basis in ancient Egyptian experience, the role of countermemory, such as in Germany's postwar treatment of the Holocaust, could contribute to explaining the collisions and indeterminacy in, and between, the Egyptian Ipuwer text and the Hebrew narrative, especially in view of their the racial and class subthemes.[2]

---

[2] On countermemory in Germany, see Young, 2000: 90-151; my argument about the erasure of, or opposition to, monumental witness in Egypt complements Young's work. I suggest that Hacking's, 1998 account of transient amnesia in individuals could also be generalised, suitably qualified for the ancient world, to mobile or disrupted populations in biographical crisis. This approach could then, combined with a thesis about countermemory, apply to the above views.

Yahweh versus Who?

The narrative of Aaron's throwing down the rod which becomes a serpent (Ex. 7:9-12) appears to engage with a mythological polemic. The magicians' rods that transmogrify into serpents are devoured by Aaron's rod. Research by Keitel (1986) on the application of psychoanalysis to literature has some implementation in this sort of context. He notes the related functions of irony, opposition, and their psychopathology can be manifested in the form of communal irony manifested with protagonists representing opposed classes and regimes. The Exodus narrative appears to presuppose dynamics of conflict, which hinge on intertexual and iconographic symbols drawn from Egyptian religious and mythic history as well as its political usage.

The most evident of these are the allegorical functions associated with the pharaoh. Various interrelated identities for the serpent and snake motif(s) in Canaan associate by mediation or contrast with the serpent and cobra archetypes in Middle Kingdom Egypt. The uraeus symbol situated on the pharaoh's headdress acted as an epitome, and in certain focuses, an epiphany of many of these snaking identities. A cobra uraeus both contrasts with, yet is aligned to be in competition with, the Mosaic serpents. To what extent Near East writers consciously articulated clusters of these functions requires further study; yet the data above and below structure properties of the material which appear intrinsic to its basic semantic dynamics which were constantly the subject of reflection and modification.

The serpent motif condenses the Mosaic versus Egyptian priestly opposition into a conflict of mythic identities, in which the projected ego-symbol of one group is eclipsed by the Other. The uraeus symbol mirrors a facet of the goddess Edjo. In some exposition of the Middle Kingdom, Edjo is seen as incarnating an archetype of pharaoh, ruler of lower Egypt. This location associates with Semitic populations in bondage that is a subtheme of Exodus 7. The god's territorial function is challenged and his identity devoured by Yahweh's agency, thus paving the way for freedom.

The Ipuwer narrative seems to address an ethos consequent on this sort of invasion by proletariat usurpers of the uraeus, linking this to a serpent function. Although the intertextual relations are complex, it is worth reflecting on the Ipuwer text's representation of the serpent and uraeus:

> Woe, magic is exposed; exorcism spells and possession spells are made ineffectual because they are repeated by ordinary people...the serpent (guardian) is taken from her hole...men rebel against the uraeus.

The term 'uraeus' (*'rti*) mirrors the role of the cobra on the pharaoh's head-dress, and the related hieroglyphic sign for a cobra is prefixed to the word. The scope of the

Hebrew *naḥaš*, 'serpent', is wide enough to permit recognition of an allusion to a cobra motif, strengthened by the presentation in Exodus of polemics with the serpent motif in the presence of the pharaoh. In positioning this cluster of nuances, one should also recall the pharaoh as the manifestation of Ptah, an incarnation which has an iconographic emphasis with the uraeus on Ptah's forehead (from Westendorf 1968). So the Exodus narrative's use of 'serpent' is not mere magic, but it interweaves theological power-politics in terms of Egyptian symbolism, no doubt with a tonal pun on the sort of primal semantic field for 'serpent' which we find developed from Genesis 3 in the Old Testament.

From the standpoint of an ancient reader familiar with the Ipuwer text or its ethos and some of the elements in the Exodus serpent narrative, Moses and Aaron fill the typology of the Ipuwer 'ordinary men', who question the uraeus and the courtly use of magic. It may be extending the possibilities of parody in tragic inversion to their limit to notice that the uraeus passed to pharaoh's eldest son on the pharaoh's death. Only in death did he fully manifest Ptah uraeus, leaving it possible to suggest a connection between these points and the tragic arc in the Exodus plagues. Yet it appears that somewhere within the Exodus narrative, some such semantics are pulsing in the intertext and subplots, though it needs more study to assess these further.

5

Generalizing about the Exodus Journey

Vagueness

It is common to suppose that the type of account of the Exodus journey found in such texts as Numbers 33 is inconsistent, confusing, and yet has historical elements. G.I. Davies (1979) clarified some of the states of debate in discussion of the possible locations of the relevant proper names. In examining of such matters, it is helpful to articulate explicit criteria of a narrative's use of proper names, including concepts associated with being the referent of a proper name. Such analysis, carried out in a manner so as not to include unnecessary controversial theses about further issues of the identity of reference, contributes to prevent ignorance about location, being confused with allegedly vague 'named' identifications made in the biblical texts. An obvious but neglected point is that one's inability to identify a location does not enable one to infer that an alleged reference to it in a text is fiction. The vagueness ascribed to an item in a narrative may be a mirror of our psychological imperceptiveness, or the absence of extant evidence, or both. Davies (1979: 1) points out that the geographical emphasis on investigation in Numbers 33 has been pursued to the neglect of the text's formal characteristics. If we are to forefront the text's purported inconsistency, then we should acknowledge more readily than we tend to do that this could amount to the problem of our ignorance of history and of the inability to identify sites. As Gebel et Tih in the Wilderness of Zin (Figure 5.1) exemplifies it, there is an absence of empirical data which dislocates our capacity to determine space-time locations. So, ignorance of temporal geography should not be made a basis for negative inference about the nonhistorical status of sites or ethnic migrations.

One's ignoring the indeterminate relations between these two options could be due, in part, to a person's being unaware of or confused about two distinct things to do with proper name use. That is, the criterion of identity, and the criterion of application. These correspond to standard distinctions in logic, devised by Dummett (1981: 547-50)

Figure 5.1   Gebel et Tih in the Wilderness of Zin

further developed by Gibson 1998b and, to mark distinctions of major importance in the examination of proper names and (definite) descriptions. It is worth giving a rough description of these two criteria, since confusion over them crops up repeatedly. They will also lead us to expose the analytical mistake in the failure to distinguish between referring and referent. A criterion of identity, roughly, is a description that has to be satisfied by a proper name of a phenomenon, if the latter is to be referred to by a proper name attached to the description. For, example, in Num. 33:22, it states that the Israelites 'set out from Rissah, and encamped at Kehelathah'. A criterion of identity for Rissah could be 'the place n from which the Israelites set out at time t to Kehelathah', where n stands for Rissah. If the criterion is satisfied, and the conditions are fulfilled, n is Rissah, and the time t is a sign for the date. We need this information in some form just in case the subjects went to Kehelathah at another time, in which case it would be possible to confuse Rissah with some other place from which they went to Kehelathah.

Criticisms that some of the names are vague in the wilderness journey route could rest on misleading conflicting recipes, or just be unclear, or non-consciously held, suppressed premises. These views may confuse the difference between a criterion of identity and a criterion of application. Another example filling in a criterion of identity is, in the case of Kadesh Barnea, 'that proper name n whose location is x miles on the way to Shur (Gen. 20:1) and at place y on the edge of the wilderness of Paran and the wilderness of Zin (on the latter, see Figure 5.1; cf. Num. 13:26; 20:1), being 11 days' journey from Horeb and Sinai via Mount Seir, and where Miriam was buried'. This should not be confused with the criterion of application for the proper name Kadesh Barnea, which would just be the above quoted specification, with the x and the y replaced by the exact number of miles and the location, respectively. Often, these two criteria are confused as though they be one thing. A criterion of identity is the type of situation in relation to others. A criterion of application is the specific test for a bit of geography that enables one, hopefully, to discover the site. History is mainly concerned with the former; and geography with the latter. Conversely, a criterion of application is a specification of the condition(s) that we need to know to implement the criterion of identity. This criterion of application might take a number of forms: it could precisely describe the geography of the place Rissah and how to recognize it.

From the above, we should appreciate that the criterion of identity is a distinct use of a test from the criterion of application.[1] We may have the linguistic knowledge which defines or exhibits the relation of a proper name such as 'Rissah' to its description, but this does not imply that we also possess the criterion of application, nor even know how to form or implement it. For example, the place to which Rissah

---

[1] Sometimes in contexts not relevant for the above, the criteria can overlap or coincide; cf. Dummett 1981: 73-78.

referred may no longer exist. Now it is surely odd to regard it as the fault of a text that the place to which it refers no longer exists. The text may be perfectly well-formed in its using, or assuming, a criterion of identity. The criterion of application, however, may not easily be used to produce or yield the geographical location to which the name refers, because of a change in the state of affairs in the site or local knowledge of it. Again, this does not show that the text has been the host for some descriptive impurity because of an alteration in circumstances outside itself. Expressed this way, of course, the point is entirely obvious. If the distinctions are merged or neglected, however, the gap between criterion for site and criterion for identity is sometimes so obscure that confusion is a function of the interpretation.

Someone might wish to reply that it is possible for mistakes to be made, so one should not assume that the narrative has a properly formed criterion of identity. A name does not cease to exist by virtue of the cessation of its referent bearer. Consequently, the absence of a site is not a sufficient condition for a name to be finally construed as fictional. The criterion of identity is usually more readily satisfied than the criterion of application. [2] 'Rissah' is a case in point. Numbers 33 explicitly positions the term in relation to the other proper names which define its linguistic relation to them in the journey-motif, but the criterion of application is susceptible of different identifications. As Davies (1979: 87-88) points out, genealogical issues stand behind options, to procure Rasa as the referent of 'Rissah', whereas on another interpretation, following Koenig's hypothesis, Bir al-Qena' might be 'al Rissah'.

The second point is that those who neglect the foregoing distinction between the identity and the application of a proper name have conflated the two different criteria. They have confused the identity specified by the proper name in language with the application of that specification to the state of affairs referred to by the proper name. The criterion of identity is about the linguistic expression of the conception of the proper name. Conversely, the criterion of application is to do with the characterization of the geographical circumstances of the state of affairs to which the name refers.

Since proper names do not cease to exist when their bearers do (even in the event of our ignorance of their function) the referring that a proper name 'does' strikes a relation of reference with regard to the location to which it refers. It is important not to anthropomorphize this relation. A name's referring has an analogy with pointing, though this manner of characterizing it is metaphoric. We do not have to succeed in pointing 'down' the past to what a proper name referred to, for the name to have a reference. The relation of reference forever stands, if ever it did for a proper name, unlike predicates attached to the name. To miss this feature provokes the collapse of

---

[2] For Frege, see a discussion by Dummett 1981; see also Linksy 1977: 71-90.

the criterion of identity and the criterion of application into one muddled 'denoting', reminiscent of Ockham's two name theory, in which description, reference, intentionality and ontology are conflated (see Gibson 1998a). A consequence of this is that an argument fallaciously charges a text with a muddle over the sites to which its proper names refer, when, through no fault of the narative, only the criteria of application are unclear.

Loughlin (2000: 91) exemplifies how such confusion is also implemented concerning the associations of the putative referents of the names. Of Kadesh-Barnea he contrarily asserts two propositions, one after the other:

(A) "Surely, if this event [Hebrew "group *wandering* around a desert" – his *italics*] as described in the Bible actually happened, *something* of the presence of so many people would have turned up by now…"

(B) "My point is, such an event might have taken place, but there is absolutely no indisputable archaeological evidence to support such a conclusion."

This polemic has the anachronistic style of some past liberal versus conservative debates. Perhaps it is too much for one to have assumed that such distracting binary counterfeits had passed away; but beyond that appearance there are also problems. Given Loughlin's adoption of the role of neutral arbiter dispensing fair reporting, it is disappointing to notice that (B) is contrary to (A). Therefore it follows that Loughlin's argument is false. That is to say, if in (B) "My point is" involves the modal operator "might" being true (i.e., 'might' with the value of 'actually could be'), then Loughlin blocks the actual possibility of this by asserting that "something would have turned up by now". So if his "point" really is in (B) as a report of some feature of (A), then what he claims is false, since it articulates inconsistent possibilities. My remarks are not a skit on method. They concern the possibilities of history: what is a criterion of Loughlin's "*something* of a presence"? Notoriously, a traces of history are complex illusive properties. They do not always bear on them criteria of their users' identity. Utility is frequently a function that has no indexical criterion of a beare's identity, or satsifies a criterion shared by differences and different bearers. Subsequent generations re-use previous traces and discard them elsewhere in transformed states etc. Loughlin (2000) at least boldly presupposes that Loughlin has precisely the precondition for always recognising an instance that satisfies this. Accordingly, under the rubric of a seemingly harmless piece of prose, Loughlin insists on a criterion for an observation-condition that allegedly indexes the remote past, for a transient changeable climate, with a shifting sandy surface subject to desert storms, that seems so strong as to suppose supervenience that perhaps only an anti-Humean supernatural observer could satisfy; but surely, that is something just like what Loughlin was attacking: a description of history that exceeds (Loughlin's) natural inductive expectations. Consequently, in terms of logic he is relying on the negation of his claim to get it off the ground. Consequently, such jackboot-theorems are not the rational and tolerant means to policing the ancient past that they seem to be.

Ten Commandments and Law Codes

A more complicated series of interrelations than the foregoing item on proper names (but one that has a family relation to it) is the description of the Mosaic law in relation to its literary parallels. One facet of this topic is of interest for present concerns. What force is deployed in evaluative types of expressions such as 'law codes of this kind', 'contained many such concepts' and the 'first such expression'? The following type of statement occurs in scholarly discussions: 'the Mosaic law is not the first such expression of law; law codes of this kind existed prior to it, and contained many such concepts as those displayed in Exodus 21–23'. Terms such as 'kind', 'concepts' and 'expression' are (metalinguistic) designations which presuppose notions of class, the relations of truth and falsity to thought, together with a questionable assumption that 'expression' is a covering term only for one type of utterance. These terms occupy the slots involved in concept-formation, in relation to the linguistic conditions for distinguishing between what it is to be a representation of the same concept, and different concepts (i.e. interpretations) of the same concept (cf. Lewy 1976: 87 and *passim*). Such distinctions are fundamental for the identification and assessment of the status of what a concept is. The vocabulary for measuring such ingredients and concepts determines the legitimacy of linking two codified laws, or legal fragments, as paraphrases, expansions, or complex 'synonyms' of one another. But little attention has been given to this terminology or this perspective on the problem by biblical or Near East scholars.

Contenders for what is the, or a, correct formulation of what it is to be a concept, have composed a perplexing history. So long as we hold to a given interpretation, however, and explicitly signify our differing grasps of our uses of 'concept', then we can usually manage to control evidence and proof. But equivocation runs riot when we unclearly, unconsciously or falsely handle 'concept' (or terms having some such use in our analytical vocabulary). A main depiction of a concept is that it is the meaning of a statement or statements—a proposition or a series of propositions. Following various scholars, we might extend this formal notion to include other literary forms of representation. So on this analysis, a concept is a linguistic expression, not a mental phenomenon (this can be gathered from study of such works as Dummett 1978: chs. 7, 9, 11). Whether one picks out the linguistic or the psychological domains as primary for couching a 'concept', this does not falsify the conclusion that to equivocate over the two domains can be fatal for inference and accurate representation of both domains. Barr (1961) and Gibson (forthcoming e) variously show that such confusion was rampant; and the situation has not fundamentally changed in certain areas of research. Although there has been an acquiescent acceptance that such mistakes in analysis are incorrect, they still recur.

In short, it is worth holding on to quite basic distinctions, even in a research context. For example, a concept is not smaller than a sentence unit—it is not a word; it may be composed of groups of sentences. Kitchen has argued that, in Exodus, the structural order of Introduction, Commandments, Code, Stipulations (Blessings and Cursings) only finds parallel in the 14th/13th centuries BC. It does not have any complete parallels prior to this date, nor are any to be found in the 1st millennium. The earlier and later law codes are either fragmentary or different in form or both. This produces the specific 14th-century chronological context in which the Bible reports Exodus to have been written. One might interpret this correspondence of legal forms around the purported time of the Exodus and the Sinai journey in two different ways. First, it might be held that the Commandments and Law Code in Exodus rely upon these contemporary sources for structural form. This need not be construed as dependence, however. For it is structural form, not semantic content of a concept, that is here the topic of parallel.

For example, imagine a totalitarian ruler who develops a legal argument, to the effect that some Human Rights Declaration (HRD) is incorrect and incoherent, and he were to replace it with some alternative which nevertheless re-used the terminology of the Declaration, while subverting its identity as a HRD. It could only perversely or mistakenly be said that the ruler had depended on, or been relevantly influenced by, the Declaration for the new ethical content (as in Gibson 2000a). So could be the case with the 'correspondences' between Exodus and other contemporary codes. Although the Exodus Law is not an HRD, there remain many tasks for research on it and the Mesopotamian paralleled codes, prior to one's being able to measure the similarities and differences. Just as juridical scholars have enormous problems in representing and comparing distinctive traditions which manifest fundamental differences, so with the above ancient contexts. Research scholarship has yet to depict what a 'value' and what conditional inference are in these narratives, in the priority of having a determinate account of those functioning properties which may or may not lead to divergences of identity in relation to deontic and comparative jurisprudences. Even when these issues are clarified, we would still need to explore if the Exodus law might merely be utilising a common structure of the time to dispute a prominent ethical world-view expressed in that structure. In law and cultural cosmology, matters of detail are often crucial in producing a fundamental difference in conceptual identity. So the occurrence of similarity between the Mosaic Law and other codes is not itself necessary and sufficient evidence of relevant levels of identity between them. Nor can this form a basis to attempt to construct the implication that such data have to be recognised as influence or dependency.

A second way of interpreting any correspondences of structure, if the early date for elements in the Exodus were to be roughly correct, would be to propose that the Exodus Commandments and Law Code had been first on the scene with a unique ethical structure, which then was used as a structural form by the slightly later Mesopotamian Law Codes of that period. Even so, the structural parallels between Exodus Law and Mesopotamian parallels are not so complete as to be identical in structure, function; nor do they match in all or even most, details. In respect of these senses, it is wrong to maintain that the Exodus narrative could not be the first such expression of an original concept.

We are concerned here with terminology common to the Mesopotamian laws and Exodus. Occurrence of identical terminology in two distinct literatures is not evidence that there is a direct causal connection of influence between the two. A modern comparison highlights this situation. Portions of vocabulary in Marx's early writings are parallel with lexical items in the Bible. Terms such as 'Christian', 'holy', 'God', 'substance', 'Christ', 'Christians', and even phrases like 'God of the Jews' (Marx 1975: 70, 80, 219, 240, 239 respectively)). This usage is not evidence of Marx's dependence on the Bible for his ideas. Rather, Marx was attacking it; but he was also redeploying terminology to express his own counter-views opposed to common ancient cultural traditions which have employed such biblical terminology. Likewise, when 'eye' is used both in Mesopotamian laws (see Hammurabi Laws sec. 199) and in Exodus Law (Ex. 21:26), this need not imply dependence. 'Eye' (and sometimes the predicate fragment in which it is employed) employs a common expression to disagree with consequences that are drawn from, for example, a man's eye being put out. The Exodus record draws the consequence that such a man, if he is a servant, should go free. Contrarily, Hammurabi states that the servant stays, and instead such a person is given a bit of silver for his eye's troubles. Therefore, if a scholar has in mind the common vocabulary, and in particular its specific context in linking Exodus to Hammurabi as 'laws of this kind' (or similar expressions to be found in scholarly judgement), then such evaluation is thereby inconsistent because it incorrectly measures and conflates distinct semantic relations, especially concerning the presupposition of 'kind' and its differentiating functions.

On the other hand, an interlocutor may have in mind concepts, that is, at least proposition length expressions; this would also have to have an identical context for one to be able to imply identity of sense. The use of 'identical' here is strictly linguistic, not a pooled polemical employment of the expression. Just because predicate fragments and phrases are 'the same' (whatever they may mean, various as are its uses) does not entail that functional sense is identical in usage between two genres. In many putative equations between Exodus and Mesopotamian laws, the presumed identity of sources neglects to develop an explicit and/or functionally accurate notion of what being a quotation is. One would have thought that it would be obvious that it is not enough to discover strings of the same words in two contexts, though examples abound where such a presupposition is the only assumption that links two items in scholarly studies. The foregoing has argued that the concepts of what the two contexts are, are disinct presuppositions that need to be made explicit as functions of distinct identities. Their merger from one source is thus a theoretical possibility, not empirical description.

Not only do we need accounts of identity and synonymy which require further refinement in philosophy as well as linguistic theories (see, e.g., Katz 1996), the type of biblical scholarship alluded to above has no explicit treatment of these parameters. We require theories of irrelevance so as to gauge what is relevance. J.P. Stern (1992: 14-17) highlights the importance of the latter for a concept of how to judge that a criticism is inapplicable. The task here is to attend to concepts of opposition pertinent to measuring ancient language. In contrast with synonymy, there is antinomy. At the strong end of antinomic cases there are the usual forms of negation (contradiction, i.e. prefixing 'not' or 'no' to an expression), but, as the contrast reduces in presentation, though not necessarily in function, there is a range of what are termed negative polarity functions. For example, in a scholastic context, we might suggest that there are 'few' or 'many' cases of identity between Mosaic and Mesopotamian law. I have here employed quantifiers; but the same sort of problem occurs with the full range of antonyms, and when differing theses compete in distinct traditions over the senses of, say, 'just', 'wrong', 'guilty', etc. A problem for mapping and exposing these negative polarity functions is that such terminology does not often occur in a source ancient narrative, since polarity mapping is not its presuppositional focus. Such polarity mapping is often a presupposition of the thematic, contextual employment of language, rather than an indexical function marked by separate terminology.

Thus the absence of 'YHWH' from the book of Esther is a function of the book's sense. This is quite different from reading this judgement as if it was a claim that the significance of the absence of 'YHWH' from the book of Esther was that its absence has no narrative relevance to the book's significance. It would be comic if one were to invent the false claim that the absence of 'Ur-Dagan' from Esther has the same sense and force as the absence of 'YHWH'. Consequently, polarity marking of a theme's meaning or context may function in the presence of apparently minimal surface semantic evidence. In sum, the occurrence of seemingly identical language in Mosaic and Mesopotamian law may function as polemic with a negative polarity marking function, rather than operate to secure a charge of juridical similarity in sense between Mosaic and Mesopotamian justice.

There are expressions which reflect similar concerns, and employ parallel terminology and phrasing; but, as the above indicated, this does not prove the alleged connection. The form of a legal proposition is immensely significant regarding its conceptual relation to a similar proposition. What may be regarded as slightly different terms and ordering of parts of propositions, and propositional order generally, can make a difference not just of concept but of legal system. Phillips (1970) has exposed structural and semantic features in the Exodus record of the Commandments and laws. He shows that the Ten Commandments hold the position of ten premises that regulate, and are conceptually extended, in the Criminal Law of the book of Exodus. For this to be present in the two connected parts of Exodus 21–23 requires a high degree of internal consistency. Such consistency and associated properties are absent or different from Akkadian law.

In the semantics of Exodus 20–23, the Ten Commandments have the status of something comparable with axioms; ones on which logical systems are founded (Quine 1950: 72). Sometimes in legal traditions and their exposition, axioms are replaced instead by theorems in natural inference systems of logical construction, but axiom and theorem in these cases are usually taken to be inter-derivable; in Quine (1950: 72), axioms are treated as theorems, however. (Obviously legal and logical uses of such terms are not identical, though it is worth employing them to make the analogy explicit, *and* the stages at which their values diverge.) These axioms are parallel with theorems that also serve to illustrate the point. The point is this: construed as premises, the Ten Commandments occupy a position comparable with axioms or theorems. An axiom is a statement that is placed at the basis of a system from which other statements are generated or presented as its consequences. It is plausible to consider that Exodus has ten such axioms. This state of affairs is not found in any of the Mesopotamian laws in their attempts at legal systematisation. Some research in the theory of modern legal systems holds analysis of logic and legal forms as a principal interest (cf. also the old traditional approach of Wortley 1967: 366-69, etc.); but this logic relation is hardly ever pursued in biblical studies.[3] Current research needs to attempt some correlation between biblical law and features in logic. Clearly, following Rawls (1972: 150-53, and 1999: 315-17), we should make a distinction between 'rational' and 'reasonable' here, and allow for its regulating effects on the concept of precept in law. Rawls' profound work in these publications does not explore how this distinction connects with issues in

---

[3] W.F. Albright made excursions into this area; see Gibson 2000b: 'Appendix'.

logic and law. This is a project for future research that bears on how one should assess notions of causal relations between distinct juridical traditions, of which the Amorite, Hammurabi and Mosaic instances are problematic instances.

Early Mesopotamian Amorite Laws

For example, the Hammurabi stele, which is a final form discovered from a Persian level, requires further assessment. The provenance of its contents is obviously much earlier than the context of its discovery. Its status as a finalised abstracted composite version, which is not identical in detail or generalisation to the more ancient copies that are in fragmentary forms, is too readily compromised by equation of this stele, sometimes without qualification, as *the* Hammurabi code sharing its presentation with its source. Lambert (1975: 193) claims that a part of Babylonian and biblical law, which had been asserted to be an example of transfer, was in fact due to quite separate parallel lines of development, employing a previous common linguistic and cultural tradition. This tradition allegedly behind the two is sometimes said to be the Amorite laws. These are comparatively fragmented, however, and cannot serve as the source for the much more intricate and logically complex biblical Law in Exodus. What is more, on the basis of the hypothesis offered in Chapter 3 above, prior to the existence of the Hammurabi law, we find that the Genesis Abraham narratives exhibit a deployment of some of these early 2nd-millennium Amorite laws. (Kitchen 1997: 68ff. has developed something partially parallel with this line of argument, namely that Canaan had absorbed some of the Babylonian laws.) Of course, the circa 12th-century BC data of the final form of the Hammurabi law is well after the appearance of Canaan parallels, which presumably arise from the earlier versions of Babylonian laws. My own preference is to notice the early provenance for the Amorite laws on which parts of the Hammurabi forms are probably based, and position the Amorite forms as the partners of the Canaanite forms. If it happened that Amorites or others absorbed these phenomena from Genesis—if an early date for the relevant parts of Genesis can be fixed—or if the relevant part of its record is derivable from the time of its history, then these Amorite sources could be influenced by some form of the Genesis laws; and not *vice versa*. Even if this time-relation is inverted so that the Amorite sources are prior to the Genesis sources, it would not imply simple dependence because the fragmentary Amorite texts do not display the type of similarity of terminology, phrasing and systematisation which are criteria of legal identity in Exodus.

Adjacent to these considerations is some research of Finkelstein's (1969), who published earlier forms of the Babylonian laws than had previously been known. Some

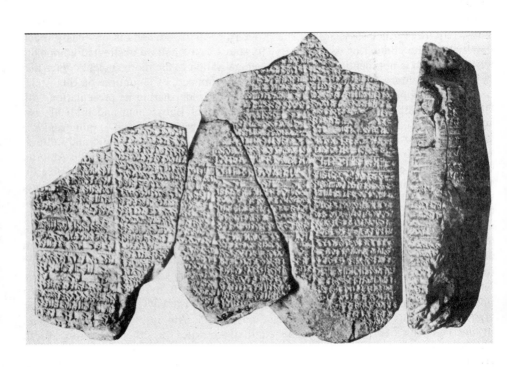

Figure 5.2   Amorite laws pre-existing the Mosaic Law

years ago in a personal communication, Finkelstein made the point that these earlier Babylonian laws portray a situation derived from judicial practice—case law, where *ad hoc* precedents were precursors of the Mesopotamian laws, foreshadowing later Mesopotamian codification of legal practice only indirectly.

An emphasis which is not often stressed in this context is that the most sophisticated Mesopotamian laws, which are matched as antecedents of the biblical narratives because of detailed similarities in phrasing and systemisation, certainly are the much later 1st-millennium versions in 7th-century tablets. Of course, these are late copies of postulated earlier forms and archetypes, and there are substantial series of parallels with vocabulary and cases in Exodus. Yet this does not justify the often-unstated presumption that the relevant earliest source is identical to the extant late form of the Babylonian legal code.

Another type of asymmetry between the Mesopotamian laws and the Exodus text which is frequently ignored is a detail which has importance for classifying the conceptual level of the two. One such example is the question of tense and abstraction (as in Prior 1971: 32; cf. 29-30). In Exodus, the conditional 'if' (*'im* or *kī*) is abstract with its associated verb (e.g. Ex. 21:2, 'buy', *ltiqneh*) in the future (or present). Conversely, usually the Akkadian laws are expressed in the past tense (preterite) in conjunction with the use of 'if' (i.e. *šumma*), though the Akkadian of Alalakh is untypically different in this respect (Giacumakis 1970: 52). Scholars often notice that this difference of tense may reflect the case-law background of the Akkadian because the tense advertises the practical background in the past in legal practice from which the laws arose as case precedents. If this accurately retrieves some of the relevant diachronic history, then the appropriate usage of the Babylonian conditional summa is tied to that origin as well. But in respect of the biblical language's future tense, with the Ten Commandments at its base, the conditional 'if' assumes the level of an abstract semantic item bound to a highly developed legal system within Exodus. Therefore the levels or status ascribed to the Akkadian and biblical laws are sharply distinct. The former is practical case law—in conceptual status as well as origin. The latter, in Exodus, is a refined conceptual, theistically-based system whose conditional inferences are relative to a different basis of rationality and ethical value (in the Ten Commandments) from the above mentioned Mesopotamian codes.

6

The Hebrew Conflict with Canaan

An Egyptian Province?

Many of the scenarios for placing elements of Joshua and related themes into other books in the Bronze Age are, to say the least, generally obscurant or highly improbable. I do not unqualifiedly advocate a Bronze Age chronology for such data. Rather, I suppose that the data and questions relating both to early and later dates are more complex, less firmly resolved and much more indeterminate, than the standard theories allow. This presupposes that there is an overdetermination of the functional status of theories, and an undetermined use of evidence. Clearly, a midpoint between such options is that there is an absence of the relevant evidence to close the gap between conjecture and proof. In such a perspective, it is not uncommon for scholars to interpret alternative conclusions as more determinate than they are, and to use interpretation as if it held the status of empirical evidence. Consequently, part of my strategy is to highlight possibly neglected areas by giving them an explicit assertoric role.

The importance of these priorities was driven home to me when Peter Geach described an encounter he had with Wittgenstein, standing as they were at the main entrance to Cambridge University Library, which is not unlike an austere modernist castle. Geach asserted to Wittgenstein that he had just discovered a small hole in the foundation wall of Frege's philosophy. Wittgenstein was vehement in his castigation of Geach: 'it is only worthy to attack an opponent via the main gates; only a rat would get in through the moat, and that would not provoke the edifice to collapse'. Wittgenstein elsewhere added that it would be a better exercise for such a critic to argue for the case to which the critic or consensus gave least probability for viability. Why? This type of exploration could expose unexpected insights and obscured merits to the person who might be least likely to find them. Even for one to argue the untenable case can have the effect of exposing hitherto neglected facets of the empirical world. This can be of value to those critical of the nonviable hypothesis. Defending such examples of the unfashionable also places a question mark against consensus; in doing so, it queries what it is to have a correct, or most relevant, assessment of the role of a consensus for a given purpose. Furthermore, those scholars who dissent from a position which is defended with unexpected means can thereby benefit, since we are sometimes attracted to re-assess features of our own position. Just as those philosophers who argue that they can prove that we do not exist, are really concerned to use this device to trigger hidden grounds for proving in what ways we exist, so analysis in archaeology can make use of unpopular or improbable scenarios. Even so, the function of ignorance in relation to justified knowledge requires that we also acknowledge, again, Popper's (1972) dictum: the most unlikely things can turn out to be true. Although there are many differences between philosophy and the archaeology of history, our capacity of failing to understand that of which we have a concept is not one of them. It might just be that we have yet to understand the relations between Bronze Age chronology, the *'apiru*, and the Hebrews, as well as the historical relations between Old Testament text and tablets. The nonconquest scenarios, not least those related to migration and/or gradualist social evolution scenarios, have been given extensive attention over the last 20 or so years. It is empirically and analytically felicitous to have a perspective that stands outside of such normalised choices, and reflect on alternative possibilities, even if only as a test-bed for measuring and challenging the strengths of nonconquest theories. And who knows? Such reflections may discover fresh identities hidden in tradition.

Wimmer (1990) has argued that his review of postulated Egyptian temples in Canaan, which range from Old to New Kingdom phases, leads to the conclusion that these are almost invariably Canaanite places of worship, with untypical exceptions in Byblos and the Gaza Strip, though of course various Egyptian artefacts and evidence of influence were found in excavations. As Wimmer observes, this generalisation requires Egyptian architecture and/or Egyptian worship to be traced in the sites for a sanctuary to be termed an Egyptian temple.

Not necessarily in tension with this position, there is a range of evidence for military and administrative operations in Canaan involving Egyptians and others in close contact with Egypt. The main inscriptional resource for this is the Tell El Amarna Letters, documented in the edition by W.L. Moran (1987; 1992), supplemented by Izre'el's (1997) edition of those of the Amarna tablets of which Moran does not explicitly treat. Although the bulk of these predate the proposed Hebrew conquest of Canaan, some of the data are helpful as a means of indexing links with literary and historical phenomena, as well as complementing other data discussed below. At the risk of treating the self-evident as neglected information, it is worth reflecting on 'obvious' points here.

Figure 6.1   Tel El Amarna tablets concerned with *'apiru*

176   *Text and Tablet*

The references to the *'apiru* number over seventy in the Amarna tablets, and this is very close to the number of references to Egypt itself, which thus embodies a quantitative sense of the scribes' ancient political priorities in the extant Amarna letters. It is not trite to note that the semantic fields of these references to *'apiru* are generally close to those of Joshua/Judges. The range of descriptions for the *'apiru* runs from that of an alien runaway dog who seizes a city—in the first reference to *'apiru* in EA 67, to the last one in EA 318 where the term indicates powerful enemies from whom one needs deliverance. (Clearly, it is too easy to see *'kaleb'* here with its folk etymology of 'dog' in direct punning usage; yet have we grounds for excluding some oblique irony here, perhaps derived from historical memory, if the records relate to some actual history?) Such a spread of data relevantly manifesting the semantic themes of Joshua/Judges for the conjectural Bronze Age synchrony of these books is remarkable.

It may be too easy to dismantle the inferential function of these data by deeming the relevant compositional forms of Joshua/Judges (i.e. the earlier part of Judges) to a late Iron Age phase. After all, as I argue elsewhere, literary criteria are not always relevantly empirical, and they have massively fewer objective criteria of application than archaeological ones have for the appropriate groups of inscriptions. It is a peculiarly uneven priority to dissolve such an empirically based hypothetical connection between Amarna *'apiru* and biblical semantic fields because of a systematised conjecture about literary evolution. Someone may respond that this isolates only one possible link from other empirical arguments against a Bronze Age basis for a suitable range of elements in Joshua/Judges. Rather, it is appropriate to argue that this response is a circular argument, even if only as a strategy for a balanced research diet that does not engender illogical deficiency diseases. What may apply to link *'apiru* and the biblical Hebrews can be redeployed to some other arguments that purport to adduce an Iron Age basis for Joshua/Judges. The central problems here are: to what extent have we generally conflated interpretation with data, and in what respects have we promoted non-empirically or weakly secured interpretation (unstably attached to archaeological data) to become *the* history of the Levant? This merger, where insufficiently exposed, obscures alternative possibilities. I argue that such archaeology is too provisional in its state of confirmation to warrant foreclosure to other options.

Na'aman (1997) is a culmination and reversal of his previous research which contributed to the reconstruction of the range of Canaanite kingdoms in the areas of Palestine in the Bronze Age. Previously he had specifically used the biblical material as a basis for construction of the Canaanite kingdoms. Now, having become convinced that this material was produced long after the later Bronze and Early Iron Ages, he has rescinded his earlier claims, and wishes principally to found his political geography of the system of Canaanite kingdoms on the Amarna tablets. Na'aman (1997) notes, yet does not evenly implement the point as a restriction, that we almost certainly have only a small proportion of the original Amarna archive. He argues that, because in any case it is selective and reflects one-sided socio-political bias, we can hardly achieve empirical certainty with this basis, though the tablets list most of the main cities of Canaan and some of their geopolitical concerns. Further, since the archive covers rather less than 30 years, this temporal window is hardly an opportunity for generalisation as a criterion of historical accuracy over the presupposed time-geography of Joshua/Judges. His proposal that Ashdod is Cypriot Enkomi, due to the former's absence from mention in the Bronze Age, exemplifies the inconsistent status of his reasoning.

This is typified, for example, by his use of such illogical arguments as: 'Since all areas of Palestine began to be settled in Iron Age I, it was logical to assume a measure of continuity between the systems of city-states and tribal allotments. However...I therefore withdraw all my former reconstructions' (Na'aman 1997: 601). He here states that it was 'logical to assume', but he employs it as a consequence—a conditional proposition in use in inference. Rather, an assumption is not itself an inference but a precondition for a premise. (An assumption may indeed be adopted as a premise, but this is precisely what Na'aman here bars from being an interpretation of his case by his use of 'it is logical to assume', which he states to be his consequence.) Accordingly, his reasoning confuses a conclusion with an assumption. So this is a vicious circle: his reasoning assumes that what is to be proved is an active component that makes the inference. This sort of logic is what Na'aman claims to have used to support a scenario for the probability of the biblical material as a resource for construction of the Canaanite system of kingdoms. And Na'aman announces that this earlier type hypothesis is untenable, so he has discounted it. Well, *it* would be untenable. But this is because of its fallacious form in Na'aman's presentation, not because of the internal properties of the empirical and narrative data, since Na'aman overlaid and suppressed the functional possibilities of the Bronze Age theory-construction by fallacious reasoning. Therefore, he has not deconstructed the possibility of a Bronze Age date for using some Old Testament narrative and other ancient data such as those at Amarna.

The detailed debate of the form and the identity of the Hebrew conquest of Canaan is somewhat adjectival to the present book's priorities, though it is relevant to its concerns to investigate aspects of the ruling paradigm which tends to dispose scholars to privilege certain diachronic models over others. Those who date the conquest in the Iron Age still recognise some close relations between the Joshua/Judges literary patterns and historical inscriptional information in the Late Bronze Age framework. This information was utilised by earlier scholars, and a few more recent writers (Mercer 1939 and Bimson 1978) to adduce the emergence of a Hebrew presence in Late Bronze Age Canaan. Herrmann (1985: 47-53), who questions among other things some of the grounds for the certainty asserted by scholars in some Iron Age scenarios, discusses the extensive list of territories and towns which remained inaccessible to the Israelites, cited in Jud. 1:27-36, and recorded by Thutmosis III. Given the criteria of proof required for certainty in interpreting the complex and incomplete excavational states of affairs in a variety of unexplored locations in what was ancient Canaan, and the way in which not only theological but also pragmatic archaeological presuppositions mould procedures that are employed to reach general value-judgements on the date, it is worthwhile considering possible features of an early-dating hypothesis to assess what elements in the refinable scope of an alternative conception could be.

One possible way of generating a new framework is to propose that early- and late-dating theorists have over-stated, and thus improperly polarised, two diachronically inter-connected groups of data. Let us call this the diachronic cross-benches view: the early date is accurate for an initial small incursion of Semitic aliens into Canaan, who linked up with Semitic residents. As Judges claims, it failed at that time to get off the ground in terms of the scale of success anticipated. In combination with this hypothesis, the late-date hypothesis should be deployed to delineate the quick Early Iron Age consolidation and growth of the Israelite settlement, with other alien Semitic elements joining the trend. Such a cross-benches view could incorporate the roles of the larger multinational groups of conflicts in which others were competing for, or relinquishing hold on, the same territories of Canaan. Within the ancient tablets, some such foment of conflicts advertises its own worlds of inclusive and exclusive relations which, as modern defence lawyers say, are entrapped in Old Testament narrative.

Some of the Amarna letters, which appear to interpret events around Jerusalem, have tantalising relations to the books of Judges and Joshua. For those who prefer an Iron Age date for the beginning of the Israelite settlement, they may wish to construe such relations as the later editorial absorption of preserved historical patterns in theological reconstruction of history. But if the thesis of a Hebrew conquest of Canaan is sustained (on either an early date or the foregoing cross-benches contention—which combines some features of early and late scenarios), then the temporal contiguity between historical documentation and Old Testament functions will be in evidence attested by causal explanatory power. Clearly, the structures of these relations would be uneven and reflect some of the presuppositions of the ancient compositions. The Amarna tablets concerning Jerusalem, particularly EA 280, 285, 287, 289, and 290, depict a state of increasing anxiety and finally panic on the part of those defending Jerusalem and its vicinity against attacks of the *'apiru*. These senders of the letters clearly want an urgent supporting response from their Egyptian lords, where presumably the 'king' is the pharaoh. Other proper names may have some importance, though their value should not be exaggerated. For example, a form akin to the proper name 'Joshua'—Yisuya—occurs in EA 256, line 19, in a letter from northern Israel, sent by Mut-Baḫlu, though the internal context is not ideal for use here; yet at least it illustrates a Bronze Age use of the name in a semantic field partly coincident with the book of Joshua.

The present study follows Cazelles' assessment of a close link between Hapiru and the Hebrews, while one should allow for metaphoric shifts in uses of the terms.[1] The scope of some tablets furnishes ample contextual criteria for this type of association. Consider samples from EA 289 and 290:

289: And now as far as Jerusalem is concerned, if this land belongs to the king, why is it <not> of concern to the king like Hazzatu? (11-17; cf. Moran 1992: 332-33).

290: the land of the king deserted [or, is passed] to the Hapiru... Let the king listen to 'Abdi-Ḫeba, your servant, and send archers to restore the land of the king...there are no archers, the land of the king will pass to the Hapiru.

This ancient source text collides, and does not read consistently, with T.L. Thompson's (1999: 150-51) statement that: 'the Palestinian highlands were plagued by such bands of bandits that ravaged and disrupted the trade routes... These "bandits" or "outlaws" (which is the meaning of the term *'apiru* used for them) were a recurrently disruptive force.' Contrariwise, it is the city, not merely routes, which the letters show to be at risk from military invasion and take-over. This is hardly the function of a bandit raid, plundering for transitory needs.

EA 289 also mentions that the pharaoh's 'nobleman' (as Cochavi-Rainey 1998: 105, translates *ir-pi*, contra Moran's translation 'official', on the basis of Egyptian usage) has departed to Gaza. This illustrates the point that, around the time of the continuing crisis, some leaders sympathetic to Egypt and Egyptian leaders, including army staff, seem to have made their way to the south of Palestine, mainly

[1] See Mercer (1939) and Bimson (1978: 19-20, 23). I do not presume that this term uniformly bears the 'Hebrew' sense throughout the Amarna letters. It could have had an ethnic reference, but at other times it was a metaphorized and emblematic motif for a group in the ways Canaanites sometime used 'piru/Ḫabiru. Even if the terms were non-ethnic, the above context in the Amarna/Jerusalem correspondence would still allow and support an equation of the terms with Hebrews on operational and contextual grounds alone. I believe that there is a punning mixture of both uses: first to the Hebrews, and secondly with an overtone (or tone) alluding to the emblematic sense applied to the Hebrews.

through the Gaza Strip. This is certainly not the expected reaction of the Egyptian super-power to something like Thompson's putative raids. Prior to this reversal, at the end of Thutmosis III's successes, just before 1500 BC, there were more than 200 garrisons in Canaanite towns, if we accept Egyptian records. Some time after Thutmosis's death, the situation changes. Eventually, the above types of attacks are manifest features of policy concern. With the Hittites pushing South and the internal strife in Canaan (together with the later instabilities, re-emerging for different reasons in the reign of Akhenaton), the Egyptian presence and influence withered. If we follow Giles's (1997: 235-38) sort of view, the Amarna tablets cover the period commencing about the last 12 years of the reign of Amenhotep III, the reigns of Ikhnaton and Smenkhkare, and the first three regnal years of Tutankhamen (excluding EA 16). On other views, the period of the letters shrinks to less than 30 years. So this Bronze Age setting is apt for the military invasion of the Hebrews, though both the Amarna, other sources and the biblical accounts present complex strategic and tactical profiles of successes and regresses, together with the intricate obscurities which fairly well-organised, civilised, yet semi-nomadic multiple groupings of aliens would readily provoke responses when variously opting for either peaceful coercion backed by the threat of violence, or a range of options including siege.

The worldview of Joshua/Judges concedes that there were territories that the Hebrews did not control. For example, Jud. 1:34-35 states that: 'the Amorites forced 'the children of Dan into the mountain...but the Amorites would dwell in...Shaalbim: yet the hand of the house of Joseph prevailed, so that they became tributaries'. The name 'Shaalbim' is rare; yet it occurs in an Amarna letter which appears to be referring to the same conflict as does Judges 1. In addition to this feature, a Semitic term for 'tributaries' is also used with the same sense in the Amarna letter, thus tying the use of the proper name to a particular type of sociolinguistic context that is mirrored in the semantic field of Judges 1. This situation can be exploited so as to furnish a criterion of identity which both Judges 1 and the Amarna letter satisfies. The proper name and common predication involving 'tributaries' yield this criterion of identity. (For 'referring' as a functional value of Hebrew, see Gibson forthcoming e: 49-50.)

Although this criterion is not a test to demonstrate that both texts record the same event, the criterion fulfils the condition that such a test would have to satisfy. So this coincidence of terms in the Amarna and Judges texts yields a principle of confirmation and justification for the usage. Judges presupposes the perspective that, while Hebrews did conquer parts of Canaan, certain areas were not conquered, were later surmounted with difficulty, or were not controlled at all. Such a perspective does not portray a simplifying mythological picture, but an operationally messy and sensitive strategic one typical of many war zones and policy games. In keeping with such a view, decisive battles are claimed for the invaders. At least one of them is suitable as a choice in its relation to the foregoing example of Jerusalem is *'Adoni-ṣedeq*. In Joshua 10, we read of the battle with the five kings, and that they are being conquered by the Hebrews. One of these kings is 'Piram king of Jarmuth' (10:3). Clearly, his territory is lost to the Hebrews as a consequence of their triumph and his death (10.23-6).

A hieroglyphic inscription, on the smaller Beth Shan stele of Seti I (Albright 1951: 24-32) communicates the claim that *'prw* now occupy Jarmuth. This latter name is a rare term, corroborated as 2nd millennium, with a specific context parallel with the text of Judges, and it belongs to a slightly later decade in the Judges' period. The hieroglyphic form in the stele for *'prw* has the determinative prefixed to it depicting a lion sign which indicates a warrior group. The stele records an urgent communication sent by the Beth Shan commander to Egypt. On the assumption that a set of the *'brym* in Joshua can be equated, even qualified, with the reference on the stele's Egyptian *'prw*, as referring to the same type of socio-political group, we have an added ingredient from within the Egyptian world-view which concurs with Joshua 10. The relevant part of the stele reports:

> This day, lo, Majesty [Pharaoh]…those *'apiru* of the mountain of Jarmuth
> with the Tiria arose in attack upon the Palestinians…

It is clear that this circumstance apparently produced by the Jarmuth attackers is specific in determination of reference and spatio-temporal function. It mirrors the type of state of affairs in which Joshua mentions Jarmuth while Canaanites are still ruling there. Nevertheless, as such, the stele's positioning of the conflict is closely related as a consequent type of event to the Joshua 10 military scenario that sketches the replacement of the Canaanite king of Jarmuth by the Hebrews. It is interesting that the very rare term 'Tiria' appears in the stele, since, in 1 Chron. 4:16, the Hebrew form of the name occurs in a genealogical sequence as a name for a relation of the tribe of Judah, perhaps marking a commando clan. Despite the incompleteness of such links, their typicality brings cumulative support for generating an expositional association with text and history. Another case of this sort connects with Jud. 3:31—significant in the present interpretative context—from yet another standpoint of Egyptian attempts to retain or regain Palestinian power-bases lost to the Hebrews.

This example depicts this part of the book of Judges as a political account of international contact sensitive to external strategic perceptions. Jud. 3:31 mentions that one of the judges 'was Shamgar ben-Anat, who slew of the Philistines six hundred men'. The Philistines sometimes, both in the narrative presuppositional world of Judges and in a range of archaeological textual references acted in coalition with, or as, mercenaries for the Egyptians. At the time of which Judges purports to write

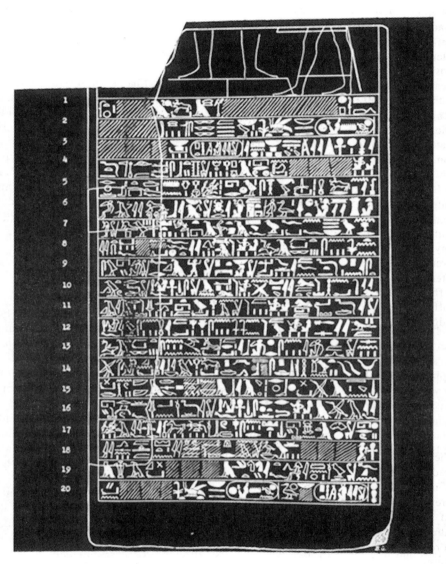

Figure 6.2   The smaller Beth Shan stele

apparently there were attempts by both groups to regain some land in Canaan. This example from 3:31 is there presupposed to relate to Beth-Shan where the stele mentioned above was originally situated, containing as it does a name and context internal to the scenario asserted in Judges. This set of interrelations highlights the closely interconnecting nature of evidence that can be selected from just one small area. Of course, we do not know about all the relevant areas; but the appropriate point is that the closely concentrated types of evidence indicate a rich set of interlocking explanatory features which complements the Judges historical presupposition and priority here. The often polemically motivated deconstruction of Joshua/Judges in such matters has not always been accurate to such a functional matrix of historically compliant empirical features.

An indication of a characteristic treatment can be cited in connection with the Judges 3 Philistine aspect. E.D. Oren (1973) published a detailed survey of the contents of a cemetery excavated at Beth Shan. The cemetery was associated with a Philistine–Egyptian garrison. Some Egyptian texts—found not in the cemetery but in Egypt (cf. Breasted 1906: III, 125-28, 214-48; cf. Moran 1992: 151-52, 117-92 and Oren 1973: 139-50)—can be used to imply that Philistines were buried in the cemetery after a battle which those in the cemetery, judging by their forms of burial, lost. The coffins have the characteristic Philistine quasi-Egyptian headmasks and mummiform coffin styles (Oren 1973: figs. 78-84). Oren's (1973: 50) analysis yields, in his judgement, the following connection with Judges 3:

> The foregoing data thus appear to establish the fact that the early coffin burials at Beth Shan belong to an early phase of military garrison manned by Egyptians and Sea Peoples...which was followed by a large-scale invasion by sea and land... It is not unlikely that a reference to the Aegean community at Beth Shan is to be found in Judges 3:31 in a report of a clash in the Galilee led by Shamgar Ben-Anat...and that the end of Beth Shan VII may be attributed to this attack.

The Jud. 3:31 reference to the Philistines comprises only a short statement. This may readily produce the response that it is a mere detail of obscurant concern and untypical of major trends in Canaanite history. Even so, the archaeological background which Oren supplies, together with the Egyptian historical records, indicate, if Oren is correct (cf. Yeivin 1971), that the presence of the verse in Judges is that of a carefully introduced selective assessment that typifies a significant category of military strategy in relation to the Hebrews' emerging political economy. Certainly, the Judges context presents its own anatomy of the perceived internal pressures on the Hebrews' identity, judged to be because of theological compromise. But all nations blend their theology

Figure 6.3   Philistine clay-anthropoid coffin found at Beth Shan

Figure 6.4   Woman's sculpted face on a Philistine coffin from Beth Shan

with operational assessment, as the Amarna letters themselves illustrate. The book of Judges introduces the above verse as an external structural feature that complements the internal state. It takes this to be a consequence of a failure in pragmatic ideology, which presupposes that internal justice can combat external threats. This is a thesis whose viewpoint is widely shared by political interpretation within most civilisations. Even in poetical passages in Judges one can isolate this type of focus, illustrated in the tribe of Asher's settlement at the haven of the sea (Jud. 5:17). On one interpretation, this may relate to a facet of the continuing Egyptian reference to Semitic Palestinians, on the chronology assumed above. Another of Seti's records, on his temple at Redesieh, refers to captive Asuru and the people of Megiddo; the former may allude to elements of the Asher tribe, possibly met in the type of raid documented in Jud. 3:31.

It is important to place Philistine/Egyptian/Canaanite relations in their international contexts; this is not the context to do this at length. However, in the priority of correctly positioning problems concerning documenting Hebrews in Egypt, as well as noting the need to provide a general historical and archaeological framework for the relations, we should not allow these matters to seem extreme and untypical compared with other contemporary Near Eastern problems. We are as yet quite unclear about the specific nature and scope of the Minoan Empire in the 2nd millennium BC. The possibility of the new site in Sicily containing evidence of Minoans, with the already attested Minoan traces on its pottery, is tantalising. While Arthur Evans was wrong about a number of matters, aspects of his contributions may have been underestimated. Probably there was a large unified Minoan empire, with considerable contact between Crete and Egypt. Reference to the Egyptian scribes studying the Cretan language (in the 34th year of Thutmosis III's reign) supports Philistine/Egyptian links that are developed in the foregoing (cf. Izre'el 1997; cp. Huehnergard 1989).

Egyptian/Hebrew relations are problematically intertwined with these and other international considerations. It might be worth offering here what is only intended as a preliminary conjecture; to be explored in future work. Although Minoan Linear A is not fully deciphered, most of the materials needed for such a decipherment are probably in the hands of scholars. Linear A is certainly not Greek, though Linear B, which is Greek, borrowed some of its sign system from Linear A, albeit in many cases with different values. Possibly Linear A is a product of a collision or engagement between Near East language and indigenous languages. The leather inscriptions found on the Gaza Strip and the Philistine anthropoid 'Egyptian' coffins are still problematic (cf. Brug 1985), though they appear to support the link, in the light of the reasonably high proportion of graphic similarities, between Linear A and the leather text signs. It would be unwise to equate the two languages, but a firm level specific direct relation is a probability. Of course, it would not follow from this relation that the Linear A script would have to have originated in the Gaza Strip, since there is probably a European influence on its emergence. Such discoveries of Cypro-Mycenaean script of Cyprus in the Late Bronze Age (see Dothan and Dothan 1992: 153), however, serve to point the way to the Aegean as a strong connection with the Philistines. It might have been influenced by Philistines or one of the many related grouping of Sea Peoples arriving in Crete any time from before the circa 1450 BC break-up of pre-Linear B Minoan Crete, after which there was some limited usage of Linear A. Of course, this picture is to be modified, for example, by the Sikils, possibly a 'Sea People' from Sicily, resident at Dor (see E. Stern 1994; cf. 1995), though this type of perspective itself lends support to an Aegean axis; and the occurrence of Minoan tablets in that territory enriches the equation.

Possibly some of the Philistines were returning to the Gaza Strip area as an ancestral home left by their ancestors. If this were so, Minoan Linear A on Crete, but not necessarily elsewhere, could partially derive from a Hamitic-Semitic language in this area of the Levant. Obviously, this hypothesis would permit pulses of change to modify Minoan Linear A over some 400 to 500 years, in both its sign-system and its semantics. If we were to continue the trend of dating the emergence of the Phoenician alphabet earlier to a period well before 1200 BC, a number of other considerations would also concur with suggesting the possibility that the sign-system, perhaps in some form not identical to Linear A, came from or derived from the Levant. Alternatively possibly, the import/export relation now attested between Ebla and Crete may have attended or succeeded some linguistic interaction, the remnants of which appear in loan-words, especially connected, for example, with the more refined aspects of the weaving trade.

Whatever the final solution about Minoan Linear A, its undeciphered state obliquely mirrors the same level of adventurous instability which attend our attempts to perceive aspects which interfere with theorisation about Philistine, Egyptian, and Hebrew relations, by which a more unified international understanding of the Aegean will contribute to restoring the map of relations between Egypt and Canaan.

City Hebrews in Evidence

A literary study of a narrative has a certain responsibility to review the claims of historicity in the text, even where the consensus is that it is a mixture of legend and historical information, since the narrative's ontology needs classification. The gap between concerns in literary functions and archaeology is often large, but archaeological discussion impinges on the assessment of a narrative's creative use of ancient historical elements. Consequently, although the interface between literary functions and archaeological analysis has asymmetries, it is worth discussing their uneven relations as an aspect of literary study of the Old Testament. The proximity or distance between the narrative and archaeological results will be a function of the Old Testament's use of counter-intuitive historical realism or fantastic realism, as well as a scholar's own presuppositions. The analytical conflict over the alleged conquest of Canaan by the Hebrews is a typical case in which external and internal presuppositions collide over ontology.

Mazar (1985: 61-71) proposed that the permanent settlement of the Hebrews might have been preceded by a semi-nomadic phase at the very end of the Late Bronze Age and beginning of the Iron Age. It may be that this notion can be modified and extended backwards in time. So the issue of formulating criteria, and how to define them, for isolating a Hebrew presence in a site need development and refinement. If the Old Testament narratives on the ethnic movement of the Hebrews into Canaan were to be taken solely as a rough reflection of historical events, or alternatively if, for example, J.A. Callaway's (1977) views on the late date of the emergence of the Israelites were followed, then we would still need more refined criteria than we have.

On the former view, let us suppose that some Semitic stock was in Egypt and moved to Canaan. They perhaps would arrive in Canaan with Egyptian cultural and behavioural influences, just as scribes who wrote Akkadian in Canaan reflected Egyptian linguistic influences (as Cochavi-Rainey 1997 demonstrates in respect of different issues). Indirectly, some Canaanite cultural and craft features had impact on Egyptian mores. Perhaps Semites in Egypt would tend to reflect many of these Canaanite elements rather than classic Egyptian functions. The resulting admixture would have a strong, albeit off-key, marginal resemblance to certain Canaanite features in the sites which they took over when arriving in Canaan. The issues of comparative influences assume increasingly complex proportions. The presuppositions of the controversial hypothesis of the Hebrews' semi-nomadic existence prior to entering Canaan, together with the notion that they had emerged from Egypt, involve proposing their previous eclectic absorption of a variable range of linguistic influences, functions and customs prior to entry into Canaan, possibly mirroring patterns from other semi-nomadic groups whose mores had also been previously selectively adopted by Canaanites. Groups of Canaanites themselves could have followed a not dissimilar route of semi-nomadic experience and expedience to the hitherto migrating Semites entering Canaan, thus entrenching patterns which the Semites adopted. These similarities could readily be misused to infer an incorrect continuity between disparate resident Canaanites and Semites who had arrived and adopted such customs. In this type of scenario, the earliest arrival of the Semitic semi-nomads might be undetected by some sorts of archaeological interpretation.

When Semites arrived in the cities in which they came to live, the resulting complex hybrid of their mores, and more particularly the historical traces of them unevenly deposited in archaeological residue, would comprise a compositional variable—with unpredicted proportionality factors and ratios to standardised stylistic Canaanites identities—that would echo, mirror, parody, and allude to similarities in the sites' previous inhabitants. In contemporary tribal and semi-nomadic environments, anthropologists have some difficulty in separating such phenomena, especially in terms of differentiating between functions manifested by groups originating mores and the copying of derivative groups, a problem much more acute in the foregoing circumstances. Kristiansen (1998: 185-209) points out that no systematic analysis and discussion of the criteria for identifying the existence and causes of migration versus internal change and information exchange have been presented for the Bronze Age, nor for any earlier period by either side of the debate, which, according to his new research, is still not well-informed. Biblical scholars who have skimmed off results from migration research tend to rely, for example, on archaeological general theory applications to the Thraco-Cimmerians. He shows that, to some degree, this situation also holds for the Iron Age. Kristiansen argues that the identity and conceptualisation of migration theory and its relation to internal change have yet to be formulated. This presses the conclusion into explicit form, that not only have biblical scholars generally not addressed the sharpened techniques and focus of such archaeological theory, these issues have yet to be connected to an explicit sophisticated analysis of the problem of Hebrew or *'apiru* migration, alienation and/or invasion, together with their significance for the date of composition of Joshua/Judges.

This therefore also affects the view held by those such as Rowlett (1996), who depend upon the composition of the book of Joshua at a time-point well into the Iron Age. The research has not yet been produced to warrant the requisite assumptions about migration either in the Bronze Age or by appeal to literary manifestations of perception of migration deconstructed into a Joshua–Josiah association. There are at least two problems that obtrude on to the foregoing group of issues. First, the types of refined, and welcome, literary analysis of Joshua, which attend such late-date Iron Age compositional scenarios are extremely intricate and internally fine-tuned to theological and sometimes ideological premises. As such they are quite separate in focus from external historical contexts, and are usually totally disconnected as criteria from many uses in assessing empirical and historical data, especially since, additionally, they are not even applied to judge the possibility of testing or supporting earlier associations of Joshua with archaeology. Secondly, nevertheless, such studies often proceed as if writing literary criticism were, at least in effect, writing out, censoring out, or displacing the proper role of historical non-literary and archaeological analysis. No doubt the tedious debate between liberal and conservative theologies has accorded us this binary division of labour; but we should not allow this schizophreniform of analysis to continue, as covertly it does on both sides, in the alienation of typical literary theologians and archaeologists from each other. Internal tuning of literary analysis will not yield history, and to presuppose that literary criticism is itself the criterion of the (ir)relevance of narrative to archaeological history is quite incredible as a technique for judgement. Certainly, many scholars are too subtle to make this bald claim; yet the more implicit the policy is, often the more unnoticed the damage it does, especially to the criteria for judging good literary analysis. Literary analysis has as little to do with achieving measurement of the historical background, say, of the semantics of Joshua, as Isaac Newton's refinement of alchemical theory had to do with reaching insights into the microphysics of metal transformation; nor are these critical remarks made by one averse to literary research but as one with a preoccupation with literary creativity (see Gibson 1987, and his forthcoming a).

The criteria for identifying the arrival of semi-nomadic Hebrews have not been and perhaps cannot be satisfactorily formulated in view of the transience of the historical situation and the inherent restrictions of archaeological reconstruction. In the absence of recognising the force and focus of these limitations, there is a tendency to offer operational recipes which ape, but do not satisfy, the standards of criteria (cf. Gibson forthcoming e: ch. 3), for a definition of such criteria). Some of the characteristics of the later more explicitly developed Israelite site have been subject to retrojection into the imagined earlier conditions for being a Hebrew site. That is to say, a genetic fallacy can easily be committed, of confusing the origin of a thing with its product.

Of course, much analytical progress has been made in some relevant areas, yet assumptions can slip into discussions which later need adjustment and are not revised sufficiently in the light of (the absence of) criteria. In 1972, Callaway had argued that the former major fortified city at Ai in the Early Bronze Age was violently destroyed circa 2400 BC, and abandoned until circa 1200, when it was settled by tent-dwellers, though presumably no tents have been found there (cf. Callaway 1977: 5, reviewing his earlier study in the perspective of subsequent research). The criteria, logically to impose such a judgement in the light of the functional nature of semi-nomads, do not exist. In 1984, Callaway (1985: 73-74) said that Ai Iron Age settlements 'were established from the beginning on a subsistence base of agriculture primarily'; yet he did not reconcile this with his statement in the same review, when he admitted that: 'How much of the valley and hills outside the ancient walls of Ai was planted with crops cannot be ascertained.' Therefore, semi-nomads who might have lived at the site could have grown crops without a trace of them being left. This clearly leaves us with the prospect of criteria of semi-nomads interfacing with criteria for populations in transition to village settlement, where there is no pertinent crop evidence to indicate this, though the empirical probability of such an historical circumstance is not thereby weakened or to be denigrated. In 1977, Callaway stated that the radiocarbon dates published in his first volume on Ai were incorrect: 'as a result, the calibrated...dates are about 500-700 earlier' (Callaway 1977: 8). He also disregarded a conflicting result that employed charcoal. Consequently, the conception he constructed contains the empirical possibility or probability of a 230-year error factor. Independently of, but in keeping with this state of affairs, Matthiae (1978: 1ff)[2] has said that the Ebla material will probably require a shifting of the date at which the Early Bronze Age started back by about 200 years, which reflects a similar differential to Callaway's mistake. The way in which such revisions should be allowed to modify a hypothesis is not always pursued.

In some respects, this type of analytical situation will mask at least two related presuppositions. First, of course, there is the issue of the relations of the narrative to actual historical ontology. Secondly, there is the role of the ancient readers in their narrative presuppositions. Concerning the second, no doubt some groups of ancient readers read the narratives of conquest as exhaustively literal history, while others disposed them as legends and metaphors. These alternatives complement the sort of conclusions reached in other semantic domains by John Day in *God's Conflict with the Dragon and the Sea* (1985: 189). It is for a future publication to explore and map the uneven contrasts and interrelations in ontological assumptions between mythic and historical presuppositions in Old Testament narratives. Frank Kermode (1990: 66-67) expresses an important insight relevant for such analytical issues, stating:

> Although the categories are never quite distinct, we know in general the differences between historical record, historical myth and historical poem...We know that we have to read it against the grain of the manifest, and because of that good poems about historical crises speak a different language from historical record and historical myth.

Consequently, the 'grain of the manifest' in narrative history contains poeticisms we perceive and misperceive as unstable narrative, ambivalent over the ontology of evaluative invention and quantitative history. The intricate web of asymmetrical presuppositions in the conquest narratives offers pitfalls to the reader intent on prematurely smoothing the ontology into archaeology *or* mythology. If the reader misjudges this difference, then he will not be able to assess the sort of realism or antirealism disposed in the narrative. If the semi-nomads farmed crops, adopted Canaanite mores, and expediently used extant Canaanite buildings, the absence of

---

[2] This form of the point was made by Matthiae to the author at Manchester University in his 1978 Ebla meeting.

uniquely Israelite residue in place of these phenomena, together with evidence of some Semitic presence, are consistent with an Israelite historical realism about the conquest. These considerations are against the 'grain of the manifest' in such a way as to warn us that we should not false-foot studies of the typologies of narrative realism in conquest contexts. A slip in contrasting archaeology with narrative invisibly assigns fantastic realism to the text, while the text may in fact be a counter-intuitive piece of irony or historical item whose form is finer than the available 'theory-net' (see Cartwright 1999, and above, pp. 4, 13, 65) of empirical site assessment. Clearly, this is not to take the view that no evidence is proof, as we have and shall see below.

It is a worthy project to return to a tired, misconstrued battleground of debate and dislocate its priorities without allowing its polarities to restrict creativity concerning empirical possibilities. The Middle Bronze Age, circa 2000–1500 BC city of Jericho, was the period of its greatest prosperity. The city had plastered earthen banks with walls on top. Later, the debris of the ruined city began sliding and washing down the slopes of the tell. Additionally, there was extreme erosion over the intervening period until the subsequent inhabitation, that left little or no Middle Kingdom Bronze Age Jericho, except a slice on the east side of the excavated city as Dame Kenyon indicated, though there has been a questioning of her selectivity in sample soundings and trenches. Some place the destruction of Jericho by fire in the Middle Bronze Age, around 1550 BC. Some infer that this destruction was by the Hyksos or Egyptians, and others suggest that the assailants were unknown. Bimson (1978: 143-55) argued that this Jericho came to an end at the hands of the invading Hebrews referred to in Joshua. At the side of these alternating options, the book of Joshua has a vexed history of interpretation on the topic, partly interfacing with archaeological disputes and naive realist interpretations of walls being blown down by trumpets, though this does not match the semantics of the narrative (Josh. 6:4-16). It is clear that some walls of Jericho in the Middle Bronze Age period collapsed and slid down the slopes, about seven metres down the hill, except on the eastern slopes. Whatever one may assume as legendary elements associated with the fall of Jericho, and the 20th-century anti-modernist conservative biblical theological historicization, we should not conflate this prejudice with neglect of empirical data[3] which in fragmentary ways mirror items in Joshua's story of the fall of Jericho. Kenyon recognised that the Jericho site was reoccupied around 1400, and separately mentioned that the second-hand walls using Middle Kingdom material would stem from this time. The unknown assailants could readily comply with the Hebrew invasion in Joshua, though Kenyon

---

[3] For some relevant logic here see Geach 1972; Hamblin 1970: 105-8, 218-23, 284-303; and Hansen and Pinto (eds) 1995.

Figure 6.5 A Bronze Age house at Jericho

did not consider this nor mention it, since she presupposed a 1200 BC emergence of the Hebrews.

In Kenyon's Report (1960: pl. 30), remains of a Bronze Age house and its contents are documented within what she identifies as an Iron Age phase. Possibly these are the ingredients for a *reductio ad absurdum* against her Iron Age scenario, not least because her excavation methods involved selective and not entirely empirically justified sampling of the site by sporadic excavation of statistically determined locations within the site. Although one should not generalise this incongruity, the unexcavated areas within Jericho, together with the selective pattern of excavation, place a question-mark against dismissing this anomaly as irrelevant to discovering Bronze Age date Semitic domestic life in Jericho, immediately subsequent to the arrival of what she deemed with characteristic autocracy the 'unknown assailants'. If they are unknown, then they could have been *'apiru*; and if *'apiru*, then possibly they were Hebrews. If there is the remnant of a Bronze House in Jericho, then it would hardly be the only one, since one city house would hardly exist on such a hill site by itself.[4]

The foregoing selection of problems are of course are only fragments from among the available data. Yet they exemplify the concern with historical ontology and its impact on the literary analysis of the Old Testament which can detect fresh hypotheses as well as new formulations of some aspects of older theses which do not collapse under the weight of traditional past versions of these theses. Incomplete archaeological excavations and their technical ramifications, intermixed with the presuppositions of opposed historical theses, can too readily be simplified into serving the needs of opposed schools, be they 'biblical archaeology' or its antagonists. It is too much to expect that the selective sample methods and archaeological theorists will have avoided all significant errors in synthesis. In a Popperian world of falsification, it is precisely the secured paradigm using inductive methods in which occasionally the most unlikely probabilities turn out to be confirmed. In addition to this, the state of the art or science of archaeology is not yet sufficiently advanced to escape the principle of revisability.

---

[4] Since we are dealing with inductive probabilities, as many of the relevant archaeologists seem to regard the assessment of the proposed circa 1200 BC date of the Israelite settlement—rather than a Popperian noninductive scenario (see Popper 1972)—it is worth keeping opposed possibilities such as the Late Bronze Age date in lively debate to tune up a test for veracity by assessing the strength of contrary ways of interpreting data. In this respect, it is worth linking Late Bronze Age sites with the Bronze Age conquest hypothesis to see if there is a probability which can be assigned to the hypothesis; for example those sites in the Wadi el Hasa survey (Macdonald 1983: 18-28).

Knowing an archaeological concept is not invariably a recognitional capacity of its all of its versions, implications, or applications. Reformulations of past possibilities sometimes contain counter-intuitive and surprising entailments. We need to be careful in prematurely foreclosing the debate about the relations between Bronze and Iron Age Semitic histories and cultures, since the inductive models presupposed in archaeological analysis and narrative interpretation are sufficiently incomplete to warrant allowance for new possible futures which are not the sum of a contemporary majority consensus. It may also be the case that induction itself, in the perspective of research, for example by Mellor (1995; 1998), as well as the work by Hacking (1994) discussed in Chapter 1, is inappropriate for fine-tuned application to the analysis of such ancient topics. It may also be that induction itself is an irrelevantly coarse-grained formalism in a major range of its forms, which needs displacing by falsification techniques devised by writers such as the above scholars—who are indeed somewhat conservative in their positions. So one need not embrace excessively controversial viewpoints to sustain this questioning of induction; and of course it will have occurred to readers that what is scientifically well-grounded inductive procedure is considerably weakened, in any case, when applied in other subjects where contemporaneous experimental controls are replaced by retrojective conjectural inference in archaeology and biblical studies.

The Language of Conquest

Clearly, various cultures which comprised the Near East of the 2nd millennium exhibited widely shared linguistic mores and styles when treating of standard situations, albeit with overtones which witness to local re-use of the patterns. A case in point is the employment of given military or regal stylistic conventions in contexts of conquest and subservience. An instance of this is to be found in Josh. 12:9-24, where a list of kings occurs. This parallel was first exposed by Ring (1977: 141-45). I here add further interpretation of the data.

The military content of Joshua 12 is to do with the invasion of Canaan and the conquest of 31 kings and cities. Tablets in Minoan Linear B found at Pylos and Knossos display the same type of style and structural features, with a regal set of subjects parallel with Joshua 12. The Middle and Late Bronze Age levels in Canaan[5] display ample evidence of Mycenaean artefacts (for example, the bichrome pottery

---

[5] I include under this scope relevant parts of the Old Testament that implicitly require this dating when their internal presuppositions are assessed as interpreted in the present study.

Figure 6.6   Minoan LB tablet An 857: I (Apijoto: king of Owoto, one)

ware). This provides an appropriate socio-cultural environment with which to match and complement the occurrence of an Aegean parallel in a Semitic text, though this is not to force a judgement on the parallel about the direction of origin for the stylistic feature in Joshua 12; it is merely to give perspective to its supporting context. For Hebrew, the style of Joshua 12 is most unusual, with a ledger-like presentation of names and numbers, as follows:

> 9. The king of Jericho, one
>   (*mlk yryḥw 'ḥd*)
>   the King of Ai, one
>   (*mlk h'y 'ḥd*)
> 10. The King of' Jerusalem, one
>   (*mlk yrwslm, 'ḥd*)
> 11. The King of Jarmuth, one
>   (*mlk yrmwt, 'ḥd*)

It is clear that the occurrence of place-names in this stylistic context has relevance for the criticism of attempted dismissal of any historical claims, when the same style recurs in contemporary Near Eastern texts. Josh. 12:7 states that this list, which is composed of 31 kings, 'are the kings of the country which Joshua and the sons of Israel smote'.

The Greek Minoan Linear B tablet An 261 (Bennett 1951; cp. An 857, Figure 6.6) exhibits exactly this style and structure, for example:

> King of U-wo-to, one
> (ke-ro-si-ja o-wo-to I)

A semantic structural feature, which is identical in Joshua and the Linear B tablet, is that each of the lists has kings who total 31. Ring presented this as characteristic of international military classification in the Near East, some of which the book of Joshua articulates. Certainly, there was much Minoan contact with the area of Palestine and Egypt from at least 1900 BC, where customs such as the above stylistic form were absorbed by Semitic peoples, as well as reflecting Semitic (probably trading) contact with Minoan civilisation (Marinatos 1976: 15 and pl. l9b; also Marinatos 1984: ch. 2). Such a pattern is already attested between Ebla and Minoan Crete of the 3rd millennium, in terms of refined woven wool and dyestuffs export.

Another Minoan Linear B tablet, that of Knossos As 1516, though fragmentary, also exemplifies the summation type of accounting found in Joshua. The ending of the Joshua (12:24) list mentions the total of kings, as do the Minoan lists:

> all the kings, 31
> (*kl-mlkym šlšm w'ḥd*)

A slight difference between the Joshua narrative's ending and Knossos As 1516 is that, instead of 'kings', the Minoan convention is to add the ideogram for MEN to the total, though the total is 31, as with the Joshua record. This possibly indicates a standard classification of grouping numbers, perhaps reflecting international patterns of military accounting, possibly combined with some cultic or iconic numerological association.

These tablets and others of their genre come from the period circa 1900–1350 BC. So we have a complex precedent for the Joshua list at a time contemporary with the stated time of the events reported in Joshua. Ring argues that these common features show that the documentary hypothesis is falsified on relevant counts because the parallels require contemporary knowledge and practice of specialised linguistic conventions which were not extant outside that period. The high incidence of common factors in the parallel, as well as the originality of their structure, present evidence that satisfies a 2nd-millennium criterion for proving that the relevant epoch supports the type of language and composition assigned to it in Joshua.

Biblical and Ugaritic Gods

There are fundamental theological, linguistic and archaeological problems about how Canaanite culture influenced the Hebrews and the production of the Bible in anti-Canaanite polemics. Often the resolution for these problems rests on disputed details or neglected minutiae that obscure a facet of a general item. For example, there is the problem of a word for 'god'—'el/'il. Is the term a proper name in the Old Testament? How does this Hebrew 'el connect or otherwise with the semantic fields and identity of Ugaritic 'il?

A related difficulty is that Ugaritic directly mirrors some Iron Age data in the Bible, but the Ugaritic culture is mostly Bronze Age. So there are delicate issues of mediation, though Hadley (2000) considers that this presents us with no special problem since preservation and mediation of texts is in considerable evidence at relevant stages. The status of the interrelations dictates whether or not there is or at what level there is discontinuity between the Bible and Ugaritic mythology. It is in this situation that the application of logic is a means to clarification of the disputes.

The literature and research are complex; for this reason, and for brevity, it is convenient to discuss one treatment of some standard approaches to the questions. So the following study selects for a review a collection of these tendencies as focused by their influence. For convenience, it is worth choosing a general review of such viewpoints in the following, as in Magnusson 1977, somewhat over-stylised though it is. For example, he asserts (1977: 83) it is noteworthy that the Old Testament never stigmatises the Canaanite worship of El, whose authority in social affairs was recognised by the Patriarchs. His consort was Asherah, the mother-goddess, represented in Canaanite sanctuaries by a natural or stylised tree (*'aserah*). Jud. 8:33-4 is a straightforward counter-example to the criteria of consistency assumed in this quoted opinion:

> And it was, as soon as Gideon was dead, that the sons of Israel turned again, and went a whoring after Baalim, and made Baal-berith their god and remembered not Yahweh their God.

Self-evidently, this passage does stigmatise a set of gods. Transcription, which elides the biblical and Canaanite apocopated near-homonyms for 'God', obscures an important difference: *'el* in Hebrew is qualified as a noun with the article, whereas Ugaritic usually treats *'il* as a proper name. Jud. 8:33-4 explicitly places the Baal-berith *'el* as a contrary of Yahweh, and condemns the people who worship the former instead of the latter. Presumably, in the semantic presupposition of 'whoring after Baalim', it is true to insist that necessarily *'El* is stigmatised by Baal-berith—the god who, within the presupposition of Judges, personifies theological prostitution.

Is *'el* a proper name or common noun? What are the principles by which the two types of word can be distinguished? Sometimes even grammarians have not always discriminated accurately between the two uses. Some opinions propose that the Patriarchs believed in the Canaanite *'el*, though it is often not made explicit that the relevant Ugaritic Canaanite use of *'il* is a proper name and not a common noun, whereas, as noted above, the biblical use of *'el* is not a proper name but a noun. I shall use the expression 'biblical *'el*' to refer to biblical usage of *'el* where reference is to Yahweh. This distinction is immensely important, since on it turns the possibility or falsehood of linking the Ugaritic *'il* with biblical *'el*. So what principles enable one to distinguish a proper name from a common noun? Immediately relevant standard tests devised by Dummett (1981: 73-80), Hale (1994, 1996) and Gibson (1981, forthcoming e) in theory of meaning are:[6]

12. A proper name is never qualified by 'the'.[7]
13. A proper name is never qualified by 'not'.

---

[6] For applied linguistics for Hebrew that reaches to the same type of conclusion from another standpoint, see Andersen 1974.

[7] The Greek use of the morpheme which is the same as the article prefixed to Greek proper names is not a semantic quantifier, rather an ossified element or a piece of syntax marking the proper name as a proper name. The proper name already refers to the identity that the introduction of an article presupposes has not been specified.

14.   A proper name is never qualified by 'all', 'some', 'every', etc.

There are other tests; but those mentioned here satisfy the present purpose. The tests all apply to biblical proper names. For example, 'Yahweh' is never modified by 'the', 'not', 'all' or 'some'. In fact, one might think that a person who said 'I read about the Yahweh' had not rightly mastered language.

'Not-Yahweh' is a nonsensical phrase, and of course is not attested in MT Hebrew. Someone might object to the second test, however, by regarding the statement that 'Baal is not Yahweh' as in conflict with it. Here, it might be supposed, Yahweh is qualified by 'not'. This is a misunderstanding about the roles of 'is' and 'not' in the proposition 'Baal is not Yahweh'. To appreciate this, suppose that a person using the proposition did believe in the existence of Yahweh and, in using it, solely wanted to deny the truth of the equation 'Baal = Yahweh'. Here, the introduction of 'not' cancels the equation: that is to say, 'not' denies the identification of Baal with Yahweh. In such uses, therefore, 'not' does not have the force of denying Yahweh's existence, but that of opposing the relation of Baal to Yahweh. So the foregoing objection does not succeed in finding a weakness in the second test. The Bible accords with this usage.

The third test is concerned with quantity. A proper name uniquely refers to one bearer in actual usage (as opposed to lists of names in a directory; but even in these cases, each name functions differently to pick out a unique individual). We do not have 'some Yahwehs', nor 'all Yahwehs' in the Old Testament. It is of central importance in relation to the thesis I am contesting to realise that all of these tests do apply to the Canaanite proper name *'el*. Of equal significance is the fact that none of the tests can functionally apply to the biblical *'el*. These tests are fundamental ways of identifying proper names by measuring their function in use. They are not trite tests devised in the abstract. They are based on what it is to be communication. For example, if we ask if a noun such as 'city' *refers* to a specific identity (rather than is true of a type of entity), we should either realise that the user is presupposing that we already know that it is by misleading brachylogy, with it going proxy for a particular proper name of a city—a city whose name we know (in which case we are assuming that the city is the one referred to be the proper name, and we need the proper name to identify the city); or, the noun 'city' does not refer at all to anything. It describes a property of a referent of a proper name, once it is correctly employed in use. By itself, 'city' does not secure an identity for the reader. Traditionally, terms such as 'denote' foggily merge the differences here. But the distinction is crucial since it is a functional fact that we thereby do not know which city it being indicated (since none semantically is referred to) by 'city', unless it is immediately contextually parasitic in the semantics of a proper name. So nouns by themselves do not function by use of reference, as do proper names. Clearly there is a question of intentionality to be assessed if there is no reference. But even here, the intentionalist question 'to which God am I [allegedly] referring in this use of the noun?' does not of itself provide any answer, which it would have to do in itself if it were an intentionalist attempt to specify the internal mentalist use of the semantic identity of 'God'. Obviously, there are adjacent conceptual topics which query certain issues here (for which see Dummett 1980), though investigation of these queries does not falsify the tests (on the latter see Gibson 1998b). It is for such reason that the above tests operate as a matter of linguistic pragmatic possibility and not as only a premise of a linguistic theory. These tests agree with other biblical usage of proper names, and God's name 'Yahweh'.

The characteristic uses of this biblical *'el* specifically contradict these tests for being a proper name. This entails a proof that this type of biblical *'el* is not a proper name. It is therefore functionally distinct to the Canaanite *'el*. The biblical non-Ugaritic *'el* is a noun, not a proper name. That is to say, those subjects of sentences that satisfy these tests are proper names. Those subjects of sentences that might appear to some to be proper names, yet to which the above three tests cannot apply, are not proper names but nouns. So this procedure of applying the tests is the way in which one can isolate proper names from common nouns, as follows.

Some forms of criticism make much of *'el* and Bethel, as though such biblical usage were the Canaanite meaning; the occurrences of this type are actually evidence against this equation. Consider the example of Gen. 31:13—'I am the *'el* of Bethel'. Here the first test fails, since 'the' (*ha-*) is found qualifying *'el*. Accordingly, this a piece of evidence for the view that this use of *'el* is a noun, not a proper name. We have seen above that the plural form sometimes appears when 'some' or 'all' is used with a noun. The plural form itself is an extension of the third test. Ex. 15:11 interrogates the reader with the question, 'who is like you among the gods (= *'elim*)?' The text could have used the standard plural *'elohim* (gods); but it did not. The text sensitively articulates a plural quantity of *'el*s; and thus fails the third test. Also, one will need a sense of contrast in the placing of Yahweh against other gods which are alleged members of the set of *'el*s throughout Mesopotamia.

The first two tests are decisive against the type, just mentioned, of collapsing Canaanite *'el* and biblical non-Ugaritic *'el* into being the identical term to El. Ps. 5:4 gives an indication of the second test which applies the term to *'el*: 'For you are not *'el* who has pleasure in wickedness'. Another case can be found in Deut. 32:21: '(that which is) not *'el*'. It is of interest that Abraham is said to have, 'called...on a name, the name of Yahweh, the everlasting *'el*' (Gen. 21:33). Noticeably, the narrative uses the singular 'name', not 'names': the presence of *'el* is not taken by the author as a warrant for designating it as a name, with 'Yahweh'. A corollary of this is that biblical non-Ugaritic *'el*, in conformity with above tests, is not designated a name by biblical usage. All these proofs fault, disintegrate and dispose of the form of assertion about the common identity of Canaanite and biblical non-Ugaritic *'el*. Further, since the functional logic (which maps what it is to be a proper name in the foregoing) is shown to be shared through patriarchal, Yahwistic and Deuteronomistic semantic fields, it is incorrect to infer that the patriarchal uses of *'el* link with the Ugaritic employment of allegedly parallel theistic terms.

This situation does not depend on ascribing to the biblical writers' cognisance of any logical distinctions. Rather, the thesis is that the internal dynamics of what it is to be able to refer, to describe and to quantify using subject-terms is already internal to the possibility and linguistic empirical conditions of what it is to use language in attempts to pick out and characterise the external world outside of language, whether or not the attempts are true or false. It is, of course, a separate issue that such a state of affairs itself presupposes criteria which are correctly or incorrectly formulated and/or applied to the semantic field in question.

One may feel uneasy, despite this evidence, for are not the Canaanite *'el* and the biblical non-Ugaritic *'el* nevertheless still identical in 'form'? They are unless we worry (as we might) over the elision from *'e'* to *'i'*. But this does not prove synonymy in the context of meaning, that is, the sense and uses of words. For example, as a comic aside we may think of an implausible set of similarities: within unpointed Hebrew, *'l* (without the vowel) has identical, form when it means: 'not' (e.g. Gen. 15:1); 'to' (Num. 25:1); 'into' (Ex. 28:30); 'towards' (Josh. 8:18); 'against' (Ex. 14:5); 'concerning' (Gen. 20:2); 'power' (Gen. 31:29); and 'God'. Of course, to say of the one word *'el* that 'it means' all these things is only a manner of speaking. In a strict sense, though the forms of the words are identical, they are homonyms. Probably, divine nouns in Canaan are polysemes, stemming from common ancestry. But this is little help in applied synchronic linguistics, when the central features of such polysemy is that a large group of competing claims are made for the particular god being the same identity or a different god, from all or some of the others. So it is precisely at the interface of deconstructing differences of identity that we have to be careful to map—and not to interfere with—the semantic field's presuppositions of collision over the question of a term's reference, where homonymy and/or polysemy provide competing or ecumenical uses.

Years ago, Barr (1961) launched his attack on what he judged to be incorrect linguistic analysis, of using form to define meaning; in 1981, I added some logic to sustain and extend this type of critique (cf. also Gibson, 1997, 1999, and forthcoming e). One should be aware, however, that any such criticism is contingent if it has not exposed—as Barr had not—an impossible state of affairs ascribed to the target subject. What he demolished could thereby, at least in principle, be reconstructed without the mistakes; whether or not that would be a worthwhile prospect would be a different issue, one Barr did not assess.

And there are certain impossible properties: for example, it is impossible actually to refer, as opposed to intentionistically referring, to a specify identity (especially where there are many linguistically expressed candidates to be the referent of this identity) external to a piece of language by standard use of a noun, such as 'God' or 'person', without imposing some unstable interpretation which disguises within it some dependency of 'God' which goes proxy for and so entirely depends on for its identification a presupposed antecedent logically proper name (cf. Magnusson 1977: 85; by 'logically proper' here, I intend a functional category which identifies a referent's identity, and not some formalist recipe). It may be that some other uses of language (such as definite descriptions, like 'the Holy One of Israel' or 'the Creator of the Universe') are functionally tautologous (though not synonymous) with a logical proper name, and they thus preserve a reference to identify the bearer of the description, but these instances do not confute the particularity of differences between other terms which do not thus identify a referent.

True or accurate criticism of a contingent property or presentation does not entail that all other versions of that property are subject to the same criticism. Barr's attack on biblical theology dismantled a project with criticism that has a contingent relation to some areas of linguistics and presuppositions, both those that Barr himself adopted and also ones that he criticised. None of this would fault his actual analysis; yet making explicit the identities of contingent presuppositions lays open the logical and empirical propriety, as well as possibility of the negation of criticism of them. It will not have escaped the reader's attention that the present analysis airs the negation of some of these presuppositions, and advocates the empirical and conceptual probity of constructing a defence of some other presuppositions. It is worth noting that the history of philosophy certainly does not have a complete grasp of how to recognise all instances of viable hypotheses that can be salvaged from demolished theories which have fallen through the contingencies of scholarly attention. Perhaps biblical scholars are not free of the same limitation. We re-write history at our peril, however, though we need to re-assess our, and previous, attempts to reproduce it.

Cross (1973: 12) insists that 'the' was not originally in the text of Gen. 46:3, which reads 'I am the God (*ha-'el*) God of your father'. Cross deletes *ha-* ('the') from the Hebrew. He does this because he is clearly averse to allowing 'the' to be prefixed to what he claims is the proper name *'el* in Gen. 46:3. In other words, he seems to accept the force of the foregoing first test—that a proper name is never qualified by 'the'—and, unwilling to relinquish his belief that negates it, he speculatively emends the Hebrew. This is not too sharp a characterisation, because there is no variant reading or corruption of the Hebrew texts (either cited in BHS or in the ben Asher MS, or in any of the Qumran MSS). Cross, even though he is required to present substantial proof, since there is no empirical evidence for his assertion, only offers the reader a short footnote stating, not proving, that the original texts 'must have had 'the' (*ha-*) in them'. This proposal is extraordinarily illogical and nihilistic with respect to linguistic evidence, since it ignores a necessary truth of linguistic usage, and invents its negation by destroying the textual evidence that presupposes the falsehood of the proposal. Such an example has been discussed to exemplify the importance of not assuming that a contingent presupposition's apparent demise is the end of its future. We may have unwittingly interfered with our own evidence to accord with false presuppositions whose non-viability has been masked from our consciousness by custom.

This could be part of a trend in which we project ecumenical fellowship onto Levant theistic identity. Such hypostatization is hardly a likely amalgam as a function in such an ancient world, pious though it would be to have had or to have such agreement. It is sometimes assumed that the biblical *'el* and the Canaanite *'el* are one identical god. For example, sometimes we find it said that: *'El*'s consort was Asherah, the mother-goddess, also represented in Canaanite sanctuaries by a natural or stylised tree. (There is of course need for sensitive discrimination of the simple equation between the deity and her alleged physical depictions, as Hadley (2000) helpfully shows.) This seeming 'El' reflects the reduction of two deities to one entity. We have seen that this equation rests on confused connections which actually display evidence that we still have two distinct deities: first, Yahweh, who has the common noun *'el* (God) applied to him; secondly, the Canaanite deity, whose proper name is *'el/'il*.

Descriptions and predicates that are applied to a subject as essential features produce criteria for defining that subject's identity (cf. Dummett 1978: 97-98). In plain terms, this states, roughly, that what is said about a subject produces a definition of which she/he is. A consequence of this is that we cannot consistently operate with descriptions without violating a text's own criterion of identity in use. High on the list of examples of this consequence is the situation where two descriptions applied to one subject are contrary: for instance, where one claims that God is both immortal and dead. Both cannot be true; at most only one is true. If it happens that a textual tradition is incoherent, and one of its gods is both immortal and dies, then naturally we should incorporate it into the presuppositions of the narrative. In this type of circumstance, texts that refer to subjects (or purport to do so) are easily prone to inconsistent handling by an outsider. A reader's view about the status of a/the deity's ontology does not prevent this consequence from applying to the text. For, if one asserts that the Old Testament's non-Ugaritic language of *'el* is compatible with or identical to certain descriptions, it is a matter of matching biblical and Ugaritic texts. An ancient text might exhibit internal contrariety. This should be preserved in characterization of it. All too often we confuse, conflate or collapse the distinctions of autonomous texts, textual families, histories and conflicting world-views. We should not pool distinct narrative traditions and their semantic fields as if they were tautologous with, or a continuum for, synonymy, since then our results will not correspond to any one generalised sense of a signifier's particular usage. There is a potential for contrariety between critical description in measuring and mapping languages (of, say, Ugaritic expressions in association with biblical terms). For example, as mentioned above, sometimes it is maintained that biblical *'el* had a consort deity, though one biblical tradition (Ex. 20:3 and 34:14) notoriously affirms that worshippers shall have no other gods in worship. These biblical passages are decisive in two respects. First, they oppose the combination of any other deities with the biblical non-Ugaritic *'el*. In this connection, the biblical non-Ugaritic *'el* cannot possibly be said to have a consort deity—Asherah. Secondly, the very terminology (*'el*) advertises an awareness of the Canaanite or Amorite *'el*, and cancels any possibility of a synchronic semantic contract between the Canaanite deity and the biblical non-Ugaritic deity. Jud. 3:7 affirms that the Israelites 'forgot Yahweh...and served Baal and Asheroth'.[8] In an Exodus passage (34:14) pertinent to the foregoing narrative frame, we have Yahweh commanding the Israelites to 'cut down their Asherah'—stated in the context where they were instructed not to worship other *'el*s. Here 'Asherah' and 'Yahweh' are in contrary opposition; in conflict, not consort. The use of 'Yahweh' is no problem, because Ex. 34:14 there identifies Yahweh as *'el*. Hence, this conflict polemically destroys the polytheistic premise, and removes the possibility of a link with Asherah and the biblical non-Ugaritic *'el*. Wherever Asherah is mentioned in the Old Testament, it is to condemn that deity, not align it with the biblical non-Ugaritic God. What is more, if one were to employ editorial hypotheses linking relevant books and contexts which mention Asherah and *'el*, then even sharper counter-evidence arises. For example, Isa. 45:22 declares 'I am *'el* and beside me there is none else'; this is incompatible with the texts in which *'il* has brother and sister gods.[9] These oppositions in the extant Old Testament Hebrew texts, and the linguistics they seem to mirror in competing Canaanite polytheistic semantic fields, and which the Hebrew attacks, are at variance with a number of trends in biblical scholarship.[10] For example, the attempts to make Ugaritic and biblical *'el* coalesce conflicts with Ugaritic texts espousing an alien Romantic nihilist world of orgies, *'il*'s drunkenness, the goddesses wading in the blood of victims and drinking it.[11] In the Baal text 76 II (de Moor 1971a), Baal enacts a magic hunting rite for rebirth

---

[8] The *-oth* ending on 'Asheroth', i.e., the plural marker for 'Asherah'. Ugaritic Asherah was one of a set; Jud. 3:7 condemns the whole set.

[9] The textual sources (except where otherwise specified) are from Herdner 1963.

[10] Magnusson 1977: 83 mirrors these trends at a popular level.

[11] Herdner 1963 sec. 23.31. Ugaritic *'el* is supposed to have 'seduced' the wives Asherah and Anat, giving birth to the gods of Canaan. Clearly there is nothing agreeing to this in the biblical *'el*'s actions, and much of the language linked to him is condemnatory of this type of arena. This origin of the gods through *'el* is in opposition to biblical *'el* who is said to be the only God. See

and fertility. The Keret text from Ugarit (1 II) informs us of how a blind man can be healed by knowing his relation to the 'zodiacal' sign or planet position. A cognate of the Babylonian term used here is *mazal* (*mazaltu*). In 2 Kgs. 23:5, the Hebrew form *mazzalot*, evoking the worship of the stars, apparently depicts and condemns the Mesopotamian influence on Israel. The employment of Asherah is also denounced in the same context. This picture is extended by, for example, Gray's (1965) association of the *Repha'im* with agriculture and magic rites. These deadened giant-figures, discussed above, stood as motifs of divinity and fertility, as well as agents of deities as noticed elsewhere in the present study, while the Ugaritic Aqhat I text affirms that '[The *Repha'im*] prayed (that) the clouds in the heat of the season, they should rain…(but) Baal failed for seven years', which may be punned on in 2 Kgs. 8:1 in its later form. Such phenomena frequently extend to match worship of Astarte, with figurines seemingly used as charms or magic amulets as aids to fertility (Magnusson 1977: 84). Such data complement the picture of the biblical non-Ugaritic *'el* as exclusive of, and in ontological and conceptual opposition to, the developments earlier in Ugaritic's pantheon.

Consequently, comparative analysis needs to make judgements that are accurate to such differences. Deconstruction, as Hobson (1998) argues, must preserve the notion of difference which itself impinges on the concepts of presence and the absence entailed by a stress on the function of presence. Otherwise, the controls on the causal relations and connections between interpretation and information will be lost amidst confident, but confused, opacities in illicit semantic mergers.

Immortal life motifs occur in the predicates which comprise biblical versus Canaanite contraries. The Old Testament pointedly discriminates between the biblical *'el* who is Yahweh, as opposed to the Canaanite *'el* who does not exist. Isa. 45:22 is in agreement with earlier biblical texts in declaring that 'I am *'el* and besides me there is none else'. These are in fundamental conflict with, for example, the Ugaritic text UM 67:VI, where the Canaanite *'el* rejoices that Baal is alive again, after his annual descent to death for the magical rebirth of the earth, proclaiming that, 'I shall sit and rest…for the Most High Baal is alive'. This is evidently in dispute with Hebrew claims for Yahweh. Appropriately, the Canaanite Baal is never once praised or even allowed to have ontological existence in any part of the Old Testament; this Baal is always condemned and made the subject of the occasion for theological prostitution (e.g. Jud. 8:33). This division of labour seems quite similar to distinctions formulated in many disparate rational traditions (cf. Geach 1975: 139-43).

Schaeffer 1968: 545-51, Text 1. Cf. Gibson 1978: 6-8, 15-14, 18-19, 31. Note that the 'logic of mythological thought' (to use J.C.L. Gibson's apt expression) entailed magic invoking rituals.

The Ugaritic and Canaanite predicates attached to *'el*, clash with, and are contrary to, the biblical occurrences of predicates linked to *'el*, when it is possible to assess these conjunctions. This commits anyone who demurs from the exclusive identities of Ugaritic and biblical *'el* to contradiction, in maintaining an equation of identity. Such contradictions arise not only on linguistic technical grounds, but also on straightforward contrasts of the senses in Ugaritic and biblical theologies. The conditions for a contrary statement are composed when the Canaanite and biblical theologies are made to code a goddess-partner Asherah for the biblical *'el*, while predicates attached to the later Hebrew traditions insist on uniqueness conditions and a ban on the seeming Canaanite partner for Yahweh or Hebrew *'el*. The equation which (falsely) combines the identities of Ugaritic or Canaanite *'il* and biblical *'el* has to be committed to the thesis that predicates in the Bible should be capable of consistent conjunction with the Ugaritic predicates. If the biblical traditions loosened this requirement, all well and good; but instead these parade a polemical conceptual war against external theistic influences.

It might be retorted that this only presupposes my notion of consistency, but the foregoing carefully avoided presuming that there is any other consistency except what the texts assert. Even where negation and contrariety were taken to be paraphrases of the aligned Ugaritic and Hebrew traditions, the terminology was matched to those texts to furnish a use within it of concurrence or opposition. Indeed, this objection can be taken too far: without assuming that there are semantic universals, the use of a term for 'not' or 'there is no other' imposes certain restrictions on the interpreter who wishes to circumvent the use of these so that they actually mean 'conjunction' instead of 'disjunction'.

This appears to be an often unconscious slide into paraconsistent language (cf. Priest 1995, as an example, and Gibson 2000a for analysis), according to which a given specific use of a particular proposition in a single semantic occurrence is presupposed by a few scholars to be true *and* false, a position which only a few philosophers favour, and even then not in the present sorts of natural language textual uses.

Additionally, a reason behind the absence or failure of the conjunction of such use of Ugaritic and biblical material concerning *'el* is that the modern academic protagonist for such Canaanite union with Hebrew monotheism has equivocated over either what identity is, what a criterion of identity is, is unaware what such a criterion is, or has conflated either of these with a criterion of (speculative) application, as explained in Gibson (forthcoming e). Identity is what a thing is, and it is a relational function in use, for example, mapping the assertion that 'Yahweh is God'. A criterion of identity is roughly a description that is presupposed in the relational identification, such as 'God created the heavens'. Sometimes the criterion of identity coincides or overlaps with the criterion of application, though it is often distinct, as with the answer to the question, 'Where is Jerusalem?'

Identity presupposes an internal non-secondary core of predicates, such as being female, for Asherah. Those who want to feminize Yahweh will find a semantic absence of any relevant predicates. It is not enough to notice that, for example, breast language (*say*, etc.) is occasionally employed of the 'male' Hebrew God, since this is not in a propositional frame which asserts or presupposes the female gender or identity for Yahweh. Thus an ironic pun on gender is not itself evidence of an ancient theologian treating God as a client for a sex-change operation. But the proximity of contemporary feminisms in attempts to merge *'ăserah* and Yahweh illustrates that the ancient Canaanite or Ugaritic urge to give binary genders to plural deity is not itself alien to our contemporary rational categories. Therefore, it is also improper to skip over the semantic field constraints of categorical denunciation by the Hebrew Old Testament, set against such claims, since they are co-extensive with relevant gender and predicative relations in our own world. Ancient writers had available to them in Hebrew the linguistic choice to re-sex God, but did not select the female gender. So we can correctly attempt to generalise the appropriate subsumed Hebrew language functions in principle to assess relevant portions of these ancient narratives, where other linguistic difficulties do not obtrude. It is of course an important truth that male domination of gender for thousands of years has done enormous damage to the function and scope of the female, and female gender. This is not corrected by non-functional measurement of ancient examples of this. (It is worth proposing some agenda for further progress in the sphere of theistic semantics of gender, however. Since language about the Christian or Judaic God's gender is metaphoric, discussion of the deity's sexuality has to be metaphoric. Consequently, much discussion about gender and God is not about gender and God: it is about metaphoric gender and God; such discussion does not succeed in addressing God's gender. Although subsequent to acknowledging this asymmetry between actual and metaphoric gender, it is obviously possible to engage with examination of important issues to do with feminism and God. Failure to notice the point that we are not discussing God's gender but metaphor has a significance, to the effect that we are not talking about what we think we are. This also relates to the ways in which the function of metaphor, or anthropomorphic imaging of deities, might have been in Canaanite and Old Testament theisms; cf.Gibson, 1997.)

Another type of contrary is sometimes present in discussion of Canaanite *'il* and Old Testament *'el*. For example, it is sometimes argued that there is ample evidence that some of the aspects of Yahweh are shared with aspects of Baal as the Divine King. To be sure, some of the liturgical language is strikingly similar, as with Ps. 68:33, 34: 'To him that rides upon the heavens of heavens', 'his strength is in the clouds' (cf. Magnusson 1977: 83-84). In its combined form, there is no evidence linguistically that the Old Testament proposes this type of language for a Canaanite deity *and* Yahweh or the Hebrew God. There is no explicit biblical acknowledgement that Yahweh reflects aspects of Baal, for instance, in the sense that it never proposes that Yahweh shares common properties with the Ugaritic Baal. In fact, we should clarify and extirpate some of the terminology which modern scholarship uses as a sort of defining metalanguage of such alleged relations: nowhere is the phrase 'Divine King' used of Yahweh in the Bible. The absence of terminology we presuppose in source texts which only occurs in one group (e.g. the Ugaritic texts) and not the other comparative range of texts (e.g. the Bible) should guide us to revise the way we have formed the comparison.

If this is done, the basic issue is simply that we should not transform two narratives that use similar types of expression into a joint statement shared by two deities. The obvious reason for this is that at least the Hebrew deity, and often the Canaanite god, is having claims made for it which are not reducible to shared properties with other deities, because they are presented as unique to the single bearer, and attended by a supposition or assertion that there is a fundamental competition between the claims applied to one god rather than the other(s). Clearly, the Old Testament traditions have no thematic development to achieve anything other than the routing of competing claims for Yahweh's and the Hebrew *'el*'s and also the theistic *'elohim*'s sole applicability of supremacy and monotheistic language. This obviously collides with the pantheism outside of the Old Testament.

Yahweh's and Baal's identities are sometimes alleged to possess common features, such as supreme power, in Ps. 68:33-34, supposing that the ending for heavens (*smy*) reflects a Phoenician stylism (Gray 1977: 17-18), together with a thesis sharing power-claims with gods beyond the Old Testament's narrow monotheism. But such 'sharing' of language does not make Yahweh and Baal the joint subject of such predicates. Why? Certainly, someone will want to side step this type of point and query it by standing outside of the internal comparative debates as here proposed, and speak of the cultural evolution of groups of societies that have overall directions and trends. As important as such a priority is, it does nothing to identify and measure the actual use of such ancient languages in actual specific texts, since they can be utilised to some degree to imply some of the thinking thus expressed. The danger in such comparative studies is that the actual subjects—what people write and edited to manifest their mentality and lives are the subject of complex equivocation, to the effect that their writings become metaphors for something other than what they contain. They become, as it were, corporate products to be packaged by probability distribution, rather than the conceptual dynamics of the consciousness that composed them. This would amount to an equivocation fallacy, in which the actual subject in narrative use was displaced by the presuppositions of the observer (cf. Hamblin 1970: 182-85). Evidently, the ancient people subject to such repression by our contemporary analysis had almost no awareness of the patterns to which they 'contributed' by their biographical functions (individual or collective) being subsumed in scenarios alien to their own semantic uses of preferences and priorities. And they made vehement uniqueness claims for their own god(s), explicitly competing against other counter-assertions. This polemical textual situation violates the scholarly disposition to make purportedly common subjects of contrary subjects.

Yahweh at Kuntillet 'Ajrud

The Old Testament of the Ugaritic, and other data about Asherah as a consort for *'il*, and of the foregoing analysis have been illuminated by the discoveries at Kuntillet 'Ajrud in southern Palestine (some 50 km south of Kadesh-barnea in Sinai). Among the extensive finds two of the inscriptions on the remains of large pithoi portray an *'Šrth* consort for a deity named 'Yahweh' (cf. Hadley, 2000; Dever 1984). Such a role of a consort for Yahweh explicitly conflicts with the narrative world of the Old Testament's monotheism as adduced above. As we have seen, from contexts such as 2 Kings 23, we find biblical references condemning polytheistic worship that incorporated worship of Yahweh with Asherah. It is important for accuracy in the presuppositional semantics of 2 Kings 23 to incorporate the function that these phenomena are condemned in such passages. Here the narrative voice sustains the foregoing type of coding for consistency and disjunction between Yahweh, the Hebrew God, versus the gods of Canaan. 2 Kings 23 describes the removal of a 'grove'—an Asherah in the house of Yahweh at Jerusalem.

Other similar situations are attested in the Old Testament, both in temples and in agricultural settings. The dating of the Kuntillet 'Ajrud site and inscriptions to around termination of the ninth and commencement of the eighth century BC. This more than sufficiently early to come roughly within the range of the internal narrative voice presupposed in the orbit of the Asherah passages in relevant contexts of 2 Kings. It also shows that the much earlier Late Bronze Age Ugaritic material therefore has parallels in Iron Age II Palestine, long after Ugarit ceased to operate as an influence. Certain expressions in the inscriptions provide striking evidence for the paganized worship of a cultic 'Yahweh' referred to in the books of the Kings. This raises the question of the occurrence of homonyms of 'Yahweh', isolatable from the theology of Yahweh which typical Old Testament writers, apprehended as true monotheism or contrary to the identity of the standard Hebrew perception of Yahweh's identity. It is significant to note that some of the Kuntillet data complementarily support the Old

Testament's own theological opposition to polytheistic worship with evidence of actual polytheistic texts.

Two of these inscriptions bear directly on the foregoing discussion. Inscriptions (a) and (b) below are positioned above the heads of the Bes figures, adjacent to or obtruding on to the headdress.

> (A) *brkt. 'tkm. lyhwh. šmrn. wl'šrth*
> 'I bless you by Yahweh of Samaria and by his Asherah'.

Note that in (A) the direct object marker *'t* is prefixed to second person plural suffix *km*; and in (B) below the second person singular suffix *k* is attached to *brkt* ('bless'). Inscription (B) is situated on another pithos , and it reads:

> (B) *'t brktk lyhwh tmn wl'šrth*
> 'Yahweh of Teman and his 'Asherah'

A proper name form of 'Yahweh' being used in such an inscription does not guarantee that it has the same reference as when it occurs in the biblical narratives. Notoriously, in the linguistic history of polemics, there is a recurrent practice of a new concept of a referent being foisted onto a previous different use of a proper name to coerce unwary users of different identity for the named bearer: same form, different subject. (Oscar Wilde makes this feature a mainstay of his final and finest play, *The Importance of Being Earnest*, in which 'Ernest' is used by two different characters, claiming that each of them is the 'true' 'Ernest'; see Gibson and O'Mahony 1993.) The conjunction of Asherah with Yahweh, in the relevant senses, I argue, precludes the term from being entered as a member of the same type of semantic field as that of Old Testament passages which were discussed in the foregoing, since they ban the possibility of such a conjunction (cf. Gibson, 1982, chapter 3). Consequently we are clearly dealing with a different and deviant subversive narrative innovation if we adopt those Old Testament passages discussed above as a basis for assessment. For in the above quoted inscriptions, all three tests for proper names presented in the above analysis are contradicted by Old Testament Hebrew usage if it is used as the basis for assessment of identity. This demonstrates that, in these inscriptions 'Yahweh' has a different reference, or no reference, in relation to Old Testament usage. A reason for this has already been introduced above: the Old Testament narratives themselves dismantle Asherah from being a cultic consort for Yahweh, whereas in the Kuntillet 'Ajrud inscriptions there are data that offer her as a function incorporated into the worship of Yahweh. Hadley (2000) has carefully distinguished various versions, icons and personifications of Asherah to which one should be sensitive. My assessment of the relations between the various expressions and identities of Asherah implements the analysis that Asherah, as with many notions of deities, amounts to a generative network of differentiable yet overlapping functions. In this perspective, the Asherah of Kuntillet 'Arjud in inscription (A) may well have its personifying source in an idol set up by Ahab in Samaria. The functions of personification here frequently facilitate inference between different manifestations of a subject that can map leakages, traces and continuities between distinctive uses of the same emblem. Equivocation and merger of homonyms and their iconic counterparts were evidently interactive components in religious development or decay in such ancient contexts. Conversely, of course, we need to avoid such slippages in description while characterising their ancient recurrence, though there are some unclear boundaries at the edges of these ancient religious uses and modern scholarly territories; yet to discover what the latter are is itself part of the resolution for problems ambiguity.

The territorial affiliations for named for *yhwh* in the inscriptions are 'Samaria' and 'Teman', and this stylism clearly jars against Old Testament usage. The latter proper name may be reflected in the punning reference to Teman in Habakkuk. 'Samaria' may have to be associated with the kingdom area of northern Israel, rather than a city; but there is no reason why this scope should not also be attended by some allusion to the city of Samaria as the focal point for the religious centre that has a national domain. There is no construct proper name in the Old Testament ('Yahweh of...') with which to yield a precedent for 'Yahweh of Teman'. The latter may be an ascription associated with a narrowed territorial sociolinguistic domain, whereas typical Old Testament uses of Yahweh, though connected to the inheritance of 'the land', is tied to a people's own identity and universalising claims. However, the construct ('of') can be construed as an item in a scope-fixing expression formed by the conjunction of two proper names. A phrase such as 'Teman Yahweh' and 'Samaria Yahweh' would accordingly concur with this view, with such uses as 'Ur of the Chaldees' (*'ur kaśdim*) to act as models. On either this analysis, or other explanations of the relation between 'Yahweh' and the place-names, it would be textually and logically impossible for us to posit the same reference for 'Yahweh' in the Old Testament and such a context as that found in Kuntillet 'Ajrud, not least if the latter is not actually a religious centre, but a way station (as Hadley 2000 suggests) if the tests and analysis offered above are correct. So, the impropriety of linking the two contexts is not the result of abstract imposition. Rather, the issue is that of drawing out the semantic conditions inherent to the two narrative situations, as well as allowing for the probability, even so, that a range of the Kuntillet 'Ajrud users may have wished to lay claim to sharing the same tradition as that manifested in mainstream areas of some Old Testament use of 'Yahweh'.

That this site appears to be a sort of visitors' centre for religious devotion, may itself advertise the polytheism, widespread through strata of Canaanite societies at a time when the prophets inveighed against polytheism—taking it to be an attack on monotheistic worship of Yahweh. Therefore possibly some of the worshipful visitors travelling through Kuntillet 'Ajrud intended the same reference to be attached to 'Yahweh' as that of some contemporary prophets and writers who criticised them in the Old Testament. Contrariwise, Kuntillet 'Ajrud inscriptions do not show that Yahweh of the Old Testament was worshipped there, even though it seems that Canaanite culture sometimes attempted to push Judah and Israel in that direction.

7

The Sense of Opposition in David

Contradiction

It is sometimes assumed that there are three somewhat contradictory biblical versions of Saul's emergence as king. Much attention has been given to these three presentations. Nevertheless, the measuring language or metalanguage by which adjudication of the 'contradictory' relations is sought has received little attention. The metalanguage, at one level, matches the uses of the vocabulary, which perform as standard rules to measure semantic relations and analytical sensitivity. A 'contradiction' is just such a mapping use. If the articulation of the metalanguage is arbitrarily adopted and is not exactly measured for its worth, then the contradictions will be traced in the metalanguage, but not in the biblical object language to which the metalanguage is applied. Of course, the metalanguage vocabulary need not be explicitly present to claim that it is normative for use in the object language—as with 'reference' in a proper name, it may be implicit but actual in function. According to the view that there are three contradictory versions of Saul's regal adoption, one of the biblical accounts states that it was at Gilgal that Saul was proclaimed the first king of Israel.

Contradiction, strictly, is when a statement is made twice (combined together), once with 'not' affixed to it: 'Saul became king at Gilgal and Saul did not become king at Gilgal', though the 1 Samuel passages do not state this, of course. It is a moot question of central importance to discover what the status of a scholarly paraphrase of an ancient text's sense is in relation to the imposition of our contemporary interpretations over against the putative sense of the ancient senses. Contrariety is where two or more related statements are incompatible because one or more of them are false by virtue of opposed predicates or subjects. Expressions such as 'varying accounts' (as used by Bright 1981: 188) are often employed to ascribe contrariety to a narrative. Two of the narrative strands are said to be respectively 'favourable' as against 'unfavourable' to Saul, by J.A. Soggin (1984: 48). The problem is that such judgements are offered without evidential support as assessments as evidence for the view that there is such an opposition. Some of the typical scholarly claims are set out in Figure 7.1 below; but note that no term in the purported three versions is in contrary or contradictory relation to another.

I.M. Zeitlin (1984: 156-59) is opposed to such claims of contrariety at relevant levels. Zeitlin also maintains that the two textual traditions, which some theologians suppose both claim distinct conflicting first meetings between David and Saul, are 'not necessarily contradictory'. He argues that the two narratives do not contain these implausible senses. It follows from these considerations that Bright's and Soggin's adoption of contrariety for the narratives is an assumption external to the texts. This has happened because they submerge explicit description of their assumed opposition ('contradiction', etc.) and inject a theological ideology that automatically generates consequences for the narrative thus programmed. This situation is disguised because scholars typically impose such ideological programs as though they were presenting analytical judgements sustained by proof; or, they are presented as if insulated by the illusion that sharing a consensus is the evidence of what history is.

1 Samuel represents Samuel as anointing Saul to be king, and yet announces that Saul later has Yahweh's Spirit withdrawn from him since Saul is rejected as king. A number of scholars construe this tension as 1 Samuel's presentation that Samuel 'repents' about his former support for Saul. The terms for 'repent' are never used in 1 Samuel of Samuel, however. But one word (*niḥamti*) is used of Yahweh (1 Sam. 15:11). The principle of linguistic choice has some importance here. This word is not the obvious choice (which would be *šub*), used for human repentance (with one exception regarding in irony: Absalom vaunting himself as if he were God, in his emotion). Ignoring this distinction between terms causes a commentator to confuse anthropomorphic with theomorphic categories. Consequently, it is held that the ancient writer, or critic, presents Yahweh to repent. The narrative emphasis in 1 Samuel exactly avoids this. Rather than employ jaded, unproved allusions to tragedy, as for example Soggin (1984) does for Saul, it is helpful to deploy Goldhill's (1984) deconstructed tragic figura from his treatment of the *Oresteia*. This sort of project would show that Samuel's descriptions of Saul cannot be identified with the coherent notion Soggin reconstructs with his Romantic view of 1 Samuel. In summary, the point is that Saul's psychological deconstruction is a function of the picture of his personal identity as represented in the narrative. The biography of Saul is not therefore an editorial ploy betrayed by alleged incongruent tensions in the Samuel text. These testimonies need interpreting outside of the purported triple versions, and integrated into a perspective which downloads the tensions into Saul's personality, instead of textual history.

This sort of alternative highlights a reason for forcing the distinction of repenting versus change or regret into the narrative arena. The simplistic 'Samuel and God repenting' aligns what is separate in the text. The term *naham*, stem of *niham*, and the form it has in 1 Samuel is not the 'turning about' sense which is associated with the term *sub* in personal human contexts. Naham reflects more a change associated with a function of grief. None of the above descriptions in the three versions of Saul has to be contrary. Being acclaimed king is not contrary to anointing; nor is Samuel's reluctant anointing contrary to his later opposition to Saul. In the putative authorial voice, God's reluctance is explicit from the beginning of Saul's career, and God's change of attitude towards Saul is causally consequent on the change in Saul's moral status and is not contingent on contrariety in divine dealings. (Rather like, in philosophical parlance, a Cambridge change in the price of butter: a price alteration, not one in butter.) Further, 'acclamation' has no fixed ritual priority in Hebrew kingship. 'Anointing' has no definitive sense that is contrary to other activities that stress or complement kingship or ascension to the throne (as it would in Egyptian ritual, for example). Thus there are no contraries in the purported three versions in 1 Samuel, if one draws on what aspects of the versions are depicted in biblical usage. With this preamble, we are now focused to assess similar relations in theological discussion of events subsequent to Saul's emergence as king yet related to Saul's kingship.

Conflicting and Irreconcilable

The confused 'contradiction' type of reasoning is often characterised by the use of assumed opinion rather than premises employed in reasoning. Assumptions rest on presuppositions that are often implicit, even to the consciousness of those who adopt them. This sort of 'contradictory' employs its own assumptions seemingly to detect lapses in others' departures from consistency. Consequently, the detection is simply a mirroring of the critic's epistemology in the target; with the supposed mistake being the gap between the target's presuppositions and the critic's. A corollary of this type of slip is found in the claim that the Davidic record gives three conflicting and irreconcilable versions of how David rose to a position of influence in Saul's Court. In one subtheme (1 Sam. 16:14-23), David is summoned to Court as a skillful harpist to soothe Saul's melancholia. In another subtheme (1 Sam. 16:1-13) David was secretly anointed by Samuel, as part of God's rejection of Saul. In the third version (1 Samuel 17), David the shepherd-boy emerges as folk-hero by volunteering to battle with the giant Philistine champion, Goliath. Such polemics do not take account of basic logical principles, nor allow for the research on motive causality in narratology such as those

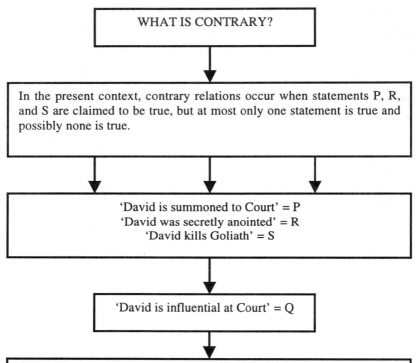

Figure 7.1   A logic diagram for David's Court promotion

implemented in comparable subjects (see for example Vitz 1989). The narrative structures of, and contrasts between, such elements as mental causality, motive, emotion and reason require explicit separation. This is not the occasion for a detailed theory (but Anscombe 1958 supplies one such applicable theory). A crucial expression in the above scenarios is, 'how David rose to a position of influence in Saul's Court'. Is there self-evidently, or necessarily, only one reason or means by which 'David rose to a position of influence in Saul's Court' obtains? Surely not. A ground for this is that a consequence Q (= David's rising to a position of influence in the royal Court) can be implied by more than one premise/antecedent. Here each above premise let us say P, B, and S (= the three reasons for David's promotion) can obviously be placed in consistent sequence, in correct conjunction. Each version about David's promotion, in other words, can be contributory, concurrent or sequential processes by which Q was achieved.

To suggest that two or more statements are contrary can presuppose that the semantics of their oppositions are internal to them. This is not the case with the three narrative forms under discussion, in view of the above; but we should consider further points. Sometimes statements are considered to be contrary because they conflict with an independent criterion that requires them to be joined, and so contrariety is generated or exposed; but the foregoing situation does not conform to this sort of conflict. Characters act in accordance with more than one univocal plot or operational function in the development of a singular end. It will assist to plot out the foregoing relations to represent this state of affairs further.

In the format of '(P and R and S) implies Q'—taking these schemata letters each to represent one of the three versions, introduced above, we have the versions of how David came to be influential in Court (i.e. Q). Namely, a set of causes of being influential in Court: (P and R and S) caused Q. More explicitly expressed, this would be: 'Q because of (P and R and S)'. Namely, David rose to a position of influence in court because of all the circumstances described in the three versions. There are a number of ways of approaching the characterisation of the three versions (as some inappropriately term them); yet there is no alternative method which yields a notion of contrary version as a requirement of the textual information and structure of David's early biography in 1 Samuel.

To deny the above position on the basis of inherent contrariety is to assume an arbitrary extra-textual presupposition that distorts the internal properties of the Hebrew semantic fields as a standardised analytical structure for the relevant Davidic data. The mistake, as exposed above, is that using what are actually contributory factors to David's success in going to and being at, Court, the presupposition illicitly deforms into mutually exclusive alternative means which are inaccurately paraphrased so as to be conflicting and irreconcilable semantic properties. The above correcting analysis is a matter of what logic there is *in* the criticised exegesis, and in biblical constructions of David's early biography. Use of such terms as 'version' artificially abstracts an internally harmonious narrative feature from the text without any proof. One cannot consistently ban the phenomenon of contributory factors from the universe of discourse to circumvent these objections, as one can see from Figure 7.1.

Who Killed which Goliath?

The record of David's slaying Goliath in 1 Samuel 17 is sometimes regarded as a contrary of the passage in 2 Sam. 21:19, where the killing of Goliath is attributed to Elhanan, the son of Jair of Bethlehem. As to translation relevant for indexing possible problems in the Hebrew Old Testament, some of the commentators have not mentioned that the differences that the texts present are only supported by some translations, such as the NEB. Conversely, the AV identifies the brother of Goliath as the one killed in 2 Sam. 21:19:

> (1) Elhanan the son of Jaare...slew the brother of Goliath. (2 Sam. 21:19, AV)
>   *'lḥnn bn y'ry...hlḥmy 't glyt*

There is no conflict in this with David's killing Goliath, because it is about Goliath's brother. In the record parallel with 2 Sam. 21:19 in 1 Chron. 20:5, even in the NEB this brother of Goliath is named:

> (2) Elhanan the son of Jaire killed Lahmi brother of Goliath. (1 Chron. 20:5, NEB)
>   *'lḥnn bn-y'wr 't-lḥmy 'ḥy glyt*

So, if the AV type of translation is correct, the combination of (1) 'Elhanan the son of Jaare...slew the brother of Goliath' and (2) 'Elhanan the son of Jaire killed Lahmi brother of Goliath' can be used to imply that in the narrative voices, and the conjectured intertextual semantic contracts, of Samuel and Chronicles David's defeating Goliath is not contrary to other Goliath deaths, because these other accounts refer to a relation of David's Goliath-victim being killed in a distinct context. Even if one employed the NEB type of translation for 2 Sam. 21:19 ([3], below), which excludes the 'brother of' expression, one still could be in a position to know of this brother if (2) is a genuine expansion of the implicit or intended sense of the Hebrew of (1) 'Elhanan the son of Jaare...slew the brother of Goliath'. There are a number of problems associated with this interpretation, which will be dealt with below, though they do not require a modification of (2).

In (1) 'Elhanan the son of Jaare...slew the brother of Goliath', the AV translation, the expression 'the brother of' is not present in the Hebrew text. The NEB renders it:

> (3) Elhanan son Jair...killed Goliath. (2 Sam. 21:19, NEB)
>   *'lḥnn bn y'ry...hlḥmy 't glyt*

This does not fully reproduce the Hebrew, however, because it leaves the term *'et* untranslated, as often it is. Here *'et* is prefixed to 'Goliath'. The varieties of uses associated with this term are sometimes difficult to reproduce in translation. Sometimes it has the sense of a preposition—'with' or 'along with'; but, as in the NEB translation (3), *'et* is often associated with another value—a piece of syntax, not translated meaning: *'et* can mark the object (here in [3] the object would be 'Goliath'). Yet, the Hebrew of 2 Sam. 21:19, *'lḥnn bn y'ry...hlḥmy 't glyt*, does not have to bear this latter interpretation.

Let us concentrate on the translational senses of 'with' or 'along with' for *'et*. Even when these senses of the word *'et* are translatable, translations often do not render them into another language, because they do not easily fit into the usual semantic frame and word preference of, say, English. (For example, the Authorized Version, along with many others, does not bring the two occurrences of *'et* into English in Gen. 1:1, 'In the beginning God created [*'et*] the heavens and [*'et*] the earth'.)

The usual and indeed proper explanation is that *'et* is the object of the verb-marker; but even here it could be that these uses also reflect tonal nuances, perhaps from their prehistory, as prepositional-like functions in terms of underlying semantic components, though I do not suggest that they should be thus rendered. This difficulty is to be emphasized when one comes across figurative uses of *'et* which are employed in some narrative presuppositional history texts. For example, in Gen. 4:1, where, as a result of Eve's giving birth to Cain, Eve is said to state: *qnyt 'ys 't-yhwh*, literally: 'I have gotten (a) person with (*'t*) Yahweh'. Embodying this instrumental sense, the AV renders *'et* with 'from', while NEB translates it 'with the help of' (cf. also BDB 86 col. A). (A 'literal' translation is still intelligible here; but perhaps the King James' translator was sensitive to the avoidance of using 'with' because it could easily ascribe too close a relationship of Eve with Yahweh, though with that sense it seems only to have an instrumental metonymic function.) In the NEB's employment of 'with the help of', it has resorted to a translation device which is akin to the AV's 'the brother of' in (1) 'Elhanan the son of Jaare...slew the brother of (*'et*) Goliath', though of course the sense is different from Gen. 4:1, in an attempt to match the force of its interpretation of the Hebrew 'et. One feature of this attempt is the introduction of 'of' in AV and NEB.

By itself, the 'of' in 'of Goliath' or 'of Yahweh' is not instructive, but it needs expansion into in what respect *'et* possibly carries this 'of' sense. In Hebrew, this type of usage comes near to being an idiom, where pun on the idiom could trigger or activate the relevant meaning—as with cut/make in the Hebrew: '*karat* a covenant'; or the expression 'to be with it' in colloquial English, which communicates sharing in a fashion. I am not linking this meaning to the Hebrew *'et*, however, but only illustrating how a preposition in relation to a piece of metaphorized syntax can acquire an idiomatic sense. BDB (85 col. B) extends this type of meaning by noticing that some of the *'et* uses can bear the sense of companionship; that is, as in 'together with'. In addition to this, even in respect of the sense 'with', the term *'et*, as BDB suggests, 'expresses closer association than *'m 't'*. This is quite compatible with the point that *'im* is the normal term for 'with' in Hebrew (cf. BDB 87 col. A). One use of *'et*, in Gen. 44:28, illustrates how a class of uses is connected with family relations at this intimate level, where Jacob laments his loss of Joseph: *wys' h'ḥd m'ty*—'one went out from me' (AV). Neither the AV nor the NEB brings *'t* through into the English translation. With these sorts of contexts and uses, the AV's 'the brother of' in (1) is a textually probable representation of the force of the Hebrew *'et* if it falls into this class of uses. Even without this translation, if the term *'et* is grouped with the foregoing class, it obviously occurs as an incomplete (syntactically metonymic) expression.

By 'incomplete expression', I have the standard logical distinction in mind (Geach 1968: 39). For example, if one says that 'x is the same as y', this appears to be complete; but it is actually functionally incomplete, because to appreciate its sense one has to know what the ingredient of being 'the same' is. The actual structure is: x is, or has, the same F [= property] as y. By analogy, but with a different meaning, the Hebrew *'et* is an incomplete expression. But, for what it is an incomplete expression? Well, judging by the previous considerations, an incomplete expression for being 'a relation of Goliath'. As the AV translation has specified it in (1) 'Elhanan the son of Jaare...slew the brother of Goliath', it is an incomplete expression whose value is: 'being a brother of Goliath'. Given the foregoing assessment, if *'et* in (1) belongs in the above category, it is a misunderstanding of (2) 1 Chron. 20:5: 'Elhanan the son of Jaire killed Lahmi brother of Goliath', to consider that text as an improper attempt at harmonisation. It has been supposed that (2) attempts to harmonise 1 Samuel 17 and 2 Sam. 21:19, because (2) 1 Chron 20:5 introduces the name 'Lahmi'. If (2) is merely supplying the name to fill the incomplete expression embodied by 'et , then this is not, in a nontrivial sense, an addition which relevantly alters the function of the word *'et* or its context. Rather, it is naming the member of the class that the text already semantically presupposes as an intertextual function, with which it forms a relational contract.

An alternative standard explanation of the difference between (3) 2 Sam. 21:19: 'Elhanan son Jair...killed (*'et*) Goliath' and (2) 1 Chron 20:5: 'Elhanan the son of Jaire killed Lahmi brother of Goliath', which removes the need for judging the texts to be inconsistent, has been proposed by Hertzberg (1964: 387). This proposal does not depend on the foregoing analysis or conclusion; yet Hertzberg's thesis can be combined with my foregoing proposals. Many commentaries fail to include a mention of Hertzberg's type of view, which is a pity, since it renders the alternative wrong, if Hertzberg is right. Hertzberg's interpretation can be stated quite briefly: the use of 'Goliath' in 1 Samuel 17 in connection with David, and in 2 Sam. 21:19 to do with Jaare, are two different meanings of the name 'Goliath'. The first is a proper name of an individual; the second is the designation of a clan called Goliath. This latter opinion accords with the foregoing assessment of *'et*, which could also indicate a member of a clan. It is interesting in this connection that the 1 Samuel 17 usage of 'Goliath' does not use *'et* with the name, which concurs with the distinction that this is a proper name of an individual, whereas the possible clan-use in 2 Sam. 21:19 does have *'et*.

A number of points tend to support Hertzberg's exposition and my reformulation of it. First, the David/Goliath context is midway through the first book of Samuel, while the 'Jaare' report is at the end of the second book of Samuel. In their presuppositional history and extant compositional intertextual relations, and in their internal diachronic time-span, an interval of a generation separates the two uses of the terms. This is quite adequate for a shift in the meaning of the term 'Goliath'. Consider a 20th-century parallel: 'Nazi' was a name of a specific ethnic military/political group in the second world war. A generation later, the word 'Nazi' had been metaphorized and became emblematic of a certain type of group activity; the term has been applied to an ethnic group or individual, and not necessarily in respect of a military role. The scope of 'nazi', as with Hertzberg's proposal for 'Goliath', has enlarged and shifted over the space of a generation. Secondly, in biblical and other Near Eastern usage, the proper name of a progenitor of a group or a leader of a clan frequently becomes the name of the group or clan (e.g. Gen. 10:15). Thirdly, in some such groups the name of the clan is also used as the name of its leader or its warriors. The mythology surrounding the giant-clan *Repha'im* employs named *Rapha'* (cf. Chapter 3, above) as it chief or king. So one may not even require the possibility of the change from an individual's proper name in David's contest with Goliath to the time of Jaire's defeating another Goliath. Fourthly, since 'Goliath' in the context of 1 and 2 Samuel is plausibly a Philistine word, and because we know so little about the syntax of Philistine proper names, it would be rash to insist on the term 'Goliath' necessarily having to possess a semantic scope that entails a conflict in its usage in Samuel and Chronicles.

In such a state of ignorance, the apparently messy condition of aspects in the textual history could be due to hitherto undetermined linguistic parameters related to Philistine semantics attaching to the Bible narratives, and puns upon them, rather than problems be the result of the transmission of the biblical text, or writer, which inadvertently or intentionally provokes the issues here addressed.

This study makes some attempt at allowing for Bakhtin's view about uncomfortable oppositions of sense in a narrative's history: 'At any present moment of the dialogue there are great masses of forgotten meanings, but these will be recalled again at a given moment in the dialogue's later course when it will be given new life. For nothing is absolutely dead: every meaning will someday have its homecoming festival' (cf. Clark and Holquist 1984: 350). My argument is that due attention to the binary dynamics of the narratives here discussed, and scholarly contributions, can supply this.

8

Military Theology

Particular Generalization

As Kristiansen (1998: 128-33) argues in the context of archaeological general theory, the ending of the Bronze Age was associated with the decline of the old orders and the emergence of new ritual centres connected to major settlements. A common ingredient in this transformation was the use of iron, not only the Levant, but also through Europe. Kristiansen (1998: 83) shows that this is well attested in, for example, Ørbaeklunde and Fuen, Denmark, with its substantial distribution hoard of iron winged axes. Although Kristiansen recognises that there is substantial asymmetry between Europe and Mesopotamia regarding the specific development and role of iron, yet there are significant similarities, and ones beyond the scope of this discussion. Anciently, this was to some degree recognised and not always taken to be a positive change, for example as with the quotation of Hesiod from early in the seventh century BC, cited by Kristiansen (1998: 130):

> Would that I did not live in this fifth generation, but had either died before it or born afterwards! This is truly a generation of iron; for men never stop toiling and wailing by day, and perishing by night. The gods will give them sore troubles. (*Works and Days* II: 174-78).

This emphasis on increased perception of death, the uniqueness of the point of experience, alienation from the contemporary, together with the looking to the past or future, we may be surprised to realise, is a set of conditions for being a modernist period. Hesiod's concern for the response of the gods to this state of affairs is not unlike some presuppositions of 19th-century French modernism (on the French aspect see Kelley 1976). In a modified sense, we can recognise that these features parallel facets of the Iron Age in Canaan. As with modernism, however, so with some relations between later Bronze Ages and particularly Iron Age II. An interaction metaphor (along the lines of Black 1961) is an apt motif to depict certain relations here. For example, in Bronze Age Ugaritic there was already some cultic use of iron (for which see below) that influenced Iron Age II. Moreover, as Mazar (1993: 510) noted, alongside the Iron Age II use of the Hebrew term for iron—*barzel*—which he suggested 'became a synonym for strength' (and I argue below, enjoys somewhat more specific significance), there is evidence of concurrent employment of bronze and other metals. So an age's metal should be seen as a dominating function among other competing subsidiary metals. This focus is especially important for the metal presuppositions manifested in a religious centre's activity and its mythological or theological polemic. Such an ancient propagandist perspective attaches to a metal in such a way as frequently to leak, condense and communicate some ancient mental elements of those concerned with religious centre and deity. As such, a study of a specific case of presuppositional attitudes to a metal like iron assists us to contextualise both retrojected and predictable general movements of agricultural and military evolution, but also to address specific conceptual tendencies in ancient human creativity.

Elisha and the Iron Axe

One qualifiable parallel of typical sites is the ludic use of the iron axe. Whereas religious centres had tended to evolve to become the temple, in the Iron Age of Canaan, the authorial voice of 2 Kings takes other religious centres as threats to the temple worship. In fact, it seems that the move from religious centre to temple site was so complex and fraught with external influences and internal indeterminacies that, at many junctures, it challenged or internally diversified the uniform notion of evolution

Elisha's narrative in 2 Kings is partially neglected, due perhaps to its bizarre character. A way of restoring it to more attention might be theological polemic against various mythological aspects of Canaanite culture. This will reveal that the bizarre features are those of the target audience and object of polemic, and not that of a presupposition advocated in the authorial voice. Each of the some 14 signs—often termed miracles, on this analysis, is an element in a synthetic campaign that performs the role of an enacted ironising parable. This, I suggest, is a component in the narrative's ideological war between two cultures: roughly, Yahweh's teachings against Baal's fertility. The theological war is itself sometimes blended with military features to enhance its relevance for the practice of Yahweh's will. In short, the perceived emergence of Yahweh as supreme judge is seen in the focus of his treatment of the affairs of war as a function of his control of religious activity. The iron axe miracle of 2 Kings 6 exemplifies this trait of miracle as parable and military polemic, disguised

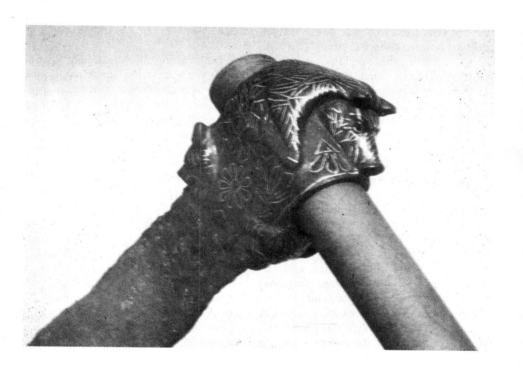

Figure 8.1   Ugaritic cultic war axe

from casual view though the nuances are. Elisha's trainee prophets coerce him into going to the Jordan to build the temple. Upon commencing construction, one of them drops a borrowed axe into the water. Elisha castigates the person, casts a stick into the water, and raises the axe so that it floats. The next event depicted in the narrative is that of Syria attacking Israel. In 2 Kings 6, *hbrzl* is the expression for 'axe'—not one of the standard Hebrew terms for 'axe'. It also has the form of a Canaanite word for iron with the prefix definite article, though the spelling *brzl* occurs elsewhere, for example in some 20 uses at Mari. The equivalent Ugaritic form occurs in a mythological votive context (Gordon 1965: 120, 1, 6). In Ugarit, a cultic axe was discovered, apparently of the type referred to by this term (Schaeffer 1939: 108-12).

It is a cultic heraldic war axe, with lion and boar motifs. A matching figurine of Baal was also found at the same time at Ugarit in the Late Bronze acropolis; this embodies a smiting-god position, holding aloft an axe (in some other occurrences, a mace). At Doliche, the god 'Teshub of the double-axe' was a catalyst in the Baal religious centre there (cf. Forbes 1960: 454-55), and Negbi (1976: 119) observes that Baal derived his smiting-god characteristic from an older war god, though he did not make the link to 2 Kings 6. As Yadin showed (1963: 352-87; esp. 352-53; cf. also Albright 1968: 97-212; and Oden 1976: 31-36), the axe with god of war motif extends well into the Iron Age. He documented a war-god at Hazor with an axe between his knees; it was found in a pottery vessel filled with votive offerings, including two arrowheads which have Hebrew inscriptions on them. The axe from Ugarit is made of 'steeled' iron, and the smiting god figure is, as is typical, made of iron—a feature not without its allusive quality with regard to the attendant mythology of this metal's function in war.

The use of Akkadian and its influences at Ugarit (see, for example, Huchnergard 1989) are important here in relation to the foregoing cluster of associations around the bestial motifs (including the remarks above pp. 6-9) concerning the archetypal role of weapon-names, not least in relation to the function of the Sumerian me (= archetype) with regard to the mythology. The Akkadian influences in the Levant survived the end of Ugarit, and exerted themselves through many more layers of influence in later semantic fields. Livingstone (1986: 49-63) elegantly depicts the *Weapon Name Exposition* in Babylonian, which has Sumerian foundations. Although this is in a Mesopotamian context rather than that of the Levant, the above series of connections and influences has some parallel with it, and it appears to articulate some of the details in the themes connected with them, not least in its extensive use of astrology. As Livingstone points out, it was because of the widespread acceptance of the importance of the theme and its connections with such matters that the *Exposition* was composed and used for such contexts. A date in the very late 2nd or early 1st millennium BC has been adduced, and there is evidence of the use of the

Babylonian duplicate texts in the reigns of Sargon II and Sennacherib, thus providing an appropriate temporal environment for its use to illustrate the mythological and cultic employment of iron weapons. We may accurately think of the Sumerian sense of me, archetype, by partially aligning it with a notion of Platonic form (as formulated by Bernard Williams 1999, rather than some more traditional approaches). This sense, together with its mystical associations, is not dissimilar to the 6th-century AD use of the divine names in pseudo-Dionysius the Areopagite. This cluster of senses approximate especially to the function of manifestation of the Mesopotamian trend to use a named archetype in a specific context. In this respect, it is significant to see that the 'axe lion-headed me' is mentioned in the text of the *Weapon Name Exposition* (after Livingstone 1986: 54-55):

^dme.sag.50* ^{d.gis}tukul.sag.pirig ^dme.sag.pirig.

Fifty-headed archetype; Lion-headed weapon; lion-headed archetype.

Renfrew's excavations at Melos (documented in Renfrew 1985) supply a more distant yet boundary of possible symbolic relation to this iconic history, with the smiting-god figurines form the Levant being found there. There even seems to be a cultic parallel in Crete at Knossos, where Arthur Evans (1928: II, 335) discovered the shrine of the double-axe. The metal-god icons types took their places amongst the many conceptual metaphors forming part of the complex ritual and mythological systems, mediating themselves through subsequent Canaanite societies. Reference to this type of symbolism appears to have been an associative trigger-device to produce an evocation of the symbolic significance of that for which it stood. The range of archaeological data above, though not resolvable into a complete solution, sufficiently map on to the 2 Kings 6's *hbrzl* so as to expedite the interpretation of related aspects, since there are many typically connected icons. Negbi (1976: 2) states that:

> Since monumental Stone sculpture is comparatively rare in the Levant before the Hellenistic period, it is usually suggested that metal figurines are miniature replicas of wooden religious statues, which have been obliterated. As such, metal figurines may have occasionally served as cult idols, but they are generally regarded as having been votive idols. In many places they were found in public sanctuaries and high-places; therefore, their ceremonial function can hardly be denied.

This complements the other sorts of statues, for example bestial ones, including monumental parallels with the lion motif on the axe; the remarks above (pp. 6-8) prepare the way for and are presupposed in the present exposition.

Figure 8.2   Baal as smiting god

The iron axe that was discovered, mentioned above, is a full-sized one, which comes from a smiting-god, similarly full-sized, statue, and was used by priests as a ceremonial emblem of the war god. With these connections and data, it is evident that the biblical term *hbrzl* for 'axe' has a historical basis that is derivable from such cultic functions as these encode. The existence of the narrative in 2 Kings 6 is relevant to theologically substantive issues in ancient Levant priorities. It rehearses the confrontation of some Canaanite theology and religion concerned with conceptual and military conflict. The borrowed axe in 2 Kings 6, with the text employing a highly specialised cultic term, specifically latches onto and manifests a disputational interest in Canaanite theology. The related Baal image, as for example Negbi judges it, was frequently to be found in accessible locations, some of which seem, as was appropriate to military and fertility associations attached to buildings or locations specialised for worship, to have been beside rivers. Such a tradition starts before Ugaritic culture, moves through its influences, is merged with other influences in and from Mesopotamian literatures, and continues well into the Iron Age.

The River Jordan was central to such textures of association; it is with nuances like these that 2 Kings 6 sets the narrative alongside the Jordan where Elisha is presented as performing the act of raising the axe. It is worth noting that the terminology of divine intervention is absent here, as is any Hebrew use of transcendental terms in a miracle scenario. This may be due to the attempted demythologisation in the writer's presupposition about the way a prophet of Yahweh made the 'miracle'-category a feature to be imposed polemically on the pragmatics of life. Perhaps this is reminiscent of an ancient pre-Greek non-dualist sense of the immanence of God and divine presence in everyday life, as in contrast with the narrative voice's premise that Canaanite life was suffused with magical dualist intervention. In other words, the field semantics of 2 Kings 6:1-5 manifests the guise of secular pragmatism. This includes the punchline appearance of the Syrians invading at the end of the scenario—a narrative suddenly injected with a floating axe. Possibly the tension is a form of ironic counterpoint interposing originality in this type of contrast.

The notions of 'water' and 'rising' play an important double role in Baal theology. Baal was deemed the Lord of fountains. It is significant that here a dispute between Yam and Baal involving 'judge Naḥar (river)' in Canaanite myth should centre on a debacle involving an axe (cf. J.C.L. Gibson 1978: 40-45). Baal was deemed the Lord of fountains as a means to maintain Baal's power over nature and nations. These motifs were localised and concretised in ritual ceremony. The rites are stylised in Baal stelae, with Baal as chief fertility god of Canaan and Phoenicia—a claim especially directed at his mastery over winter rain and water (Moor 1971a: 9-28). In a characteristic pose adopted by a statue which is usually taken to be in his likeness, Baal stands as an epitome of Rasap's war power wearing Egypt's gods' white crown (see Negbi 1976: 31, and his reference to Schaeffer). As mentioned above (p.90) in relation to Ea, river symbolism of this sort in relevant senses matches, and is probably partially derived from, Sumerian influence mediated by Akkadian (for the best review of the overall background see George, 1999: *xxxi*, etc). Akkadian was entrenched at Ugarit in such ways as to indicate its increasing influence on Canaanite literature (see Huehnergard, 1989; cf. Driver 1978: 12-13).

From early times, rivers such as the Jordan were personified either individually or as a class. 'Nahar' was a usual Northwest Semitic name for Jordan functioning as a personified river, as were others. Such a river could be deemed either a deity or be treated as an extension of Baal's dominion or power. (The deification of the sea, associated with Yam, is also identified with Nahar, though this aspect is not developed in the present context; see Ap-Thomas 1973: 273, n. 47.) In the linguistic flow-charts which document such trends, hypostatization attracts corporate agglomeration of relatable properties. These semantic fields were fertile grounds for originating and sustaining thematic metaphors. Earlier motifs in the ministry of Elisha have already prepared some of this thematic ground. In 2 Kings 2, the water seems to turn red, mirroring the Egyptian plague language, but it also finds a parallel with a river near Phoenician Byblos, called Nahr Ibrahim and later Adonis, which was supposed to turn red as a sign of the death and rising of the god (Aqhat II.vi, 45-6; see Baal II, iv, 20-2 as well).

Rites were associated with such myths, whereby rulers/priests/soldiers stood in the river to associate them with the god's rising, and this ritualised typology recurs in the Ugaritic 'Palace of Baal' myth. This myth itself pertains to another theme in 2 Kgs. 4:18-16 (CTA 2: I, 13-39), that of the death of the child by sunstroke, whose mother, having been provided with this—now dead—child by Elisha's previous word, warns him, when requesting her son's revival, 'Do not deceive me'. She, in these words, is quoting the liturgy from the 'Palace of Baal', and the narrative voice simultaneously puns upon Genesis 3. There is no space here to illustrate the extent of this sort of interplay and thematic comparative polemic which constitute a complex pattern throughout the 14 signs in Elisha's ministry, but we should note that the axe motif is part of a rich use of condensation and displacement devised in 2 Kings to provide a framework for theological warfare using Canaan's symbols from polytheistic traditions. One well-known aspect of the Baal/Nahar is where Baal and Nahar are in conflict; Baal as smiting god attacks Nahar with an axe. Ceremonial rites were connected with this mythology. Here it seems that we have part of the background for Elisha's power over the axe in 2 Kings 6. It is appropriate to quote at some length from this Baal myth:

Depart, young men, do not tarry head straight for
the Assembled Convocation (of the gods)
Standing up, tell what you have to inform
(them) what you know.
And say to the Baal, my father *'il*
A message of your Master Judge Naḥar
Give up Baal the son of Dagan
The gods lowered their heads
Baal rebuked them lift up, gods, your heads
For I am going to answer the envoys of Judge Naḥar
His Highness [Zebul] Baal became angry
and took an axe in his hand, in his right hand
he raised a slayer[1] of the young men.

Subsequently in the Baal myth, attention is turned directly at Naḥar:

I say to you, O Highness [Zebul] Baal...slay your foes...
take your eternal...kingship, your everlasting dominion.
Kotar [the speaker] brought down a double-headed
axe and proclaimed its name:
you, your name is Yagruš ['to drive away' or 'cast out']
(CTA 2: IV, 8-17, 2 75)

Yagruš, drive away...Naḥar...
leap from the hand of Baal,
like an eagle from his fingers.
Strike Judge Naḥar between the arms.
The axe leapt from the hand of Baal
It hit Judge Naḥar between the arms[2]

This gambit is not fully successful, so the myth reports that another axe is deployed:

Kotar brought down a double-headed axe
and proclaimed its name: You, your name
is Ayyamur [= do anything to destroy].[3]

---

[1] The stem of the term for 'slayer' is used in Isa. 57:20 in connection with sea, where there may be some punning-allusion to the Baal/Yam/Naḥar motifs.
[2] The term for axe in this myth is a general term (*smdm*) and not the biblical *hbrzl*. Of course, the two narratives, Ugaritic and Hebrew, use related though distinct language dialects and the former uses derive in extant texts from usage antecedent to the Hebrew. This allows for some diversification and shift of scope. *smdm* metaphorically indicates the blade of an axe, and is used metonymically of the whole axe.

Ayyamur, expel...Naḥar
leap from the hand of Baal
like an eagle from his fingers
hit...Naḥar between the eyes
And the axe leapt from the hand of Baal,
Like an eagle from his fingers.
It hit...Judge Naḥar between his eyes.[4]

So Baal appears to triumph over river water and has it in his power by virtue of acquiring the right axe. Here and in other contexts the axe is theologically and emblematically symbolic of the state of affairs partly depicted here. In related rites, characters stand in water with the axe, either in rivers or in a mirroring of this in temple ritual worship, Baal ruling by association with his personified identity.

In 2 Kings 6, then, Elisha's raising the axe was a phenomenon set against and connected with those complex widely spread cultural motifs in Canaanite use. The Hebrew term for axe itself is directly drawn from Canaanite usage, and thus, we have seen, it reflects the water-god, river power, and the rising-god. In other words, the axe symbol in 2 Kings 6 was perceived as a numinous sublime symbol of divine presence. In the narrative world, Elisha demonstrates that Yahweh—not Baal or Naḥar—has power to raise the axe. And the mere fact of the axe's being in the river—in Naḥar, so to speak, together with its terminological identity, and thereby theological attachment to Baal—showed, even in the river god's personified body, that Yahweh can exercise power over the river and Baal's implement. Hence, 2 Kings 6 is debating a matter of fundamental structural importance in the Palestinian mythological scene—grappling with, and surmounting it, by means of the theology of Yahweh.

Nevertheless, the axe-motif is not solely a theological issue. We have seen how closely war and smiting components fit into the general Baal theology. In ancient Canaan, mythology was closely linked with military and political activity. In military strategy, mythology was a ritual and policy-making function, and this is a focus produced in 2 Kings 6, not least when we position as relevant the closing and otherwise apparently irrelevant remark that the Syrians came to war against Israel, and noting also the ways in which early chapters in 2 Kings had already paved the way for the

---

[3] There are two stems in the term *Ayyamur*: *'ay*—'anything'; *mr*—'to expel'. The above 'do anything to destroy' is a paraphrase concisely to catch the force of the expression.

[4] This representation and role appear early, for example at Ebla (see Matthiae 1977, with reference to the photograph of a relief of a king-figure with axe regarding the Ebla tablet TM.74.G.1000); see also Yadin 1963: 386 for a relief representing the axe in active Iron Age combat contexts.

amalgamation of theology and war, not least with the reference in 3:27 to the king of Moab's offering of his eldest son in human sacrifice—mirroring the custom described on the Moabite Stone. Throughout the account of his ministry, Elisha uses theology to confront politics, as well as the envisaged military status of Israel and Israel's neighbours. It is as though the borrowing of the axe is seen as a dependence on pagan relic; obliquely encapsulating Israel's degraded status before Yahweh. Elisha's raising the axe exhibited the autonomy and power which Israel had neglected or rejected, with a result that Yahweh sends the Syrians to judge Israel. This theme was to continue to Elisha's death. Later, in 2 Kgs. 13:17-20, Elisha's death heralded the return of the Moabite attack; and eventually the Syrians would invade again.

The AV 1611 translators, consciously or not, rendered the text with the pun in a sensitive way that is tantamount to exposing the nuance on the likely significance attached to the iron axe ossified in the word *hbrzl*. As observed above, in 2 Kgs. 6:5, *hbrzl* is translated 'axe', whereas in verse 6 it is translated into English as 'iron' when the floating axe is highlighted. Here both the tension of iron's floating, and its being iron as a metallurgical power-motif reflecting mythology and military ceremony, break the surface semantics and emerge as nuances which are code-signs for aspects of the foregoing. The tactical and strategic importance of iron at the military level contributed significance to and strengthened the emphasis on ancient Levant perception of these nuances, sharply contrasting with Bronze Age instruments of war, since properly smelted iron would be perceived as a major contrast with the old fashioned or past means of warfare. This pattern stretches in various ways from Genesis to the use of iron in Daniel's image (Daniel 2). Accordingly, this metal's links with mythology and its operational use are valuable resources for further research.

The elements for such a synthetic construction of polemical interplay had been laid down in other cultures whose later influence on the Old Testament world downloaded at polemic junctures to utilise the potential for a narrative stream of consciousness when subsequent ancient technology harnessed this past potential. Muhly *et al.* (1985) report that the iron blade of the above mentioned Ugaritic axe—shown in Figure 8.1—has a nickel content of 3.25% and 0.41% of carbon. He contends that this is sufficient carbon to classify it as mild steel. Muhly observes that, though an early view was that the nickel content was too low for it to be meteoritic iron, this is now disputed. Quite independently of whether or not the meteoritic source of iron is itself mythology, is the ancient apparent belief that iron was from heaven. So, behind this applied utility of iron was a forceful legacy of mythology and etymology that merged mystique with metal. This is idiosyncratically reflected in the Sumerian KU-BI AN-NA. Traditional scholarly ascription of sense to the expression is that of 'heaven metal'; that is, meteoric iron, putatively speaking. One would have thought that this is obviously open to, or is sourced from, astral considerations, rather than excavation by the ancients of actual meteoric iron. This Sumerian is reproduced and paraphrased into Hittite hieroglyphic, though the usage is not consistent. It comes through into Akkadian as a cognate of *brzl*, and *parzillu*. The Sumerian AN, and possibly BAR, are already in Syrian Sumerian at Ebla in the 3rd millennium, though the Sumerian references perhaps do not indicate smelted iron. Egyptian etymology literally matches the Sumerian 'heaven metal', with *bi' n pt*. Such allusive potential is no doubt distant from the Old Testament; yet combined together, the multiple layers facilitate mediated access for complex pun in ancient creative mythic polemic.

Sennacherib

In the Hebrew of 2 Kings and Isaiah, Sennacherib's name is Sanherib, and Sin-ahhe-eriba in Akkadian. The use of the *s* (as opposed to *shin*) may indicate that the biblical writer adopted the Babylonian form of the name as standard (cf. Gurney and Kramer 1976: 15, 83). If the components of the name are assigned senses, then the meaning is 'Sin has given us [two] brothers'. 'Sin' is the name of a Mesopotamian moon god, traceable to the Sumerian Suen (or Zuen; see J.C.L. Gibson 1975: 28) associated with Haran. This deity was also familiar to West Semitic people, for example, this god is called upon to witness a treaty struck by a king of Arpad who was a son of Attarsamak (e.g. Moorey 1975: 104) in the 8th century BC. (The form '*Altar-*' in this name is parallel with '*Adr-*' in the name of Sennacherib's son Adrammelech, allowing for the expected shift of *tt* to *r*; cf. Millard 1976: 8-9). The naming motif in 'Sennacherib' aptly falls into line with Isaiah's treatment of the king as a politico-theological threat to Judah. The third campaign of 701, which Sennacherib brought against Canaan, is thrown into mythological priority by the biblical record's treatment. This is reflected in Isaiah's report that the Assyrian chief of staff, Rabshakeh, challenges Jerusalem by claiming that Sennacherib had destroyed the gods of Arpad, Hamath and Sepharvaim. He argues implicitly that Yahweh will not be made an exception of in this practice.

That Sin was a god at Arpad is not noticed as a possible contrary detail—for Sennacherib had opposed one of his own gods there. Names of gods have homonyms (as we found with 'Yahweh' above), because a range of such gods are cultic functions of imagination for ancient mythology, whose form migrates to new identities: a god of the city religious centre is ultimately a function of the dynamics of both imagination and external societal pragmatism. Once a god was absorbed as the, or an, object of worship in a city, it was deemed to be a transcendent inhabitant, or a remote honorary one, and thereby a construct of that city's social identity. For example, a god might be positioned as a territorial god. In this perspective, if the god Sin at Arpad and the god Sin at Nineveh were defined in terms of their social and religious contexts, then they would be two different gods. A reason for this is because the explanation of a god in such terms identifies it as a god of that city's religious centre. The criterion of identity for Sin, nested in the mythological texts, appears to operate with the bits of local world-view as part of the criterion. So the definition of Sin as god of Arpad, as well as the attendant territorial claims, is a limiting feature that explains Sin as a construct of, and production from, the elements of the city religious centre and culture. Clearly, for us, this necessitates treating the concept of the god as an intentionalistic identity, because his identity is defined in terms of phenomena that are not reducible to an existing deity. In keeping with this sketch, though the term 'Sin' was used to name icons in different cities, 'Sin' occurs in different locations as homonyms where the city religious centre in each city is incorporated into a definition of that particular god Sin. Particularly is this the case because Nineveh's mythology of Sin does not recognise, for example, the Arpad mythology of Sin as a function of Nineveh's Sin's identity. Nevertheless, Sennacherib is typical of Assyrian monarchs in supposing the contrary, that his gods had universal power, a power which held sway over the lands of other monarchs, but this is in opposition to the cultural form such gods take. Universal power requires a specification of a god as 'the one and only such object', whereas the Sin type of deity is a cultic symbol with a relativistic foundation—there are sets of such symbols which form a class of gods. So the political 'philosophy' of this type of Mesopotamian deity extends outside the legitimate scope of the deity's basis. Of course, it is a moot question as to whether or not senior politicians and scholars in such ancient societies actually fully, or partially, believed what we would call the ontological uptake of the declarative forms of theistic propositions. There are some signs that they were as capable as modernist humanity of partial belief dispositions, and this could be a way of construing relativistically the above contrary tendencies in the functional claims of the ancient social theologies. To this, we can readily add the pragmatic use of ritualised polemic.

Sennacherib's Return to Nineveh

It is both in the polemical loss of face and in personal devotion to the little-known god Nisroch in Assyria, that Sennacherib had his deathly homecoming as viewed by the Isaiah narrative. The Hebrew MT presentation of the causes of Sennacherib's return to Assyria (2 Kgs. 19:6-7, 32-35) does not thereby omit some of the putative complex historical relations which surround the events merely because a miracle is there presupposed. In 2 Kgs. 19:7, a rumour, which impresses Sennacherib, is presented as a central reason for his return to Nineveh. It is not known what this rumour was, though crises often occurred at Court in Nineveh, as elsewhere. These at the time frequently revolved around the claims as to who was to become the crown prince; accordingly, various sons instigated revolts. These eventually escalated into a major conflict that appears to have brought about the murder of Sennacherib.

An immediate military candidate which could have produced the rumour was the rebellion by the Babylonian vassal Bel-ibni whom Sennacherib had put on the throne the previous year (702) after having made Babylon subservient. When Sennacherib returned from Jerusalem to Nineveh, the Assyrian army marched on Babylon—a move that would tend to support the foregoing type of assessment. Moreover, Sennacherib's eldest son, the crown prince Assur-nadin-sumi, went to Babylon and was placed on the throne. This latter point might relate in part to the removal of the crown prince from Nineveh for reasons of safety, or to establish him publicly as crown prince. Subsequently in 694, Assur-nadin-sumi was taken captive to Elam, and never returned. This left the sons Adrammelech, Sharezer and Esarhaddon to develop the dispute as to who would be king after Sennacherib's death. The eldest remaining son was Adrammelech. Sennacherib's wife Naqi'a-Zakutu, however, favoured her own son Esarhaddon, over Adrammelech. Eventually, Esarhaddon was publicly proclaimed crown prince, though he went to live in, or fled to, a distant province it seems in order to avoid assassination by his brothers.

On 20 Tebet 681, Esarhaddon's two brothers murdered Sennacherib instead, in an attempt to get around Esarhaddon's status as crown prince, though their ploy was unsuccessful. They fled to the land of Ararat (as 2 Kgs. 19:37 mentions). The recurrence of conflict between the sons of Sennacherib may indicate why 2 Kgs. 19:37 affixes a note concerning the murder of Sennacherib—an event which occurred twenty years after the siege of Jerusalem. There is nothing in the Hebrew to suggest that the biblical author is assuming that the siege of Jerusalem and the murder were close together in time. The narrative appears to place the two topics next to one another because it presupposes that there is a causal relation between Sennacherib's return to Nineveh (the rumour) and his murder. Perhaps the time-compression is an ironic evocation of cause and effect, temporally separated, though primary in the writer's viewpoint. His sons' scheming and his embroilment in military politics, which emerged as the focus of his concern and recall in 701, culminated in his murder in 681.

Parpola (1980: 171-82) has drawn attention to and analysed an important Neo-Babylonian letter, first published in 1911, but was incorrectly described and so was ignored and eclipsed, until Parpola's study, in which he identifies the name of Sennacherib's murderer. The text transcribed by Parpola is as follows:

	Front:	**Reverse:**
1	[..]⸢x x⸣ *ti* ⸢x x⸣] x⸢...]	*i-na pa-ni* 1-ARAD-d-NIN⸢.LÍL⸣-[*ma*]
2	[. ŠE]Š-MEŠ-*ni* URU-TIN.TI[R-KI-MEŠ]	*ul-te-zi-zi-šú um-ma a-mur* x [.]
3	[1-DI-*m*]*u*-PAB-MEŠ *i-na* É [. . .]	*im-ma-šá⸣ina pi-i-ka qi-b*[*i*]
4	[*a*]-*de-e šá s-i-hi šá* x[. . .]	*šú-ú iq-ta-bi um-ma* 1-ARAD-⸢d⸣-[NIN.LÍL]
5	*ki-i iš-mu-ú* 1+*en i-na* [ŠÀ-*bi-šu-nu*]	DUMU-*ka i-dak-ka pa-ni-*[*šú*]
6	*i-na pa-<an> né-er-ti a-mat* LUGAL *ut*-[. .]	*ki-i ip-tu-ú* 1-ARAD-d-NI[N.LÍL]
7	1-d+AG-MU-*iš-kun ù* 1-*ṣil*-[*la-a*]	*ki-ú-sa-niq-šú a-na šá*-[*a-šú*]
8	*ki-i il-li-ku-nu i-šá-a*-[*lu-šú*]	[*ù*] ŠEŠ-MEŠ-*šú i-d*[*u-ku*]
9	*um-ma a-mat* LUGAL-*ka a-na* U[GU *man-ni*]	[. .] 4 ERIM-MEŠ 1-ŠE-BAR? 1-DUG-*ia* 1-x [. .]
10	*šu-ú ma-a a-na* UGU 1-ARAD-⸢d⸣-[NIN.LÍL]	[. .]1-d+AG-ŠEŠ-APIN –*eš ki-i* [. . .]
11	*i-na* TUG-KUR.RA-*šú pa-ni-šú i*-[*ter-mu*]	[. .]-*qi-pi* ERIM-MEŠ *šá* É 1-AR[AD-d-NIN.LÍL]
12		[..] [. .]-*tu šá al-la* : *en-n*[*a*. .]
13		[. .]-*ma? bab-ba-nu-ú šá* x[. . .]
14		[..*a*]-*nu hur-ru a-na* LU[GAL . . .]
15		[*ki-i*] *iš-pu-ru* LUGA[L . . . .]
16		[ ]x[ ]x x[ ]

Translation:

Our Babylo[nian broth]ers [....] [Salam]u-eres in the house..[..]

After they had heard about the treaty of rebellion which [...], one of [them] bef<ore> the murder [announc]ed (that he had) a king's word.

After Nabu-sum-iskun and Sil[la] had come and enquired[ed of him]: '[Whom] does your king's word concern?', (and after) he had answered: "Arda-[Mulissi]", they [covered] his face with his cloak and took him before Arda-Mulissi [himself], saying: 'Look [...], speak up!' So he said: 'Arda-[Mulissi] your son is going to kill you.'

After they had uncovered [his] face, and Arda-Mu[lissi] had interrogated him, they kil[led] him [and] his brothers.

The writer seems to be a brother of the 'Babylonian brothers' which are referred to who had come to know of a covert covenant of rebellion involving the murder of king Sennacherib. Within the perspective of the above record, the king had already been murdered, and the letter is a later report attempting to divulge and clarify the nature of the conspiracy to a subsequent king, who probably is Esarhaddon.

Parpola (1980: 172, 176 n. 11) notices that Postgate identified the expression for 'king's word' (line 6) to be employed where a person is to be taken directly to the king. The covering of the face of a commoner before the king was customary. Unfortunately, the above witness is not taken to Sennacherib to whom he thought he was revealing the plot, but he was placed—with his head covered—before the son who was planning his father's murder. The witness is questioned to discover the names of others who knew of the conspiracy; subsequently he is murdered. This scenario fits well with the above considerations concerning Sennacherib's domestic problems.

Although transliteration is usually the only transcription problem for proper names, its being a logogram which can be the medium for distinct values complicates the description of the murderer's name. Nowhere does the name occur complete, but it appears to be ARAD-d-NIN.LIL in logographic form, though the LIL sign is missing from all forms. So the last element is disputed; and this fact should be employed to qualify the following. Parpola adopts Reiner's proposal that the component d-NIN.LIL should be read *Mulissu* or *Mullesu* (Parpola 1980: 174), and ARAD as *arda* or *ardi*. Parpola combines these features to argue for Arda-Mulussi as the correct value for the Neo-Assyrian name. Parpola regards this as the source of the biblical Adrammelech. He assumes that a metathesis of *d* and *r* occurred in the transfer, which is attested in related uses. The Hebrew '*k*' in the ending of 'Adrammelech', Parpola considers to be a corruption of ss in 'Arda-Mulissi'. Although the termination for the logogram on which the *ss* is based is a hypothetical restoration, scholars such as Salvesen (1998: 157-58) agree with the conclusion. (Parpola also observes that '*Malkat*' is a proposed reading for NIN.LIL, though he discards this suggestion.) If Parpola's equation is adopted, this aligns the Hebrew *k* exactly with the equivalent Akkadian *k*; but most parallels which Parpola cites in the use of ^dNIN.LIL preserve the reading with an *s* ending. Of course, this somewhat uneven descriptive state of affairs surrounding the proper name is not necessarily a vagueness within Parpola's, or the biblical, usage of the name. It largely arises because of the complex graphic problems which this type of Akkadian logographic formation attracts, together with the issues posed in the frequent propensity for ambiguous matching of a foreign language proper name referred to in a narrative whose linguistics naming conventions do not mirror those of the language of origin.

Millard (1976: 11) raises the possibility that 'Adrammelech' is the West Semitic translation of an Akkadian name which the murderer of Sennacherib bore, and he notes that Sennacherib's wife's names are a case of this mode of translation, where the Akkadian *zakutu* matches the western *naqi'a*. This would account for some of the differences of form in the various expressions of the name of Sennacherib's murderer. The western *t* could go into the Akkadian as *d*; this is reflected in the Syrian name 'Atarmilki', which is related to the Ugaritic deity 'Athirat' (i.e. *atrt*). Athirat was a female deity as was NIN.LIL, and these linguistic features long survived Ugaritic usage and influenced later Mesopotamian and Northwest Semitic proper name usage in the sphere of the present discussion.

The collision between military language and political prose has always been a species of subversive instability whose presence mimics a subversive absence (see Gibson 2000b). Sennacherib's none too courtly demise manifests how such departures from consistency have, for us, a semantics which not only code this *différance* between presence as absence, but it also contains our inadequate attempts to anticipate how ancient deviance is hidden by literary order. We need to give further to developing concepts that can alert us to unpredicted turbulence within ordered discourse—or, allow for a more various ancient world than many standardised views encourage, a world that differs from a variety of our interpretations of more recent past literatures.

9

Babylonian and Aramaic Records of Daniel

Belshazzar and Nabonidus

The book of Daniel is written from the assumed standpoint of contemporary knowledge of the Jewish captivity in Babylon. On the other hand, it has been customary to maintain that Daniel is a very late composition from four centuries after the exile, on some views having little if any historical value. The infamous examples of Belshazzar not being son of Nebuchadnezzar, but the son of Nabonidus, and his not being king but viceroy, are cited to support such criticisms. The data are fairly well known; yet tuning in aspects of presentation is a worthy reason for reviving the pertinent issues, particularly concerning the use of terms for 'king' and 'son', as well as the book's language and its date.

    The Persian and Babylonian records contemporary with the last phase of the Babylonian kingdom and Cyrus are relevant regarding Nabonidus and the use of terms for 'king' and 'son'.[1] The Persian Verse Account of Nabonidus, Column VI (Smith 1975: ll. 18-20), states:

> Ka-ra-as ip-ta-qid a-na res-tu-u bu-kur-suamelummani(-ni) ma-ti-tan u-ta' ir itti-suip-ta-ta-ar qat-su ip-ta-qid-su sarru-tam.

> He [Nabonidus] entrusted a camp to his eldest firstborn son [Belshazzar]; the troops of the land he sent with him. He freed his hand; he entrusted the Kingship to him.

So we have a contemporary official royal annal recording that Belshazzar had the kingship transferred to him by Nabonidus. It is incredible that some scholars omit this

---

[1] The relevant Aramaic was invariably used in the Persian era, and this may be reflected in the Babylonian text's term.

text as evidence, especially in its contradiction of the assertion that Belshazzar was viceroy, not king. The cuneiform text does not employ the word for 'viceroy'; it utilises the standard, official term for kinship: *sarru-*.

Two texts, which were produced for Nabonidus himself when king, provide the basis for proof of this sense of 'kingship'. The first, an inscription from the Moon god's temple at Haran, contains the statement (Haran, Nabonidus H 2, A and B, ll. 5-11, after Gadd 1958: 56-57, cf. 1923):

> [The god] Sin, lord of the gods and goddesses...[thou art he] who, in front of Nabonidus king of Babylon, camest from the heavens. I (am) Nabonidus, who have not the honour (?) of (being a) somebody and kingship (sarru-u-tu) is not within me, (but) the gods and goddesses prayed for me, and (the god) Sin to the kingship called me.

Clearly, this text is not announcing that Nabonidus has been called by the god Sin to be viceroy—but to be king. Hence, when Nabonidus gives the kingship to Belshazzar (using the same expression), it is false to deem this an appointment for viceroy.

The second citation is a royal annal from the archives of Nabonidus, composed by him. It is most important, since it is a description of his coronation; and it employs the relevant term 'kingship' (after Langdon 1912: 276-75, col. V, ll. 1-13):

> Unto the midst of the palace (?) they brought me
> and all of them cast themselves at my feet and kissed my feet
> (and) paid homage to my kingship. At the command of
> (the god) Marduk, my lord, I was raise 1 to the sovereignty
> of the land...

Since the term 'kingship' has the specific associations of coronation and sovereignty, it would be an indication that Belshazzar was being given the role of king when this term was used of him by Nabonidus. In the foregoing quotation, we can see that the scope of the term 'kingship' is fixed by reference to the instituting of Nabonidus as king and the institution of being king. One can hardly wish for more precise evidence that the first inscription quoted in this chapter (where Belshazzar receives the kingship) recorded Belshazzar as king, and not viceroy. Why, then, was the kingship passed on to Belshazzar from Nabonidus, and how is it possible that this occurred while yet Nabonidus still lived? Accurately determined answers to these questions await further discoveries; but certain features are ascertained. First, Nabonidus spent many years of his reign away at Haran (cf. Haran, Nabonidus H 2, A and B; Gadd, 1958: 72-78), which period Daniel 5 covers, and also at Tema. The latter location and journey are given as the reason, implicitly, for Belshazzar's receiving the kingship, according to the Persian record cited above, which continues (after Smith 1975: 1. B 21-8):

> Then he [Nabonidus] himself undertook a distant campaign...towards Tema and toward the midst of the Westland he set his face. He undertook a distant campaign on a road not within reach since ancient times. He slew the prince of Tema with the [sword]; the dwellers in his city (and) country, all of them they slaughtered. Then he himself established his dwelling [in Tema]... That city he made glorious...they made it like the palace of Babylon.

Another possible cause of Nabonidus's being away from Babylon might have to do with his unpopularity and his unpopular command, namely to restore the Moon god temple at Haran, which the people apparently refused to execute. As Nabonidus himself states (Haran, Nabonidus H 2, A ll. 11-27):

> In the night season he [the god Sin] caused me to behold a dream saying: thus 'E-hul-hul the temple of Sin which (is) in Haran quickly build... (But) the sons of Babylon [etc.] against his great divinity offended...they forgot their duty... But I went quickly myself far from my city of Babylon (on) the road to Tema, Dadanu, Padakku[a], Hibra, Iadihu, and as far as Iatribu [i.e. Medina]; ten years I went about amongst them, (and) to my city Babylon I went not in.

The closed world of Mesopotamian gods here recycles Sin from the Sumerian Zuen, mentioned in the foregoing chapter. It appears, in the final year of his 'reign' (year 17) in the Spring of 539 BC, that Nabonidus returned and celebrated the New Year's Festival, at which he seems to have disgraced himself. This was the year in which, on 13 October, according to the royal Babylonian annals, Cyrus—through the efficient offices of Ugbaru—took Babylon. Despite Nabonidus's return, however, there is no textual evidence that he withdrew the kingship from Belshazzar. It may be, with Cyrus's military in the vicinity prior to the invasion of Babylon (cf. Stronach 1978: 286-91, 281-82), that Nabonidus was alerted to the danger for Babylon and decided to return at this time of impending crisis, perhaps too late to regain the kingship and restore his power-base. Whether or not he was in Babylon when it was invaded is not certainly known. Records are ambiguous, incomplete or require further analysis with regard to the last months of Nabonidus's activities at the fall of Babylon. Some texts suggest that he fled;[2] others declare that he was exiled (cf. Stronach 1978: 291); and one interpretation of a text suggests that he returned subsequent to the conquest of

---

[2] For a discussion of these possibilities, see Dougherty 1929: 138-200; regarding Nabonidus's possible fleeing see p. 180, and Josephus, *Contra Apionem* 1.20.

Babylon and was arrested by Cyrus.[3] Another account proposes that, while Ugbaru took Babylon, Cyrus pursued Nabonidus to Borsippa. The current options hardly leave one with grounds for the conclusion that Nabonidus was the normalised ruler practising his kingship prior to or at that time of crisis. It should be mentioned that the tablet which is used to date Nabonidus's return and celebration of the New Year festival to his 17th year, does not itself specify that date, having been broken at the relevant point, though the date is taken by a number of scholars to be the probable original reading. If this assumption is wrong, it permits further rearrangement of Nabonidus's closing years, in the light of future discoveries·

If we mark our interpretations as possible worlds, and the ancient writers as having articulated another set of such worlds, we can recognise ourselves in binary or binary plus multiple relation to the ancient narratives. Actual history itself is a further spacetime domain, that of an absence which interpreted by texts that attempt to retain or retrieve a sensible trace of history's identities. When a text that presupposes historicity for itself is investigated by modern scholars, there is a tendency to impose what, one might term, negative nostalgia on the narratives. We need further conceptions of disinterestedness and objectivity, so as to be less disposed to impose our theories on other spacetimes.

'King' and 'Kingship'

An objection to the foregoing might be that the cuneiform texts employ the term 'kingship' for Belshazzar, not 'king' as with the Biblical Aramaic's translation. So, it might be argued, the residual problem still remains, because, though Belshazzar might have received the 'kingship' he did not become 'king'. This is an extremely thin distinction for the protagonist to sustain, not least because, on a functionalist analysis, Nabonidus's lengthy absence and his own transfer of the office of the kingship comes—at the least—very near to the recipient's being king.

Nevertheless, assessing the counter-theory as it stands, it has two refutations. First, Biblical Hebrew and Aramaic do not have a term for 'kingship', so the absence of an abstract noun for 'kingship' in the vocabulary of Daniel could be a central reason why it does not appear in Daniel 5. This point is often neglected in assessment of differences between forms of words. Linguistic choice to some extent dictates the matching of an Aramaic word with a Babylonian term. The absence of the abstract

---

[3] This is based on a particular interpretation of the Nabonidus Chronicle in Smith 1975: 117.l.16: as Dougherty 1929: 170-71 explains, it is translated as 'Afterwards Nabonidus, when he returned to Babylon, was taken prisoner'.

noun-form 'kingship' from Biblical Aramaic does not necessarily create a (lexical) gap in Aramaic vocabulary. In other words, the sense of kingship might still be covered by the word for king because the usage of 'king' is often extended to indicate the institution of being king, or kingship. Therefore the choice of 'king' in Daniel 5, as opposed to 'kingship' (*šarru-tam* or *šarru-u-tu* [or *-ti*]) in Babylonian, is not even a possible or consistent objection to the historicity of Daniel 5's use of 'Belshazzar'. That is to say, only if the vocabulary of Biblical Aramaic had an abstract noun formation for 'kingship' could it be consistent to draw the possible conclusion that Daniel 5 had improperly chosen the wrong form of the expression 'king'. Since the form does not exist, and with king functioning in its place, the Aramaic noun for 'king' is a proper replacement for the Babylonian word rendered 'kingship'.

A second point, which secures the refutation of the 'king' versus 'kingship' distinction, is linguistic and practical, as well as logical. This parallels a medieval debate scrutinised by Peter Geach (1972: 296), who demonstrated that 'the King's Majesty just is the King', and being Lord Mayor exactly is the mayoralty. He argues that, it 'would be manifest nonsense to say that the mayoralty a man assumes could go on existing after he had laid it down' and itself be a Lord Mayor, and to deny this involves equivocation. This equivocation is about the pragmatic scope of actual use, not some abstract theory. The force of this demarcates the type of link between kingship and king.

If Nabonidus entrusts his kingship to Belshazzar, Belshazzar does not respect the trust nor preserve the kingship for his father by locking up the kingship for safe keeping, as though it were some separate phenomenon from being king. The linguistic and pragmatic function entailed by kingship just is being king. Likewise, the practical entrusting of the kingship is not like a person's being a legal trustee of it, in the sense of protecting it but not utilising himself of it. Of course it is easy to imagine a situation where a king might metaphorically speak of his entrusting kingship; presumably he did not intend that the institution of monarchy be abolished in his absence. There is no evidence that he gave instruction to have it suspended; nor are there data to show that he replaced the kingship with 'governors' or trustees. Rather, the cuneiform record of Nabonidus explicitly transfers the kingship as a political pragmatic construct to be performed by Belshazzar. Many texts describe Belshazzar's employment of the office, and what the kings of Babylon (as well as Belshazzar) did in that office. So this counter-move is not relevantly sensible. Hence the hypothesis that defends the existence of Nabonidus as king, so as to oppose the Daniel narrative's report that Belshazzar was king, are involved in a misapprehension about linguistics and practical reason in relation to the relevant extant texts in application to their historical referents. The kingship's identity does not solely consist in doing what the king does. Rather, doing what the king does, and by his assent via Nabonidus's specifically transferring the kingship, expressed by using the coronation nomenclature. This, with internal historical royal command and precedent, warrants the use of the term 'king' in Daniel 5.

Those who still feel that there is some infelicity in Dan. 5:1, because it terms Belshazzar 'the king', should notice that the Aramaic there does not employ the article usually represented by 'the'. The text states 'Belhazzar king'. So it would be a false move or assumption to impose the interpretation that the writer of Daniel presupposed that Belshazzar was the (one and only) king. We should notice that the narrative does not designate Belshazzar as the 'king of Babylon'—a characteristic title typically reserved for Nabonidus. Implicit in some criticisms of Belshazzar as king is the assumption that there can only be one king. In practice—in the cuneiform texts—Nabonidus destroys that claim by using the term of himself and of Belshazzar. Moreover, the Aramaic of Daniel cannot rightly be committed to that position for, as indicated above, it does not even posit Belshazzar as 'the king' yet alone 'the one and only king'.

Of course, no one has produced their criticism by suggesting the converse, that is, the 'one and only king' for Daniel's use of the term 'king'. My point is that Dan. 5:1 would need to have that quantification of 'the one and only' for the proposal to be true that Nabonidus's being king excludes the truth of Belshazzar's being king. Why? For the reason that there is no universal rule by which a kingdom is limited to having to having only one king, especially in the circumstances described by the cuneiform records. That objections sometimes trade on this 'implicit' quantification of 'the one and only', or are committed to requiring it, reveals how structurally muddled they are.

Belshazzar's Father

Within the conceptual world of the view which was depicted at the beginning of this chapter, Belshazzar was not the son of Nebuchadnezzar; yet, in Dan. 5:22, with the genetically construed English translation 'son', Belshazzar is indeed made out to be Nebuchadnezzar's son. Noting that Nebuchadnezzar is also called Belshazzar's 'father' in Dan 5:2, 11 and 18 can exacerbate the apparent severity of this problem. This (mis)apprehension is due, however, to misunderstanding about the scope of the English imposed on Aramaic terms and their Babylonian counterparts. For example, the old BDB lexicon (120 cols. A–B) points out cases where the Hebrew *ben* means 'grandson'. For example, Gen. 29:5 has, 'Laban the son of Nahor'. Here, *ben* means 'grandson', as we can see from Gen. 28:5, where Laban is the son of Bethuel, who is the son of Nahor. BDB also lists other cases, and this semantic range is also true generally for Aramaic, relevant because of the Aramaic portion of the book of Daniel, 2:4 to the end of chapter 7. The general term for son, *bar*, can mean 'grandson', as is the case in the Aramaic of Ez. 5:1: 'Zechariah the son of Iddo'. Further, from Zech. 1:1, we discover that Zechariah's father was Berechiah; and Berechiah's father was Iddo. Therefore the domain of the Biblical Aramaic word *bar* includes the sense of grandson, because the actual usage of *bar* is applied to males—other than sons—who are descended from the specified presupposed ancestor. Obviously each language has its own semantic field and internal spread that focuses and overlaps opposition of words and synonyms for each word. Actual usage in a specific language is the rule by which we ought to permit or preclude senses for words. Hence *bar*, by virtue of how it is used in the Old Testament, actually does have the meaning of 'grandson'. We should not work back, for instance, from some external presupposition of a narrow sonship scope for *bar*, and accept this situation as an exception which has to be justified, in the light of the evidence we have assessed. Rather, the expression *bar* starts out as a derestricted semantic specifier whose scope initially is wider than a Eurocentric literalism. Therefore, the sense of the Aramaic of Dan. 5:22, which terms Belshazzar Nebuchadnezzar's *bar*, has the semantic property that is consistent with being used to classify Nebuchadnezzar's grandson.

The pertinent extant ancient records, though incomplete and partly problematic for the relevant period, exhibit data that do show that Belshazzar was the grandson of Nebuchadnezzar. This type of analysis concurs with Dougherty's (1929: 194) view that, 'if the inferences which have been drawn are valid, Belshazzar was a grandson of Nebuchadnezzar. Should this prove to have been the relationship between the two, one need not be surprised that the fifth chapter of Daniel calls Nebuchadnezzar the father instead of the grandfather of Belshazzar as this is entirely in harmony with Semitic usage under the circumstances.' Dougherty's (1929: 194 n. 642) treatment of this position contains the following helpful considerations:

> The Hebrew and Aramaic word for father is used in the sense of ancestor. See 1 Kings 15:11; 2 Kings 14:3; 18:3; Is. 51:2. In Gen. 28:13 Abraham is called the father of Jacob. In 2 Sam. 9:7 Saul is called the father of Mephibosheth, who was in reality the grandson of Saul. In Tobit 1:15 Sennacherib is referred to as the son of Shalmaneser, omitting Sargon, the king who came between them. It was customary for Babylonian kings to refer to any one of their predecessors as their father. Thus Nebuchadnezzar called Naram-Sin his a-ba-a-am la-beri, 'ancient father'. Note sarrani ab-bi-e-a, 'the kings, my fathers'.[4] In using the term 'father' for 'ancestor',

---

[4] For the bibliographical reference Dougherty supplied, see Langdon 1912: 78, col. III, l. 27 for the former cuneiform expression, and p. 110, col. II, l. 77 for the latter.

particularly of a royal predecessor, the fifth chapter of Daniel is in harmony
not only with Hebrew and Aramaic, but also with Neo-Babylonian custom.

It seems, then, that what in some Eurocentric biblical scholarship has been
misleadingly framed on both sides as a conservative versus liberal debate, should be
deconstructed into Mesopotamian semantic field perspectives.

Daniel's Date

The question of the date of the book of Daniel is closely bound up with what is deemed
to be its theology and its relation to both Old and New Testament developments.
Accordingly, the possibility that the late date proposed for its composition (circa 167
BC) is too late, is a matter which warrants further questioning.

The discovery and contents of the Deir 'Alla Aramaic texts, from circa 700
BC, can revolutionise a central aspect of the nature of the evidence for dating the book
of Daniel. This text has been the subject of numerous reports since 1967 (Franken
1967: 480-81; Hoftijzer 1976: 1-17), together with the major publication of the texts
and extensive analysis by Hoftijzer and Kooij (1976). The text is from the East Side of
the Jordan. It states that it is a prophecy of Balaam; presumably, *if* this claim were
accurate, it would have been mediated in oral or written form from the 2nd millennium
BC.

The most important feature of the text, for present purposes, is that its
language is parallel at points with aspects of the Aramaic of the book of Daniel. This
shows the claim that even prior to the 6th-century BC date in which the book of Daniel
depicts itself to have been composed, there is a comparable contemporary Aramaic
form to its use of language. Such a fact queries the credibility from a main hypothesis
which has been deployed in the past to support a late-date 167 BC composition for
Daniel. This hypothesis purports on one view to explain that the Aramaic of Daniel is
not earlier Eastern or Royal Aramaic, but is circa 167 BC Western Aramaic, though
there has never been a systematic scientific formal linguistic analysis to demonstrate
this thesis. In sum, aspects of the language of Daniel are centuries older than 167 BC
partly because Aramaic of 700 BC displays some of the same characteristics as of the
Aramaic portion of the book of Daniel.

Franken (1967: 12) reports that there is a prospect for a maximum time-spread
for the date of the Aramaic in the Deir 'Alla inscription of between 700 to 500 BC, so
this later time limit is no later than the internal dating of the book of Daniel (cf. Hackett
1984). The time-spread scholars usually give for the inscription's language, however, is
late 8th or early 7th century BC (cf. Franken 1967: 271). The Aramaic dialect in which

the inscription is written is the first of its type to be discovered. It strikes a new precedent in non-Biblical Aramaic. Hoftijzer (1976) stated, as a consequence of this discovery, that:

> The value of our neat linguistic classifications for this period was already seriously affected, and I believe that the data of our texts [i.e. ones comprising the Deir 'Alla inscription] will show us all the more how shaky the basis for our classifications was.

Aspects of these classifications were precisely those in part which have been assumed, or deployed, to argue for the 167 BC date for the book of Daniel, and those for which some scholars assume certainty as firm evidence of a late date for Daniel. There is need to balance one's account with these more recent excavations and research which can be shown to point to the Babylonian 6th-century origin for the Aramaic of Daniel.[5]

So, what is the concept of classification that Hoftijzer is here presupposing among earlier scholars? The criteria for distinguishing between two slightly different registers and/or forms of a dialect or two related dialects at distinct periods or in different geographical contexts are problematic for a dead language. This is sharply true where a people is moved from Judah to Babylon. The detection would likely be relatively easy for a native contemporary speaker, but acutely difficult for a scholastic 'foreigner' who knows not what standard dialect is. To define the differences—to offer a criterion that measures the difference of sound, idiom, etc.—is much more problematic. With regard to the Aramaic of 700 BC to 100 BC, we are not completely certain what it is to be standard Aramaic of certain dialects and literary forms. Therefore we have problems deciding what actually it is to be a dialect, and hence to be a given dialect of, Aramaic. The reason for this is evident: the principles embodied in Aramaic by which one might measure differences of Aramaic in dialect are not yet defined for Semitic linguistics, though inductive suppositions abound in quantitative analysis. The value of these approaches is at times unclear in their value for qualitative semantics. So sometimes it is unclear what Aramaic is being classified, because initial assumptions of what the necessary internal properties of a given range of Aramaic usage are stipulative, not descriptive. This is why the Deir 'Alla inscription has, and should, provoke reassessment.

By insisting that the Aramaic in the book of Daniel embodies the linguistic styles of circa167 BC, and building this stipulation into definition of classification of Aramaic of the 167 BC period, one internalises a suppressed empirical inconsistencies into definition, because some features in the Aramaic of Daniel have been found in the

---

[5] Some work for the 6th–4th-century Aramaic has been done earlier by Kitchen 1997: 152 n. 10.

Figure 9.1   Portion of the Deir 'Alla Balaam inscription

earlier 700 BC period. The situation for defining time-periods in Aramaic inscriptions is additionally complicated by other factors, one of which concerns what it is to be a shift in the nature of some subset of the dialects as synchronic and/or diachronic influences or needs change. For example, there are obviously a wide range of differences in grammar between Old Testament Aramaic and other Aramaic literatures of the period from 200 BC to 100 AD.

An instance in this group of differences is that a particular sᵉgolate noun formation and variety in Biblical Aramaic is much more complex and diverse in range of forms than what are classified as other dialects of Aramaic. These other dialects have a much more straightforward and simpler set of forms for this noun type. As Muraoka's study (1976: 226-35) proves, there is considerable room for refinement over definition of the sᵉgolate noun categories, especially because of the disagreements that obtain in the diachronic formal linguistics of Aramaic. If some of these relevant differences impinge on the assumed principle of development by increasing simplification of Aramaic forms, as they easily may do, then incorrect dating of narratives provokes false description of what it is to be a criterion of a given period's usage. Even without a restricted quantitative framework, an early date concurs with sample data. Muraoka's case of the sᵉgolate noun yields only a few circa 167 BC uses, whereas the biblical Aramaic text has comparatively more. If a linguist ignores this disparity between the texts in Daniel and non-biblical 167 BC narratives, while grouping all uses as self-evidently from one period, then his logic will be fallacious, and the difference of incidence in the two groups will be obscured. Muraoka's analysis provides grounds to question the conflation of the varied statistics at this stage in discussion. So a wedge is driven between the texts of Daniel and the possibly later 167 BC occurrences of sᵉgolate nouns.

The foregoing type of evidence is highly unstable, since complex theological theses act as suppressed premises behind the linguistic data. One ought to strip the linguistics of theological assumption when attempting to determine the time axis of the source. The Deir 'Alla inscriptions give at least some provisional warrant for pressing the above anxiety. Here are some summary parallels with Daniel and the Deir 'Alla inscriptions:

haddamῑn ti'abdῡn ('cut in pieces'): Dan. 2:5, offers the same grammar, on many standard views, as an expression in the Deir 'Alla Inscriptions Combination 1, line 6.[6] This grammar is also the same as in Dan. 3:29 and the Aramaic version of the Behistan text II. 17f. The Biblical Aramaic in Est. 2:5 also follows this type.

---

[6] See Hoftijzer and Kooij (eds) 1976: 225. The following initial data are largely drawn from Hoftijzer, while re-analyzed and modified, and taken on to comparative interpretations that he did not address.

An unusual form of verb (itpeel) occurs in Dan. 2:5: This is translatable as 'shall be made'—*yitte'amun*, and Deir 'Alla Inscriptions Combination I, line 9; cf. Dan. 4:9 and Ezra 5:8.[7]

A problematic form in Deir 'Alla Inscriptions Combination II, line 15: It is [*l*]*lqsh*. It is probable that this parallels either the root *qsh*, a form *qṣt* that occurs in Dan. 2:42 rendered 'part', or the two other occurrences of the same form *qst* in Dan. 4:26 and 31 (vv. 29 and 34 in the English), where they have the sense 'end'. Another possibility is 'cut off' with the stem *qṣṣ* in Dan. 4:11 (English v. 14). It is not impossible that Daniel 4, with these related forms, is punning on 'end' and 'cutting' (or breaking) in a way which might reflect a pun on the Deir 'Alla type of usage. The reading of the Deir 'Alla text at this point is uncertain, but probably is (lines 15-17): 'For the end of the plastered wall [on which the inscription was written]...they said to Balaam...it will be impossible for you to curse anymore.' On this interpretation, the initial *l* in '*lqsh*' would be a preposition, roughly, marked as 'for'.[8]

Deir 'Alla Inscriptions Combination II, line 13 smh: This term matches the verbal form exactly in Dan. 4:16. (v. 19 in English), translated as 'astonished' or 'horror'. It is worth noticing that in this Daniel context the term 'king' appears, as it does in the Deir 'Alla text, line 15, within the scope of the context of 'astonished'. The ways in which a context and its semantic field display a choice of words, their combinations and their collocations are important as an indicator of common background and source usage.[9] When more than one term appears to be common to two contexts, this cumulatively increases the probability of a common background or setting in time. One should take account of the possibility of intertextual quotation or allusion. In addition and in combination with this prospect, is the way in which common stylistics in syntax and semantics can be a result of textures of cross-synchronic influences, which can serve as evidence for the same temporal contextualization of otherwise thematically distinct narrative such as Daniel and the Deir 'Alla Inscriptions. If we accept the Levant origins of some of the Jewish captivity in Babylon, it is evident that this would carry with it a socio-linguistic domain which, even after a generational gap, would mirror some of the intertextual semantic contracts of a cultic inscription from Deir 'Alla if they had similar temporal contexts. The present selective list from the Deir 'Alla Inscriptions meets this set of requirements and as such has cumulative force, since a continuous stream of related contexts in Daniel

---

[7] See Hoftijzer and Kooij (eds) 1976: 242-44.

[8] On another interpretation, the expression *lqs* would be parsed as a root *lqs*, which Hoftijzer (1976: 244 n. 165) suggests would be a newly attested Aramaic root.

[9] See Hoftijzer and Kooij (eds) 1976: 240. On the theoretical foundations for the above, see Lyons 1977: 261ff.

matches the inscription, even after we allow for the distinct thematic concerns in the two semantic fields.

The term used in Daniel to represent Nebuchnezzar's 'dwelling' (mdr): This term appears in Dan. 4:22, 29 (vv. 25, 32 in English), and is used in the Deir 'Alla Inscriptions, Combination II, line 5, if one follows Hoftijzer's first interpretation (Hoftijzer and Kooij [eds] 1976: 222).

One interpretation of the Deir 'Alla Inscriptions, Combination I, line 12 has styw.hmr: These two terms, with the senses of 'drank wine', appear in Dan. 5:4 with exactly the same suffixes (*yw*: singular suffix, 'of') as does the Deir 'Alla text (Hoftijzer and Kooij [eds] 1976: 207-208).[10] The order of the two terms in the phrase is the same in Daniel here and in Deir 'Alla. In addition, the two words in the phrase also recur in Dan. 5:1 and 23, but in reverse order from 5:1 and the Deir 'Alla text, l. 7.

In Dan. 6:20 (v. 19 in English) 'very early' (ngh): Here is a term that matches Deir 'Alla Inscriptions, Combination I, 8-9, and the thematic element of tension and apprehension is common to the contexts of both (Hoftijzer and Kooij [eds] 1976: 196).

Deviant grammar: In some biblical grammar, there is an apparently intended violation of what we usually (perhaps primitively) take to be plural rules or declensions for nouns for special purposes of emphasis or nuance. In Dan. 7:10, 'ten thousand times ten thousand...[stood] up' (*ribbō ribwan...yᵉqumūn*) we have such a case. Hoftijzert (Hoftijzer and Kooij [eds.] 1976: 295 n. 21) parallels this usage with the phrase in the Deir 'Alla Inscriptions, Combination I, line 16.

Deir 'Alla Inscriptions, Combination I, line 2: A special sense of the term for 'fire' occurs in Dan. 7:11, where it has the meaning 'flame', 'blaze' or 'blazing fire' (*'š*). This sense appears in the Deir 'Alla Inscriptions, Combination I, line 2 (Hoftijzer and Kooij [eds] 1976: 187).[11]

Deir 'Alla Inscriptions, Combination I, line 9 'for ever' ('d.'lm): This phrase is matched by the expression as it occurs in Dan. 7:18 (Hoftijzer and Kooij [eds] 1976: 200).[12]

Of course, there is yet earlier Aramaic before the Deir 'Alla Inscriptions with the variety of texts that has been available for some time, albeit sometimes in fragmentary or problematic states of preservation, but even with respect to this type of data, evidence is forthcoming. Still, it can easily be eclipsed because of an interpretative assumption which one might regard as untenable, or for which there is an alternative construction. An example of this is to be found with regard to the Aramaic of the Dan. 7:13 expression, the 'son of man': *bar 'ᵉnaš*. This phrase is often collapsed

---

[10] Note that Daniel's *hmr'* has an ', whereas the Deir 'Alla text does not.
[11] There is no ' on the end of *'s* in the Deir 'Alla text, such as there is in Daniel.
[12] In Daniel there is a termination ' in *'lm,* which is absent from the Deir 'Alla text.

into the later modified form *br-nš*, which omits the consonant *'aleph*. Conversely, at least for some uses with the *'naš* formation, this conflation is incorrect; indeed, there is no wide semantic field of parallel uses of the phrase with the *'aleph* to show that the two designations have the same sense or register of meaning. The expression *br-nš* has the indefinite sense of 'a man', 'anyone', 'someone', with the overtone or tonal sense of 'peasant', etc. This tone and value are often imposed on the Dan. 7:13 occurrence, but there is no warrant for this merger. There is an explicit heavenly regal specificity contracted in the field of the Daniel usage. If this hypothesis is right, then a possible approach to its earlier pre-Babylonian Aramaic regal usage becomes a significant support for the hypothesis.

In the circa 760 BC Aramaic Arpad Sefire iii inscription (J.C.L. Gibson 1975: 46-50), there is an occurrence of *br 'nš*. J.C.L. Gibson translates this with the expression 'someone'; but this merely appears to assume, without argument being offered, that it automatically complies with the sense of the much later *br-nš*. Against this, a number of features are worthy of mention. We here have an ancient regal precedent as a parallel with the regal function of Dan. 7:13. The Sefire inscription possesses regal features. Its context is the possible or envisaged assassination attempt on the king of Arpad by another ruler. As line 16 of the text states:

> wys' 'l sptwh lhmtt 'qry whn ysq 'l [l]bb mlky 'rpd bkl mh zy ymwt br 'nš
> sqrtm lk

> and if he lifts up to his lips to put my descendant to death, or indeed if this idea is upon the heart of any of the kings of Arpad—that my son of man dies—you have been false to all[13]

The context explicitly links these words to two kings and their sons. This fixes the range of the semantic field in a way that is quite different from the scope and nuances of the later *br-ns* usage. So here is an 8th-century BC occurrence of *bar-'nas* which exhibits and highlights features in Dan. 7:13 that can easily be missed as distinguishing elements in the phrase's use. This evidently gives considerable weight to a hypothesis that the Aramaic of Daniel embodies pre-exilic Aramaic, and it matches linguistic mores in particular semantic registers of royal Courts. Between Sefire and the time presupposed in the putative authorial voice of Daniel, however, we should allow for some possible diachronic change of sense and scope, yet the limited short time-frame separating them does not present a problem for substantial continuity. This latter point is strengthened by the consideration that semantics in which ritualised or institutional

---

[13] See J.C.L. Gibson 1975: 48. The above translation is my own, which departs from his paraphrastic rendering.

linguistic custom tend to hold a regular position even in an ironized polemical context such as Dan. 7:13. Without wishing to push the point as primary evidence, it is worth weighing the evidence for the conclusion that the contexts in Daniel and Sefire iii share a background thematic strand which may be a subsidiary item in regulating or complementing the choice of br-'nš. This strand is the inset theme of death and politicized violence of Sefire iii, lines 11-18, and of Dan. 7:11, 17-21 which, in the latter, are directly explained in connection with the use of 'ancient of Days', occurring in 7:13 and 22, in (only partial) parallel with the threat of the established senior king in the Sefire inscription. My qualification of the parallel here, of course, is to emphasise the thematic asymmetry at a general level. Narrowly yet contextually isolated, the subject and lexical spread shared between the two texts is clear, and within such limits, significant as evidence of an equivalent purpose

An extensive review of the diachronic implications is outside the scope of the present remarks. Nevertheless, the foregoing conclusions are of some value for a fresh approach to 'Son of Man' issues, and their implications for New Testament study. The 1st-century AD reading of Daniel in a range of institutional, traditional, or revolutionary, ancient communities could have interpreted a regal sense from within the narrative of Daniel 7, with its admixture of heir-apparent usage and deconstructing revolutionary breakdown of coronational ritual language. The foregoing argues that such a regal contextualisation is not an external imposition of late date on the text. Rather, it genuinely articulates western and eastern Aramaic regal customs already in place by the time of the Babylonian exile. Internalised as such dynamics are in Daniel 7, this chapter originally lodged a question-mark against failure to retrieve regal and other language from Daniel's own putative Aramaic background in the Levant.

More than a few traces of such examples in the history of Semitic languages had been revived by the impact of Greek invasion, and by rabbinic employment or absorption of Roman regal aspirations in Palestine. Such tendencies of an indigenous group to 'go native' with the invading occupants can readily act as causal triggers for many situations. Derrida (1998: 57) has portrayed a situation of a French north African Jew that one might take as a motif for such issues, both as we read the ancient world and as they performed their speech acts as well as compositions: "And that jealous guard that one mounts in proximity to one's language, even as one is denouncing the nationalist politics of language..., demands the multiplication of shibboleths as so many challenges to translations, so many taxes levied in the frontiers of language, so many alliances assigned to the ambassadors of idiom..., where the event of its prosody only takes place at home, in the very place where its "being home" [son *"chez elle"*] disturbs the co-inhabitants, the fellow citizens, and the compatriots?".

It is apt and perhaps ironic that features of the Roman, sometimes divine, regal semantics could be seen ironically to coincide with the New Testament's subversive divine invasion of the regal semantic field by use of another external semantics — the Aramaic of Daniel, for deployment in the New Testament's Christological polemic. And quite unlike an unidentified peasant tagged as a son of man.

If the above parallels are correctly exposed, they can be used as a stencil to approach other, perhaps obscured linguistic elements, in a range of narratives and inscriptions to produce a generalised hypothesis about the 6th-century BC Aramaic provenance of features to be found in Daniel, not least because the foregoing examples are selective and typical of other cases in the book. If the origin of the Aramaic of Daniel rests in the 6th century, then one would expect that a composition, which emerged from a people in captivity, would reflect in a suitable way the language used by them in the land from which they had been taken, not least since the notion of being confronted by an alien language is no Romantic imposition. Rather, it is a thematic function of Daniel from its inception. Aspects of the Deir 'Alla text's semantic field comprise just such evidence for certain features of Daniel, even though it is a cultic inscription, and is written in a genre not entirely matched by Daniel's own. The mythological elements in the Deir 'Alla text are very different from Daniel, however, since they at least entertain an element of child human sacrifice (see Hackett 1984).

Given the need for fresh study of the originality of the language of Daniel—that is, a creativity thesis somewhat submerged by over-emphasis in many scholarly studies of Daniel's editing presuppositions—this is to be expected, and should not be not used as a foil to deflect direct investigation of Daniel's historical provenance within its own compositional presuppositions. So, hypothetically allowing for the earlier date of the book to be that of a time-point soon after the Babylonian captivity of the Jews, the linguistics of the Sefire inscription typifies some of the grounds for reassessment of pre-exilic Palestinian influences on the Aramaic of Daniel. No doubt the postulated origin of the book of Daniel involves analysis of the influences from Babylonian Aramaic in Babylon, as well as Persian use of Babylonian Aramaic, which are in any case explicit in the book and the thematic subject of polemic. Given these multifarious factors, commentators of Daniel should consider reading it as an original historical synthesis of pre-exilic Babylonian with Jewish-Babylonian Aramaic and Hebrew. The carefully planted thematic presence of Hebrew circumscribing the beginning and the end of Aramaic and Babylonian in the book of Daniel ironically complements this view and provides an internal narrative start for such an analysis of influences.

On this interpretation, Daniel witnesses to a desire to preserve conceptual autonomy as well as position some of the contrasting influences mirrored in it. In this perspective, we should explore its use of ironised polemic as a genuine historically based manifestation of *difference* and presence. Consequently, we should not read the book of Daniel as a recipe to suit a committee of editors preoccupied with a later Greek dominated Palestine, alien to Daniel's linguistic world and theological agents. The text of Daniel, not least in its use of two languages, and two cultures, stands over the gulf between alienation and empathy, between ludic presence and tragic absence. These relations can attract competing binary responses from scholars and readers. A problem is that we presuppose our own world as the point of contrast and similarity to assess the ancient world. We need to probe our responses so as to gain entry to alien universes of discourse, to achieve some grasp of what being present in its world involves. In this respect, concentration on the creative identities within narratives will help alert us to ways in which original narratives tend to encode their origins at one level, yet obscure them at another. Our assumptions in this sphere about what is relevant, or irrelevant, could accordingly do well to allow for counter-intuitive depths, rather than traditions of smoothed out uniformity in semantics. Our choices in interpretation might then be nearer the ancient authorial voice.

10

Conclusion

We have seen that the Near East 'sense' is composed of very many differing universes of discourse. The last hundred years or so have seen quite amazing progress in the recovery and presentation of the ancient Near East and related areas. This progress should not be under-estimated, not least since it is unique in cultural history. As we look to the future, however, we need to have new perspectives on the scale of our ignorance and the provisional identities of our perceptions. The analysis and understanding of these spheres are at an early stage. And no doubt the many original suggestions proposing new approaches in this book suffer from these drawbacks.

The policing and institutionalising of the Old Testament by a variety of theological traditions has often not had a liberating effect on the narratives. There are many issues here, and three of them suffice to compose an impression of the need for further changes in perspective. First, not infrequently in such criticism there is a mythic sense of unity and stability of understanding of the ancient world. Secondly, there is an artificial series of differing approaches that often stress formal editing and Eurocentric or Anglo-American perceptions to the detriment of the functions of creativity or identity in the ancient narratives. Thirdly, some post-structuralist enterprises impose their Third Millennium deconstruction of non-relativist values as if this were an objective discovery, rather than the imperious drift of culture that it is. Certainly, when such competing approaches are pooled, as they often are not, a sort of international balance of diet can be achieved. Although variety can be the spice of scholarship, such a consensus is hardly the means to successful assessment and generalisation.

In such a situation the relations of the Near East narratives to the Old Testament cannot be relevantly or sensitively measured, despite a growing awareness of to what degree the latter is a member of the former. Accurate perception of this membership is a counter-intuitive unstable affair in the light of the restrictions under which we labour. Explicit measurement of the collision of ancient ideologies and the roles of creative confrontation requires more fundamental attention that it is generally given, if we are to excavate elements in ancient creativity. A specific feature of this is that Old Testament scholarship has tended to mirror its own academic patterns as a function of the ancient world, and by so doing neglected to isolate the radical operation of individuality in authorial dissent from ancient centres of influence. The tendency of theological Enlightenment and institutionalised modernist traditions to invent methods which are in-house almost 'private-language' procedures—often inferior to their indirect specialist counterparts in other subjects—has not been fully nullified by later developments. Quite unfounded speculations that were absorbed in the first flush of theological modernisms are sometimes still unquestioned presuppositions. The exciting advances in the latter third of the 20th century should be seen as the basis for fresh and fundamental shifts of perception and theory, as well as one's having the sense to realise that our pasts were mistaken.

The presuppositions of Genesis require reinvestigation in the light not only of archaeological discoveries such as Elba, but with the use of techniques of analysis which do not prejudge the origins and internal values of the book. Just as some archaeologically founded exegesis of Genesis in earlier decades has been too ready to present Genesis as a by-product of some ancient society like Mari, so it is unwise to structure Elba as a library which contain all the requisite properties for examining Genesis. Conversely, a position of scrutiny midway between these two stances may be too bland and institutionalised to take account of the merit of facets in the discoveries in Syria and elsewhere. Hypotheses that in the twentieth century A.D. seemed untenable in principle, now appear possible consequences of conjoining Genesis, refined analysis and archaeological data. So, speculative investigation under the aegis of explicit reason and archaeological investigation is a permissible way to test both the foundations of scholarly explanation and expository routes to exposing the presuppositions of Genesis. A major presupposition that has been eclipsed by some previous treatments is the 3rd-millennium provenance for parts of Genesis—or at least one can deem this as a radical proposal that requires sustained attention. If it is correct, it has ramifications which generate implications for theses about other parts of the Old Testament that have been made to impinge wholly or partly on a historically later background for the earlier parts of Genesis.

Even where there is relative paucity of extant documents from an area or period relevant for a narrative in the Bible, as with the Egyptian axis of the Old Testament, one can discover archaeological data with varying strengths and weaknesses that nevertheless permit inferences for expositional progress as well as re-assessment of hypotheses that hold or have held the field. Nevertheless, in this domain it is imperative for analysis to operate an explicit notion of reasoning and assessment, though this point does not warrant a growth-industry of methodology. Bits of world-view in some scholarship, which hold a dogmatic position—and may at times appear to have little else to support them—should not be allowed to function as normative premises authorising, or blocking in principle, the airing and possible viability of new, old or reconstructed discoveries and theories. In particular this is the case where controversial notions are being considered. The present work has on occasions tended to concentrate on issues that require further attention in this perspective, or unstable ones that compete with standard views: they boldly vary between completely new, unfashionable, neglected or standard. This approach has been taken merely to balance against some established positions. The book's perspectives are also to exemplify an exercise in analytical and creative options, irrespective of whether or not they concern radical possibility or conservative choice. An effect of this is to scramble separated world-views or lines of demarcation. I do not suppose in doing this that all such territories should be re-landscaped. Rather, we should query the notion of territoriality and lines of disengagement, and explore the consequences of changes for interpreting ancient sites and texts. There are tendencies within many institutional traditions, in which a dominating fashion can be censorship, or at least have a coercively corrosive effect on those who explicitly question leading authorities or influences. It is true that a certain mentality that is preoccupied with dissent from and dismissal of accepted paradigms is not itself a discovery-procedure for what is true; and those who have a penchant for the negation of this truth display and remarkable inability to think objectively.

Correspondingly, understanding of a narrative is not exclusive either to radical reaction, or to reactionary norm. There is need for an explicit comprehension and account of consistency and empirical criteria of assessment, and their attendant distinctions. This obtrudes on, and yet is an ideal for any complex analysis. The Exodus journey narratives and the subsequent appearance of Hebrews in Canaan is a group of such interlocking cases. The present book's concern to air this viewpoint in discussion of such matters may seem an unnecessary hostage to fortune. Conversely, this sort of topic was chosen precisely because of the certainty its negation holds in many central trends. My presupposition is, of course, that knowledge of the ancient world is far less secure in such domains than we usually assume. A good way to inject this priority into discussion is take just such an example. Even if the view turns out to be incorrect, it should give us cause for pausing over our grounds of thinking about our basis for certainty or predilection in taste. If readers seriously entertain theories that they do not believe to be correct, then there will be real assessment of our grounds for taking a certain view of the ancient world. I have supposed that our views are more precarious than we often wish them to be, and that we accordingly tend to insulate them and ourselves with over-determined assumptions and description. In this type of analytical context, the logical classification of expositional categories quite clearly enables one to isolate and order points that might otherwise be confused and ignored. In studies where quite varied phenomena are wrongly classified under one heading—where superficial similarities 'hide' deep structure—there is urgent need for criteria identity and application to the situation (as I argue in Gibson 1997a, 1998b and forthcoming e).

One reason, this book claims, why there is a larger than appropriate, or necessary, amount of disagreement in biblical scholarship is because the same form is taken as a basis for the same meaning, when actually there are differences within the same form. This familiar point has unfamiliar realisations using familiar data. The study of *'el* as a noun and the Ugaritic counterparts which function as proper names are examples of this category. This sort of example is especially instructive because such a mistaken conflation results in two different identities being collapsed into one other. In other words, confused form is used to imply false identity. This is at the very foundations of our deepest confusions, usually confidently held because we do not see into the relevant deep structure. We look into ancient semantics and produce a mirror of our own presuppositions, and, seeing only the surface and its dark potential, we may fail to notice the differences of shade which can produce deconstruction of the mirror into the world beyond it. Accordingly, this book has not been a negative quest to conclude that this narcissus is in our perceptual natures. It has also attempted to circumscribe the profound and exciting developments on which we all stand, with appreciation.

The book advocates reconstruction and synthesis for new futures in which reason is harnessed to imagination and the originality, both in our world and in application to the ancient narratives and their external world. In relation to the degree of originality in the Old Testament, we come hopefully at the end of what effectively is a totalitarian editorial tradition of excessive censorship by Eurocentric 19th-century theological institutionalism, though there have been exceptions to this corporate trend. One problem with such uniform corporate consensus of technique and opinion is that what are frequently assumed to be eccentricities in the Old Testament narrative and are ascribed to its intentionality, could be apprehended as the Old Testament's characterization of what is to be criticized by irony. Here the irony is invisible to a surface reading of the narrative. Chapter 7 offered the Elisha axe-raising narrative as an illustration of this. The peculiarity of the narrative was a function of the Canaanite mythology that was being denounced. The alleged eccentricity arose as a characteristic of the Canaanite mythology that was being punned upon in the polemic. This no more reflects on the psychology or theology of an author than does the three witches' motif in Shakespeare. Further, to obscure the thematic emphasis by misunderstanding the origin of the axe-motif is bound to induce a reader incorrectly to presume that the narrative articulates crude notions of relevance, coherence and creativity. So a close reading of such a narrative could revolutionise our perception of its identity.

Nevertheless, the foregoing has attempted to show that a close reading of the Old Testament narrative will often concur with a person's first reading. This view is counter-intuitive, since modernism typically and rightly instructs the reader in how to access subtle originality and alienation in a literary work. Rather, my point has more to do with the attempted retrieval of this literary state's identities, as well as the need to interrogate the influence of modernisms. Certainly our contemporary scholarship has made enormous gains in understanding. This retrieval has, however, to varying degrees been attended by what typically happens with large corporate traditions, as with empires: the observer-culture is conflated with the culture observed.

Conversely, with great literary work, the ingredients which access the inner and originating functions of the internal dynamics of the literary narrative are just those which are its communicative identity. A virgin reading, informed though it could ideally be of some of the internal forces of the composition, is distinct from self-conscious explicitly presuppositional theory-constructed and tradition-driven editorial theses, much though we learn from contemporary scholarship. Reading the Old Testament as a work of art partly achieved by attempting to locate a criterion of consciousness that accurately functions within the ancient world. It is a good thing to aspire to detect properties of some ancient unconsciousness, complex and problematic though our attempts often are.

This does not rely on a prior assumption that parallels between the Old Testament and the ancient world have to be found nor that if parallels exist. Rather, it challenges the tired realism that has imploded into subjective ahistorical taste, or into dogmatic assumptions. It is not enough for scholars and readers to invent their sense of an ending, so that it becomes the relation of a narrative to its originating world; neither is it rational to invent a history for the narrative's world-view, which has never occupied space-time. Both these extremes may force on us a diet of mediocre compromise that masks familiar terms such as 'parallel'—and such expressions as 'not a convincing parallel'—with a fictional or counterfeit self-evidence they usually do not or rarely, possess. Conviction is a function of the observer's psychology, and it should be isolated from the measurement of narrative and from empirical analyses. The reason for this is that evidence and proof are functions of the actual world; they are only our inventions when we have failed to observe. When the negation of these points is practised, anything goes. And thereby the ancient world has unnecessarily gone from our grasp. What we need is a counter-intuitive renaissance by which to construct a future of open possibilities for the past.

Bibliography

Abusch, T.
1995   'The Socio-Religious Framework of the Babylonian Witchcraft Ceremony: Some Observations on the Introductory Section of the Text, Part II', in Z. Soviet, S. Gating, and M. Sokoloff (eds), *Solving Riddles and Untying Knots* (Winona Lake, IL: Eisenbrauns): 45-65.

Akurgal, E.
1962   *The Art of the Hittites* (London: Thames & Hudson).

Albright, W.F.
1951   'The Smaller Beth-Shan Stele of Sethos I (1309–1290 B.C.)', *BASOR* 125: 24-32.
1954   'Northwest-Semitic Names in a List of Egyptian Slaves from the 18th Century B.C.', *JAOS* 74: 222-53.
1968   *Yahweh and the Gods of Canaan* (London: Athlone Press).

Algaze, G.
1993   *The Uruk World System* (Chicago: University of Chicago Press).

Alter, R.,
1981   *The Art of Biblical Narrative* (New York: Basic Books).

Alter, R., and F. Kermode (eds)
1997   *The Literary Guide to the Bible* (London: Collins).

Ambraseys, N.N. and C.P. Melville
1982   *A History of Persian Earthquakes* (Cambridge Earth Sciences Series; Cambridge: Cambridge University Press).

Amiet, P.
1980   *Art of the Ancient Near East* (trans. J. Shepley and C. Choquet; ed. N.N. Richard; New York: H.N. Abrams).

Amitai, J. *et al* (eds)
1985   *Biblical Archaeology Today: Proceedings of the International Congress on Biblical Archaeology, Jerusalem, April 1984* (Jerusalem: Israel Exploration Society).

Andersen, F.I.
1974   *The Sentence in Biblical Hebrew* (The Hague: Mouton).

Anscombe, E.
1958   *Intention* (Oxford: Oxford University Press).

1970   *Philosophical Writings/Descartes* (trans. and ed. E. Anscombe and P.T. Geach; London: Nelson University Paperbacks of the Open University).

Ap-Thomas, D.R.
1973   'The Phoenecians', in Wiseman (ed.), *Peoples of Old Testament Times*: 259-86.

Archi, A.
1979   'The Epigraphic Evidence from Ebla and the Old Testament', *Biblica* 60: 556-66.
1981   'Further Concerning Ebla and the Bible', *BA* 44.3: 5-54.

Arom, S. and Khalfa, J.
1998 "Une raison en acte" (in *Review de Musicologie* 84.1): 5-17.

Astruc, J.
1753   *Conjectures sur les mémoires originaux dont il parait que Moyse s'est servi pour composer le Livre de la Genèse. Avec des remarques, qui appuient ou qui éclaircissent ces conjectures* (Bruxelles: Chez Fricx).

Austin, L.
1987   *Poetic Principles and Practices: Occasional Essays on Baudelaire, Mallarmé and Valery* (Cambridge: Cambridge University Press).

Bahrani, Z.
1998   'Conjuring Mesopotamia: Imaginative Geography and a World Past', in L. Meskell (ed.) *Archaeology under Fire* (London: Routledge): 159-74.

Baines, J.
1989   'Ancient Egyptian Concepts and Uses of the Past: 3rd to 2nd Millennium BC Evidence', in R. Layton (ed.), *Who Needs the Past? Indigenous Values and Archaeology* (London: Unwin Hyman): 131-49.

Bakhtin, M.
1984   *Problems of Dostoyevsky's Poetics* (ed. and trans. C. Emerson; intro. W.C. Booth; Theory and History of Literature 8; Manchester: Manchester University Press).

Banfield, A.
1982   *Unspeakable Sentences* (London: Routledge & Kegan Paul).

Bar-On, D.
1999   *The Indescribable and the Undiscussable* (Budapest: Central European University Press).

Barr, J.
1961   *The Semantics of Biblical Language* (Oxford: Oxford University Press).
1964   *Old and New in Interpretation: A Study of the Two Testaments* (London: SCM Press).
1968   *Comparative Philology and the Text of the Old Testament* (London: SCM Press).
1993   *Biblical Faith and Natural Theology* (Oxford: Clarendon Press).

Barthes, R.
1970   *S/Z* (Paris: Editions du Seuil).
1977   *Images–Music–Text* (London: Fontana).
1999   *The Grain of the Voice* (trans. L. Coverdale; New York: Hill and Wong).

Bataille, G.
1975   *Essential Writings* (ed. M. Richardson; London: Sage).
Baudrillard, J.
1996   *The Perfect Crime* (trans. C. Turner; London and New York: Verso).
Bennett, E.L
1951   *The Pylos Tablets* (Princeton: Princeton University Press for the University of
        Cincinnati).
Biggs, R.D.
1974   *Inscriptions from Tell Abu Salabikh* (Chicago: University of Chicago Press).
Bimson, J.J.
1978   *Redating the Exodus* (Sheffield: JSOT Press).
Binford, L.R.
1977   *For Theory-Building in Archaeology* (New York and London: Academic Press).
1982   'Objectivity-Explanation-Archaeology 1980', in C. Renfrew, M.J. Rowlands, and B.
        Abbot-Seagraves (eds.), *Theory and Explanation in Archaeology* (New York and
        London: Academic Press): 125-38.
1983   *In Pursuit of the Past* (London: Thames & Hudson).
Black, J., George, A., and Postgate, J.N.,
1999   *A Concise Dictionary of Akkadian* (Wiesbaden: Harrassowitz Verlag).
Black, M.
1961   *The Scrolls and Christian Origins* (London: Nelson).
Blackburn, S.
1998   *Ruling Passions* (Oxford: Clarendon Press).
Blazer, V.
1999   'Elam: A Bridge between the Ancient Near East and India', in R. Blench and M.
        Spriggs (eds), *Archaeology and Language. IV. Language-Change and Cultural
        Transformation* (London and New York: Routledge): 48-78.
Bloom, H. and D. Rosenberg
1990   *The Book of J* (London: Faber).
Boghossian, P.
1989   'The Rule-following Considerations', *Mind* 98: 507-49.
Bono, P.
1999   *Esercizi di differenza* (Milan: Costa and Nolan).
Bouveresse, J,
1987   *La force de la regle* (Paris: Editions de Minuit).
1995   *Wittgenstein Reads Freud* (trans. C. Cosman; Princeton: Princeton University Press).
1996   *La demande philosophique* (2nd ed.; Paris: Editions de l'eclat).
Bowie, A.
1990   *Aesthetics and Subjectivity: From Kant to Nietzsche* (Manchester: Manchester
        University Press).
1997   *Philosophy of German Literary Theory: From Romanticism to Critical Theory*
        (London: Routledge).

Bowie, M.

1972   *Henry Michaux* (Oxford: Oxford University Press).

1978   *Mallarmé and the Art of Being Difficult* (Cambridge: Cambridge University Press).

1   'The Question of *Un Coup de Dés*', in M. Bowie, A. Fairlie and A. Finch (eds.), *Baudelaire, Mallarmé, Valery* (Cambridge: Cambridge University Press).

2   *Psychoanalysis and the Future of Theory* (Oxford: Oxford University Press).

Boyde, P.

1984   "Predisposition and Prevenience: Prologomena to the Study of Dante's Mind and Art" (in *Proceedings of the British Academy*. Italian Lecture 1983; LXIX): 327-54.

Bradford, R.

1997   *Stylistics* (London: Routledge).

Breasted, J.H.

1906   *Ancient Records of Egypt* (5 vols.; Chicago: University of Chicago Press).

Bright, J.

1981   *A History of Israel* (OTL; London: SCM, 3rd edn).

Brown, F., S.R. Driver, and C.A. Briggs

1952   *Hebrew and English Lexicon of the Old Testament* (Oxford: Oxford University Press).

Brug, J.F.

1985   *A Literary and Archaeological Study of the Philistines* (Oxford BAB International Series 265: Oxford: Oxford University Press).

Buccellati, G.

1966   *The Amorites of the Ur III Period* (Naples: Istituto Orientale di Napoli).

1996   *A Structural Grammar of Babylonian* (Wiesbaden: Harrassowitz Verlag).

Bullinger, E.W.

1898   *Figures of Speech Used in the Bible* (London: Eyre & Spottiswoode).

Burkert, W.

1984   *The Greek Religion* (Oxford: Oxford University Press).

Burnyeat, M.F.

1994   "Enthymeme: Aristotle on the logic of persuasion" (in D. J. Furley and A. Nehamas (eds.) *Aristotle's Rhetoric*; Princeton: Princeton University Press): 3-55.

Callaway, J.A. and J.M. Weinstein

1972   'The Early Bronze Age Citadel at Ai (Et-Tell)', *BASOR* 207: 41-53.

1977   'Radiocarbon Dating of Palestine in the Early Bronze Age', *BASOR* 225, 5: 1-16.

1985   'Radiocarbon Dating in Ai', in Amitai *et al.* (eds.) 1985: 2.73-74.

Cartwright, N.

1999   *The Dappled World: A Study of the Boundaries of Science* (Cambridge: Cambridge University Press).

Catagnoti, A.

1998   'The 3rd Millennium Personal Name from the Habur Triangle in the Ebla, Brak, and Mozan Texts', European Centre for Upper Mesopotamian Studies. *Subartu*. IV. (Bruxelles: Brepots).

Caverero, A.
1995   *In Spite of Plato* (trans. S. Anderlini-D'Onofrio and A. O'Healy; Cambridge: Polity).
Cazelles, H.
1973   'The Hebrews', in Wiseman (ed.), *Peoples of Old Testament Times*: 1-28.
Chadwick, J.
1987   What Do we Know about Mycenaean Religion?', in MorPurgo Davies and Duhouy (eds) 1985: 191-202.
Chinca, M.
1997   *Gottfried von Strassburg: Tristan* (Landmarks in World Literature: Cambridge: Cambridge University Press).
Chomsky, N.
1995   *Language and Mind* (New York: Harcourt Brace Jovanovich).
1995   'Language and Nature', *Mind* 104: 1-62.
2000   *New Horizons in the Study of Language and Mind* (Cambridge: Cambridge University Press).
Clark, M and M. Holquist
1984   *Mikhail Bakhtin* (Harvard: Belnap Press).
Clements, R.E.
1977   'Review of J. van Seters, Abraham in History and Tradition (New Haven: Yale University Press 1975)', *JSS* 22.1: 90-92.
Clines, D.J.A.
1992   'Story and Poem', in P.R. House (ed.), *Beyond Form Criticism* (Winona Lake, IL: Eisenbrauns).
Cochavi-Rainey, Z.
1998   'Egyptian Influence in the Amarna Texts', *UF* 29: 95-114.
Cohen, L.J.
1977   *The Provable and the Probable* (Oxford: Clarendon Press).
1993   'The Semantics of Metaphor', in A. Ortony (ed.), *Metaphor and Thought* (Cambridge: Cambridge University Press, 2nd edn): 58-70.
Conti, G.
1992   *Index of Eblaic Texts (published or cited)*, with A. Catagnonti and M. Bonechi (Quaderni di Semistica Materiali 1; Florence: Dipartmento di Linguistica, Universita di Firenze).
Cross, F.M.
1973   *Canaanite Myth and Hebrew Epic* (Harvard: Harvard University Press).
Culler, J.
1980   'Prolegomena to a Theory of Reading', in S.R. Suleiman and I. Crosman (eds), *The Reader in the Text* (Princeton: Princeton University Press).
Cumming, R.D.
1992   'Role-playing', in C. Howells (ed), *The Cambridge Companion to Sartre* (Cambridge: Cambridge University Press): 39-66.

Dahood, M.
1979   'The Ebla Tablets and Old Testament Theology', *TD* 27.4: 308.
Dalley, S.
1989   *Myths from Mesopotamia* (Oxford: Oxford University Press).
Dalley, S. *et al.*
3   *The Legacy of Mesopotamia* (Oxford: Oxford University Press).
Danto, A.
1994   *Embodied Meanings* (New York: Noonday Press).
Davidson, D.
1980   *Essays on Actions and Events* (Oxford: Oxford University Press).
Davies, G.F.
1992   *Israel in Egypt* (Sheffield: JSOT Press).
Davies, G.I.
1979   *The Way of the Wilderness* (Cambridge: Cambridge University Press).
Davies, G.
1953   *Vers une explication rationelle du Coup de Dés* (Paris: J. Corti).
Davies, P.R.
1985   *Daniel* (Old Testament Guides; Sheffield: JSOT Press).
Day, J.
1985   *God's Conflict with the Dragon and the Sea* (Cambridge: Cambridge University Press).
Deimel, P.A.
1947   *Sumerische, akkadische und hethitische Lautwerte nach Keilschriftzeichen und Alphabet* (Rome: Pontifical Bible Institute).
Delaney, C.
1998   *Abraham on Trial* (Princeton: Princeton University Press).
Deleuze, G.
1986   *Cinema 1: The Movement-Image* (trans. by H. Tomlinson and B. Habberjam; London: Athlone Press).
Deleuze, G. and F. Guattari
1994   *What is Philosophy?* (trans. G. Burchell and H. Tomlinson; London: Verso).
Derrida, J.
1967   *L'écriture et la différance* (Paris: Editions du Seuil).
1990   *Writing and Difference* (London: Routledge).
1982   *Margins of Philosophy* (Chicago: University of Chicago Press).
1978   *The Truth in Painting* (Chicago: University of Chicago Press).
1983   'The Time of a Thesis: Punctuations', in A. Montifiore (ed.) *Philosophy in France Today* (Cambridge: Cambridge University Press): 34-50.
1998   *Monolingualism of the Other, or The Prosthesis of Origins* (trans. P. Mensah; Stanford: Stanford University Press).
Descombes, V.
1996   'Foreword' to Bouveresse 1995: vii-xiii.

Dever, W.
1984   'Asherah, Consort of Yahweh? New Evidence from Kuntillet 'Ajrud', in *BASOR* 255: 21-38.
Devereux, G.
7   *Dreams in Greek Tragedy* (Oxford: Oxford University Press).
Donnington, R.
1979   *Wagner's 'Ring' and its Symbols* (London: Faber, 2nd edn).
1990   *Opera and its Symbols* (New Haven: Yale University Press).
Dothan, T., and M. Dothan
1992   *People of the Sea* (New York: Macmillan).
Dougherty, R.P.
1929   *Nabonidus and Belshazzar* (Yale Oriental Series 15; Yale: Yale University Press).
Driver, G.R.
1978   *Canaanite Myths and Legends* (Edinburgh: T. & T. Clark, 2nd edn).
Drury, M. O'C.
1973   *The Danger of Words* (Oxford: Oxford University Press).
1981   'Conversations with Wittgenstein', in R. Rhees (ed.), *Ludwig Wittgenstein* (Oxford: Oxford University Press): ch. 6.
Dummett, M.
1981   *Frege: Philosophy of Language* (London: Duckworth, 2nd edn).
1975   'What Is a Theory of Meaning?: I', in S.D. Guttenplan (ed.), *Mind and Language* (Oxford: Oxford University Press): 97-138 = M. Dummett, *The Seas of Language* (2 vols.; Oxford: Clarendon, 1993, 1996): 1: 1-33.
1978   *Truth and Other Enigmas* (London: Duckworth).
1993   *Frege and Other Philosophers* (Oxford: Oxford University Press).
Dupré, J.
1993   *The Disorder of Things* (Cambridge, MA: Harvard University Press).

Eco, U.
1984   *Semiotics and the Philosophy of Language* (London: Macmillan).
Eidem, J.
1997   'Appendix B: The Inscriptions [on the Early Glyptic of Tell Brak]', in Matthews 1997: 307-11.
Emerton, J.A.
1971   'The Riddle of Genesis 14', *VT* 21: 431-34.
Empson, W.
1953   *Seven Types of Ambiguity* (London: Chatto & Windus, 3rd edn).
Evans, A.
1928   'The Palace of Knossos and its Dependencies in the Light of Recent Discoveries and Reconstitutions: Resume of Communication', *Journal of the Royal Institute of British Architects* 3rd series: 91-102.

Everett, H.
1997 'The Theory of the Universal Wave Function', in B.S. DeWitt and N. Graham (eds), *The Many-worlds Interpretation of Quantum Mechanics* (Princeton: Princeton University Press).

Fales, F.M., and Postgate, J.N.
1992 *Imperial administrative Records. Part I: Palace and Temple Administration* (F. M. Fales and J.N. Postgate (eds).; J. Reade, illustrations ed.; State archives of Assyria Vol. VII; Neo-Assyrian Text Corpus Project of the Academy of Finland, and Deutsche Orient-Gesellschaft; S. Parpola and R. M. Whiting (eds.); Helsinki: Helsinki University Press).
Falkenstein, A.
1936 *Archaische texte aus Uruk* (Berlin: Deutsche Forschungsgemeinschaft).
Fine, K.
1985 *Reasoning with Arbitrary Objects* (Aristotelian Society Series 3; Oxford: Blackwell).
Finkelstein, J.J.
1969 'A Late Babylonian Copy of the Laws of Hammurapi', *JCS* 21: 39-48.
Finley, M.I.
1985 *Ancient History* (London: Penguin Books).
Foley, H.P.
1988 *Ritual Irony* (Cornell: Cornell University Press).
Forbes, R.J.
1960 *Metallurgy in Antiquity* (Leiden: E.J. Brill).
1965 *Studies in Ancient Technology. III.* (Leiden: E.J. Brill, 2nd edn).
Forrester, J.
1980 *Language and the Origins of Psychoanalysis* (London: Macmillan).
1997 *Dispatches from the Freud Wars* (Cambridge, MA: Harvard University Press).
Forte, M. and A. Siliotti (eds)
1997 *Virtual Archaeology* (London: Thames & Hudson).
Foster, B.R.
1996 'Appendix B: Volcanic Phenomena in Mesopotamian Sources?', in Polinger Foster and Ritner 1996: 12-14.
Foucault, M. [Note: where the French version is listed first, this is because references in the book derive from the French edition since it seemed more appropriate.]
1961 *Folie et deraison* (Paris: Plon).
1963 *Naissance de la clinique* (Paris: Presses universitaires de France).
1965 *Madness and Civilization* (trans. R. Howard; London: Routledge).
1966 *Les mots et les choses* (Paris: Gallimard).
1972 *The Archaeology of Knowledge and The Discourse on Language* (trans. S. Smith and A. Mark; London: Tavistock).
1989 *The Birth of the Clinic* (trans. A. Sheridan; London: Routledge).
1989 *The Order of Things* (London: Routledge).

1969   *L' archéologie du savoir* (Paris: Gallimard).
1979   *The Will to Knowledge* (London: Allan Lane).
Franken, H.J.
1967   'Texts from the Persian Period from Tell Deir 'Alla', *VT* 17: 480-81.
Frankfort, H.
1939   *Cylinder Seals* (London: Macmillan).
Freedman, R.E.
1996   *Life of a Poet: R.M. Rilke* (New York: Farrar, Straus & Girox).
Freud, S.
1974   *The Standard Edition of the Complete Works of Sigmund Freud* (ed. J. Strachey with
         A. Freud; London: Hogarth Press for the Institute of Psycho-analysis). [References to
         Freud's works in the present book refer to this edition by year of publication in this
         series.]
Freud, S. and J. Breuer
1998   *Studies in Hysteria* (trans. A.A. Brill; Boston: Beacon Press).
Frevel, C.
1995   *Aschera und der Ausschließlichkeitsanspruch YHWHs*. Biblische Beitrage 94
         (Weinheim: Bonner).
Friedman, R.E.
1996   'Some Recent Non-arguments Concerning the Documentary Hypothesis', in M.V. Fox
         et al. (eds), *Texts, Temples and Traditions* (Winona Lake, IL: Eisenbrauns): 87-101.

Gadd, C.J. (ed. and trans.)
1923   *The Fall of Nineveh: Babylonian Chronicle, no. 21,901, in the British Museum*
         (London: British Museum).
1958   *Anatolian Studies* 8: 56-57.
Gallois, A.
1998   *Occasions of Identity* (Oxford: Clarendon Press).
Gardin, J.-C.
1980   *Archaeological Constructs: An Aspect of Theoretical Archaeology* (Cambridge:
         Cambridge University Press).
Gardiner, A.H.
1900   *The admonitions of an Egyptian sage : from a hieratic papyrus in Leiden: Pap. Leiden
         344 recto* (Leipzig: J.C. Hinrichs)
1961   *Egypt of the Pharaohs* (Oxford: Oxford University Press).
Gatens, M. and G. Lloyd
1999   *Collective Imaginings* (London: Routledge).
Geach, P.T.
1968   *Reference and Generality* (Cornell: Cornell University Press).
1972   *Logic Matters* (Oxford: Oxford University Press).
1971   *Mental Acts* (London: Routledge and Kegan Paul, 1st edn).

1975   'Names and Identity', in S. Guttenplan (ed.), *Mind and Language* (Oxford: Oxford University Press): 139-58.

Gelb, I.J.

1988   'Thoughts about Ibla', *SMS* 1.1: 3-30.

George, A.

1999   *The Epic of Gilgamesh: the Babylonian Epic Poem and other Texts in Akadian and Sumerian* (London: Allen Lane, Penguin Press).

Giacumakis, G.

1970   *The Akkadian of Alalah* (The Hague: Mouton).

Gibson, A.

1981   *Biblical Semantic Logic* (1st edn; Oxford: Basil Blackwell; New York: St. Martin's Press).

1987   *Boundless Function* (Newcastle: Bloodaxe Books).

1997a   'The Semantics of God: Some Functions in the Dead Sea Scrolls', in S.E. Porter and C.A. Evans (eds), *The Scrolls and the Scriptures: Qumran Fifty Years after* (RILP 3; JSPSup 26; Sheffield: Sheffield Academic Press): 68-106.

1997b   'Archetypal Site Poetry', foreword to J. Milbank, *The Mercurial Wood: Sites, Tales, Qualities* (Salzburg Studies in English Literature, Poetic Drama and Poetic Theory; Salzburg: University of Salzburg): vii-xi.

1998a   'Ockham's World and Future', in J. Marenbon (ed.), *Routledge History of Philosophy*. III. *Medieval Philosophy* (London: Routledge): 329-67.

1998b   'Modern Philosophy and Ancient Consciousness: I Think, Therefore Am I Gendered?', in M.A. Hayes, W.J. Porter and D. Tombs (eds), *Religion and Sexuality* (RILP 4; STAS 2; Sheffield: Sheffield Academic Press): 22-48.

1999   'Logic of the resurrection', in S.E. Porter, M.A. Hayes and D. Tombs (eds), Resurrection (RILP 5; JSNTS 186; Sheffield: Academic Press): 166-94.

2000a   *God and the Universe* (London and New York: Routledge).

2000b   'Philosophy of Psychotic Modernism: Wagner and Hitler' (in S.E. Porter and B.W.R. Pearson (eds) *Christian-Jewish Relations down the Centuries*; (RILP 6; JSNT 192; Sheffield: Sheffield Academic Press): 251-86.

forthcoming a   *What is Literature?*

forthcoming b   'Archaeology of Asia Minor, Greece, and Italy', in C.A. Evans and S.E. Porter (eds), *Dictionary of New Testament Background* (Downers Grove, IL: InterVarsity Press).

forthcoming c   *Counter-Intuition.*

forthcoming d   *Beyond Human Meaning.*

forthcoming e   *Biblical Semantic Logic* (Sheffield: Sheffield Academic Press, 2nd edn 2001; includes a new chapter: "Logic, literary creativity and philosophy of mathematics" [1981 1st edn., as above]).

forthcoming f   'Rhetoric and Philosophical Logic', in S.E. Porter and D. Stamp (eds), *Proceedings of the Florence Rhetoric Symposium* (JSNTSup; Sheffield: Sheffield Academic Press).

Gibson, A. and N.A. O'Mahony
1995   'Lamentation sumerienne (vers–2004)', *Dedale: Le pardoxe des representations du divin—L' image et l'invisible*, 1–2: 13-14.
1993   'Style and Substance under the Veneer', *Times Higher Education Supplement* 1064 (March 26): 21.
Gibson, J.C.L.
1975   *Textbook of Syrian Semitic Inscriptions*. II. *Aramaic Inscriptions* (Oxford: Oxford University Press).
1978   *Canaanite Myths and Legends* (Edinburgh: T. & T. Clark).
Giddens, A.
1984   *The Constitution of Society: Outline of the Theory of Structuration* (Cambridge: Polity).
Giles, F.J.
1997   *The Amarna Age: Western Asia* (Australian Centre for Egyptiology Studies 5; Warminster, UK: Aris and Phillips).
Giveon, R.
1976   'New Egyptian Seals with Titles and Names from Canaan', *TAJIA* 3: 127-34.
Goldhill, S.
1984   *Language, Sexuality, Narrative: The Oresteia* (Cambridge: Cambridge University Press).
1986   *Reading Greek Tragedy* (Cambridge: Cambridge University Press).
1990   *The Poet's Voice* (Cambridge: Cambridge University Press).
Gombrich, E.
1977   *Art and Illusion* (Oxford: Oxford University Press, 5th edn).
Gordon, C.H.
1958   'Abraham and the Merchants of Ura', *JNES* 17: 28-31.
1963   'Abraham of Ur', in D. Winton Thomas and W.D. McHardy (eds), *Hebrew and Semitic Studies* (Oxford: Oxford University Press): 77-84.
1965   *Ugaritic Textbook: Revised Grammar, Paradigms, Texts in Transliteration, Comprehensive Glossary* (Rome: Pontifical Biblical Institute, Supplement, 1967).
Gottwald, N.K.
1979   *The Tribes of Yahweh* (London: SCM Press).
Gray, J.
1977   'A Cantata of the Autumn Festival: Psalm LXVIII', *JSS* 22.1: 2-26.
1965   *The Legacy of Canaan* (VTSup 5; Leiden: E.J. Brill, 2nd edn).
Gruber, M.I.
1992   *The Motherhood of God and Other Studies* (South Florida Studies in the History of Judaism 57; Atlanta, GA: Scholars Press).
Gurney, O.R. and S.N. Kramer
1976   *Sumerian Literary Texts in the Ashmolean Museum* (Oxford: Oxford University Press).

Hackett, J.A.
1984   *The Balaam Text from Deir 'Alla* ̄ (Harvard Semitic Monographs 31; Chico, CA: Scholars Press).

Hacking, I.
1994   *Rewriting the Soul* (Princeton: Princeton University Press).
1998   *Mad Travellers: Reflections of the Reality of Transient Mental Illnesses* (Charlottesville: University Press of Virginia).

Hadley, J.M.
2000   *The Cult of Asherah in Ancient Isael and Judah: Evidence for a Hebrew Goddess* (Cambridge: Cambridge University Press).

Hale, R.
1994   'Singular Terms', in B.F. McGuinness and J.L. Oliveri (eds), *Philosophy of Michael Dummett* (Dordrecht: Kluwer Academic Publishers): 17-44.
1996   'Singularity Terms (1)', in M. Schirn (ed), *Frege: Importance and Legacy* (Berlin: de Gruyter): 438-57.

Hallo, W.W.
1983   'Lugalbanda Excavated', *JAOS* 103: 165-80.

Hamblin, C.L.
1970   *Fallacies* (London: Methuen).

Hammond, G.
1983   'The Bible and Literary Criticism: I and II', *Critical Quarterly* 25.2: 5-20 and 25.3: 3-15.

Hansen, H.V. and R.C. Pinto (eds)
1995   *Fallacies* (University Park, PA: Pennsylvania State University Press).

Haran, M.
1978   *Temples and Temple-Services in Ancient Israel* (Oxford: Oxford University Press).

Harland, R.
1987   *Superstructuralism* (London: Methuen).

Harris, A.C. and L. Campbell
1995   *Historical Syntax in Cross-Linguistic Perspective* (Cambridge: Cambridge University).

Hattem, W.C. van
1981   'Once again: Sodom and Gomorrah', *BA* 44.2: 87-92.

Hawking, S., and R. Penrose
1996   *The Nature of Space and Time* (The Isaac Newton Institute Series of Lectures; Princeton: Princeton University Press).

Hayes, W.C.A.
1955   *Papyrus of the Late Middle Kingdom in the Brooklyn Museum: Papyrus Brooklyn 35.1446* (New York: Department of Egyptian Art, Brooklyn Museum).

Healey, J.
1978   'MLKM/RPUM and the KISPUM', *UF* 10: 89-92.

Herdner, A.
1963   *Corpus des tablettes en cunéiformes alphabétiques* (2 vols.; Bibliotheque archeologique et historique 79; Paris: Imprimerie Nationale Geuthner).

Herrmann, S.
1985   'Basic Factors of Israelite Settlement in Canaan', in J. Aviram *et al.* (eds), *Biblical Archaeology Today: Proceedings of the International Congress on Biblical Archaeology, Israel Exploration Society* (Jerusalem: Israel Exploration Society): 47-53.

Hertzberg, H.W.
1964   *1 and 2 Samuel* (OTL; London: SCM Press).

Hess, R.S
1994   'Asking Historical Questions of Joshua 13–19', in A.R. Millard, J.K. Hoffmeir, and D.W. Baker (eds), *Faith, Tradition, and History* (Winona Lake, IL: Eisenbrauns): 191-206.

Hesse, M.
1995   'Past Realities', in I. Hodder *et al.* (eds), *Interpreting Archaeology* (London: Routledge): 45-57.

Hiddleston, J.A.
1999   *Baudelaire and the Art of Memory* (Oxford: Clarendon Press).

Hintikka, J.J.
1998   'Who is about to Kill Analytic Philosophy?', in A. Biletzky and A. Matar (eds), *The Story of Analytic Philosophy* (London: Routledge): 253-69.
1998   *The Principles of Mathematics Revisited* (Cambridge: Cambridge University Press).

Hobson, M.
1982   *The Object of Art* (Cambridge: Cambridge University Press).
1990   'On the Subject of the Subject: Derrida on Sollers in *La dissemination*', in D. Wood (ed.), *Philosophers' Poets* (London: Routledge): 111-39.
1995   'What Is Wrong with Saint Peter's, or Diderot, Analogy and Illusion in Architecture', in W. Pape and F. Burwick (eds), *Reflecting Senses* (Berlin: W. de Gruyter): 53-74, nn. 315-41.
1998   *Jacques Derrida: Opening Lines* (London: Routledge).

Hodder, I.
1982   *The Present Past* (London: Batsford).
1985   'Postprocessual Archaeology', in M.B. Schiffer (ed.), *Advances in Archaeological Method and Theory.* VIII. (Orlando, FL: Academic Press).
1999   *The Archaeological Process* (Cambridge: Cambridge University Press).

Hoftijzer, J.
1976   'The Prophet Balaam in a 6th Century Aramaic Inscription' [Note that the sixth-century BC date attributed to the inscription in this title was an editorial error, for which the editor later apologized and corrected to the intended circa 700 date], *BA* 39.1: 11-17.

Hoftijzer, J. and G. van der Kooij (eds)
1976   *Aramaic Texts from Deir 'Alla* (Documenta et Monumenta Orientis Antiqui 19; Leiden: E.J. Brill).

Horn, L.R.
1996   'Presupposition and Implicature', in S. Lappin (ed.) 1996: ch. 11.

Huehnergard, J.
1989   *The Akkadian of Ugarit* (Atlanta: Scholars Press).
Hume, K.
1984   *Fantasy and Mimesis* (London: Methuen).
Hutcheon, L.
1984   *Formalism and the Freudian Aesthetic* (Cambridge: Cambridge University Press).

Ingraffia, B.D.
1995   *Postmodern Theory and Biblical Theology* (Cambridge: Cambridge University Press).
Iser, W.
1972   *Der implizite Leser* (Munich: Fink).
1974   *The Implied Reader: Patterns of Communication in Prose Fiction from Bunyan to Beckett* (Baltimore: Johns Hopkins University Press).
Israelit-Groll, S. (ed.)
1990   *Studies in Egyptology: Presented to Mirian Lichtheim* (2 vols.; Jerusalem: Magnes Press/Hebrew University).
Izre'el, S.
1997   *The Amarna Scholarly Tablets* (Gröningen: STYX Publications).

Jacobi, F.H.
1787   *David Hume über den Glauben oder Idealismus und Realismus ein Gespräch* (Breslau: G. Loewe).
Jacobsen, T.
1939   *Sumerian King List* (Chicago: University of Chicago Press).
1976   *The Treasures of Darkness* (Yale: Yale University Press).
1981   'The Eridu Genesis', *JBL* 100.4: 513-29.
James, H.
1986   *The Art of Criticism* (ed. W. Veeder and S.M. Griffin; Chicago: University of Chicago Press).
James, S.D.T.
1984   *The Context of Social Explanation* (Cambridge: Cambridge University Press).
Juhl, P.D.
1980   *Interpretation* (Princeton: Princeton University Press).

Kabbani, R.
1986   *Europe's Myths of Orient* (London: Pandora).
Katz, N.M.
         16. *Rigid Local Systems* (Annals of Mathematics Studies 139; Princeton: Princeton University Press).

Keitel, E.
1986   *Reading Psychosis* (Oxford: Oxford University Press).
Kelley, D.J.
1964   *Charles Baudelaire's Salon de 1846* (2 vols.; unpublished PhD thesis, University of Cambridge).
1975   *Baudelaire: Salon de 1846. Texte établi et présenté par David Kelley* (Oxford: Clarendon Press).
Kempinski, A.
1990   'Two Scarabs of Yakubum', in Israelit-Groll (ed.) 1990: 2.632-34.
Kennedy, R.
1998   *The Elusive Human Subject* (London: Free Association).
Kenyon, K.M.
1960–65 *Excavations at Jericho* (2 vols.; London: British School of Archaeology in Jerusalem).
Kermode, J.F.
1964   *The Sense of an Ending* (New York: Oxford University Press).
1979   *The Genesis of Secrecy* (Cambridge, MA: Harvard University Press).
1983   *Essays on Fiction* (London: Routledge & Kegan Paul) = *The Art of Telling* (Cambridge, MA: Harvard University Press).
1985   *Forms of Attention* (Chicago: University of Chicago Press).
1990   *Poetry, Narrative, History* (Oxford: Blackwell).
1996   *Not Entitled: A Memoir* (London: Harper Collins).
2000   *Shakespeare's Language* (London: Allen Lane, Penguin Press).
Kershaw, I.
1997   *Hitler* (London: Allen Lane).
Khalfa, J. (2000) "Deleuze et Sartre: idée d'une conscience impersonnelle" (in *Les Temps Modernes* 55.608):190-222.
Killen, J.T.
1985   'The Linear B Tablets and the Mycenaean Economy', in Morpurgo Davies and Duhoux (eds) 1985: 241-310.
Kinnier Wilson, J.V.
1979   *The Rebel Lands* (University of Cambridge Oriental Publications 29; Cambridge: Cambridge University Press).
1989   "Fish rations and the Indus script", *SAS* 3:41-46.
1996   "'seven cities' and the Indus Valley script", in *SAS*: 99-104.
Kirjavainen, H.
1978   *Certainty, Assent and Belief* (Helsinki: Luther-Agricola-Society).
Kirk, G.S.
1974   *The Nature of Myth* (Harmondsworth: Penguin).
Kitchen, K.A.
1990   'Early Canaanites in Rio de Janeiro...', in Israelit-Groll (ed) 1990: 2.635-43.
1998   *The Bible in its World* (Exeter: Paternoster Press).

Klein, J.
1997 'The Origin and Development of Languages on Earth: The Sumerian versus the Biblical view', in M. Coggin, B.L. Eichler and J.H. Tigay (eds) *Tehillah le-Moshe* (Winona: Eisenbrauns): 77-92.
Kosak, S.
1982 *Hittite Inventory Texts* (Heidelberg: Winter).
Kramer, S.N.
1963 *The Sumerians* (Chicago: University of Chicago Press).
1968 'The Babel of Tongues', *JAOS* 88: 108-11.
1983 'The Sumerian Deluge Myth: Reviewed and Revised', *AS* 33: 114-21.
1990 *Sumerian Mythology: A Study of Spiritual and Literary Achievement in the Third Millennium B.C.* (Westport, CT: Greenwood Press, rev. edn).
Kristeva, J.
1982 *Powers of Horror* (New York: Columbia University Press).
Kristiansen, K.
1998 *Europe before History* (Cambridge: Cambridge University Press).
Kugel, J.L.
1982 *The Idea of Biblical Poetry* (Yale: Yale University Press).

L'Heureux, C.E.
1979 *Rank Among the Canaanite Gods* (Harvard Semitic Monographs 21; Missoula. MT: Scholars Press).
Lacan, J.
1971 *Écrits: A Selection* (trans. A. Sheridan; London: Routledge [1966]).
1976 *Scilicet 6-7* (Paris: Minuit).
1991 *Le Séminaire de Jacques Lacan. VIII. Le transfert* (Paris: Éditions de Seuil).
Lambert, W.G.
1960 *Babylonian Wisdom Literature* (Oxford: Oxford University Press).
1995 'Some New Babylonian Wisdom Literature', in J. Day, R.P. Gordon and H.G.M. Williamson (eds), *Wisdom in Ancient Israel* (Cambridge: Cambridge University Press): ch. 2.
Langdon, S.
1912 *Die Neubabylonische Konigsinschriften. Vorderasiatische. Bibliothek. IV.* (Leipzig: J.C. Hinrichs).
Lappin, S. (ed.)
1996 *The Handbook of Contemporary Semantic Theory* (Oxford: Blackwell).
Lear, J.
1980 *Aristotle and Logical Theory* (Cambridge: Cambridge University Press).
Legge, E.M.
1988 *Max Ernst: The Psychoanalytic Sources* (Ann Arbor: University of Michigan Press).
Leick, G.
1994 *Sex and Eroticism in Mesopotamian Literature* (London: Routledge).

Lemoine-Luccione, E.
1985–86 'The Social Bond', *SG* 1.
Lewis, D.
1980   *Collected Works*. I. (Oxford: Oxford University Press).
1986   *Worlds in Plurality* (Oxford: Oxford University Press).
Lewy, C.
1976   *Meaning and Modality* (Cambridge: Cambridge University Press).
Lichtheim, N.
1976   *Ancient Egyptian Literature*. II. (Berkeley: University of California Press).
Linsky, L.
1999   *Names and Descriptions* (Chicago: University of Chicago Press).
Livingstone, A.
3   *Mystical and Mythological Explanatory Works of Assyrian and Babylonian Scholars*
          (Oxford: Clarendon Press).
Loughlin, J.C.H.
2000   *Archaeology and the Bible* (London, New York: Routledge).
Lyons, J.
1977   *Semantics* 1 (Cambridge: Cambridge University Press).
Lyotard, J.-F.
1984   *The Postmodern Condition* (Manchester: Manchester University Press).

MacDonald, B.
1983   'The Late Bronze Age and Iron Age Sites of the Wadi el Hasa Survey 1979', in J.F.A.
          Sawyer and D.J.A. Clines (eds), *Midian, Moab and Edom* (JSOTSup; Sheffield: JSOT
          Press): 18-28.
Magnusson, M.
1977   *BC: The Archaeology of Bible Lands* (London: British Broadcasting Corporation).
Marinatos, N.
1984   *Art and Religion in Thera* (Athens: D. and I. Mathioulakis).
Marinatos, S.
1976   *Excavations at Thera* (Athens: He en Athenais Archaiologike Hetaireia).
Marx, K.
1975   *Early Writings* (ed. L. Coletti; London: New Left Review).
Matthews, D.M.
1997   *The Early Glyptic of Tell Brak: Cylinder Seals of Third Millennium Syria* (Orbis
          Biblicus et Orientalis 15; Series Archaeologica; Fribourg: University Press of
          Fribourg; Göttingen: Vandenhoeck & Ruprecht).
Matthiae, P.
1991   'Masterpieces of Early and Old Syrian Art: Discoveries of the 1989 Ebla Excavations
          in a Historical Perspective' (in *Proceedings of the British Academy* 1989 LXXV;
          Oxford: Oxford University Press for the British Academy): 75: 25-69.

1979   'Princely Cemetery and Ancestors Cult of Ebla during Middle Bronze II', *UF* 11: 563-69.
1978   'Preliminary Remarks on the Royal Palace of Ebla', *SMS* 2.2: 1-20.
1980   *Ebla* (London: Hodder and Stoughton).
1997   'Ebla: A Rediscovered City', in Forte and Siliotti (eds) 1997: 76-83.
Mazar, A.
1993   *Archaeology of the Land of the Bible* (New York: Doubleday; Cambridge: Lutterworth).
1985   'The Israelite Settlement in the Light of Archaeological Excavations', in Amitai *et al.* (eds.), *Biblical Archaeology Today*: 61-71.
Mazar, B.
1986   *The Early Biblical Period: Historical Studies* (trans. R. and E. Rigbi; ed. S. Ahitov and B.A. Levine; Jerusalem: Israel Exploration Society).
McAllister, J.W.
1986   'Theory-Assessment in the Historiography of Science', *BJPS* 37: 315-33.
McGinn, C.
1984   *Wittgenstein on Meaning* (Oxford: Oxford University Press).
Meiroop, M. Van De
1999   *Cuneiform Texts and the Writing of History* (Approaching the Ancient World; London and New York: Routledge).
Mellor, D.H.
1982   'Probabilities for Explanation', in C. Renfrew, M.J. Rowlands and B.A. Segraves *Theory and Explanation in Archaeology: The Southampton Conference* (London: Academic Press).
1995   *The Facts of Causation* (International Library of Philosophy; London: Routledge).
1998   *Real Time II* (International Library of Philosophy London; New York: Routledge, rev. and extended edn [1st edn: Cambridge: Cambridge University Press, 1981]).
Melzer, T.
1995   'Stylistics for the Study of Ancient Texts', in W. Bodine (ed.), *Discourse Analysis of Biblical Literature* (SBLSS; Atlanta: Scholars Press).
Mercer, S.A.B.
1939   *The Tell el-Amarna Tablets* (Toronto: Macmillan).
Meyers, C.
1988   *Discovering Eve: Ancient Israelite Women in Context* (Oxford: Oxford University Press).
Milbank, J.
1997   *The Word Made Strange* (Oxford: Blackwell).
Millard, A.R.
1976   'Assyrian Royal Names in Biblical Hebrew', *JSS* 21: 1-14.
Mitchell, B.
1985   *Old English Syntax*. I. (Oxford: Oxford University Press).

Molyneaux, B.L.
1997   'Representation and Reality in the Private Tombs of the Late Eighteenth Dynasty,
        Egypt: An Approach to the Study of the Shape of Meaning', in B.L. Molyneaux (ed.),
        The Cultural Life of Images (London: Routledge): 108-29.
Moor, J.C. de
1971a   *The Seasonal Pattern in the Ugaritic Myth of Ba'lu according to the version of Ilimilku*
        (Kevelaer, NL: Butzon & Bercker).
1971b   *Baal* (Berlin: de Gruyter).
Moorey, P.R.S.
1975   *Biblical Lands* (Oxford: Oxford University Press).
Moran, W.L.
1987   *Les Lettres d'El-Amarna* (Paris: Editions de Serf).
1992   *The Amarna Letters* (Baltimore: Johns Hopkins University Press).
MorPurgo Davies, A. and Y. Duhoux (eds)
1985   *Linear B: A 1984 Survey* (BCILL 26; Louvain-la-Neuve: Cabay).
Muhly, J.D., R. Maddin, T. Stech and E. Ozgen
1985   'Iron in Anatolia and the Nature of the Industry', in *AS* 35: 67-84.
Muraoka, T.
1976   'Segolate Nouns in Biblical and Other Aramaic Dialects', *JAOS* 96.2: 226-35.

Na'aman, N.
1997   'The Network of Canaanite Late Bronze Age Kingdoms and the City of Ashdod', *UF*
        29: 599-625.
Negbi, O.
1976   *Canaanite Gods in Metal* (Tel Aviv: Tel Aviv University Press).
Nicholson, E.
1998   *The Pentateuch in the Twentieth Century* (Oxford: Clarendon Press).
Nili, Sh.
1993   *Where Can Wisdom Be Found? The Sage's Language in the Bible and in Ancient
        Egyptian Literature* (Orbis biblicus et orientalis 130; Fribourg: Göttingen University
        Press/Vandenhoeck & Ruprecht).
Nilsson, M.P.
1971   *The Minoan–Mycenaean Religion and its Survival in Greek Religion* (New York:
        Biblo and Tanner, 2nd rev. edn [1st edn: Lund: C.W.K. Gleerup]).
Nussbaum, M.C.
1999   *Sex and Social Justice* (New York, Oxford: Oxford University Press.)
4   *Women and Human Development: the Capabilities Approach* (Cambridge: Cambridge
        University Press).

Oden, R.A.
1976   'The Persistence of Canaanite Religion', *BA* 39.1: 31-36.

Oppenheim, A.K. *et al.*
1970   *Glassmaking in Ancient Mesopotamia* (New York: Corning Museum of Art).
Oren, E.D.
1973   *The Northern Cemetery of Beth Shan* (Leiden: E.J. Brill).
Owen, D.I.
1992   'Syrians in Sumer', *Bibliotheca Mesopotamia* 1992: 107-75.
Özgüc, N.
1980   'Seal Impressions from the Palace at Acemhöyük', in E. Porada (ed.), *Ancient Art in Seals* (Princeton: Princeton University Press): 61-100.

Parkinson, R.B.
1997   *The Tale of Sinuhe and Other Ancient Egyptian Poems* (Oxford: Clarendon Press).
Parpola, A.
1994   *Deciphering the Indus Script* (Cambridge: Cambridge University Press).
Parpola, S.
1980   'The Murderer of Sennacherib', in B. Alster (ed.), *Death in Mesopotamia* (Mesopotamia 8; Copenhagen Studies in Assyriology; Copenhagen: Akademisk Forlag): 171-82.
Pearson, B.W.R.
1999   'Resurrection and the Judgment of the Titans: ἡ γῆ τῶν ἀσεβῶν in LXX Isaiah 26.19', in S.E. Porter, M.A. Hayes and D. Tombs (eds.), *Resurrection* (RILP 5; JSNTSup 186; Sheffield: Sheffield Academic Press) 33-51.
Pettinato, G.
1977   'Gli archivi reali di Tell Mardikh-Ebla', *RBI* 25.3: 225-43.
1979   *Catalogo dei testi cuneiformi di Tell Mardikh-Ebla* (Materiali epigrafici di Ebla 1; Napoli: Istituto universitario orientale di Napoli).
1981   *The Archives of Ebla* (New York: Doubleday).
1980a   'Ebla and the Bible', *BA* 43.4: 203-16.
1980b   *Testi amministrativi della biblioteca L. 2769* (Materiali epigrafici di Ebla 2; Napoli: Istituto universitario orientale di Napoli).
1991   *Ebla: A New Look at History* (Baltimore: Johns Hopkins University Press).
Phillips, A.
1970   *Ancient Israel's Criminal Law* (Oxford: Oxford University Press).
Picchioni, S.A.
1997   *Testi Lessicali Monolingui "és-bar-kin"* (Materiali Epigrafici di Ebla 1; Rome: Universitá degli di Roma).
Pierce, C.S.
1931–58   *Collected Papers* (Cambridge, MA: Harvard University Press).
Polinger Foster, K. and R.K. Ritner
1996   'Texts, Stories and the Thera Eruption', with an appendix by B.R. Foster, *JNES* 55.1: 1-14.

Pollock, S.
1999   *Ancient Mesopotamia* (Cambridge: Cambridge University Press).
Popper, K.R.
1963   *Conjectures and Refutations* (London: Routledge & Kegan Paul).
1972   *Objective Knowledge* (Oxford: Oxford University Press).
1994   *The Myth of the Framework* (ed. M.A. Nottarno; London: Routledge).
Porada, E.
1980   *Ancient Art in Seals* (Princeton: Princeton University Press).
Porter, B. and R.L.B. Moss
1985   *Topographical Bibliography of Ancient Egyptian Hieroglyphic Texts, Reliefs, and Paintings*. II. (Oxford: Griffith Institute, Ashmolean Museum).
Postgate, J.N.
1992   *Early Mesopotamia* (London: Routledge).
Priest, G.
1995   *Beyond the Limits of Thought* (Cambridge: Cambridge University Press).
Prior, A.N.
1971   *Objects of Thought* (Oxford: Oxford University Press).
Pritchard, J.B. (ed.)
1969   *Ancient Near East Texts Relating to the Old Testament* (Princeton: Princeton University Press, 3rd edn).

Quine, W.V.O.
1950   *Methods of Logic* (New York: Holt).

Rainey, A.
1994   'Remarks on Donald Redford's *Egypt, Canaan, and Israel in Ancient Times*', *BASOR* 295: 81-85.
Rao, S.R.
1994   *New Frontiers of Archaeology* (Bombay: Prakashan PVT).
Rast, W.E. and R.T. Schaub
1973   *Survey of the Southeastern Plain of the Dead Sea* (Annual of the Department of Antiquities of Jordan 19; Amman: Department of Antiquities).
Rawls, J.
1972   *A Theory of Justice* (Oxford: Oxford University Press).
1999   *Collected Papers* (ed. S. Freeman; Cambridge, MA and London: Harvard University Press).
Redford, D.B.
1967   *History and Chronology of the 18th Dynasty* (Toronto: University of Toronto Press).
1973   'The Temple of Osiris at Karnak', *JEA* 59: 16-30.
1992   *Egypt, Canaan, and Israel* (Princeton: Princeton University Press).

1996   'A Response to Anson Rainey's "Remarks on Donald Redford's *Egypt, Canaan and Israel in Ancient Times*"', *BASOR* 301: 77-82.

Rees, M.
1999   *Just Six Numbers* (London: Weidenfeld and Nicolson).

Renfrew, A.C.
1973   *Before Civilisation* (London: Cape).
1982   *Towards an Archaeology of Mind* (Cambridge: Cambridge University Press).
1985   *Archaeology of Cult: The Sanctuary of Phylakopi* (with contributions by P.A. Montgomery *et al.* London: British School of Archaeology at Athens and Thames and Hudson).
1987   'Problems in the Modeling of Socio-Cultural Systems', *European Journal of Operational Research* 30: 179-92.
1994   'Towards a Cognitive Archaeology', in A.C. Renfrew and E.B.W. Zubrow (eds), *The Ancient Mind: Elements of Cognitive Archaeology* (New Directions in Archaeology; Cambridge: Cambridge University Press): 3-12.

Rescher, N. and R. Brandom
1980   *The Logic of Inconsistency* (Oxford: Oxford University Press).

Reynolds, D.
1995   *Symbolist Aesthetics and Early Abstract Art* (Cambridge: Cambridge University Press).

Riffaterre, M.
1991   'Undecidability as Hermeneutic Constraint', in P. Collier and H. Geyer Ryan (eds), *Literary Theory Today* (Cambridge: Cambridge University Press): 109-24.

Ring, Y.
1977   'The Biblical List of 31 Kings in the Book of Joshua against Parallels in Mycenaean Greek Tablets', *Tarbiz* 46.1–2: 141-44 [Hebrew].

Robson, E.
1999   *Mesopotamian Mahematics, 2100–1600 B.C.* (Oxford: Clarendon Press).

Rogerson, J.W.
1985   'The Use of Sociology in Old Testament Studies', in J.A. Emerton (ed.), *Congress Volume: Salamanca, 1983* (VTSup 36; Leiden: E.J. Brill): 245-56.
1991   *Genesis 1–11* (Sheffield: JSOT Press).

Rooth, M.
1996   'Focus', in Lappin 1996: ch. 10.

Rorty, R.
1984   'The Historiography of Philosophy: Four Genres', in R. Rorty, J.B. Schneewind, and Q. Skinner (eds), *Philosophy in History* (Cambridge: Cambridge University Press): 49-76.

Ross, J.
1997   *The Semantics of Media* (Dordrecht: Kluwer Academic Publishers).

Rowland, C.C.
1982   *The Open Heaven* (London: SPCK).

Rowlands, M.J. and B. Abbot-Seagraves (ed.)
1982   *Theory and Explanation in Archaeology* (New York: Academic Press).

Rowlett, L.L.
1996   *Joshua and the Rhetoric of Violence* (JSOTSup 226; Sheffield: Sheffield Academic Press).

Saggs, H.W.F.
1962   *The Greatness that was Babylon* (London: Sidgwick and Jackson).
1960   'Ur of the Chaldees', *Iraq* 22: 200-209.
Salvesen, A.
1998   *Origin's Hexapla and Fragments* (TSAJ 58; Tübingen: J.C.B. Mohr [Paul Siebeck]).
Sangali, A.
1998   *The Importance of Being Fuzzy* (Princeton: Princeton University Press).
Save-Soderbergh, T.
1951   'The Hyksos Rule in Egypt', *JES* 37: 53-74.
Schacter, D.L.
1997   *Searching for Memory: The Brain, the Mind, and the Past* (New York: BasicBooks).
Schaeffer, F.A.
1939   *Ugaritica. I. Études relatives aux découvertes de Ras Shamra. Première série* (Bibliothèque archéologique et historique 31; Mission de Ras Shamra 3; Paris: P. Geuthner).
1968   *Ugaritica. V. Nouveaux textes accadiens, hourrites et ugaritiques des archives et bibliothèques privées d'Ugarit* (commentaires des textes historiques J. Nougayrol *et al*; Bibliothèque archéologique et historique, Institut français d'archéologie de Beyrouth 80; Mission de Ras Shamra 16; Paris: P. Geuthner).
Shapiro, E.R.
1997   *The Inner World in the Outer World* (New Haven: Yale University Press).
Shennan, S.
1997   *Quantifying Archaeology* (Edinburgh: Edinburgh University Press, 2nd edn).
Shoesmith, D.J. and T.J. Smiley
1980   *Multiple-Conclusion Logic* (Cambridge: Cambridge University Press, corr. edn).
Shuttleworth, S.
1984   *George Eliot and Nineteenth-Century Science* (Cambridge: Cambridge University Press).
Simons, J.
1959   *The Geographical and Topographical Texts of the Old Testament* (Leiden: E.J. Brill).
Skorupski, J.
1976   *Symbol and Theory* (Cambridge: Cambridge University Press).
Smiley, T.J.
1982   'The Theory of Descriptions', *Proceedings of the British Academy (1982)* 67: 321-27.
Smith, S.
1991   *Babylonian Historical Texts* (Hildesheim: Olms).

Soggin, J.A.
1984   *A History of Israel from the Beginnings to the Bar Kochba Revolt, AD 135* (London: SCM).
Sparks, M.
1970   *In the Driving Seat* (London: Macmillan).
Sperber, D.
1985   *On Anthropological Knowledge* (Cambridge: Cambridge University Press).
Spitz, E.H.
1985   *Art and Psyche: A Study in Psychoanalysis and Aesthetics* (New Haven: Yale University Press).
Steiner, G.
1990   *Real Presences* (Cambridge: Press Syndicate).
Stern, D.G.
1995   *Wittgenstein on Mind and Language* (Oxford: Oxford University Press).
Stern, E.
1994   *Dor: Ruler of the Seas* (Jerusalem: Israel Exploration Society).
1995   *Excavations at Dor, Final Report* (Jerusalem: Institute of Archaeology, Hebrew University of Jerusalem and Israel Exploration Society).
Stern, J.P.
1992   *The Heart of Europe: Essays on Literature and Ideology* (Oxford: Blackwell).
Stronach, D.
1978   *Pasargadae: A Report on the Excavations Conducted by the British Institute of Persian Studies* (Oxford: Oxford University Press).

Tanner, M.
1997   *Wagner* (London: Flamingo).
1979   'The Total Work of Art', in P. Burbidge and R. Sutton (eds), *The Wagner Companion* (London: Faber).
Tardieu, J.
1991   *The River Underground* (trans. and ed. D. Kelley; Newcastle: Bloodaxe).
Thody, P.
1977   *Roland Barthes* (London: Macmillan).
Thompson, T.L.
1999   *The Bible in History* (London: Cape).
1978   'A New Attempt to Date the Patriarchal Narratives', *JAOS* 98.1: 76-84.
Thomsen, M.-L.
1984   *The Sumerian Language* (Mesopotamia 10; Copenhagen: Akademisk Forlag).
Tigay, J.H.
1985   *Empirical Models for Biblical Criticism* (Philadelphia: University of Pennsylvania Press).
Tilley, C.
1999   *Metaphor and Material Culture* (Oxford: Blackwell).

Ucko, P.J.
1968   *Anthropomorphic Figurines of Predynastic Egypt and Neolithic Crete* (London: A. Szmidla).

Van Seters, J.
1964   'A Date for the "Admonitions" in the Second Intermediate Period', *JEA* 50: 13-23.
1975   *Abraham in History and Tradition* (New Haven and London: Yale University Press).
Vitz, E.B.
1989   *Medieval Narrative and Modern Narratology* (New York: New York University Press).

Walton, J.
1992   'The Antediluvian Section of the Sumerian King List and Genesis 5', *BA* 44.4: 207-208.
Watanabe, C.E.
1998   *Aspects of Animal Symbolism in Mesopotamia* (Cambridge: Cambridge University Faculty of Oriental Studies [Ph.D. Thesis])
Ward, G.
5   *Barth, Derrida and the Language of Theology* (Cambridge: Cambridge University Press).
Watterson, B.
1999   *Amarna: Ancient Egypt's Age of Revolution* (Stroud, UK., Charleston, SC.: Tempus).
Weidemann, H.
1994   *Peri hermeneias, Aristoteles. Übersetzt und erläutert von Hermann Weidemann* (Aristoteles Werke in deutscher Übersetzung 1.2; Berlin: Akademie Verlag).
Westendorf, W.
1968   *Painting, Sculpture and Architecture of Ancient Egypt* (New York: Harry N. Abrams).
Whedbee, J.W.
1998   *The Bible and the Comic Vision* (Cambridge: Cambridge University Press).
White, A.
1981   *The Uses of Obscurity* (London: Routledge & Kegan Paul).
Williams, B.
1998   *Plato: The Invention of Philosophy* (London: Phoenix).
Williams, R.J.
1983   *The Eastern Mediterranean: Where Ancient Cultures Met and Mingled* (Southam Lectures; Ottawa: Canadian Mediterranean Institute).
Williamson, T.
1996   *Vagueness* (London and New York: Routledge).
Wimmer, S.
1993   'Egyptian Temples in Canaan and Sinai', in S. Israelit-Groll (ed.). 1990: 2.1065-1106.

Winlock, H.E.
1948   *The Treasures of Three Egyptian Princesses* (New York: Metropolitan Museum of Art).
Wiseman, D.J. (ed.)
1973   *Peoples of Old Testament Times* (Oxford: Oxford University Press).
Wittgenstein, L.
1958   *Philosophical Investigations* (Oxford: Oxford University Press, 2nd edn).
1999   *The Collected Manuscripts of Ludwig Wittgenstein on Facsimile CD-ROM* (ed. Wittgenstein Archives, University of Bergen: Oxford: Oxford University Press).
Wortley, B.A.
1967   *Jurisprudence* (Manchester: Manchester University Press).
WozÅniak, S.
1979   'Ugaritic Parallel of Jahwe *melek oÔla ˜m*', *FO* 20: 171-73.
Wyatt, H.V.
1977   'Vaccines and Social Responsibility: Here are Some Answers. What Are the Questions?' (in *Monist* 60): 81-95.

Yadin, Y.
1963   *The Art of Warfare in Biblical Lands* (London: Weidenfeld and Nicolson).
Yeivin, S.
        17. *The Israelite Conquest of Canaan* (Istanbul: Nederlands Historisch-Archaeologisch Instituut Istanbul).
Young, J.E.
2000   *At Memory's Edge* (New Haven, Mass.: Yale University Press).

Zeeman, C.E.
1979   'A Geometric Model of Ideologies', in A.C. Renfrew and K.L. Cooke (eds), *Transformations* (New York: Academic Press): 463-80.
Zeitlin, I.M.
1984   *Ancient Judaism* (Cambridge: Cambridge University Press).